PETER TAYLOR has reported on terrorism for nearly 40 years. His Troubles trilogy – *Provos*, *Loyalists* and *Brits* – is considered to be the definitive account of the Northern Ireland conflict. Since then he has presented five television series on the Islamic terror threat. In 2002 he received an OBE for services to broadcasting, and in 2008 he was awarded the highly prestigious James Cameron Memorial Prize 'for work as a journalist that combined moral vision and professional integrity'.

PETER TAYLOR

Talking to Terrorists

Face to Face with the Enemy

Harper
Press

HarperPress
An imprint of HarperCollinsPublishers
77–85 Fulham Palace Road
Hammersmith
London W6 8JB

This HarperPress paperback edition published 2011
1

First published by HarperPress in 2011

A catalogue record for this book
is available from the British Library

ISBN 978-0-00-732553-5

Typeset in Minion by G&M Designs Limited,
Raunds, Northamptonshire
Printed and bound in Great Britain by
Clays Ltd, St Ives plc

MIX
Paper from
responsible sources
FSC® C007454

FSC is a non-profit international organisation established to promote the
responsible management of the world's forests. Products carrying the FSC
label are independently certified to assure consumers that they come
from forests that are managed to meet the social, economic and
ecological needs of present and future generations.

Find out more about HarperCollins and the environment at
www.harpercollins.co.uk/green

To my family, friends and colleagues

CONTENTS

ILLUSTRATIONS

IRA press conference in Derry in June 1972. *(Keystone/Getty Images)*

The author and his Thames Television crew come under attack from Loyalists in Lenadoon Avenue, West Belfast, in 1972. *(Victor Patterson)*

Brendan Duddy, the vital secret conduit between the British government and the leadership of the IRA. *(John Thynne)*

Michael Oatley, the MI6 officer who worked with Duddy. *(Paul Cooper/The Times/nisyndication)*

Martin McGuinness and Ian Paisley after being sworn in as Deputy First Minister and First Minister of the Northern Ireland Assembly. *(Bloomberg/Getty Images)*

The FBI's Pat D'Amuro and his team looking over the ruins of the US Embassy in Nairobi after it was destroyed by an Al Qaeda suicide bomber on 7 August 1998. *(Federal Bureau of Investigation)*

Kenyan soldiers searching through the ruins of the US Embassy in Nairobi. *(Federal Bureau of Investigation)*

The author interviewing Salim Boukhari in gaol in Germany. *(BBC Photo Library)*

Al Qaeda's suicide attacks on New York and Washington on 11 September 2001 were intended to deliver a blow that America and the West would never forget. *(Chao Soi Cheong/AP/Press Association Images)*

Osama Bin Laden. *(AP/Press Association Images)*

Bin Laden with his closest associate, Ayman al-Zawahiri. *(AP Photo/Al-Jazeera/APTN)*

The Sari Club at Kuta Beach, Bali, after the bombings of 12 October 2002. *(AP/Press Association Images)*

On 16 May 2003, ten suicide bombers attacked targets in central Casablanca. *(Denis Doyle/AP/Press Association Images)*

The author with General Ahmidou Laanigri, the head of Morocco's Interior Ministry. *(BBC Photo Library)*

The author in the shanty town of Sidi Moumen, outside Casablanca. *(John Stapleton)*

Attacks on four crowded commuter trains in Madrid on 11 March 2004 left 191 people dead and almost two thousand injured. *(Denis Doyle/AP/Press Association Images)*

A surveillance camera captures three of the four London bombers as they enter Luton station on their way to the capital on the morning of 7 July 2005. *(Getty Images)*

Hasib Husain, the fourth bomber, detonated his bomb on the number 30 bus in Tavistock Square. *(Peter Macdiarmid/Press Association Images)*

Matazinhos and Maria, the parents of Jean Charles de Menezes. *(Peter Taylor)*

Abu Hamza. *(Matt Dunham/Reuters/Corbis)*

Sheikh Omar Bakri Mohammed. *(Hussein Malla/AP/Press Association Images)*

Sheikh Abdullah al-Faisal. *(Reuters/Ian Waldie)*

Belmarsh prison in south-east London, where many of Britain's convicted terrorists and terrorist suspects are held. *(Stefan Rousseau/Press Association Images)*

Abu Qatada. *(Press Association)*

Al Qaeda and Taliban detainees at Guantánamo Bay. *(Shane T. McCoy/AP/Press Association Images)*

Mohammed al-Awfi, who alleges that he was tortured by the Americans while he was being held in Afghanistan. *(HO/Reuters/Corbis)*

The radical American-Yemeni cleric Anwar Al-Awlaki. *(Tracy A. Woodward/The Washington Post/Getty Images)*

A computer printer cartridge containing the explosive PETN (pentaerythritol tetranitrate) that was found in a cargo plane bound from Yemen to Chicago in October 2010. *(AP Photo/Dubai Police via Emirates News Agency/AP/Press Association Images)*

A pilotless 'drone', of the type increasingly used by the CIA to target suspected terrorists in Afghanistan and the border regions of Pakistan. *(Reuters/Corbis)*

Forsan et haec olim meminisse iuvabit
'One day it will be good to remember these things'

VIRGIL, *AENEID*, BOOK ONE, LINES 203–4

(see page 45)

PREFACE

The title of this book, *Talking to Terrorists*, is intended to suggest a broad compass. I've talked to many terrorists face to face in nearly forty years of covering the phenomenon that has scarred the lives of so many during the latter years of the twentieth century and the first decade of the twenty-first. I've talked to terrorists not because I sympathise with them – I believe that conflicts should be resolved through dialogue, not destruction – but in order to try to understand their motivation, and to explore why individuals are prepared to kill for a cause, be it secular or religious, in which they believe. In the case of suicide bombers, they're prepared to kill themselves too. I've always hoped that the programmes I've made and the books I've written may also help others to understand and perhaps reconsider the stereotype of the 'terrorist' – the deranged, fanatical gunman, or the bloodthirsty bomber who kills for the sake of killing. The reality is far more complex. I hope that this book may contribute to the continuing debate about how liberal democracies should respond to threats of terrorism and, where appropriate, engage in the process of conflict resolution.

This book isn't just about me talking to terrorists. It's also about the security and intelligence agencies – the 'spooks' – talking to terrorists face to face, both to obtain evidence to bring them to justice and to elicit information: a process that in some cases has involved torture and serious abuses of human rights.

It's also about governments talking to terrorists as part of the process of resolving conflict. The British government talked to the IRA (as detailed in the first chapter of the book); the South African Prime Minister F.W. de Klerk talked to Nelson Mandela; the Americans talked to the insurgents in Iraq; and British diplomats – and no doubt American ones too – are talking to the Taliban, although at this stage perhaps only through intermediaries. Which raises the question, will we at some time in the future talk to Al Qaeda? In my view, talking to terrorists may sometimes be a necessary prerequisite of conflict resolution.

I have not set out to write a global study of terrorism, which has been done by many others, but to focus on the IRA and Al Qaeda as they are fundamentally different 'terrorist' organisations which I have covered in my work over many years. The book is not intended to be an academic or sociological analysis of terrorism and terrorists but, I hope, a readable and accessible narrative that may illuminate some of the complexities and contradictions of the phenomenon and bring a degree of clarity to the confusion and incomprehension that often surround it. I've also endeavoured to provide the all-important historical context to the origins and evolution of these contrasting movements. The conflict with the IRA has, at least for the moment, been resolved, and in the first chapter I concentrate on the mechanisms by which this was achieved, and suggest that they may act as a template for the resolution of other conflicts. The conflict with Al Qaeda remains ongoing despite the death of Osama Bin Laden.

Finally, this book is not an autobiography but the story of a journey of almost 40 years from the IRA to Al Qaeda, illustrated with personal anecdotes and observations, of coming face to face with the 'enemy'. That journey has led me from ignorance in 1972, when as a green young journalist I covered 'Bloody Sunday', to, I hope, a greater understanding on the tenth anniversary of 9/11 in 2011. I make no apology for making Al Qaeda and the emergence of Islamist extremism the main focus of the book, since that is the direction from which the current threat comes, and it is likely to do so for the foreseeable future. I hope that readers may share my journey and emerge at the end, like me, with a better understanding of these vital issues that have unfortunately become part of the fabric of all our lives.

INTRODUCTION

Recognising Reality

The popular perception of terrorists and terrorism is often at variance with the reality. In combating the threat, be it from the IRA, Al Qaeda or other insurgent groups, the keystone of any government's strategy is to demonise and marginalise the enemy, in the hope of denying it moral and political legitimacy and eroding support for its cause. Over the years I've seen governments' attitudes change following their recognition that the 'terrorists' had a cause whose roots had to be addressed, and that a compromise had to be reached if there was to be a stop to the unending shedding of blood and haemorrhaging of human and financial resources. Recognising reality is a prerequisite of ending conflict. As I've found on my journey, it's also a prerequisite of reporting and analysing terrorism. The recognition of these facts did not come early for me, but gradually emerged as the result of a long process in which I engaged with some of those who were regarded as terrorists at the time. Occasionally I was caught up in their attacks. Yes, the journey was long, difficult and at times dangerous. But whatever the setbacks and frustrations along the way, it was always revelatory, not just in my understanding of the terrorists themselves but in my acquaintance with governments' efforts to combat them.

At the outset, I recognise the need to define my terms – most importantly of all, what is a terrorist? The legal definition of terrorism is the use of violence for political ends. But what colours the perception of the word depends on two primary considerations. First, what were the circumstances out of which that violence grew? These can range from the denial of civil rights to Catholics in Northern Ireland, the inequities of Apartheid in South Africa or the uprooting of Palestinians from their homeland, to the plight of Muslims living under occupation following the invasion of Iraq and Afghanistan by America and other Western nations. The IRA never regarded themselves as terrorists, and took exception to those who described them as such. They argued that their 'armed struggle' was a legitimate strategy to achieve a political end that was, they maintained, unattainable by peaceful constitutional means.

Another consideration that makes the word difficult to define is that some 'terrorists' go on to become Presidents and Prime Ministers. There's a long history of the transformation of 'terrorists' into 'statesmen'. In 1963 in Kenya, Jomo Kenyatta, believed to be one of the leaders of the Mau Mau insurgents who fought British colonial rule, became the country's first Prime Minister after independence. In 1977 in Israel, Menachem Begin, the leader of the Irgun, who resisted the British presence in Palestine, became Prime Minister. In 1994 in the Middle East Yasser Arafat, the leader of Fatah, became President of the Palestinian National Authority covering the West Bank and Gaza. In the same year in South Africa, Nelson Mandela, the former leader of the African National Congress, became the nation's first black President. And in 2007 in Northern Ireland Martin McGuinness, formerly the IRA's most prominent leader, became Deputy First Minister in the province's power-sharing government.

All judgements about the word 'terrorist' are subjective. It's a word I try to avoid using in my work – and it's one that is effectively banned on the BBC's World Service and by Reuters, since many listeners, viewers and readers around the globe may not agree with the definition as applied to certain conflicts, not least that in the Middle East. But it can't be avoided in writing a book with the title *Talking to Terrorists*. A terrorist is, literally, a person who uses the weapon of terror to target a state's political, social and economic institutions. Invariably terrorists are driven by a mixture of political, social or religious grievances that they seek to rectify by the use of violence either to overthrow the state or to force it to address the issues that lie at the root of the recourse to violence. The IRA finally recognised that its atavistic aim of driving the

British out of Northern Ireland was not going to be achieved by violent means, and in the end settled for compromise. But the politically uncomfortable reality remains that it was the IRA's military campaign that finally forced the British government to negotiate. Although the IRA would split hairs to deny it, the fact is that the IRA waged a terrorist campaign to try to achieve its end. So were the IRA terrorists? In the strict sense of the word, the answer has to be yes, however vehemently they and their political wing, Sinn Féin, would deny it.

However, cause and motivation apart, there is a fundamental difference between the terrorist violence used by the IRA and that perpetrated by Al Qaeda, its affiliates and those who support its ideology. There are degrees of terrorism, although that may be of scant comfort to its victims. With notable exceptions, the IRA did not deliberately set out to kill innocent civilians, although when tactically convenient it would, for example, brand workmen employed to repair security-force installations that the IRA had bombed as 'legitimate' targets. In stark contrast, Al Qaeda deliberately sets out indiscriminately to murder as many civilians as possible, to create maximum outrage and maximum publicity. The attacks on New York and Washington on 11 September 2001, and the suicide bombings on London Transport on 7 July 2005, are but two of the most glaring examples. Bali, Madrid, Casablanca and Mumbai have also been the sites of terrorist violence carried out by Islamist groups that, if not directly affiliated to Al Qaeda, are supportive of its ideology. Al Qaeda is, as the IRA was, a terrorist organisation, although of an entirely different order. After 9/11 I asked Gerry Adams if he would describe Al Qaeda as terrorists. He said without hesitation that he would. He would never describe the IRA in the same terms.

However, in writing this book I sometimes put the words 'terrorist' and 'terrorism' in inverted commas – to indicate a degree of equivocation over the definitions at particular points in the narrative. Again, this indicates the subjectivity of the definition. This may not be an ideal solution, but at least it illustrates that 'terrorism' is not always black and white.

* * *

Nelson Mandela is the most famous personification of the cliché 'from terrorist to statesman'. In 1981 I made a *Panorama* programme about Mandela and the ANC when he was still a prisoner on Robben Island. I remember looking out to sea from a clifftop in Cape Town at the tiny speck on the horizon seven miles away that had been Mandela's prison for fifteen years. I asked the then South African Prime Minister, P.W. Botha, about the possibility of releasing his most famous prisoner. 'We don't talk to terrorists,' he replied. In the end, his successor F.W. de Klerk did.

The reason for making the film was to mark the fifth anniversary of the massacre in the Soweto township outside Johannesburg in June 1976, when South African police opened fire on students who were protesting against the Apartheid government's insistence that the Afrikaans language be taught in Soweto's schools. I'd heard that many students had subsequently fled South Africa to join the insurgents of the ANC, Africa's oldest liberation movement, and I wanted to track down and talk to some of them. Were they 'terrorists' or 'freedom fighters'?

My contact in the ANC, based in the Zambian capital Lusaka at the time, was Tabo Mbeki, then its press officer. I met him in London with Archbishop Desmond Tutu and Oliver Tambo, then ANC President, and I remember bringing Mbeki a paper cup of BBC coffee in the *Panorama* office, never imagining that one day he would become President of South Africa. I remember too being surprised that an Archbishop seemed to be so closely associated with an organisation committed to the use of violence to overthrow the Apartheid regime.

After months of protracted negotiations, I finally got the ANC's agreement to let me film some former Soweto students training in the bush in Angola, on condition that I never disclosed where they were. Other conditions were that I was to go alone, and to do the filming and sound recording myself. I got my visa from the Angolan authorities in Paris, booked a flight and was ready to go. Then, the day before my planned departure, I received a phone call from Tabo Mbeki, who told me that the trip was off. No reason was given. I rang my ANC contact in Paris and arranged to meet him at Charles de Gaulle airport the following day, in the hope of getting the decision reversed or at the very least receiving an explanation. He said he was unable to enlighten me. The ANC, like Sinn Féin, was centrally controlled and highly disciplined. Orders were given and obeyed. My flight to Luanda was leaving in an hour. I had a ticket and a visa, so I decided to take my chances.

On the long journey south to Angola, I had plenty of time to work out my plan of action when I arrived in Luanda. I would not be met, and I would have no Angolan government minder, so I would be on my own, and would have to play things by ear. I didn't need a cover story, as I had an official invitation from the ANC, rubber-stamped by the Angolan government. I just needed a convenient lapse of memory that I'd received the phone call cancelling the whole thing. I managed to talk my way through immigration and security by waving the original piece of paper from the ANC, but once I was through passport control I discovered that I couldn't book into a hotel without the authorisation of the Angolan authorities. Again, I managed to talk my way around this, ending up in a hotel that had seen better days and more guests, ironically named the Hotel Panorama. My room had a commanding view and aroma of the harbour's less than fragrant mudflats.

The following morning I made my way to the ANC office just outside Luanda, where I found a very surprised-looking ANC Commissar. 'What are you doing here?' he asked. 'Didn't you get the message?' 'Message? What message?' I replied disingenuously. There followed a knife-edge discussion over two hours in which I tried to persuade him to let me do what I'd come to do, and he tried to convince me that orders were orders. It was one of those times when you do everything you can to avoid returning to base empty-handed. I was thinking too of the financial cost of the trip. In the end, to my amazement and relief, the Commissar seemed to relent, and told me to come back the following morning, without intimating what might or might not be in store. He said a driver would pick me up at the hotel at the crack of dawn.

A grey, humid morning broke over the mudflats. It didn't seem like a good omen. I checked my 8mm Bolex camera, cassette recorder, batteries and spare film and sound cassettes. Those were pre-video days, when film and sound had to be synchronised back in London. I dreaded the thought of achieving my goal, but returning to London with blank tapes because I hadn't checked the equipment thoroughly, or had pressed the wrong button.

My driver arrived as arranged, and beckoned me into a battered vehicle which, like the hotel, had seen better days. We then drove for what seemed forever, out of Luanda and into the bush. The car finally stopped at a clearing in the middle of nowhere, where my friend the Commissar was waiting. 'Good morning,' he said. 'Please wait here.' I still had no idea what was going to happen, but did as directed with fingers crossed, camera and tape recorder at the ready. Then suddenly I heard singing, and a column of around a dozen young men and women emerged from the bush about two hundred metres away. They were dressed in green and khaki combat fatigues, wearing camouflage caps and carrying AK-47s, the signature weapon of insurgents the world over. I nervously started to film, hoping I'd got the focus and aperture right. 'Mandela, Mandela, Mandela. Freedom is our song,' they sang as they marched to a spreading baobab tree right in front of me.

There, shaded from the early-morning sun, another Commissar proceeded to give them a lesson in Marxist economics, outlining how, when the revolution came, South Africa's banks and mines would all be nationalised so the wealth would be in the hands of the people. There was then a question-and-answer session on the 'struggle'. 'We shall not submit,' one of the student guerrillas told the teacher. 'We will fight back with every means in our power in defence of our freedom, our country and our future.' 'Precisely! Great, comrade!' exclaimed the teacher, waving his arms in enthusiastic appreciation.

The lecture over, it was time to do what I had come for, to talk to the young ANC recruits about the Soweto massacre and their intentions. They sat in a semi-circle and first sang a song about 1976. I talked to one young woman in combat fatigues with three of her top teeth missing. 'In 1976 we were schoolchildren fighting with stones against guns,' she said. 'I saw the necessity to go out and take guns and face a gun with a gun.' One of her comrades echoed the sentiment. 'Our people, the African majority, have become convinced out of their own bitter experience they will have to reply to the gun by the gun, and that the thousands of young people* who were murdered in 1976 shall surely be avenged.' But what made them think they could defeat the most powerful army in Africa? 'There's not even a single enemy who can defeat a people who are fighting a just cause, no matter how powerful it may be,' the young woman replied. 'It was proved in Vietnam.' She and her comrades had obviously been well schooled in what to say. I pointed out that in Vietnam the Americans weren't defending their own country, as white South Africa was. 'Even the Boers themselves, we're going to defeat them,' she said. 'We are determined to fight and kill them.' I then asked if she thought that one day Nelson Mandela would be released. 'Yes,' she said. 'The government will not release Nelson Mandela, but we will release him.'

I had what I came for, but there was no guarantee that film and sound would come out. Had I pressed the right buttons? Had I got the focus right? Had I remembered to turn the tape recorder on? All those things went through my mind as I was driven back to my hotel by an ANC driver. When he dropped me off, I asked him to wait while I went to get a bottle of Scotch I'd bought in case I was in a position to say thank you to someone. I handed it to him and asked him to give it to the Commissar with my thanks. He promised he would, and said he would pick me up in the morning and take me to the airport.

The following morning he arrived late, and almost paralytic. I suspected he'd drained the bottle himself. What should I do? Risk going with him, or try to find a taxi at the risk of missing the plane? I wanted to get out of Angola as quickly as possible with my valuable material, so I decided to take the risk, and jumped into his car. It was the hairiest ride I've ever taken, but we made it, and I caught the flight. Touching down at Heathrow never felt so good. Then there was

---

*The figures are heavily disputed.

an agonising wait of a week while the film was being processed. Would it come out? To my enormous relief it did. It's the only footage in existence of ANC guerrillas training. But I wouldn't like to go through the experience again.

The reality of reporting terrorism is that it occasionally involves facing danger. I'm sometimes asked if I've ever felt my life was at risk. The answer is yes.

My producer David Wickham and I had been making a *Panorama* programme on Israel's withdrawal from Lebanon in 1985, following the incursion three years earlier, codenamed Operation Peace for the Galilee. We were filming with an Israeli convoy in South Lebanon that was going to resupply a forward base. I was in a car with an Israeli army minder at the front of the convoy, and David and the film crew were in an armoured personnel carrier (APC) at the back. In the middle was a large tanker bringing precious fresh water to the troops at their forward base. We were driving through a beautiful orange grove, heavy with sweet scent, when suddenly there was an explosion, and a shower of dust and rocks. The tanker had been hit by a land-mine. The explosion was immediately followed by the rattle of gunfire from the orange groves. We had been ambushed by Shiite 'terrorists' who were resisting the Israeli occupation of their land. My Israeli minder instinctively threw open the door of the car and pushed me out into a shallow ditch, telling me to keep my head down. He then opened up with a burst of defensive fire from his automatic rifle.

The ditch afforded only a minimum of cover, and I remember lying there and looking up into the orange groves from where the bullets were flying, and being aware that I was probably right in the line of fire. I had been under fire before, in Northern Ireland, but never quite like this. My most immediate concern was for David and the film crew in the APC. Had they been hit? Was it their vehicle that had been blown up? I couldn't see because of the dust and general chaos. Were they dead or alive? If they were dead, I felt an odd onrush of incipient guilt that it was them and not me. In almost the same flash I thought of my wife, Sue, and my children, Ben and Sam. Would I ever see them again? All these thoughts rushed through my head in the noise and confusion of the gun battle. I had often wondered how I would react in such a situation, and in a strange kind of way it was almost a relief that at last it had happened. I found, to my surprise, that although I was shaken, I didn't panic. In fact I felt strangely calm and clear-headed. I accepted that there was nothing that I could do except keep my fingers crossed and my head down, and lie there until the shooting stopped.

After a while an Israeli officer gave the all-clear. The gun battle must have lasted for ten or fifteen minutes. All I know is that it felt much longer. For the soldiers in South Lebanon such an ambush was almost routine. They knew they were sitting ducks as they drove through the territory of the enemy, whom they invariably referred to as 'terrorists'. The 'terrorists' used the same term to describe the Israelis. To my relief, as I climbed out of the ditch I saw David's head popping out of the turret of the APC. Each of us shouted to check that the other was all right. We both were. The driver of the water tanker was only slightly injured, as the armour protecting the vehicle had served its purpose. The orange groves suddenly seemed to smell even sweeter.

From time to time I'm also asked if I ever feel uncomfortable about the moral dilemmas I inevitably face in reporting terrorism. Again, the reality is that I do.

In 1977 I made a series of documentaries for Thames Television's *This Week* programme on security policy in Northern Ireland. I investigated allegations of ill-treatment at police interrogation centres, the impact in Nationalist areas of the Queen's visit to the province in her Jubilee year, and conditions inside the Maze prison, where IRA prisoners were refusing to wear prison uniform, insisting that to do so would brand them as criminals. In protest they wore only blankets. As a result of these three programmes the Labour government of the day privately suggested to Thames Television that it was time for someone else to cover Northern Ireland, since my reporting had been 'unhelpful'. The moral dilemma I faced was whether I should be making such programmes, given their propaganda value to the IRA. I decided that I should, as I believed they raised legitimate questions about security policy which the British government preferred not to be asked.

The abuses during interrogation that I investigated were a far cry from waterboarding and the other 'enhanced interrogation techniques' authorised by the Bush administration post-9/11 and used by the CIA against Al Qaeda suspects – which I analyse in the final chapter of this book. I got a lot of flak at the time from the government and from Sir Kenneth Newman, the Chief Constable of the Royal Ulster Constabulary (RUC), for my investigation, the findings of which were subsequently confirmed by Amnesty International. In the wake of the programme, the Northern Ireland Office (NIO) issued an unprecedented personal attack on me and the programme: 'It is significant that the producers and reporter of this programme have produced … programmes in quick succession which have concentrated on presenting the blackest possible picture of events in Northern Ireland.' But they were dark days, and there was little positive to report.

My investigation into prison conditions raised an additional and even more acute moral dilemma. One of the people I interviewed was the Secretary of the Prison Officers' Association, Desmond Irvine. I met him in 1977 at Belfast's Europa Hotel, and talked to him at length a few days before the interview to make sure he would be happy to be filmed despite the fact that the NIO was strongly opposed because of the risk, given that the IRA were targeting prison officers. I decided to go ahead, however, because Mr Irvine wanted to do the interview and I believed that it was important that his message got across, not least because it was coming from a Protestant prison officer. Remarkably, in the interview he described the IRA protesters not as common criminals, which was the NIO's spin, but as men who had been fighting a war. He believed that he and his members were dealing with an army. Astonishingly, he said he understood why the prisoners felt the way they did.

After the programme he wrote me a letter thanking me for representing his views responsibly, and for giving 'an accurate description of life at the Maze'. Two weeks later the IRA shot him dead. I was shattered when I heard the news.

At the funeral I stood at his graveside and silently cried. One Belfast journalist rang me at home and asked me how it felt to have 'blood on my hands'. The pain and loss suffered by Desmond Irvine's family, friends and colleagues, hit me hard, and I seriously considered packing up reporting Northern Ireland and 'terrorism'. I later confronted the IRA about why they had shot dead a man who had given an interview expressing views that were consistent with the IRA's own. I was told that he was killed not because of my interview, but because he was the Secretary of the Prison Officers' Association. It was no consolation.

In Northern Ireland, the final recognition of reality was the British government's realisation that it would have to talk to the IRA, and make the compromises necessary to bring the conflict to an end. This it ultimately did as the result of a long, sensitive and secret process played out over many years, in which the key link between the British government and the IRA was a remarkable man from Londonderry – or Derry. His name was Brendan Duddy, codenamed 'the Mountain Climber'.

ONE

Talking to the IRA

There are moments that stick in the memory forever. At the time you may sense their significance, but it's only long afterwards that their real importance sinks in. Standing by a public telephone in a new shopping mall in the centre of Derry in 1998 was one of those moments.

I'd made sure that I had enough coins in case the conversation was long, but I suspected I wouldn't be needing them. I remember the empty feeling in the pit of my stomach. The reason for my apprehension was that I thought that, after months of trying, I'd finally identified the shadowy figure, known only as 'the Mountain Climber',* who for almost a quarter of a century had been the key link between Britain's Secret Intelligence Service, MI6, and the IRA. I was about to ring him to see if he would meet me. His name was Brendan Duddy.

I put the coins in the slot, and remember hearing them go 'clunk' one after the other. I held my breath as I heard the ringing tone. Then someone at the other end picked up the phone. I suspected it would be in an office, and tried to sound as composed as I could. I asked if I could speak to Mr Brendan Duddy. 'Can I say who's calling?' replied the person on the other end of the line. I thought it best to be open and say who I was. There was a pause, and I was asked to hold. The wait seemed endless, as lunchtime shoppers filed past me. Then another voice came on the line. 'Brendan Duddy speaking.' I took a

---

*He was given the nickname because as part of his daily run he would often ascend Grianán of Aileach – 'Fortress of the Sun' – a hill a dozen miles west of Derry on top of which are the remains of an ancient fort. It also refers to the mountainous task he undertook in bringing the British government and the IRA together to negotiate.

deep breath and told him who I was, again trying to sound composed and calm. I expected to hear a 'click', marking the end of the conversation, but I didn't. 'I've been waiting to hear from you,' he said. I could scarcely believe what I was hearing. To my surprise, he was familiar with my work in Northern Ireland over the years. I asked if I could come and see him to have a chat. He said that would be fine. When? 'Today?' I asked. He suggested I go to Rafters, one of the restaurants he owned, and someone would come and get me.

I put down the receiver, let out a huge sigh of relief that must have been audible to the shoppers, and went off for a cup of tea to collect my thoughts. I had to work out what I was going to say, and how I was going to present myself, to a man whose identity and top-secret work were known to no one apart from the handful of IRA men and spooks with whom he had dealt over so many years. The identity of 'the Link', as Brendan became known, was one of Northern Ireland's most closely guarded secrets.

I drove to Rafters, a modern, barn-like steakhouse on the edge of the city, sat down at a table and ordered some food, although I wasn't hungry. I had too much on my mind. My meal arrived, and so did a young man who introduced himself as one of Brendan's sons and asked me to follow him downstairs. That was the first time I set eyes on Brendan Duddy. He was discussing finance with a banker from Dublin. He stood up, greeted me with a warm smile and a handshake, and introduced me to the banker, his wife Margo and others sitting at his table as if he had known me for years.

His financial business done, Brendan suggested we go to his home, where we could talk in private. In the hallway we were met by Tara, a Great Dane of Baskervillian dimensions. We adjourned to Brendan's 'wee room' at the back of the house, with a peat fire smouldering in one corner. Margo brought us cups of tea and biscuits – as I was to learn she had done on many occasions for IRA leaders and assorted spooks. Then Brendan began to talk, a facility he has in abundance. I stressed that anything he said would be off the record, and that I would never repeat or publish any of it unless he gave me the green light to do so.

His story was extraordinary – the stuff of fiction. But as I was to discover, this was fact, not fantasy. He said that the seeds of peace had been planted in the very room in which we were sitting. They had been ripped up and then replanted on numerous occasions down the years before they finally grew into what became known as the peace process. He told me how IRA leaders had been smuggled across the border for secret meetings with the British at the height of the IRA's campaign; how his family had learned never to ask questions about what was going on in their home, and never to utter the names of some of the most wanted IRA men who had taken tea with the British under the Duddy family roof; and of how he'd known Martin McGuinness for around thirty years. As the night wore on, Brendan produced a bottle of Irish whiskey and started to pour. I don't normally drink whiskey, but under the circumstances it seemed both impolite and impolitic to refuse. As the alcohol hit home, I struggled to keep my mind clear: I did not want to miss anything. I seldom use a tape recorder – I usually take notes – but in these exceptional circumstances I feared that the presence of a notebook and poised pen might inhibit the conversation.

At about 4 a.m. I must have been visibly flagging, unlike Brendan. I thought it was time to go, but after several whiskeys I did not want to drive back to my hotel. Brendan said his son would take me, and I could pick up my car later that day. He also said that I should meet his family and, crucially, his close friend and accomplice in the Link, Bernadette Mount, so I could get the full picture. I woke up in my hotel room, not surprisingly, with a headache, scarcely believing what I had heard the night before, and started to make notes of my recollections. Brendan rang and asked if I'd like to have dinner at Bernadette's house that evening.

We ate roast lamb. Bernadette is not only a very good cook, but a remarkable woman. She later told me of how she had given bed and breakfast to IRA leaders like Billy McKee and Seamus Twomey, and their less notorious counterparts in the IRA's political wing, Sinn Féin, like its President Rory O'Brady.[1] Brendan's wife Margo and one of their sons were also at the dinner. It was a bitterly cold evening as we talked round the fire. I asked if there was ever any chance of my telling their astonishing story, knowing that the answer would almost certainly be no. The time was not right. The peace process was at an uncertain stage, and it would have been far too dangerous for Brendan to have broken cover at that time. But they said they would think about it, if the time ever came. Ten years later, it did.

Brendan Duddy was born on 10 June 1936 and raised in the city of Derry, on the very edge of the United Kingdom, on the border with County Donegal in the Irish Republic. In the late 1960s it was an impoverished and neglected place, as if its distance from Westminster relegated it to an inferior status. The majority of its inhabitants were Catholic, and considered themselves to be Irish, not British. Discrimination against Catholics was institutionalised in the political, economic and social fabric of the city, and the electoral boundaries were rigged in a way that guaranteed a Protestant majority on the council. Fourteen thousand Catholic voters elected eight councillors, while 9,000 Protestant voters elected twelve.[2] This reflected the gerry-mandering of Northern Ireland itself.* The province is made up of roughly a million Protestant Unionists, who wish to remain part of the United Kingdom, and half a million Catholics, most of them Nationalists and Republicans who wish to be part of a united Ireland. Nationalists favour bringing this about by peaceful means, while Republicans believe that violence is justified to achieve the goal.

In Derry, broadly speaking, Protestants got the best jobs and the best houses. These glaring inequalities, largely ignored by Westminster, and about which the majority of citizens in the rest of the United Kingdom remained unaware and indifferent, were the dry tinder that led to the explosion of the civil rights movement in 1968 and the subsequent re-emergence of the IRA. Brendan was simply one of the thousands of Catholic victims of the system. 'I had no work in Derry. There was no work,' he told me.[3] To fill the emptiness of the days he

---

*The boundaries of Northern Ireland, established by the 1920 Government of Ireland Act, were drawn under Unionist pressure to guarantee a Protestant majority.

used to go running in the beautiful countryside outside the city with a friend, Bobby Daly, who was a bin man. 'I was hoping that some day I might get a job as his assistant.' That was Brendan's dream.

London called him, as it had so many young Irish men and women in the past. 'It was the feeling of being boxed in in Derry. No work. No home. No house. England was a different world.' It was an alien environment for Brendan, but at least there were jobs there. He finally found work at the Bush factory in Ealing, 'putting the little knobs on brown Bakelite television sets'. He'd been expecting a replication of the discrimination he'd left Derry to escape, and that the English would look down on him because he was Irish. When it came to overtime, he assumed there wouldn't be any for him. But he was wrong. The way he was treated in England conditioned forever the way he thought of his fellow citizens on the other side of the Irish Sea. 'I met a group of people who were honest, easy to get on with and fair to me.' This, combined with the experience of learning the Irish language at the feet of the IRA veteran Sean Keenan, equipped Brendan to understand and interpret both sides of the conflict, and made him a valuable intermediary in the secret dialogue between the British government – via its spooks and diplomats based at the Northern Ireland Office residence at Laneside outside Belfast – and the IRA's ruling Army Council.*

Like many Derry men and women who leave the city, the urge to come home proved irresistible to Brendan. He returned, and opened a fish-and-chip shop in William Street, on the edge of the Bogside area where the majority of Catholics live. 'I loved every second of it. I was the best, and still am. I understand potatoes. I understand fish.' In London he had been earning £11 a week, and now he was making £10 or £12 a night. But the shop was more than just a chippie. It was a salon for the emerging leaders of the civil rights movement, who would discuss politics way into the night. Brendan never put the

---

*The IRA body that ran the 'war'. It normally consisted of six senior Republicans, although the number could be flexible. They were elected by the Army Executive, which in turn was elected by the Army Convention, made up of rank-and-file 'Volunteers' from the North and South of Ireland.

chairs on the tables. The teenaged Martin McGuinness was a regular visitor, not to take part in the greasy political salon but to deliver the sustenance for it through the back door, in the form of beefburgers from James Doherty's butcher's shop down the street. 'He was an innocent, handsome young boy,' Brendan remembers. 'He'd come in with the box of burgers, put them on the counter and chat up the girls, and I'd say, "Come on, Martin, there's work to do here."' Did he have any interest in politics? 'Absolutely none.'

The chip shop endured turbulent times in the late sixties and early seventies, with regular riots on its doorstep as the increasingly radicalised Nationalist youth of the Bogside fought pitched battles with their hated enemies the police (the RUC) and the British Army. It was ironic that the army was seen as the enemy only a few months after British soldiers had intervened in August 1969 to defend Catholics from Loyalist mobs in Derry, Belfast and elsewhere. British soldiers were initially welcomed as saviours, but the honeymoon was soon over. The army referred to the opposition as the 'Derry Young Hooligans' (DYH). Margo and Bernadette both served in the chip shop, and regarded the street battles as entertainment. 'We used to sit upstairs and watch,' Margo remembers. 'The riots were fierce, but you didn't feel in any danger. It was good fun.'

But on 30 January 1972, the fun ended. The day became known as 'Bloody Sunday'.* Everyone knew there was trouble coming. The army had made its own controversial assessment. Three weeks previously, Major General Robert Ford, the Commander Land Forces (CLF), who had visited Derry on 7 January, wrote a secret memorandum to his boss, Lieutenant General Sir Harry Tuzo, the General Officer Commanding Northern Ireland (GOC). He didn't mince his words: 'I am coming to the conclusion that the minimum force

---

*The original 'Bloody Sunday' took place at Croke Park in Dublin on 21 November 1920, when a mixed force of Royal Irish Constabulary, military and the notorious 'Black and Tans' opened fire on a crowd watching a Gaelic football match between Dublin and Tipperary. Twelve civilians were shot dead. Earlier that morning, the IRA under the leadership of Michael Collins had wiped out nine members of the British secret service in Dublin. The Croke Park massacre was seen as a reprisal.

necessary to achieve a restoration of law and order is to shoot selected ringleaders amongst the DYH after clear warnings have been issued.'[4]

The 'enemy' was ready too. By this time, both wings of the IRA – the Officials and the Provisionals* – had grown in strength, their ranks swelled by anger at the British policy of internment (the arrest and detention without trial of hundreds of Catholic Nationalists, and far fewer Loyalists) and allegations of torture being used by the army to extract information from detainees. Martin McGuinness had now risen to become second-in-command of the Provisionals' Derry Brigade. His former lack of interest in politics had been transformed by internment and what he saw on the streets of his city, where British soldiers were now seen by Catholics as the aggressors and no longer their saviours. Brendan had grown increasingly concerned at the potential consequences of a showdown between the army and the IRA. And so had his old friend, the police officer in charge of Derry, Chief Superintendent Frank Lagan, who was one of the few Catholics in the almost exclusively Protestant RUC at the time.

As tension in the city mounted in advance of a huge anti-internment march that was being planned for Sunday, 30 January, Lagan came to see Brendan to seek his help. 'He said, "I'm terrified. The IRA must not be there. There must be not a gun in that area." I said that was a tall order.' Lagan waved his hand, smiled and said, 'You can do it.' Brendan did his best. He talked to both wings of the IRA, and got assurances that guns would not be in the Bogside that Sunday. He reported back to Lagan that, as requested, there would be no guns. But there were guns – in the hands of soldiers of the First Battalion of the Parachute Regiment. And they used them. The army said the paratroopers came under fire from the IRA as they deployed into the

---

*The 'old' IRA were the descendants of those who had fought to get the British out of Ireland since the 1916 Easter Rising in Dublin and had carried on the fight for independence in 1919. This they failed to achieve, as Ireland was partitioned in 1921, divided into the six counties of the North, known as Ulster, with its inbuilt Protestant majority, and the twenty-six counties of the South that made up the Irish Free State. In 1969 the 'old' IRA split over its failure to defend Catholics in the North from Loyalist attacks. The 'new' IRA became known as the Provisionals and the 'old' IRA as the Officials. The Officials were revolutionary socialists. The Provisionals, though left wing, were more nationalistic.

Bogside to arrest rioters, the 'Derry Young Hooligans', who had been stoning soldiers stationed at the entrance to the area. The paras returned fire at what they claimed were gunmen and bombers. As a result thirteen civil rights marchers were shot dead. In his epic report into the shootings almost forty years later, Lord Saville concluded that all the dead were unarmed and innocent.* His definitive findings ran to 5,000 pages, took twelve years to produce and cost £195 million. I was relieved when I first read his summary, which confirmed much of what I had concluded in 1992 in my own investigation into the events of Bloody Sunday on its twentieth anniversary, and about which I had given evidence to Lord Saville's tribunal sitting in the Guildhall in Derry. A senior member of the Official IRA in the city told me that some weapons had been left in the Bogside for 'defensive' purposes.[5] I had concluded that there was at least one Official IRA gun in the Bogside, and that a single shot was fired at paratroopers. I had wrongly deduced that the Official IRA had fired first. Lord Saville's report stated that the first shots were fired by the paras, and the Official IRA's shot was in response.

The day after Bloody Sunday, Frank Lagan came to Brendan's house again. Brendan was furious, having arranged, as he thought, the removal of all IRA weapons from the Bogside. Lagan was shattered, and had no explanation of what had happened or why. 'This is an absolute disaster,' Brendan told him. 'We are going to have a war on our hands.' That is precisely what happened.

Bloody Sunday was my introduction to the conflict in Ireland. I was then a twenty-nine-year-old journalist, most of whose previous TV experience was limited to reporting for Thames Television's *Today* programme, presented by the legendary Eamonn Andrews. I covered local government, social issues and lighter subjects too – from the 'pumpkin nobblers' sabotaging a village's 'biggest pumpkin'

---

*Lord Saville's inquiry into Bloody Sunday reported on 15 June 2010. His conclusions were universally welcomed by Nationalists in Derry, who praised the dignity and forthrightness with which the new Prime Minister David Cameron announced and welcomed the report.

competition to a man building a flying saucer in the Berkshire woods, with his coalshed acting as Mission Control. I hardly felt equipped to cover what I found when I arrived in Derry late that Sunday evening after the shooting was over. By then I was working for Thames's *This Week* programme – ITV's *Panorama*. We'd been planning to cover the march that day with three film crews – one with the army, one with the marchers and one just floating, since it was clear that there was going to be trouble. But our plans were stymied by the militant television technicians' union, the ACTT, which demanded danger money on such a scale that the company refused to pay. The plan therefore was called off.

I remember shivering in my London flat that cold Sunday afternoon, sitting on the night-storage heater to keep warm, when I heard the news that there had been shootings and deaths in Derry. My programme editor, John Edwards, and I spoke on the phone, and along with a phalanx of other journalists I caught the next plane to Belfast. I confess I had to look at a map to find out where Derry was, such was my ignorance of Ireland. Like most of my fellow citizens, and many journalists too, I was equally ignorant of the roots and history of the conflict. I arrived in Derry just before midnight and checked into a B&B. As I undressed to go to bed I glanced at the window, wondering if an IRA sniper had me in his sights. I smile when I think of it now.

The following morning I went down into the Bogside. I found a scene I will never forget. There was not a soul around. I could almost touch the silence. Fresh blood was still on the ground. Nervously, I started knocking on doors to try to talk to people. Being a journalist from a country whose soldiers had just killed thirteen of their neighbours, I expected a hostile reception, but I was surprised to find the opposite. People asked me in, and gave me tea, biscuits and buns. They were eager to talk, wanting the world to know what had happened. I met some members of the IRA's Derry Brigade. They were not what I'd expected. They weren't hooded or threatening. Many of them were the sons or fathers of the families I had been speaking to. They were part of the community, and now after Bloody Sunday they were seen more than ever as its defenders. I also interviewed the Provisionals' Commanding Officer, who was adamant that they had removed all their guns from the Bogside. He was a nervous man with no great natural authority, and first had to make a phone call to the IRA high command in Dublin to check that he could do the interview. It was the first time I had talked to an active 'terrorist'. I remember being acutely embarrassed before filming began when my producer insisted on combing my hair.

I watched a torchlit procession wind its way through the Bogside and up to the church on the Creggan estate on the hill above, where thirteen bodies were lying in their coffins. I was standing next to the Nationalist politician John Hume, who in 1998 would jointly win the Nobel Peace Prize with his Unionist counterpart David Trimble. John pointed out one of the mourners, and said he was someone I should talk to. It was Martin McGuinness. Shortly afterwards I met McGuinness in the disused gasworks in the Bogside which was a sort of IRA gang hut. It was a bizarre experience to meet a senior member of the IRA in such unlikely surroundings, within sight and range of British Army rifles stationed high on the city walls above the Bogside. The army had made a decision not to go into the areas dominated by both wings of the IRA. The twenty-two-year-old McGuinness was charming, articulate and impressive, and seemed terribly young. Even then his eyes, into which I was to look on and off over the next thirty years, had the capacity to harden at a moment's notice, and seemed capable of taking you out at ten paces. He talked passionately about the 'armed struggle' and why he was engaged in it. To my surprise, at the end of our conversation he said he'd much rather be washing the car and mowing the lawn on Sundays than doing what he was doing. I believed him, although I thought that I shouldn't. I never imagined that one day one of Britain's most wanted 'terrorists' would become Northern Ireland's Deputy First Minister.*

* * *

---

*Later that year McGuinness was sentenced to six months' imprisonment for IRA membership. In court he said: 'I am a member [of the IRA] and very, very proud of it … We firmly believed we were doing our duty as Irishmen.' It was only many years later, while giving evidence to the Saville Inquiry, that he admitted he was second-in-command of the IRA in Derry at the time of Bloody Sunday.

The events of 30 January 1972 made Brendan Duddy determined to do all he could to help bring peace to his city and the province. 'That feeling was as strong as it could be. It was not that I could fail. It was that I was going to do it. I think it came from years of running over the hills. You had to get there.' After Bloody Sunday, the violence escalated as young men and women queued up to join the IRA. Retribution for the killings that day was swift and savage. The IRA, in which the Provisionals now made the military running, thinking they were close to achieving their goal of driving the British out of the North, declared that they were ready to call a ceasefire and talk peace. The British decided they had nothing to lose, and secretly took up the Provisionals' offer, arranging to meet the IRA leadership – which included Martin McGuinness and Gerry Adams (belying Adams' insistence that he was never a member of the IRA) – in the unlikely setting of fashionable Cheyne Walk in London's Chelsea. The meeting, held on 7 July 1972, got nowhere. The IRA said they wanted the British out of the North on or before 1 January 1975. The Northern Ireland Secretary, William Whitelaw, later said that meeting and talking to the IRA was the greatest mistake of his political career. Brendan wasn't surprised at the failure of the talks, as he felt the IRA leadership were living in cloud cuckoo land. 'It was a disaster. "Brits out" politically couldn't happen. I just said, "They're crazy!" Nobody had taken the time to think what would happen to a million Protestant Unionists if the Brits left. It was their lack of understanding of politics.' He was to spend the next twenty years trying to educate the IRA in political realities.

Two days after the fiasco of Cheyne Walk the ceasefire was over, and it was back to the 'war' with an even greater savage intensity. On Friday, 21 July, the IRA exploded twenty-two bombs across Belfast, killing eleven people and injuring 130. The disturbing scenes of the carnage, with charred body parts being shovelled into black plastic bags, could not be shown in their entirety on television. The IRA claimed that warnings had been given but not properly heeded. There were warnings, but they were hopelessly inadequate. I had been looking for an IRA contact the previous evening and was told he was at a meeting in a school in the Nationalist Andersonstown area of

11

predominantly Catholic West Belfast. I went along, and stumbled upon what seemed to be a high-level gathering of the IRA's Belfast Brigade sitting around a table and, I subsequently imagined, possibly finalising the plans for what became known as 'Bloody Friday'. What happened shocked me, and shattered Brendan. 'It wouldn't add one centimetre to Irish freedom,' he said. 'When I was looking at that black bag, that was somebody's mother, father or brother.'

By the summer of 1972, the British had decided that the army would have to enter the 'no go' areas not just in Derry but in Belfast and other places in the province that the IRA had made its fiefdom, and from which its units could operate with impunity. The government feared that moving into uncharted territory dominated by the IRA was potentially a recipe for disaster on a scale that would dwarf Bloody Sunday. Once again, Chief Superintendent Frank Lagan pressed Brendan into service. He told him the army was coming in with tanks and 5,000 men. 'All the heavy stuff,' he said. 'We need the IRA's guns removed.' Brendan was understandably sceptical, given what had happened on Bloody Sunday, but Lagan convinced him that this was different. He went to Dublin to see Seamus Twomey, the IRA's Belfast commander and member of the Army Council, and convinced him that his men would face overwhelming force, and the loss of life would potentially be great. He explained that the British had no objection to the IRA removing its weapons – presumably across the nearby border into the Irish Republic, where they would hang on to them. Twomey said he would do what he could. Shortly afterwards Brendan received a 'mysterious' visitor who told him that the weapons were ready for removal. When I asked him how this was brought about he was cagey, admitting that he had faced a desperate moral dilemma, given that some of the weapons had probably been used to kill people and might well be used to do so again. 'I had two choices,' he said. 'Either do it or not do it.' He decided to do it. All he would say was that the process wasn't interfered with by either the army or the police.

On 31 July 1972, ten days after Bloody Friday, 12,000 soldiers with bulldozers and tanks moved into the so-called 'no go' areas across the province and re-established control. It was called Operation Motorman, the biggest British military operation since Suez.[6] The IRA offered no resistance. For the moment, Brendan's work was done.

A year later, Brendan's life was to change forever. Although it was known to only a tiny handful of people, in October 1971 Britain's Secret Intelligence Service (SIS) had stationed one of its officers in the province alongside the diplomats living at Laneside. The IRA's increasingly violent campaign clearly indicated the need for improved intelligence-gathering on those who were killing British soldiers and policemen, and bombing the hearts out of its cities, with Derry in the front line. The first MI6 officer to be posted there was Frank Steele, a former Foreign Office diplomat who had served in the Middle East and Africa, and now found himself seconded to Northern Ireland, about which, as he told me, he knew virtually nothing. It was Steele who had organised the abortive meeting between William Whitelaw and the leadership of the Provisional IRA at Cheyne Walk in July 1972. He was a remarkable man. I interviewed him not long before he died of cancer in November 1997. Knowing that he had only a few months to live, he sat in a wheelchair and talked, wishing to place on the public record what he had done and what he had tried to achieve. He told me how depressed he was after Cheyne Walk, and how he left the province in May 1973 with a heavy heart. 'I don't think either community had suffered enough to make peace an absolute imperative,' he said wearily, 'and so we settled down to twenty-five years of waste and murder.'[7]

Steele was succeeded by his fellow MI6 officer Michael Oatley, who was very different in temperament and style, but equally accomplished. At Laneside he found a message from Steele suggesting that he might find it useful to look up a businessman in Derry called Brendan Duddy. Oatley made enquiries, and found that one of the contacts he had met through Steele, a prosperous local businessman, knew Brendan. A meeting was arranged at the businessman's house. That was where Brendan first met Michael Oatley, and where a relationship that was to last for almost twenty years began. At the time

Brendan was not aware that Oatley was an MI6 officer. He thought he was simply a British diplomat who had come to Derry to find out more about Northern Ireland. Brendan was impressed by Oatley, who he said had the appearance and polished manners of a film star: 'He could listen for approximately five hours, drinking tea without once going to the toilet. The perfect spy man.' Brendan learned a lot from Oatley, and Oatley learned a lot from Brendan. They both came to need each other. Oatley carried on where Frank Steele left off in working towards the long-term aim of finding a way of getting the IRA to end its campaign. Brendan became the key to that end as they walked the tightrope together between the British government and the IRA's Army Council.

Oatley admitted that he was inexperienced when he first set foot in the province. 'I knew nothing about Northern Ireland,' he told me. 'In that sense I was typical of most of the people who went to help the Secretary of State with this new problem.' But he was clear about what he had to do. 'I thought that it was a situation in which intelligence would not be a matter of simply reporting on situations, but trying to influence them. If I was going to spend two years or longer in Northern Ireland, I ought perhaps to try to concentrate on seeing whether my particular skills and background could enable me to find a way to influence the leadership of the IRA, or to make some kind of contact through which they could be influenced.'[8] Brendan was to become that contact. He was perfectly placed. He had established his credibility with the IRA on two critical occasions, in the days leading up to Bloody Sunday and Operation Motorman. He had met senior members of the Army Council like Seamus Twomey and, perhaps most importantly, he knew Martin McGuinness well from the days when he used to deliver burgers to his chippie in William Street. He also knew Rory O'Brady, the President of Sinn Féin, whom he'd met during his earlier negotiations over the removal of weapons. Brendan was Oatley's means to a very distant end, although at the time Oatley probably had little idea just how distant that end was likely to be. He knew that at some stage he, and ultimately the British government, would have to talk to the 'terrorists' if they were to bring an end to the conflict. It could be seen as a win-win situation. If talking to the IRA led to a lasting peace, that would be a win. If, on the other hand, it led to a series of ceasefires and splits that weakened the IRA through internal divisions, that would be a win too. But he was under no illusions that difficult and dangerous political terrain lay ahead.

I asked Brendan what he thought Michael Oatley's game plan was at the time. 'I don't think he had one. My job was to teach Michael, and Michael's job was to teach the Prime Minister or whoever he could get access to. The idea was to share this information.' And that meant talking to the IRA? 'Absolutely. That was the point. I was not an IRA man, not a Sinn Féin man. At the end of the day my job was to get these people talking.' I asked if he felt that Oatley was using him for his own purposes and the purpose of the British government. He was frank. 'Yes. Absolutely. And I was perfectly happy with it.' He was happy because he and Oatley shared a common view of the way forward. There had to be engagement with the IRA. 'I was saying all the time, "You've got to talk to them. This has got to stop, and the way to stop it is to talk to them."' But for Oatley there was a problem. After the fiasco of Cheyne Walk, and subsequent political embarrassment when news of the meeting with the IRA leadership was leaked, a strict prohibition was placed on any further contact with the 'terrorists'. Oatley was well aware of this, and used metaphors and analogies when he talked to Brendan. 'It's very cold at the moment,' he would say. 'Put on your woolly [long] Johns.' This was his way of warning Brendan that the government wasn't interested in any political initiatives.

By 1974 the weather was positively arctic following the IRA's bloody campaign in England. On 4 February a coach carrying military personnel along the M62 from Manchester to Catterick army camp in North Yorkshire was bombed. The fifty-pound bomb concealed in the boot of the coach killed nine soldiers, one woman and two children aged five and two.[9] By the autumn the IRA had intensified its mainland campaign. On 5 October it struck at two pubs in Guildford – the Horse and Groom and the Seven Stars – which it claimed were 'military targets', as they were used by off-duty soldiers from nearby camps. Four soldiers, two of them women, were killed. A civilian also died and fifty-four people were injured. A month later, on 7 November, there was a further bomb attack on the King's Arms pub in Woolwich, killing a soldier and fatally wounding a part-time barman. Two weeks later, on 21 November, came the most shocking IRA attack of all, when two pubs in Birmingham were bombed – the Mulberry Bush and the Tavern in the Town. A warning was given, but only minutes before the explosions. Twenty-one people died and 182 were injured.

In such a climate it seemed unthinkable that any representative of the British government should put out feelers to the IRA, let alone meet them. Oatley knew full well what the IRA was up to. 'One of the things that I'd come to understand at a fairly early stage was that the continuation of a violent campaign was not inconsistent with the IRA's willingness to consider political options.'[10] But he and Brendan agreed how tightly those political options were circumscribed, and accurately reflected the British government's position in terms of negotiating any settlement to the conflict. Brendan spelled out two unshakeable principles. 'The British made it clear that they were not going to speak as violence continued – and Michael and I made it clear too.' The second principle was that the British weren't going to 'get on their boats in Belfast', sail away and abandon the Unionists. These principles remained the cornerstones of the British government's position right through to the Good Friday Agreement of 1998 that was designed to settle and end the conflict. It was the first of them – no talks while violence continued – that, as we will later see, almost derailed the process.

Oatley faced a conundrum. He had been forbidden to have any contact with the IRA, but he knew that as the security situation spiralled from bad to worse, both in the province and on the mainland, something had to be done, and done urgently. He devised a way of communicating with the IRA without ever talking to them directly, by inventing a metaphorical bamboo 'pipe'. The 'pipe' was held by Oatley at one end and Rory O'Brady at the other, with Brendan in the middle conveying and interpreting the messages that were passed down it from the British to the IRA, and vice-versa. 'What we were in fact able to do was to blow gently down the "pipe", and the person at the other end would be able to feel the draught and blow back,' Oatley said. 'This seemed to me not much more than a slight bending of the Secretary of State's rules.' Oatley went to his boss, Frank Cooper, the senior British civil servant in Belfast, and got clearance from him to use the arrangement. 'It's quite a nice pipe,' he assured him, 'so can we perhaps put a bit of material down it to see if we can develop a relationship?' Cooper, as flexible and inventive as Oatley, agreed, and as a result of messages sent down Oatley's pipe, the groundwork was laid for an IRA ceasefire and talks.

The IRA declared a ceasefire over Christmas 1974, expecting the 'Brits' to reciprocate at once with dialogue. But there was no movement, and the IRA leadership became increasingly frustrated. Brendan was made abundantly aware of their anger, and their suspicion that the perfidious 'Brits' were at it again. He became worried that the credibility and the trust he had so carefully built up over the previous two years was about to evaporate. On Christmas Eve he rang Oatley in the middle of the night, as Oatley says was his wont, and warned him that things seemed about to fall apart. He wanted to know what the IRA wanted to know: what were the British prepared to discuss, and crucially, was a British withdrawal on the agenda? The phrase Oatley used on behalf of the British was 'structures of disengagement from Ireland'. To him, this meant the disengagement of the security forces and their withdrawal from Catholic areas in response to a cessation of violence. So when Brendan asked the $64,000 question of whether 'withdrawal' was on the agenda, the answer wasn't yes and it wasn't no. Oatley's basic message to Brendan, and therefore to the IRA, was that once violence stopped, anything could be discussed. He admitted to me that he was being intentionally ambiguous. 'I think that was the nature of our dialogue, and I think that the ambiguity was recognised by both sides, so that each could make of it what it wanted. Ambiguous phrases were very much the currency we were involved in.'[11] As Oatley knew, there was a world of difference between discussing withdrawal and actually carrying it out. But his message was enough to lead the IRA to believe that the phrase 'structures of disengagement' meant the beginning of the road to their goal, the ending of British rule in Northern Ireland. By this time Brendan knew that Oatley was working for MI6, although the IRA was still under the impression that he was just a political adviser seconded from the Foreign Office. Oatley had had to tell Brendan of his real affiliation, as Brendan had to know about what Oatley described as 'certain procedures'.

The following day, Brendan climbed into his battered Datsun and began the long journey south through the snow to see Rory O'Brady at his home in Roscommon in the seemingly endless flatlands of central Ireland. But first he had to get petrol. It was Christmas Day, and the petrol stations were shut. He was forced to call on a local garage owner whom he knew, and who obliged by filling up his car. 'He said, "I'm taking no money," and he didn't know what I was doing. People sensed that something that might alter their lives was happening.'

Brendan arrived at O'Brady's house just as the family was sitting down to Christmas dinner, and tapped on the window. Brendan Duddy was the last person Rory O'Brady expected to see staring through his window on Christmas Day, but he invited him in, put an extra plate on the table and told him to tuck in. The dinner seemed to last forever as O'Brady went on about the weather, with Brendan bursting to give him Oatley's message. The plates put away, the two adjourned to a room where they could sit alone and talk. Brendan told O'Brady he had had a message from Michael Oatley, and produced a piece of paper with notes of the telephone conversation he had had the previous evening. The note was not detailed, in case it was intercepted by the police on either side of the border. Brendan said that everything the IRA wanted to talk about was on the table. That included withdrawal – although there was no indication that the British ever intended to carry it out. O'Brady explained that he couldn't make a decision himself on a face-to-face meeting with the 'Brits', but would have to consult and get permission. 'Consulting' meant talking to the IRA's Army Council. 'I thought the best thing was to confront them with the primary source, the intermediary himself,' O'Brady told me. The Army Council wanted to see the whites of Brendan's eyes.

On New Year's Eve 1974 Brendan made the journey with O'Brady to the IRA's inner sanctum. Brendan says he didn't look out of the car window, and kept his eyes on the floor, as he didn't want to know where it was or the route they were taking to get there. These were his rules for staying alive. 'I didn't want to know the road signs, and I didn't want to ask.' They finally arrived at a big country house outside Dublin belonging to a businessman who had presumably allowed it to be used in the name of the cause. 'It was the most enormous house I'd ever seen,' Brendan said, 'almost a castle.' He was shown into a huge drawing room where the IRA leadership was waiting. It seemed an unlikely setting for a meeting with the most wanted men in Ireland. 'They were sitting round this big table, just like a board of directors. Everyone was very polite.' O'Brady waited in the wings, as it wasn't normal for the President of Sinn Féin to be there as a member of the Army Council, although he could be present *ex officio*, in his political capacity. Seamus Twomey was in the chair, alongside his fellow Belfast Republican Billy McKee. McKee told me of his surprise when Brendan walked in. 'We were just finishing up an Army Council meeting. He looked bloody scared when he came into that room. I'd never seen Brendan Duddy before, and I was amazed, because it isn't on the books to bring anybody to an Army Council meeting. There was nobody at these meetings except Army Council men.' Nevertheless, they soon got down to business, as O'Brady remembers. 'They didn't give him an easy time. They questioned him very closely. It was a very serious matter.' I asked him if they suspected that Brendan might be a British spy. 'The question didn't arise. They were aware that he was the person who had been conveying these messages for a number of years, and that this channel was totally reliable.'

Brendan explained that he had been talking to Michael Oatley, whom he described as 'a servant of the British government' (techni-cally, Oatley was referred to by the government as 'the British government representative'). The IRA was more interested in the message than the man, and Brendan duly conveyed the ambiguous communication, although I suspect the ambiguities were not dwelt on. At this stage both parties wanted to get on with the business of dialogue. Brendan insisted that he make all the security arrangements for the meeting, which he said would take place at his house in Derry. This was the point at which he enlisted the services of his friend Bernadette Mount, to drive some of the IRA leaders across the border. Bernadette is a most unlikely IRA courier, which is why Brendan chose her. Attractive, quick-witted, feisty and brave, she's the last person to arouse suspicion at army checkpoints on either side of the border. 'She was very cheerful and in no way anxious or fearful,' says O'Brady. 'She just rose to the occasion, and that was appreciated highly by all of us and still is.'

There were some hairy moments as they approached army check-points: 'It was nerve-racking,' says Bernadette. 'I'd write my car regis-tration on the front of the dashboard, as I'm hopeless at numbers.' She hid O'Brady's notes and papers by stuffing them under her jumper. Bernadette not only ferried the IRA leaders to Derry, she put them up in her house as well. She remembers the sheer ordinariness of it all, and showed me some photographs she'd taken at the time. Seamus Twomey was singing Irish songs – 'He was a nice singer.' Billy McKee helped clear out the grate, insisting it was man's work – 'Billy lit the fire every day.' And Rory O'Brady was wandering around in his paisley pyjamas, which Bernadette found very amusing – 'I told him I'd send the photo to Ian Paisley, and he thought it was funny.' She was clearly a great fan of Michael Oatley: 'He was tall, thin and perfectly dressed. Everything about him was just like James Bond. He was so relaxed he made you feel that everything was fine. He was very nice.' Brendan's family were also mesmerised by the British visitor who was to become so much a part of their lives. Brendan's wife Margo felt ashamed to give him tea in a mug, and on one of her trips to London she went into Selfridges, where there was a sale on, and bought a Royal Albert china tea-set called 'Old County Roses'. The set still stands in her kitchen cupboard.

The first encounter between the British and the IRA since the abortive meeting in Cheyne Walk took place at Brendan's house on 7 January 1975. The participants were Billy McKee and Joe McCallion, a senior IRA man from Derry who along with Martin McGuinness had been convicted in Dublin of IRA membership in 1973, and Michael Oatley in his capacity as the 'British government representative'. This was a preliminary meeting about meetings, in which both sides set out their *bona fides*. Further encounters followed in Brendan's tiny 'wee room' over the next few weeks, with Oatley joined by James Allan, the diplomat who operated from Laneside and was Political Adviser to the Secretary of State. So the talks could be held in absolute privacy, Brendan had sent his family off for two weeks to a three-star hotel in Torremolinos, with £100 to spend. Torremolinos in January was freezing. Meanwhile the secret talks back home in Derry were warmed on those cold winter days and nights by the peat fire in the corner, which Oatley became accustomed to tending, just as Billy McKee did in Bernadette's house. Brendan stood in his 'wee room' and told me about its significance:

> It's a simple room in a simple family house. This is where it all happened. Hard as it is to believe, there was always a rush for this little chair here. There's a notion that big things happened in the Oval Office in Washington or the Grand Hall in the Kremlin, but it doesn't happen that way. It happens less formally and more simply. And when you get a situation where eventually somebody is dying for a cup of tea and says, 'I'll make a cup of tea,' and you have to ask somebody who you are not very happy about, 'Would you like tea?' it breaks it down. And then, of course, what happens is somebody says, 'When you're there, would you get a bucket of coal?'

Brendan normally absented himself from sensitive and secret negotiations once he believed his job as facilitator had been done.

Republicans always took careful minutes of meetings, and those held in Brendan's house in the mid-1970s were no exception. I tried for a long time to get access to them, and finally succeeded in 1996. It involved a long drive across the border into a remote corner of the Irish Republic. I arrived at the seaside location to which I'd been directed, and waited. At last a car arrived, and I was told to get in. Once I was in the front passenger seat, I was told to look down, and not to make any mental note of the route we were taking. It was the same routine Brendan had followed when he went to meet the Army Council. I was told that the reason I was kept waiting at the rendezvous was so my minders-to-be could make sure I hadn't been followed. We finally arrived at a large detached house in the country. I was made welcome, and shown into a bedroom. On the table was a red file which contained the minutes of the historic meetings. I was allowed to dictate them into my tape recorder, as annotating them by hand would have taken more time than I was to be afforded. I felt a slight tingling sensation as I read the minutes, seeing the record of history, albeit from one side. I was kept going by endless cups of tea and fruit cake brought in by the woman of the house. The minutes recorded what was said at the meetings in Brendan's 'wee room' at the beginning of 1975, after which the IRA declared a ceasefire or 'cessation of hostilities'. At the time this was, and continued to be for the next twenty years, the British prerequisite for any private face-to-face talks with the IRA. They stated that the British agreed the following on the basis of 'a genuine and sustained cessation of violence and hostilities':

- [In that event] the army would gradually be reduced to peacetime levels and withdrawn to barracks.
- Discussion will continue between [government] officials and representatives of Provisional Sinn Féin and will include the aim of securing a permanent peace.
- Once violence has come to a complete end, the rate of release will be speeded up with a view to releasing all detainees [from internment].

This was not a million miles from what was discussed and agreed at the secret talks almost two decades later that finally led to the Good

Friday Agreement and the 'permanent peace' that was the aspiration inherent in those minutes from 1975. I scoured them for any sign of a reference to 'structures of disengagement' and British withdrawal from Ireland. I finally came across one dated 2 April 1975. It read: 'The British government cannot say they're leaving Ireland because the reaction would prevent that happening. The tendency is towards eventual British disengagement but it would stop if the Republican Movement [the composite name for the IRA] goes back to war.'

I was surprised that a British official would say such a thing quite so baldly. I asked Brendan if he was also surprised. He said he wasn't. 'I'm not an apologist for the IRA, [but] basically they don't tell lies about things like that.' Billy McKee was adamant that withdrawal was discussed. '[The word] "withdrawal" was used during the whole negotiations with Oatley and others. They said that was what they wanted, and they needed the IRA to help them so there wouldn't be a bloodbath. I can tell you that if they hadn't mentioned withdrawal there'd have been no ceasefire and no truce at the time.'[12]

The 1975 cessation lasted for almost a year, but became increasingly meaningless as Loyalist paramilitaries, suspecting a British sellout to the IRA, stepped up their campaign of sectarian slaughter, killing 120 Catholics, most of them innocent civilians. The IRA retaliated, sometimes under so-called flags of convenience,* while stepping up its attacks on London until the unit responsible was besieged in Balcombe Street before surrendering on 12 December.

By the beginning of 1976, the cessation was over. It had marked a turning point in the history of the IRA. Its former Belfast commander, Brendan Hughes, who was in prison at the time of the truce, told me it was the nadir for Republicans: 'In the 1975 period there was a great deal of disillusionment among a lot of people in the gaol. When the

---

*On 4 September 1975 the 'South Armagh Republican Action Force' (i.e. the Provisional IRA) shot dead four Protestants in an attack on the Tullyvallen Orange Hall near Newtonhamilton. Two of the dead were aged seventy and eighty. On 5 January 1976 they struck again, machine-gunning to death ten Protestant workers at Kingsmill in South Armagh who were travelling home from work in a minibus. The killers identified one Catholic, and let him escape to make their sectarian point.

ceasefire was on, the whole machine slipped into sectarianism and a lot of us were very, very unhappy with the situation.'[13]

The leadership that had taken the IRA into the truce was discredited. There was no 'permanent peace', but the IRA had largely stood down its units, rendering most of its volunteers inactive. Frustration at the lack of political progress grew, as did impatience with IRA orders to refrain from attacks. The result was disillusionment and dissension in the ranks. This was the point at which the IRA's new leadership emerged to challenge O'Brady, Twomey and McKee and the others who supported and advised them.

Gerry Adams and Martin McGuinness were untainted by the truce. Adams was in the Long Kesh prison camp,* and McGuinness had been released from gaol in the Irish Republic on 13 December 1974, having served nine months of a twelve-month sentence for IRA membership – his second such sentence. After McGuinness emerged he was not involved in the preliminaries to the secret dialogue with the British, or the subsequent negotiations that led to the truce. The new leadership believed that the IRA had been duped by the 'Brits', and vowed that it would never happen again. Brendan looks back on the period, and the failure of the negotiations and the truce, with sadness. 'The leadership of McKee and O'Brady did everything in their power within their Republican remit to get a track going similar to the track twenty years on. The difficulty was that when the young men came along, Adams and McGuinness, they simply saw the O'Bradys of this world as being past it. They said, "We're running this campaign."' And they did. Ironically, twenty years later, on 31 August 1994, the 'new' IRA leadership, which had remained in place over all those years, did the same as the old leadership, declaring 'a complete cessation of military operations',[14] and finally set Northern Ireland on the road to peace.

* * *

---

*The internment camp set up in 1971 that subsequently became a prison before having its name changed to the Maze.

Although the 'old' leadership had been discredited, Brendan thought that Rory O'Brady, Billy McKee, Seamus Twomey and others had done all they could through Michael Oatley to try to establish a permanent peace. He didn't think it was their fault that it had all fallen apart by the beginning of 1976. The bloodshed that had marked the months of the truce continued unabated through the rest of the 1970s, with a further three hundred deaths,[15] including the assassinations of Christopher Ewart-Biggs, the UK Ambassador to the Republic of Ireland, and Lord Louis Mountbatten, the last British Viceroy of India.*

By 1980 a new crisis had arisen that was to have momentous consequences for the future course of the conflict and the long and bloody road to peace. IRA prisoners in the Maze were still refusing to wear prison uniform, claiming that it criminalised them and their 'struggle'. They insisted that they were not criminals but prisoners of war, and as such demanded that they should be allowed to wear their own clothes, a demand that the new Conservative government under Margaret Thatcher steadfastly refused. In 1972 a previous Conservative government, confronted with Billy McKee's thirty-day hunger strike in Crumlin Road prison, granted 'Special Category Status', under which prisoners were allowed to wear their own clothes and were given other privileges. This was taken by the IRA to be the political status they demanded. In 1976 the Labour government rescinded these concessions and insisted that prisoners wore prison uniform. The protest began when prisoners rejected uniforms and wrapped their naked bodies in the blankets provided for the beds in their cells. The government was unmoved. In 1978 the prisoners escalated the blanket protest by smearing their excreta on the cell walls in the

---

*Ewart-Biggs was killed on 21 July 1976 by an IRA remote-control bomb while on his way to the Embassy in Dublin. With him in the car were Brian Cubbon, the Northern Ireland Permanent Under Secretary, and Cubbon's private secretary Judith Cook. Cubbon survived, but Cook did not. Lord Mountbatten, aged seventy-nine, was killed on 27 August 1979 when the IRA detonated a remote-control bomb on board his boat, *Shadow V,* off Mullaghmore, County Sligo, where he had a holiday home. Three others died with him, two of them family members. Later that same day the IRA killed eighteen soldiers of the Parachute Regiment in a double bomb ambush near Warrenpoint, County Down.

so-called 'dirty' or 'no wash' protest. Again the government stood firm. In 1980, with no sign of movement from Mrs Thatcher's new administration, IRA prisoners took the step of last resort and embarked on a hunger strike, the weapon of ultimate protest, to put pressure on the British. Their use of the tactic went as far back as 1920, when Terence MacSwiney, the Sinn Féin Lord Mayor of Cork, arrested on charges of sedition during the Irish War of Independence, died in Brixton Prison after seventy-four days on hunger strike.

Brendan was deeply depressed. Throughout the period he had remained in touch with his 'old' IRA contacts and with Michael Oatley, who had kept his 'bamboo pipe' in good working order. Oatley had made it clear to Brendan that he was always available as a point of contact, wherever he happened to be in the world. He believed he had the confidence of the new IRA leadership: 'I think that people on the IRA side thought I had come out of it as a reasonably reliable person with whom they could deal, and I for my part had been quite clearly convinced that people on the other side were able to keep secrets.'[16]

As the crisis over the hunger strike escalated, Billy McKee came to see Brendan at his home. 'He was really upset about hunger strikes due to his own experiences in gaol,' Brendan remembers. 'He said, "You've got to do something about this. I prefer a man to die on the front line rather than die in prison."' Brendan had feared the worst during the lead-up to the hunger strike, before Mrs Thatcher came to power. Labour's tough, Yorkshire-born Northern Ireland Secretary, Roy Mason, had a visceral loathing for the IRA. He once described squeezing them like a tube of toothpaste: 'We are squeezing them out of their safe havens. We are squeezing them away from their money supplies. We are squeezing them out of society and into prison.'[17] 'We had that awful man Roy Mason here,' Brendan recalls. 'We had the sides getting further and further apart. The IRA didn't want to know. They didn't want to be involved in anything. I saw the hunger strike as a possibility for reopening negotiations. That's how I read it.'

Brendan picked up the phone to Michael Oatley, as usual in the middle of the night, told him what McKee had said, and stressed the urgency of trying to break the impasse. Christmas 1980 was approaching, and some of the seven original hunger strikers appeared to be near death.* 'We spent two or three hours discussing it in veiled language,' Oatley told me. 'It seemed that one might be able to develop a formula, with no doubt some ambiguities in it, which would be a gesture by the British government to the demands of the hunger strikers.'[18]

Oatley went to see the Permanent Under Secretary at the Northern Ireland Office, Sir Kenneth Stowe, to attempt to work out a solution that would bend the prison rules and provide a face-saving formula for both parties. While talking to Stowe – a pragmatic civil service mandarin, not a dogmatic ideologue – Oatley kept in touch with Brendan over the phone to make sure that the 'escape hatch' being devised would be acceptable to the IRA. A formula was agreed, with the question of what constituted the prisoners' 'own clothes' being left imprecise, or as Oatley described it to me, 'fairly open-ended and in some ways ambiguous'.[19] Stowe got in touch with Prime Minister Margaret Thatcher, whose Private Secretary he had previously been. She signed off the deal, no doubt reluctantly. All this, of course, was done in the utmost secrecy. Oatley was then driven at top speed along the M4 to Heathrow, from where he would take a plane to Belfast's Aldergrove airport to deliver the compromise formula to the IRA via another intermediary, Father Brendan Meagher, a priest from Dundalk in the Irish Republic.

Brendan had driven from Derry, and was waiting at Aldergrove with Father Meagher. When Oatley arrived he handed the envelope containing the formula to Brendan, who gave it to Father Meagher, who conveyed it to the Provisional leadership waiting in Belfast, who relayed its contents to the hunger strikers in the Maze. The strike was called off at the eleventh hour, and no one died. But that was only the beginning of the tragic story. When families and relatives subsequently arrived at the prison carrying their loved ones' clothes, the

---

*Six of the original hunger strikers were members of the Provisional IRA: Brendan Hughes, the IRA's Officer Commanding (OC) in the Maze, Tommy McKearney, Raymond McCartney, Leo Green, Thomas McFeeley and Sean McKenna. The seventh, John Nixon, was a member of the Irish National Liberation Army (INLA).

prison authorities would not let them put them on. There was a total breakdown in communications. Brendan was desperate, as he knew what the consequences would be. 'It fell apart because the language of the prison governor and prison warders was quite different from the language of the Republican prisoners.' The prisoners thought they were getting political status, but they weren't. The prison authorities did not share Oatley's and Stowe's flexibility, and apparently the government was not minded to force the issue, as it depended on the cooperation and goodwill of the prison administration and officers to run the gaol.

Brendan was thrown into even deeper despair when he heard that there was to be a second hunger strike, as he knew that this time there would be no compromise, and it would be to the death. He had no illusions about Mrs Thatcher's determination: 'The British government had moved away from thinking of any form of agreement in Northern Ireland. They thought they were on the winning trail. They felt, "The IRA is beaten, and we're going to hammer this."' Perhaps the government thought it was going to finish rolling up Roy Mason's tube of toothpaste.

Brendan was right. Matters were now out of his hands. The epic second hunger strike began on 1 March 1981, led by the IRA's new Officer Commanding (OC) in the Maze, Bobby Sands. Nine of his comrades subsequently joined the protest, which became the second great watershed that transformed the conflict, Bloody Sunday being the first. From the outset it was clear that if the British did not give in to the prisoners' five demands, Sands was prepared to die.* As the days went by and Sands grew weaker, media interest in his condition and the reasons for his determination to give his life for the cause he believed in became huge. The hunger strike became an international story, with camera crews flying into Belfast from all over the world. It became an even bigger story when in a by-election held on 9 April,

---

*As well as the right to wear their own clothes, the prisoners demanded the right not to do prison work, the right to free association on the wings, the right to receive one letter or parcel a week, and the restoration of full remission lost through the protest.

forty days into his hunger strike, Sands was elected as Member of Parliament for the Fermanagh-South Tyrone constituency. This was a momentous political event, as it appeared to give the lie to the long-established government spin that the IRA were a bunch of murdering terrorists with no popular support. Sands died on 5 May, the sixty-sixth day of his hunger strike. Around 100,000 mourners came to his funeral, which became a global media event. The implications for the future evolution of the conflict, and the inexorable rise of the IRA's political wing, Sinn Féin, were immense.

In the weeks and months that followed, nine other hunger strikers followed Bobby Sands to their graves.* Mrs Thatcher, known not without reason as 'the Iron Lady', accused the IRA of playing their 'last card'. But her adversaries were just as determined as she was. History shows that in the medium term IRA prisoners gradually won their demands, in particular the right to wear their own clothes: in the longer term, Sinn Féin grew over the next thirty years to become the largest Nationalist party in Northern Ireland.

To his eternal regret, Brendan felt powerless to affect the course of the agonising second hunger strike. Michael Oatley had been replaced, and the 'new' IRA leadership apparently had little rapport with the person who took over from him (whom I cannot name for security reasons). Brendan believed that Gerry Adams and Martin McGuinness 'lacked experience at the time' in dealing with the 'Brits'. But even so, he thinks intervention would have made little difference. 'It was a political strike, and Bobby Sands knew what he was doing. He went on that hunger strike to die. He set the agenda. It was a strike to politicise the people of Ireland. That's what he set out to do, and that's what happened.'

One of Brendan's prize possessions is a 'com', a personal communication from Bobby Sands, written on toilet paper a few days before

---

*The other nine who died were Francis Hughes after fifty-nine days; Raymond McCreesh and Patsy O'Hara (INLA), both after sixty-one days; Joe McDonnell after sixty-one days; Martin Hurson after forty-five days; Kevin Lynch (INLA) after seventy-one days; Kieran Doherty after seventy-three days; Thomas McElwee after sixty-two days; and Michael Devine (INLA) after sixty days.

he died and smuggled out of the prison. As he read it to me, he found it difficult to hold back the tears. Sands wrote:

> To you and yours. May I be permitted to say a last goodbye. If my passion is to mean anything may it mean peace and freedom for you and all of yours. And may I be permitted to say how much I appreciate all the efforts you've done on our behalf.

It was signed with Sands' codename, 'Marcella', the name of his sister.

Michael Oatley was in Africa when Bobby Sands died. In April 1981 he had been posted to Salisbury (now Harare) in Zimbabwe, but before leaving he had made it clear to Brendan that he could be contacted at any time, although the back-channel relationship between the two remained purely informal. Throughout the 1980s, Oatley watched the conflict intensify and observed the rise of Sinn Féin. He returned to London in 1984 as MI6's Controller Middle East, to which was added a year later Controller Counter-Terrorism. In 1988 he became Controller Europe, the largest of MI6's Controllerates. Throughout this time he maintained an ongoing unofficial interest in the conflict in which he had invested so much. Brendan knew he was always there should his services be necessary, and sensed that at some stage the British would be back: 'I knew it. It was simply a matter of waiting.'

The ten hunger strikers who died effectively achieved the political status for which they had so dramatically starved themselves to death. Almost a decade later, in 1990, I was allowed into the Maze to make a BBC documentary, *Enemies Within*. My producer Steve Hewlett and I were given unrestricted access to both IRA and Loyalist prisoners on the segregated wings of the 'H Blocks' (so called because of the configuration of the four wings in the shape of an 'H'). It was an extraordinary experience. We were able to go onto the wings without any minders from either the prison service or the Northern Ireland Office, and my interviews were never monitored or recorded by the prison authorities. This remarkable access had taken me over a decade to negotiate. I finally got the green light after a meeting in London with the Northern Ireland Secretary, Peter Brooke. It was in the early evening, and he was wearing evening dress for a dinner he was due to attend. He said he trusted me not to abuse the privilege, and warned that if I did, I need never ask for any such facility again.

Steve and I spent several weeks inside the prison, getting to know and to gain the trust of the prisoners on both sides. We had had to clear the project with the Republican and Loyalist leaderships outside the prison, which wasn't easy. The gaol was not the hell hole of Republican propaganda. It was more like a holiday camp, with the prisoners from both sides, now wearing their own clothes, effectively running their own wings. For the prison authorities it was easier that way, and they had little choice anyway. The prisoners on each wing had their own paramilitary command structure and hierarchy, unlike any other prison in the United Kingdom. Every lunchtime the inmates were locked in their cells for a couple of hours while the prison officers went off to have lunch, liquid or otherwise. Often we opted to be locked in with the prisoners, taking a rare opportunity to spend 'quality time' with 'terrorists'.

Two encounters stand out for me. One was with a young IRA man from Derry, Eamonn MacDermott, whose father was a GP in the city. As I looked around his cell, I noticed the lines of literary classics on his bookshelves, from *War and Peace* to *The Mayor of Casterbridge*. 'What's an IRA man doing reading Tolstoy and Hardy?' I asked. He looked me straight in the eye with an expression that, like his reply, I will never forget: 'Because an IRA man is normal just like anyone else.' When Eamonn was released he went on to become a journalist with the *Derry Journal*. In 2010 his conviction for the murder of a police officer was overturned.

Equally memorable, though in a different way, was my meeting with the Loyalist Ulster Volunteer Force (UVF) prisoner Billy Giles, who was doing life for the sectarian murder of a Catholic workmate. He had shot him through the back of the head, and was full of remorse for what he had done. 'It was quick and it was dirty and a guy lost his life,' he told me, sitting on the bed in his cell. 'I lost part of myself that

I'll never get back. I felt that somebody had reached down inside of me and ripped my insides out. You can't stop it. It's too late.'[20] I met Billy again after his release. He looked fine, and seemed determined to make something of his life. But it was not to be. On 24 September 1998 he hanged himself, leaving a four-page suicide note. It concluded:

> I was a victim too. Now hopefully I'll be the last. Please don't let any kid suffer the history I have. Please let the next generation live normal lives. Tell them of our mistakes and admit to them our regrets. Steer them towards a life that is 'Troubles' free. I've decided to bring this to an end now. I'm tired.[21]

Sadly, Billy Giles never lived to see the peace that he craved.

Most of the Maze has now been bulldozed to the ground, leaving a few buildings that are expected to become a centre for conflict resolution. But the memories will never be erased from the minds of those who were locked in there. Or from mine.

While filming in the Maze in the summer of 1990, I was aware from talking to the IRA leaders inside that a new political direction was gradually emerging. I was told that the armed struggle had gone as far as it could, and the time for politics and talks was not far distant. Brendan Duddy was ready, as was Michael Oatley with his 'pipe', which he admitted had 'rusted up' from lack of use during the Thatcher decade, at the end of which there seemed to be military stalemate.

At Christmas 1990, a few weeks after the transmission of *Enemies Within*, the IRA declared a Christmas ceasefire. It seemed that what I had picked up in the Maze was about to become real. Once again noises began to come down Oatley's now rusty 'pipe', with the initiative coming from the Derry end. Word reached Oatley, now MI6's Controller Europe, that Martin McGuinness might be interested in sounding out the 'Brits' after the Northern Ireland Secretary, Peter Brooke, had made this remarkable statement:

It is difficult to envisage a military defeat of the IRA. If, in fact, the terrorists were to decide that the moment had come when they wished to withdraw from their activities, then I think the government would need to be imaginative in those circumstances as to how that process should be managed … Let me remind you of the move towards independence in Cyprus. A British Minister stood up in the House of Commons and used the word 'never'. Within two years there had been a retreat from that word.[22]

Brooke made other conciliatory noises too, no doubt intended for the IRA's ears.

Oatley was due to retire in February 1991, and decided to visit Derry to say goodbye to Brendan after all they had gone through together. He was also aware that there might be revised thinking within the IRA leadership. 'It seemed to be a pity just to walk away and leave it all as something one simply remembered,' he told me. 'It did seem that there might be a mood developing within the Provisional leadership where a political strategy, as an alternative to violence, might be something that they would consider pursuing.' He got in touch with Brendan and a dinner was arranged, with Bernadette Mount acting as hostess and cook. The dinner over, there was a knock at the back door. Bernadette asked Brendan who it might be. 'I forgot to tell you,' he said, 'that's Martin.' Bernadette expressed some concern. 'We don't have enough dinner for him,' she said. 'We've eaten it all.' Brendan told her not to worry: 'He's not here for the dinner.' The visit was no accident – Brendan had carefully planned it. Oatley and McGuinness settled down to talk, as Oatley remembers: 'I'd never met McGuinness before, and I was considerably impressed by his intelligence and firmness of manner. I thought him very serious and responsible, and I didn't see him as someone who actually enjoyed getting people killed. I found him a good interlocutor. It was rather like talking to a middle-ranking army officer in one of the tougher regiments, like the Paras or the SAS.'[23]

Brendan watched the two of them – traditional enemies on opposite sides of the dinner table. Oatley had no brief to do what he was doing or say what he was saying, while McGuinness had a strictly limited brief from the IRA – to listen, and that was all. Brendan couldn't believe what he was seeing and hearing. 'It was like a couple wanting to get together to enter a courtship. Dignified. Friendly.' As well as business, there was small talk about McGuinness's passion for fishing: he had only ever crossed the Irish Sea once, for a two-week fishing trip to Scotland. It was all part of breaking the ice. Then Oatley confronted McGuinness with the harsh reality that although the IRA had killed a lot of people, and continued to give the government a hard time, it had achieved nothing tangible. 'Clearly the government was willing to go on forever, if necessary, with a policy of containment, but if the IRA wished to pursue a political course, there might be things the British government could do to help.' In other words, there was a military stalemate, with neither side capable of winning and neither side prepared to give in. The alternative was politics. Brendan recalled: 'I'd never seen Martin interested in politics in my life. He held his own with Michael, and put forward his points of view. Michael very firmly told him, "You'll not beat the Brits, you'll not drive them out of here, and really and truly, would it not be better to find a better way?"' Brendan was profoundly impressed by McGuinness, who had clearly travelled a long way since delivering beefburgers to his chip shop: 'I'd known him for twenty-five years, and this was someone I've never seen before. I'm watching McGuinness emerging.'

This landmark meeting set the scene for what was to happen over the following decade and beyond. The British were going to have to talk to the 'terrorists' once again, but this time with the IRA recognising what the realistic limitations of such talks were: a complete cessation of violence, no sell-out of the Protestant majority, and no breaking of the Union. Most other things would be up for discussion.

Oatley returned to London, and briefed the Permanent Under Secretary at the Northern Ireland Office, John Chilcot, who was destined to become one of the architects of the subsequent peace process. McGuinness said that if the British wished to appoint a successor to Oatley when he retired, the Republican movement was 'morally and tactically obliged not to reject their offer'.[24] A week after the Derry dinner, Michael Oatley retired and departed the scene. On 7 February 1991, with Oatley scarcely gone, the IRA staged a mortar attack on Downing Street and came perilously close to wiping out the British Cabinet, now chaired by the new Conservative Prime Minister, John Major, who a few months before had emerged to seize the crown after the coup that toppled Mrs Thatcher. As with most insurgent organisations, fighting went hand in hand with talking, the aim being to pile on the pressure in the hope of entering negotiations from a position of strength. Neither Major nor Chilcot was surprised.

Brendan was in London on his way back from a trip abroad on the day Downing Street was mortared, and although he too wasn't surprised by it, he was 'pretty fed up with the divergence of, on the one hand, trying to talk peace and, on the other, trying to bomb London'. Oatley had called Brendan while he was out of the country and told him that there was someone who would take his place, and that he'd like to introduce him. But he never did. By now matters were out of his hands. The new Director General of the Security Service, MI5, Stella Rimington, took the view that if it was advisable to renew the contact with Brendan, the officer who did so should be from MI5, not MI6. The anomaly of the involvement of Britain's foreign intelligence service in a domestic conflict had probably only arisen because Michael Oatley had established his relationship with Brendan back in 1973, when MI6 ran intelligence operations in the province. Rimington had support for the new initiative to resuscitate Brendan's role from John Major and his Northern Ireland Secretary, Peter Brooke, and John Deverell,* MI5's Director and Coordinator of Intelligence (DCI) in Northern Ireland.[25] Now the back channel had mainstream political support.

---

*Deverell was one of twenty-five senior British intelligence officers who died on 2 June 1994 when their helicopter crashed on the Mull of Kintyre on the way to a counter-terrorism conference in Scotland.

On his return to Derry, Brendan received a phone call from a man who said he was interested in bringing employment to the city and thought that Brendan, as President of the Chamber of Trade, might be able to help. He talked of creating a hundred jobs. Brendan said he was too busy. The caller said it would only take half an hour, but Brendan still said no. The man rang back repeatedly, and eventually Brendan gave in and said he would see him: 'My purpose was to get him in, be polite and get him out again.' When the visitor arrived, 'He was very nice, very soft, very gentle.' He said he represented a company called Euro Assets. Brendan was beginning to switch off when the man suddenly reached into an inside pocket, pulled out a letter and handed it to him. 'I looked at it, and it was from Peter Brooke, the Secretary of State.' The letter praised Brendan for all his efforts over the years, and expressed the hope that he would continue them, now working with the bearer of the letter, who became known as 'Robert'. 'Robert' was a former MI6 officer who had been seconded to MI5 and tasked by Stella Rimington to carry on where Michael Oatley had left off. 'I knew that John Major and Peter Brooke wouldn't be sending over someone to talk to me unless it was the beginning of the beginning. I knew. People talk about the wonderful work that Tony Blair has done. Wonderful, everybody knows that. But John Major is the guy who really took the courage in his hand and did this – and after the IRA tried to kill him.'

And the IRA kept on sending John Major the military message with increased ferocity. The day after his unexpected general election victory on 9 April 1992, the City of London was rocked by a huge explosion at the Baltic Exchange. Three people were killed in the blast, which caused £800 million worth of damage, eclipsing at one stroke the £600 million that had been the total cost of the damage in Northern Ireland since the outbreak of the Troubles in 1969.[26] As the daunting sweep-up operation began, Major reshuffled his Cabinet and gave the job of Northern Ireland Secretary to his old friend Sir Patrick Mayhew, who had been Attorney General since 1987. Mayhew thought he was being summoned to Downing Street to be given the sack, and decided to put a brave face on it, picking a fresh camellia and sticking it in his buttonhole to make the blow more fragrant. He was astonished but delighted when he was offered the job. 'I didn't say any of the solemn things that people are supposed to say on these occasions,' he told me. 'I simply said, "Whoopee!"'[27]

Mayhew carried on where Peter Brooke had left off, sending barely coded messages to the IRA in speeches, advance knowledge of which was fed to the IRA via Brendan. The key speech was made on 16 December 1992 at Coleraine:

> It is not sensible to believe that any British government will yield to an agenda for Ireland prosecuted by violent means … provided it is advocated constitutionally, there can be no proper reason for excluding any political objective from discussion. Certainly not the objective of a united Ireland through broad agreement freely and fairly agreed … in the event of a genuine and established cessation of violence, the whole range of responses that we have had to make to that violence could, and would, inevitably be looked at afresh.[28]

The IRA's apparent response to this message came just over two months later, on 22 February 1993. John Major was working at his desk on, as he told me, a 'pretty miserable, dreary, dark day', when his Private Secretary came in with a piece of paper on which was written a message. The Prime Minister was told it came from the IRA. It read:

> The conflict is over but we need your advice on how to bring it to an end. We wish to have an unannounced ceasefire in order to hold dialogue leading to peace. We cannot announce such a move as it will lead to confusion for the Volunteers as the Press will interpret it as surrender.[29]

Major checked with MI5, who assured him that the message was genuine, and had been sent by Martin McGuinness. When it became public later that year, McGuinness was incandescent, since it gave the impression that the IRA was surrendering. Brendan, who had been working with 'Robert' for almost two years, building confidence as he had with Michael Oatley, is adamant that McGuinness did not in fact send the message, and that its publication, which was never intended, 'practically wrecked the peace process'. He knows exactly what the provenance of the message was, and says it definitely wasn't McGuinness who sent it, and it definitely wasn't him. Any message to the British government had to be conveyed through 'Robert'.

I finally managed to see the original draft of the note, which had been scribbled in pencil on a piece of paper when Brendan met 'Robert' in a hotel room in London. It was 'Robert' who wrote it, and then sent it, presumably neatly typed or rewritten in ink, via MI5 to John Major. 'Robert' may also have added a gloss to give the government added encouragement. He then gave the original historic piece of paper to Brendan. The words on it reflected what Brendan believed the IRA's broad position to be – with the exception of the unfortunate phrase 'we need your advice on how to bring it to an end', which may have been 'Robert's' own amendment, '*pour encourager*'.

Despite the embarrassment and confusion the message subsequently caused, it had the desired effect. The government took almost a month to consider it, and finally responded in a communication via 'Robert' dated 19 March 1993. It said the government was prepared to engage in dialogue, but only within the limits it had already made clear: that an end to the partition of Ireland would not be on the agenda, and the principle of the consent of the majority was taken as read. Crucially, given what was about to happen, the government emphasised that any such dialogue could only take place following 'a halt to violent activity'.[30]

The following day, 20 March, the IRA exploded two bombs planted in waste bins in Warrington city centre, near Liverpool. It was a Saturday, and the town was packed with shoppers. Warnings were given, but they proved inadequate. Two young boys died in the blast. One of them, Jonathan Ball, was only three years old. The other, Tim Parry, was twelve. Brendan was horrified. 'A disaster. A total disaster. Warrington actually spurred me on. This is crazy. This has to end. Warrington practically stopped the process. I just said to Martin, "This is absolutely not on," and he said, "Yes, you're right."'

The reason Warrington almost brought the peace process to an end was that following the government's response the previous day, arrangements were already in place for a meeting between 'Robert' and his boss, John Deverell, and Martin McGuinness and another senior Provisional, the former IRA gun-runner and Maze escapee Gerry Kelly. Both sides were keen for things to move as quickly as possible, and the meeting had been scheduled to take place at Brendan's house in Derry the following Monday, 22 March. The government had made it clear in its response of 19 March that dialogue could only take place following 'a halt to violent activity'. With two young boys dead in Warrington and the nation outraged by the IRA's murderous activity, going ahead with any such meeting was utterly unthinkable. 'Robert' knew it, and John Deverell knew it. But Brendan was convinced that the meeting had to take place, despite Warrington. McGuinness and Kelly were all geared up, and to cancel it risked destroying the whole process. Inevitably, the IRA would accuse the British of bad faith, and McGuinness's judgement in going along with the relationship with 'Robert' and Brendan, and perhaps even his leadership, would be called into question. McGuinness knew he was walking a tightrope.

'Robert' let Brendan know, probably by coded fax, that he couldn't come to the meeting. But Brendan was desperate: 'We've a situation where two senior Republicans are prepared to meet you – and there can be progress. If you don't come, I'm finished.' 'Robert' said that under the circumstances he couldn't come, but he would make a call and then ring Brendan back. Ten minutes later, the phone rang. 'Robert' said he still couldn't make it. Brendan laid the situation on the line: 'I'm totally serious about this. These people [McGuinness and Kelly] are in Derry at the moment, and I've organised it.' 'Robert' said he would call back in half an hour. 'He rang back in four minutes and said, "I'll come."' But he would be coming on his own, without John Deverell. 'Robert' was breaking the government's cardinal rule, that it would only talk directly to the IRA once it had declared an end to violence. 'That's why I admire the guy so much,' said Brendan. 'The world is full of everybody who does the right thing, and then occasionally there's people who cross the line. If he hadn't done what he did, we'd still be hearing the bombs going off today – and there'd be no Good Friday Agreement. "Robert" is the kind of guy who in other days you would pin medals on.' The government didn't find out about the meeting until many months later, and was horrified that its emissary had broken its vital precondition.

True to his word, 'Robert' arrived in Derry for the crucial meeting. McGuinness and Kelly were waiting at McGuinness's mother's house in the Bogside. When they heard that 'Robert' was alone, and Deverell hadn't turned up, they were furious, scenting British double dealing. The spectre of Michael Collins was probably in their minds.* A message was conveyed to Brendan that the Republican delegation wouldn't come until Deverell arrived, and that they would wait until the following day. 'Robert', who was waiting at Brendan's house, said he would go and explain the situation to McGuinness and Kelly. Brendan was worried at the prospect of his going into the Bogside on his own: 'Robert' had told him two years earlier that if he was captured the IRA would kill him, but that they would torture him first to get him to reveal the names of MI5's agents within the IRA, which were stored in his head. It was therefore decided that a former Catholic priest, Denis Bradley, who played a peripheral role in the Link, would accompany him to Mrs McGuinness's house. 'Robert' must have been persuasive, as they returned with McGuinness and Kelly.

Northern Ireland is a dangerous place, and not just for 'spooks'. It can be dangerous for journalists too. In 1993, around the time 'Robert' was meeting Martin McGuinness and Gerry Kelly at Brendan's house, I was in the province researching a documentary called *Dead or Alive* for my series *States of Terror*, which was transmitted in autumn that year. I had no idea about the secret contacts between MI5 and the IRA that were taking place in the shadows of Derry.

---

*Collins was the IRA leader who negotiated with the British Prime Minister, David Lloyd George, leading to the treaty of 1921 which ultimately resulted in the partition of Ireland. Republicans believe that he was duped by the British. The IRA had believed that the treaty was based on the 'freedom to achieve freedom', and that ultimately Northern Ireland and the Irish Republic would be one. It didn't happen. Hence Republican mistrust.

Ironically, given that 'Robert' from MI5 was in Derry on a very different mission, *Dead or Alive* investigated the ways in which MI5 and the RUC's Special Branch recruited and ran informers from within the ranks of the IRA, and how the IRA hunted them down and 'executed' them. As part of the evidence for the documentary, I needed to get my hands on taped interviews that I'd heard the IRA had recorded with three alleged informers before they put bullets in the back of their heads and left their naked bodies in black bin liners in remote country lanes in South Armagh.

The bodies were found on 2 July 1992, and were those of three Republicans from Portadown in County Armagh: Aidan Starrs (twenty-nine), John Dignam (thirty-two) and Gregory Burns (thirty-three). I wanted to find out who these men were, what had happened, and whether they really were informers or 'touts'. The tapes of their 'confessions' would obviously be vital evidence for the documentary I was making.

Getting access to the tapes was a long process that involved clandestine meetings with masked IRA men in council houses in Belfast and Dublin. These meetings invariably began with my being picked up in a pub and then being taken to the rendezvous, whose location I was told to forget. The IRA finally gave the go-ahead for me to hear the tapes. However, the plan wasn't for me to listen in the comfort and relative safety of a council house, but at some remote location in the wilds of South Armagh, where the tapes were apparently being held.

I met my escorts in a pub on the Irish side of the border, and was driven to another meeting point, where I was directed to get into another car. It was late at night, and very dark. I was told to get in the back and to cover myself with a blanket that was lying there. I was then driven across the border and, I assumed, through a maze of narrow country lanes. I remember lying under the blanket nervously wondering what would happen if the SAS was aware that they had two IRA men in their sights, and whether I was about to become 'collateral damage' in the alleged 'shoot to kill' policy.

We finally came to a halt, and I was told I could come out from under the blanket. I was ushered inside a derelict, isolated 'IRA safe cottage'. The room was bare, with only an old sofa and a peat fire smouldering in the corner. I was met by three or four IRA men wearing balaclavas and armed with AK-47s. One of them said, 'I know you, but you don't know me. We met in the Maze.' I've often wondered who he was, but I never found out. It was probably best that I didn't. In one corner of the room was an ancient Alba tape recorder, the kind that you would once have found in Woolworths. After some technical problems with the machine, not surprising given its age, I was played a brief section from each of the three interrogations. Chillingly, each began with the sound of a spoon striking a saucepan, which was the signal to start 'conferring'. The voices of the men making the confessions sounded disembodied and stressed, and I suspected they had been elicited under some form of torture. I asked if I could take the tapes away with me. The answer was no, but I was assured that I would get them in due course. I was then driven back across the border, again under the blanket, this time thinking that I'd come so close to getting the tapes, but failed to return with them. Had all this been for nothing?

Some time later it turned out that my hazardous journey had not been in vain, when the redacted tapes and the IRA's redacted transcripts of them were duly handed over to me after another trip to Dublin. At last I had the material for the documentary. And were Starrs, Burns and Dignam really informers? I suspected that they probably were. Ironically, it was later speculated that the leader of the IRA team that interrogated them was probably the British double agent, codenamed 'Steak Knife', who was the alleged head of the IRA's Internal Security Unit, better known as the 'nutting squad'.

When 'Robert' returned to Brendan's house from the Bogside with Martin McGuinness and Gerry Kelly, they adjourned to the room where Brendan usually held his business meetings. 'Robert' began by outlining the government's position, and trying to reassure McGuinness and Kelly that there would be no repetition of what happened during the truce in 1975, when the 'new' Provisional leadership under Adams and McGuinness believed the Brits had tricked them. On the Republican side, McGuinness did most of the talking while Kelly took notes. Sinn Féin's account of the meeting, based on Kelly's notes and the Republicans' joint recollection of what was said, is remarkable. When I later read it, I was astonished at one particular paragraph that purported to record what 'Robert' told the Republican delegation (the emphasis is mine):

> Any settlement not involving all of the people North and South won't work. A North/South settlement that won't frighten unionists. *The final solution is union. It's going to happen anyway* ... The historical train – Europe – determines that. We are committed to Europe. Unionists will have to change. *This island will be as one.*[31]

Even allowing for a degree of accentuating the positive on the part of McGuinness and Kelly, I could not believe that 'Robert' had actually said this. But Brendan, who was present, assured me that he had. He went on to tell me that 'Robert' had also emphasised that the British government would never abandon the Unionists, nor would it become an advocate for a united Ireland. I later asked Sir Patrick Mayhew about the meeting, and what 'Robert' had allegedly said. Sir Patrick had had no knowledge of it until many months later: 'If it was true, it would have been dangerously and damagingly outside the remit. It may have been an expression of this man's personal views. It was certainly not an expression of the views of the British government or fulfilment of anything he'd been authorised to do or say.'[32]

Sir Patrick and the Prime Minister, John Major, were kept in the dark about the meeting until news of it burst onto front-page headlines in the *Observer* eight months later, on 28 November 1993, when Belfast journalist Eamonn Mallie ran his scoop that the British had met the IRA. Presumably the story was leaked by Sinn Féin. This explains why on 1 November 1993, less than a month before Mallie's scoop, Major had been able to tell the House of Commons in all honesty, 'To sit down and talk with Mr Adams and the Provisional IRA ... would turn my stomach.'[33] His remarks followed the IRA's bombing of Frizell's fish shop on Belfast's Loyalist Shankill Road a week earlier that killed ten people and injured fifty-seven. The news of 'Robert's' unauthorised meeting caused Sir Patrick Mayhew acute embarrassment. But, fearing being fed to the lions when he faced the House of Commons, he was astonished to find that he got what amounted to a hero's welcome. It was as if Honourable Members on both sides of the House were applauding a government that was prepared to take great risks for peace.

However, senior mandarins in London who were monitoring and guiding 'Robert's' dealings with Brendan subsequently took a very different view. One of them told me that 'Robert' had 'severely damaged' government policy by having the face-to-face meeting. 'Our whole strategy was to be straight with them [the Provisionals] and build up trust. We were "banging on" about no face-to-face meeting before an IRA ceasefire, and they couldn't understand that because they'd already had one. It just made things more difficult.'[34]

Whether or not history would have been different had 'Robert' not broken all the rules and gone to the meeting, we will never know. Brendan had built up trust with the IRA not just in the two years or so since 'Robert' took over from Michael Oatley, but over almost two decades since he first nervously faced the IRA's Army Council at the country house outside Dublin. Had the meeting in Derry not gone ahead, that trust would have been destroyed, with the result that the conflict may have gone on even longer, although it was destined to end at some stage, once both sides had tacitly agreed on what was possible. But it would still be almost another eighteen months until the IRA finally declared its historic ceasefire on 31 August 1994.

And what of Brendan? He remained in the loop until almost the end of 1993, when the 'conflict is over' message was revealed to the world, to the fury of McGuinness and the acute embarrassment of Sir Patrick Mayhew. Shortly afterwards, four very senior IRA men paid Brendan a visit at his home. I asked him who they were. 'Think of four senior Republicans,' he said, 'and you won't be wrong.' I assumed that two of them would have been McGuinness and Adams. In an upstairs room, they grilled him 'very intensively' for four hours about the message, which they suspected him of having sent. He finally convinced them that he had not. His life was probably on the line, as there were suspicions that he might have been an MI5 agent. His wife Margo remembers seeing him afterwards. 'He was very upset after that for a long time,' she told me. 'I still don't know what happened.' I asked Brendan if he was an MI5 agent. 'I'm glad you asked me that,' he said. 'I am Brendan Duddy. Northern Irish. My own person in my own right. I didn't have to be MI5 or MI6, and I never was.' Did they ever try to recruit you? 'Never.' Did they ask you to join them? 'No. Not my job. Nor did they ever ask me a question that would have put someone in gaol for the rest of their lives.'

After his interrogation by the IRA, Brendan's role was over. McGuinness told me that the government had 'abused the Contact to destruction'. By this time Brendan had had enough anyway. His role was finished, his self-appointed duty complete. I asked him why he had done it over all those years. Tears welled up in his eyes. 'When you ask questions like that, I choke. I get emotional. I find it hard to answer.' He paused as he tried to compose himself. 'I had no choice.' Then he broke down.

And 'Robert'? Far from receiving the decoration Brendan thought was his due, he was, in Brendan's words, 'court-martialled' for disobeying orders.

At what turned out to be their final meeting, 'Robert' told Brendan, 'This is the last time you will see me.' In what must have been an emotional farewell, he presented Brendan with a book: *The Laurel and the Ivy*, Robert Kee's biography of the legendary nineteenth-century Irish constitutional nationalist Charles Stewart Parnell, who almost succeeded in bringing Home Rule to Ireland. The book is one of Brendan's most treasured possessions. Inside 'Robert' had written a Latin inscription from Virgil's *Aeneid* which translated means, 'Perhaps one day it will be good to remember these things, through all their vicissitudes and endless ups and downs.'[35] Brendan never saw 'Robert' again. He believes he became a 'non-person' because he had broken the rules.

I knew that somehow I had to find 'Robert' to try to get his side of the story. Did he really say what the Sinn Féin minutes recorded? Did he really send the infamous 'conflict is over' message with the killer words 'we need your advice on how to bring it to an end'? There were many other things I wanted to ask him. But what was his real name – and where was he? Brendan did not know, and even if he had, he would have kept the confidence. It seemed an impossible challenge. Luckily I was working with a remarkable young researcher called Julia Hannis, for whom the word 'impossible' does not exist. We decided that the starting point had to be the Latin inscription in the book 'Robert' gave Brendan, and it was that which led me to him in the end. I can't reveal the remarkable piece of detective work by which Julia found 'Robert', as it might lead others to do so. He lived some distance from London. I took a train, hired a car, and approached the house with my heart thumping. I knocked on the door several times. No reply. Tried again. Still no reply. The house seemed empty. I had a copy of my book *Provos* with me that I wanted to leave as a calling card. I had also written him a letter describing everything I had done with Brendan. I left them with a neighbour who told me the owner of the house was away on holiday, and would be back in a couple of weeks. I returned to London with an empty feeling inside. I knew I had to try again.

Two weeks elapsed, and then I retraced my journey. As I approached the house the weather was appalling, with rain sheeting down. I saw someone outside whom I took to be 'Robert', and explained who I was. To my astonishment he replied, 'I'm afraid you've got the wrong man.' I said politely that I was sure I hadn't, and that I had come all the way from London to see him. He insisted that I was wrong, and that Brendan's name meant nothing to him. I asked if he'd got the book and the letter I'd left with his neighbour. He said he had, and that he would let me have them back. He went inside, leaving me standing on his doorstep in the pouring rain. By now I felt like a drowned rat. He emerged with the book and said goodbye. I drove away crestfallen. We couldn't have got it wrong – or could we? It was only on the long journey back to London that I realised that perhaps we hadn't. If he really had not been the man I was looking for, surely he would at the very least have asked me in, out of politeness and curiosity, to dry off and have a cup of tea. He seemed that kind of man. But he didn't.

In 2008, when I was making a documentary about Brendan for BBC2 called *The Secret Peacemaker*, I decided I had nothing to lose by writing to the man I still assumed was 'Robert' to ask if he would see me. I concluded by saying, 'I suspect your answer will be no, and you may not even feel disposed to answer this letter. Dum spiro, spero … [While I breathe, I hope].' But astonishingly he did reply, in a letter dated 6 March 2008, three weeks before the programme went out, although I didn't receive it until long afterwards – it had, I assumed, been vetted by MI5 first. He wrote: 'You guessed correctly in the final paragraph of your recent letter. I would not welcome a further meeting (though thank you for the good-natured way in which you proposed it).' It was signed with his real name. The writing matched the signature in the book he had given Brendan as a farewell souvenir. It was a small consolation, but at least I knew we had got the right man. I recalled the translation of the Latin inscription that 'Robert' had written in the book: 'One day it will be good to remember these things …'

The abiding memory of, and the wider lesson I learned from, my association with Brendan over the years and my investigation into the covert mechanisms behind the Northern Ireland peace process, is that apparently intractable conflicts can be resolved. The crucial prerequisites are that the 'terrorists' agree to end violence, and the warring parties are prepared to engage in a dialogue that may lead to some form of compromise. Northern Ireland offers a possible template for the resolution of other conflicts, which would inevitably involve states 'talking to terrorists'. In the occupied territories, Hamas (the acronym for the Islamic Resistance Movement) would have to recognise Israel and declare an end to violence, while in Afghanistan the Taliban would have to engage in dialogue, end their insurgency and undertake to deny Al Qaeda access to its former training base in Afghanistan.

But what about Al Qaeda? After thirty years covering Northern Ireland, I've spent the decade since 9/11 investigating and reporting a very different form of 'terrorism'. Al Qaeda is the subject of the rest of this book. What is it? Where did it come from? How did it evolve and change? How has the West responded to it, to what extent has torture been used to elicit intelligence, and what is the threat that it currently poses? Those are some of the questions I will endeavour to answer in the second and more recent part of my journey from the IRA to Al Qaeda. It also addresses some of the questions that arise from the killing of Osama Bin Laden.

TWO

From the IRA to Al Qaeda

As I watched the Northern Ireland peace process move towards its close in the late 1990s, I never suspected that events unfolding thousands of miles away would determine what I was to do for the next decade. Little did I think that Al Qaeda would come to dominate my working life as the IRA had done for the previous three decades, and that I would be faced with the task of trying to understand and analyse a terrorist organisation that was very different from the IRA.

As the name Osama Bin Laden began to emerge in the mid-1990s, I was about to embark on a television trilogy for the BBC, *Provos*, *Loyalists* and *Brits*, which examined the histories of the three parties to the conflict, and was starting to write the three accompanying books. Al Qaeda was barely on my radar. I didn't know at the time that the IRA was about to put itself out of business just as Al Qaeda was beginning to make its bloody and indiscriminate mark. I was aware of Al Qaeda's existence, and had heard of Bin Laden from newspaper reports and mentions on radio and television, but I never took either seriously enough to think that I should start focusing my attention on them. I was too busy concentrating on whether the efforts and hopes of Brendan and Michael Oatley would finally bear fruit.

On the eve of Good Friday, 10 April 1998, I stood in the freezing rain outside Government Buildings at Stormont, where negotiations between Sinn Féin and Northern Ireland's other political parties were balanced on a knife-edge. I remember watching through the distant windows as the silhouetted outlines of Gerry Adams and Martin McGuinness paced back and forth, deliberating whether enough was on offer to enable them and their Sinn Féin and IRA comrades to do a deal. I noted in my diary that I didn't sleep for thirty-six hours, not wishing to miss the dénouement of the events I had covered for the previous twenty-five years. I tried to catch some sleep in the middle of the night, lying on the floor of the press tent, and being awakened by the booming voice of the Reverend Ian Paisley, obviously far more wide awake than I was, who swept in and declared that as far as he was concerned, the talks were doomed, and he was not going to be party to any agreement with Republicans and the IRA.

The historic Good Friday Agreement (or Belfast Agreement) was signed after long and tortuous labours through the night between Tony Blair, the Irish Prime Minister Bertie Ahern, and Northern Ireland's political parties. It was a remarkable achievement. Essentially, the compromise was that the IRA and Sinn Féin recognised partition as the political *status quo*, and agreed to share power with Unionists in a devolved assembly and government at Stormont. This did not mean that in the longer term they had to abandon their historic aspiration to achieve a united Ireland; the difference was that now they agreed to pursue it via political, not violent, means.

Two fundamental principles underpinned the Agreement: first, that any change in the constitutional status of Northern Ireland could only be implemented following a vote in favour by the majority of its citizens; second, that all parties were committed to use 'exclusively peaceful and democratic means'.[1] These cardinal principles were a vindication of all that Brendan Duddy and Michael Oatley had impressed upon the IRA over so many years. The IRA, despite great reluctance in many quarters, finally came to accept them.* In return, Unionists agreed to share power with the Nationalist Social Democratic and Labour Party (SDLP) – which believed that Irish

---

*Some IRA members, however, did not, and split to form a new dissident organisation called the 'Real IRA'. Another dissident grouping, the 'Continuity IRA', had been formed many years earlier, in 1986, after the IRA and Sinn Féin agreed to recognise the Irish Parliament in Dublin. Rory O'Brady led the walkout from the Sinn Féin conference at which that decision was taken, and formed Republican Sinn Féin (RSF). The Continuity IRA became RSF's military wing.

unity could only be achieved by peaceful means – and with Sinn Féin, which most Unionists regarded as the IRA in suits, and which they insisted on always referring to as 'IRA/Sinn Féin'. As part of the deal, all prisoners belonging to organisations from both sides were to be eligible for conditional early release, and all Loyalist and Republican paramilitaries were to decommission – or 'put beyond use', as the phrase later became – all weapons within two years. Unionists' political sensitivities were calmed by Dublin's agreement to drop its long-standing constitutional claim to the North,* and the establishment of institutional links between the United Kingdom and the Irish Republic, in the shape of a British–Irish Council. On the security front, Republicans were assuaged by a decision to reform the Royal Ulster Constabulary,† an organisation they hated – and over three hundred of whose members they had killed – and the reduction in the number of British troops to peacetime levels. It was 'Brits Out' of Nationalist areas, but not the whole province. On the political front they were mollified by the setting up of a North-South Ministerial Council – separate from the British-Irish Council – and cross-border bodies covering health, transport, agriculture, education, environment and tourism. Nobody got all of what they wanted. If they had, there would have been no deal. As the opening to the Good Friday Agreement began: 'We, the participants in the multi-party negotiations, believe that the Agreement we have negotiated offers a truly historic opportunity for a new beginning.' It was subsequently ratified with referenda on both sides of the border.

True to his word, the Reverend Ian Paisley was not a signatory. It was all the more remarkable therefore when almost ten years later, on 8 May 2007, he was sworn in as First Minister in the new Northern Ireland devolved government, with his old IRA enemy Martin

---

*Articles 2 and 3 of the Irish Republic's 1937 constitution claimed that the whole of the island of Ireland formed one national territory, which was always an affront to Unionists.

†The RUC became the Police Service of Northern Ireland (PSNI) following the recommendations of the Patten Report, headed by the former Conservative Minister Chris Patten.

McGuinness as his Deputy. I was filming in America at the time, and could hardly believe what I heard, read and saw. Why did Paisley perform such an astonishing *volte-face* and embrace his long-hated opponents? I heard one (probably apocryphal) story that he had been very ill, possibly close to death, but had made a remarkable recovery, and believed it was because the Lord had saved him for one final mission – to help bring peace to the tortured province. It is more likely that he believed the Union was secure, given that any change to the status of Northern Ireland would have to be agreed by the majority of its population – which remained firmly Protestant and Unionist – and that the IRA was effectively beaten once it had finally put its arms 'beyond use'. In other words, although the phrase never passed Paisley's lips, the Protestants had won. Nationalists, however, pinned their hopes on Catholics one day becoming a majority in Northern Ireland, although predictions put that far in the future. In his remarkable opening speech as First Minister, Paisley said, 'I believe Northern Ireland has come to a time of peace, a time when hate will no longer rule. How good it will be to be part of a wonderful healing in our province.'[2] On 4 March 2008, at the age of eighty-one, Paisley announced that he was stepping down as First Minister. Martin McGuinness paid tribute: 'The decision he took to go into government with Sinn Féin changed the course of Irish history forever.'[3]

Perhaps in the case of Paisley and McGuinness the mellowing effects of age also played their part. Some young Republicans, however, of the age that McGuinness and his contemporaries were at the outset of the Troubles in the late sixties and early seventies, were alienated and disaffected, feeling that the peace process had done nothing for them, and seeing any hope of a united Ireland disappearing over a distant horizon. As a result, a growing number of them were inclined to give their practical and moral support to the dissidents of the Real and Continuity IRA, whose increasingly sophisticated military campaign risks threatening the stability of the power-sharing government at Stormont.

* * *

On 7 August 1998, four months after the signing of the Good Friday Agreement, Al Qaeda suicide bombers in trucks loaded with explosives blew up America's embassies in Kenya and Tanzania, killing over two hundred people. I suddenly became aware of a threat potentially far more deadly than that posed by the IRA, a threat confirmed by Al Qaeda's subsequent suicide attack on 12 October 2000 on the US Navy destroyer the USS *Cole*, refuelling in Aden harbour, in which seventeen American sailors were killed. But I remained focused on Ireland. Al Qaeda still seemed far away. Then came 9/11.

Al Qaeda's attacks on New York and Washington on 11 September 2001 changed the world, and shook me as they did the untold millions who watched the scenes of unimaginable horror taking place before them. Everyone remembers what they were doing when they heard of the assassination of President John F. Kennedy in Dallas in 1963. It's the same with 9/11.

I was at the BBC with my producer Sam Collyns, editing *True Spies*, a series on Britain's intelligence services, when someone rushed into the edit suite and asked breathlessly if we'd seen what had happened. We switched on BBC News, and were transfixed as we watched events unfold. First reports had indicated that an aircraft had crashed into the World Trade Center, possibly as a result of pilot error, but this was immediately discounted the moment the second plane hit home. I remember speculating about who might lie behind the attack, and what their motives could have been. It was not long before Osama Bin Laden and Al Qaeda came into the frame, and I knew that I would have to turn my attention from Ireland to Al Qaeda. The prospect was daunting. I was almost starting from scratch. It was reminiscent of the moment on Bloody Sunday almost thirty years earlier when I realised how little I knew about the Irish conflict, and how much I would have to learn even to begin to catch up. As with Ireland, I had to start at the beginning – the difference being that with Ireland the beginning was many centuries earlier. By contrast, Al Qaeda was barely a quarter of a century old.

Where did it come from? Just as it's necessary to consider the history of the IRA in order to understand it, it's equally important to look at the much shorter history of Al Qaeda. In the process of doing so I talked to a 'terrorist' – who believes the USA still regards him as such – who has first-hand experience of the controversial origins of Al Qaeda, since his father was Osama Bin Laden's spiritual and military mentor, and ultimately became his rival. His name is Hutheifa Azzam, a former *jihadi* whose father, Abdullah Azzam, is widely regarded as the father of *jihad*. But first, a brief history.

Al Qaeda was conceived in the mountains and sand of Afghanistan, where the superpowers America and the Soviet Union were fighting out their ideological and geopolitical rivalries through their proxies. Afghanistan has been the cockpit of conflict from the late nineteenth century to the present day because of its crucial strategic position, sandwiched between the former Soviet Union and Asia.

In 1978 a pro-Moscow Communist government was established in Kabul, but was no more able to exercise control over the whole country than the pro-Western regime of President Hamid Karzai is today. The lesson of history is that Afghanistan appears to be unconquerable and ungovernable. To maintain its grip on its key strategic client, the Soviet Union sent in troops the following year, triggering fierce resistance from Muslims not only in Afghanistan but from all over the world. In 1979 the Afghan *jihad* was born. At the time there was no question as to its legitimacy. *Jihad* was to be waged in accordance with the tenets of the Koran against the infidel invaders of a Muslim land. Thousands of volunteers poured in to join the *mujahideen*, most from the Arab world, primarily from Saudi Arabia, Yemen, Algeria and Morocco. They were known as the 'Afghan Arabs', and came to exercise the key strategic and military role in the *jihad* and subsequently in Al Qaeda.

One of these volunteers was called Osama Bin Laden. He came from one of Saudi Arabia's richest families, its wealth based on a conglomeration of construction companies that had grown fabulously wealthy in the oil boom of the 1970s, and beyond that financed the Kingdom's infrastructural development. The Bin Laden Group built 13,000 miles of roads and was responsible, among many other things, for the refurbishment of the Muslim world's most sacred mosques at Mecca, Medina and Jerusalem. The Group was the Saudi royal family's builder of choice. Its founder, Mohammed Bin Laden, was originally a poor immigrant from Yemen who had twenty wives and sired fifty-four children. Osama Bin Laden was his seventeenth son.[4] Osama's main contribution to the Afghan *jihad*, although he did take part in some of the fighting[5] – notably at the battle of Jaji in 1987, when a small group of *mujahideen* stopped a Russian advance – was to provide finance and construction expertise, not least in the building of a vast network of caves and tunnels in the mountains of Tora Bora, in which he and his inner circle took refuge and from which they subsequently escaped following the American invasion, Operation Enduring Freedom, in the months after 9/11.

Osama was educated at Abdul Aziz University in Jeddah, Saudi Arabia, where he was powerfully influenced by the Palestinian Sheikh Abdullah Azzam who was teaching at the university at the time. Azzam was a political cleric who practised what he preached. He was one of the co-founders of Hamas in Gaza, and he saw Hamas through the same prism as the *jihad* in Afghanistan.[6] No doubt the Israelis had marked his card.

Azzam had been influenced by the writings of the Egyptian Sayyid Qutb, the leading intellectual force behind the Muslim Brotherhood, founded in 1928 by Hassan al-Banna, among the aims of which was to reclaim 'Islam's manifest destiny: an empire founded in the seventh century that stretched from Spain to Indonesia'.[7] In 1949 Qutb spent some time in the United States, and concluded that Western civilisation had led humanity to 'corruption and irreligion from which only Islam can save it'.[8] Qutb was executed in 1966 as the leader of a group that was plotting to overthrow the Egyptian government. Six other Muslim Brotherhood members were executed with him.

Qutb's brother Mohammed also taught at Abdul Aziz University, where he spread his brother's word. Osama Bin Laden attended Mohammed Qutb's public lectures.[9] The influence on Bin Laden of the Muslim Brotherhood and Egypt's violent insurgent groups cannot be overestimated. The relationship was cemented when the leader of

Egyptian Islamic Jihad (EIJ), Ayman al-Zawahiri, joined Al Qaeda in 1998 (see p. 84). He subsequently went on to become Bin Laden's number two, credited with being the military brains behind the organisation. Zawahiri, a surgeon and a committed revolutionary, was arrested following the assassination of the Egyptian President Anwar Sadat in 1981. He was convicted of dealing in weapons, and sentenced to three years' imprisonment. On his release he spent time practising medicine at a clinic in Jeddah before travelling to Peshawar in Pakistan's Tribal Areas to treat the wounded in the anti-Soviet *jihad*. It was there that he first met Osama Bin Laden, and forged the ideological bond that was later to elevate him to a terrorist status second only to that of Bin Laden himself. Each man came to rely on the other.[10] Zawahiri was a seasoned revolutionary who brought with him an equally experienced cadre of militants. Bin Laden had all the money and contacts in the Afghan *jihad* that Zawahiri lacked.

These were the powerful radical influences that lay behind the evolution of Osama Bin Laden's ideology, cemented by his close association with Abdullah Azzam. Together in the mid-1980s Bin Laden and Azzam established the Bureau of Services (Mektab al Khidmat) in Peshawar, through which money and *mujahideen* recruits were channelled into Afghanistan. The Bureau also provided humanitarian aid to the thousands of refugees who streamed across the border. Initially Azzam was the Bureau's titular head, until Bin Laden effectively took it over. In time fundamental differences developed between the two allies. Bin Laden wanted the Arab contingents of *mujahideen* to train and operate separately, and not as part of joint forces with the native Afghan *jihadis*. Azzam opposed this, on the grounds that the Arabs would bring greater Islamic understanding to the Afghans, who were not necessarily *au fait* with the ideologies espoused by himself and Bin Laden. Meanwhile Bin Laden secretly set about putting together an organisation in his own image made up entirely of a small group of Arab *mujahideen*. It became known as Al Qaeda Al Askariya, 'the Military Base'. It seems to have been established during a three-day meeting in mid-August 1988 held at Bin Laden's house, believed to have been near Kandahar. One of its purposes was to compile a directory of trusted *mujahideen*, initially a list of those who had fought in Afghanistan but subsequently including many more who had proved themselves in *jihadi* campaigns elsewhere.

Remarkably, the minutes of that meeting were recovered among computer files in Bosnia in March 2002 as part of a US investigation into a Muslim charity based in Chicago known as the Benevolence International Foundation which had long supported *jihadis* around the world.[11] They show Bin Laden and a handful of his closest Arab associates deciding on the new organisation's initial military strategy. Recruits were to be trained at a camp on the Pakistan–Afghanistan border before they joined the *jihad*. They would then enter a 'testing camp', and the 'best brothers' would be chosen to enter Al Qaeda Al Askariya. Requirements for admission included an open-ended commitment, the ability to listen and obey, good manners, recommendation from a trusted source, and agreement to abide by the statutes and instructions of Al Qaeda. It was estimated that within six months, '314 brothers will be trained and ready'. To what extent Abdullah Azzam was aware of all this is unclear. Just over a year later he was dead, killed by a car bomb in Peshawar. Who or what agency was behind his death has never been satisfactorily established. Some believe that Bin Laden wanted his main rival out of the way, and sanctioned the attack. Others see in the methodology the hand of the Israeli intelligence agency, the Mossad,* which is certainly possible given that Abdullah Azzam was a founder of Hamas, whose aim is the destruction of Israel. Whatever lay behind Azzam's assassination, the way for Osama Bin Laden and Al Qaeda was now clear, with no powerful figure to oppose him.

On 15 February 1989 the Soviet Union withdrew from Afghanistan, the second most powerful army in the world humiliated by a guerrilla band of Islamic fighters financed, supported and equipped by the

---

*The car bomb was a method favoured by the Mossad to eliminate its 'terrorist' enemies, like Abu Hassan Salameh, whom Israel believed to have been the mastermind behind Black September's attack on the Munich Olympics in 1972. He was killed by a car bomb in Beirut on 22 January 1979. Salameh also had links to the CIA.

United States and the West, largely channelled through Pakistan's controversial intelligence agency, the Inter Services Intelligence Directorate (ISI).* Afghanistan had been the Soviet Union's Vietnam. Bin Laden could point to the victory of the *mujahideen* as an illustration of how the power of Islam could defeat the armies of the ungodly, however powerful they were and however great the odds. He subsequently drew on the precedent to convince his increasing number of followers that America, the Great Satan, could be defeated too.

In 2006 I secretly met Abdullah Azzam's son Hutheifa at his flat in Amman, Jordan. Given his father's fate, he was meticulous about security. He told me he'd been to Bosnia – I assumed, as he was the son of the father of *jihad*, that he had been there to do more than just observe. When I asked if he'd fought *jihad* in Iraq, he was suitably evasive. *Jihadis* tend not to give details about their military activities, and often explain their presence in a theatre of conflict by claiming they were involved in the delivery of humanitarian aid. In some cases this may be true. In many others it most certainly is not. Hutheifa was nervous: 'I am considered by the United States as a terrorist. I can't move freely to any of the Western countries because I know they [the Americans] will get me and send me to Guantánamo.'

Hutheifa was not what I expected. As so often, he didn't fit the popular stereotype of a terrorist. He was urbane, charming and, as my colleague Patricia de Mesquita, who had arranged the meeting, pointed out, 'very good-looking'. He was married, but we never set eyes on his wife, who according to custom was kept well out of sight. Patricia was adept at finding her way into the kitchens of strict Islamic households and chatting to wives who I was never allowed to meet or see. One wife once told her that she and her daughters secretly listened to Western music, but said that her husband would be furious if he ever found out.

---

*The most lethal piece of equipment supplied to the Afghan *mujahideen* by America via the ISI were Stinger missiles. Fired from the shoulder, they could bring down helicopters, thus denying the Soviet Union control of the skies.

Hutheifa made us welcome, and brought a tray with small glasses of thick black Arab coffee and an array of incredibly sweet biscuits. It was getting close to midnight, and coffee usually keeps me awake at night, but it would have been ill-mannered to refuse. I also calculated that several draughts of hot, sugary coffee would see me through what looked like being a very long evening. It brought back memories of listening to Brendan Duddy in his 'wee room' in the small hours of a Derry morning.

We sat on the sofa and talked. I wanted to know more about my host and his father. Had Hutheifa fought in Afghanistan too? He said he had. As a teenager? Perhaps he noted a degree of incredulity in my voice. He got up, left the room and returned with a large, battered brown suitcase. He flicked its old-fashioned clips, opened it and scattered its contents on the floor. Strewn in front of me were piles of photographs, maps and memorabilia, a historical treasure trove of the Afghan *jihad*. He went through many of the objects, talking animatedly as the memories came flooding back. Here was his father, kneeling on the ground and holding an AK-47. Here he was surrounded by his close friends and, I assumed, his bodyguards. And here was Hutheifa in combat fatigues, looking every inch a young, handsome, poster-boy *jihadi*.

He then went to a cupboard in the corner of the room and took out a *keffiyeh*, an Arab headdress, and a torn jacket. He said his father was wearing them the day he was assassinated. He pointed out some dark stains. 'This is the blood of my father,' he said. Hutheifa had been with his father when he died, and holding the jacket and headdress clearly brought back painful memories. He explained that he had been in a car with his father in a motorcade heading for the mosque in Peshawar. His father changed vehicles a few minutes before the bomb went off. Why he did this, Hutheifa did not know. I asked who he thought was responsible. 'The Mossad,' he said without hesitation.

Although it was now getting very late, I wanted to talk about Abdullah Azzam's views on *jihad* and his rulings on its meaning, given that he was regarded as not only the Father of *Jihad* but its leading spiritual interpreter. Hutheifa got up and left the room again. This time he returned with two or three massive volumes of his father's writings, not just on *jihad* but on a whole range of Islamic issues. Every page was neatly written by hand in immaculate Arabic script. He flicked through one of the books, muttering quietly to himself until he found the relevant page. 'Look,' he said, pointing to a passage with his finger. 'The rules of how a *mujahid*, a freedom fighter, should fight *jihad*. "Don't kill any child or any woman," it says.' He said his father would never have sanctioned the Madrid train bombings of 2004, or the attacks on London's transport system in 2005. He went on to explain that his father believed it was lawful to fight the invaders of Muslim lands, and that he himself could understand why young men were prepared to become *shaheeds*, martyrs or suicide bombers: 'The nearest way to heaven, to Paradise, is by being *mujahideen*, being killed in battle with the non-Muslim occupiers, the attackers.'

Just before we said goodbye in the early hours of the morning, Hutheifa left me with an unequivocal message. 'Let me tell you clearly. America won't win the war. Hundreds of millions in the Muslim countries are ready to be terrorists because of America's policies. The problem started in Palestine, spread into Afghanistan and is now spreading into whole countries.' He said that if the United States changed these policies, there would be no problem. 'Just be fair,' he said, referring to American policy. I knew it wasn't quite as simple as that.

I thought of my meeting with Hutheifa when I later talked to one of the young, wannabe *shaheeds* he had referred to and said he understood. To meet a *shaheed* face to face was a chilling exposure to the murderous power of his determination to blow himself up, slaughter those around him and thereby, he believed, enter Paradise as a martyr. It felt a million miles from talking to the IRA. I met him secretly in a middle-class home that sympathisers had made available for the interview. He was, I guess, in his late teens or early twenties, and very nervous. He covered his face with a *keffiyeh* so that only his eyes were visible. His host told me his story. He'd tried to get into Iraq via Syria, and been turned back at the border, but remained determined to try again. 'I planned to go to Iraq to support our oppressed brothers, raise the banner of Islam and *jihad* and send the usurping, renegade enemy out of Muslim lands and fight in the name of God asking for entry to Paradise,' he told me through an interpreter. 'This is an order that God obliges us to follow. The important thing is to be killed as a martyr.'

The more I read the last testaments of suicide bombers, and the more interviews I saw with them on the internet recorded before they embarked upon missions from which they never returned, the more convinced I became that they had to believe that the gates of Paradise, with all its pleasures and delights, would be opened for them in order to give them the courage to press the button and blow themselves to pieces, and many others with them. However, there is, contrary to popular assumption, no reference in the Koran to the seventy-two virgins who await the pleasure of the new entrant.* I asked the young man if he had received any training. 'The training operation was going to be in Iraq,' he told me. 'There men are prepared physically and ideologically, and then sent to fight.' Why didn't he want to live a normal life, instead of being prepared to go to Iraq and die? 'This life is cheap,' he said. 'It lasts for a moment, and after it there is death. And what is after death? Nothing. But if you fight on behalf of God, in the afterlife there are many gardens of Paradise and a higher Paradise joining [the Prophet] Mohammed and all the Muslims to whom God has promised Paradise.'

I later wondered what had happened to him. Had he succeeded in getting into Iraq, joined the resistance, blown himself up and gone to Paradise? Had he added to the long list of terrorist victims, whether blown up by suicide bombers or living the nightmare of being hijacked by Islamist extremists? I never found out.

---

*The Koran (Surah 56, verses 22ff) describes the spiritual joys and pleasures of Paradise, but not in the carnal sense. The reference to seventy-two (or seventy) virgins comes from the *hadiths* (the sayings of the Prophet). The Koran refers only to 'companions' who are 'virgin pure (and undefiled)' and have 'beautiful big and lustrous eyes like unto pearls'. It should also be noted that these pleasures are available to all, and not just *shaheeds*.

THREE

Talking to Hijack Victims

Talking to terrorists is not just about governments or their intelligence services engaging in dialogue with their enemies. Innocent citizens have found themselves in situations where they have come face to face with terrorists, in a siege or aircraft hijacking, and talked to them in the hope of securing their survival and release. They too are the victims of terrorism: the experience of staring death, and the terrorists, in the face often colours the rest of their lives. In such circumstances, talking to terrorists can be a matter of life or death. The hijacking of an Air France Airbus by four Algerian Islamist extremists on Christmas Eve 1994 provides a unique insight into the mindset of the terrorists who carried it out, and the political situation from which they emerged. It was also a prophetic event. The Berlin Wall had fallen five years earlier. The Cold War was over. Few foresaw the emergence of the new threat that was to overshadow the next two decades: Islamist extremism and the rise of political Islam. In Algeria, the conditions were ripe for both, and it is in Algeria that we first see the emergence of the phenomenon.

The hijackers of the Air France Airbus had possibly never even heard the name Al Qaeda. In 1994 Osama Bin Laden was exiled in Sudan, building his organisation and extending its global reach. Nevertheless, the hijackers did regard themselves as *mujahideen*, adopting the mantle of their Algerian brothers who had fought *jihad* against Soviet troops in the 1980s – Algeria had provided one of the largest contingents of Arab *mujahideen*. When the Soviet Union withdrew from

Afghanistan in 1989 and many of these Algerian veterans returned home, few had any notion of global *jihad*. Their cause was indigenous. *Jihad* was primarily about local regime change. The target was the military government of the FLN – the Front de Libération Nationale.

The social and political conditions in Algeria were slow-burning incubators for revolt. By the late 1980s, 40 per cent of the population of twenty-four million were under the age of fifteen. Many were in school, being educated for jobs that didn't exist. They became known as the *hittistes*, 'those who prop up walls'. They were a potential reservoir of recruits for revolution.

France had been the colonial power in Algeria since 1830, when it invaded the impoverished North African country and scorched its earth to stamp out resistance and ensure the subjugation of the native population. In 1954 insurgents embarked upon a savage guerrilla war in which atrocities were committed by both sides, graphically illustrated in Gillo Pontecorvo's film masterpiece *The Battle of Algiers*. The insurgents of the FLN were the ultimate beneficiaries, taking power when France granted Algeria her independence in 1962. But for most of the country's impoverished people the sweetness of independence soured over the years. Growing discontent among the urban population in Algiers and elsewhere resulted in strikes and demonstrations. There was little work, no regular water supply, and food was running out.[1] In the 1980s radical clerics seized the opportunity to build support for the Islamist cause through a network of neighbourhood mosques. They provided soup kitchens, food, clothing and welfare, building a political base as Sinn Féin was doing in Northern Ireland at around the same time. Political Islam began to flourish in the fertile soil provided by dire social conditions and endemic political repression.

The military government of the FLN ruthlessly put down the protests, that seemed uncannily like an Algerian *intifada*,[2] with the army being given free rein to shoot demonstrators and torture those who had been arrested.[3] The protests climaxed on 10 October 1988, when the army fired into a crowd of 20,000 people, killing fifty.[4] The slaughter fuelled rather than stemmed the rise of political Islam. 'Black October' became Algeria's equivalent of Northern Ireland's Bloody Sunday or South Africa's Soweto massacre.

The government saw the warning signs and began to ease off, legalising political parties to give voice to the dispossessed and discontented. By far the largest and most prominent of these was the Front Islamique du Salut (FIS – the Islamic Salvation Front), which campaigned for an Islamic state based on *sharia* law, the legal code derived from the Koran and the teaching and example of the prophet Mohammed. In 1991, in the hope that it would serve as a political safety valve, the government allowed multi-party elections for the first time since independence. In the first round, the FIS won such a clear victory that success in the final round seemed inevitable. The party accepted the principle of one man one vote as a means of achieving power, but once in power it would abolish democracy forever. The government cancelled the final round of the elections, probably fearing a repetition of Iran's Islamic revolution, led by Ayatollah Khomeini, over a decade earlier.

Far from drawing the sting of the Islamist opposition, the cancellation made it even stronger. Many leaders of the FIS were arrested, and in response to the military crackdown various militant groups emerged, the most significant of which was the Groupe Islamique Armé (GIA – the Armed Islamic Group). Its core consisted of veterans of the Afghan *jihad*, who trained and indoctrinated young Algerians in the skills and ideology of guerrilla war. The GIA had no shortage of recruits or targets. France had become an additional enemy, as the FLN's ally in a civil war that became a terrible showdown between the Islamists and the military government. About 200,000 people are believed to have died in the violence.[5] The scene was set for the hijacking that was to be a harbinger of 9/11.

The four GIA terrorists who hijacked Air France Flight 8969 at Houari Boumediène airport in Algiers on Christmas Eve 1994 planned to crash it into the Eiffel Tower, forcing the pilots to aim for it at the point of a gun. Even if they hadn't managed to hit the tower, which realistically was a nigh-impossible task, the plane would have crashed on the French capital, with horrendous consequences. The outrageously ambitious plan came perilously close to succeeding.

I wanted to find out what such an experience was like for the passengers and members of the crew who had lived through the nightmare and come face to face with the terrorists. I also wanted to speak to members of the French special forces whose mission had been to storm the plane and rescue the hostages. They weren't in the business of talking to terrorists – just killing them.

I met some of the passengers, crew members and elite commandos at a hotel in Paris, ironically in the shadow of the still-standing Eiffel Tower, and interviewed them over two intense days. We set up the camera in a room in the bowels of the hotel, and stuck a 'Please do not disturb. Filming in progress' notice on the door in both English and French. We do this more in hope than in expectation that the request will be heeded, and filming had to be stopped on several occasions because of the clinking of glasses or noisy exchanges outside the room. It always seems to happen at a crucial point in an interview.

The interviews in Paris over those two days were harrowing, long and exhausting. I felt for my interviewees, who gave so much of their emotions as they recalled the most terrifying three days of their lives.

* * *

65

The first indication that all was not well had come at 11.15 a.m. on Christmas Eve as the Airbus waited on the tarmac at Algiers, ready to take off for Paris. Four men dressed like officials came on board carrying Kalashnikov automatic rifles, and ordered the passengers to produce their passports, as they said they were carrying out routine checks. Some of the cabin crew were immediately suspicious, as Kalashnikovs weren't normally carried by the police or customs officers. The captain, Jean-Paul Borderie, told me he feared the worst when one of them entered the cockpit: 'He turned round for a moment and I saw something that looked like sticks of dynamite sticking out of his coat pocket. A stick of explosives! This was really weird.' The crew's suspicions were soon confirmed when one of the four announced who they really were over the plane's intercom system. 'We are the Soldiers of Mercy,' he proclaimed. 'Allah has selected us as his soldiers. We are here to wage war in his name.'

The hijackers were armed with guns, grenades and twenty sticks of dynamite. Their leader was twenty-five-year-old Abdallah Yahia, a petty thief and former greengrocer from one of Algiers' most impoverished neighbourhoods, Les Eucalyptes.[6] It was also an Islamist stronghold. Yahia had joined the GIA two years earlier, and had risen rapidly through its ranks. His notorious local unit was known as 'Those who Sign with Blood', and was responsible for the brutal murder of several foreigners, five of whom were French. Yahia demanded that the plane should take off for Paris immediately. But it was going nowhere. The Algerian authorities were determined not to give in to terrorism, and the aircraft could not move from the tarmac until the passenger steps that were attached to it were removed.

Inside the plane, Islamic law ruled. The women were ordered to cover their heads. One Algerian passenger, Zahida Kakachi, who had been looking forward to midnight Mass in Paris, objected. 'I don't want to wear a headscarf,' she said. 'I won't wear it. It's out of the question.' But her cousin, who was travelling with her, entreated her to do as instructed. 'At this point I realised that this was not the time to make a stand,' Zahida remembered. One of the stewardesses, Claude Burgniard, also objected: 'It was really degrading to put something on my hair because of an old-fashioned, ancestral belief. I disliked it very much, but I did it to be like the other women, to support them.'

By 2 p.m., with no sign of movement, Yahia was losing patience, and decided it was time to show that he meant business. One of the passengers, an Algerian policeman, was singled out, taken to the front of the aircraft and told to kneel down behind a curtain. The passengers and crew could not see what was happening, but they heard the policeman pleading for mercy: 'Don't kill me. I have a wife and child.' A shot rang out, and his body was dumped on the tarmac. Shortly afterwards, a Vietnamese diplomat was ordered to the front of the plane, where Yahia's second-in-command was waiting. The man, thinking he was on his way to freedom, wanted to take his bottles of wine with him but was not allowed to remove them from the overhead locker. He then asked if he could have his passport back. 'You won't need that where you're going,' he was told. He was then shot in the back of the head and thrown out onto the tarmac.

Half an hour later, with two lifeless bodies lying on the runway outside the plane, there seemed to be signs of progress. Yahia agreed to let some of the hostages leave in exchange for the release of two prominent Islamist prisoners. At 2.30 p.m. sixty-three passengers, all of them Algerian, got off the plane. But that was it. Stalemate followed. The hijackers refused to give themselves up, and the authorities refused to let the aircraft leave. The Algerians then tried another approach. At 9 p.m. they brought Yahia's mother to the control tower to plead with her son over the radio. 'For God's sake, Yahia, my son, I'm afraid you will die. You're abandoning your family, your son. Yahia,' she cried, 'I can't bear the thought of you dying.' Yahia remained unmoved. 'No, I'm sorry. You are my mother and I love you, but I love God more than you, and we will see each other again in Paradise.' The stalemate continued.

Despite the two brutal murders, there was still deadlock as the Algerian authorities refused to remove the passenger steps and give clearance for the plane to depart. The silence of that first long night was broken only by the sound of one of the hijackers walking up and down the aisles, reciting verses from his Koran and talking to the male passengers. 'We are the *mujahideen*,' he kept saying. 'We have come here to die. Do you realise how lucky we are? We are going to die as *mujahideen* for our faith, for Allah. And can you believe it, there are seventy-two virgins waiting for us.' None of the terrified passengers saw fit to question the certainty of his belief.

One of the cabin crew, Christophe Morin, had vivid recollections of that claustrophobic night in captivity. 'It was hellish. The night seemed endless. The passengers were silent. It was like being trapped by a lead weight, drowning in those prayers. It was a world with no freedom, forced to listen to these endless verses.' Zahida Kakachi remembers how still and beautiful the night outside looked. 'There was a full moon. The ground seemed to be made of silver. There were all these white birds, and the tarmac was shimmering from the light of the moon.' One of the hijackers noticed her looking transfixed out of the window. 'Each of those birds will take a soul up to Paradise,' he said. Zahida was not reassured.

On Christmas Day, the second day of the hijack, with the plane still grounded in Algiers, the French government had finally got its counter-terrorist plan in place after long deliberations involving the Interior Minister, Charles Pasqua. Members of France's elite anti-terrorist police unit, the Groupe d'Intervention de la Gendarmerie Nationale (GIGN), had been flown to a disused military airport in Majorca to be on standby ready to storm the plane when the opportunity arose. Majorca was the closest the GIGN could get to Algeria without infringing Algerian sovereignty. The French had offered the Algerians assistance, but this had been politely refused. It would have been embarrassing and impolitic for the FLN government, that had fought the French in a bloody eight-year guerrilla war for independence, to be seen to be seeking assistance from its former colonial master. Pasqua told me that at this stage intelligence had been received from the Algerian secret service about the real purpose of the operation. 'It was very worrying,' he said. 'The true aim of those terrorists was to crash the plane on Paris.' Subsequently Metropolitan Police officers would raid a safe house in London believed to be connected with the hijackers and retrieve a propaganda pamphlet the front cover of which showed the Eiffel Tower in flames.

Christophe was convinced that he was going to die, and summoned up the courage to confront one of the hijackers and tell him that he did not want to meet his end with a shot to the back of the head: 'Whoever my murderer turns out to be, I want him to look me straight in the eye as he kills me.' The hijacker appears to have been surprised by the request. 'Don't worry,' he said. 'Even if you do die, you will go straight to heaven where you will find seventy-two virgins waiting for you. You will die as a martyr, so there is nothing to be afraid of. So why are you scared?' Christophe simply replied, 'All I know is that we seem to be on a journey that will end in death.'

By the end of Christmas Day, with the plane still on the ground, the hijackers were getting desperate. Two bodies on the tarmac, visible proof of their determination to carry out their threats, had not been enough to persuade the Algerian authorities to let the plane depart. At 9 p.m. Yahia issued an ultimatum. Unless the plane was allowed to depart by 9.30 he would start executing the hostages one by one, at half-hour intervals, until they were allowed to take off for Paris. The deadline came and went. Yahia picked out a French hostage, Yannick Beugnet, a cook from the French Embassy in Algiers who was flying home to spend Christmas with his wife and children. At gunpoint, Yahia marched him to the cockpit and forced him to address the control tower, where his words were recorded: 'Our lives are in danger now. If you don't do something, they are going to execute us. Something must be done as soon as possible.' Yahia then snatched the microphone and shouted, 'I swear we will take him and we will dump him out of that door. And we don't give a damn about you. See how we can hit you where we want and how we want. OK, so now we are going to throw him out. The door is already open. Now just listen to how we shoot him and dump him.' A single shot is then heard on the recording.

With three bodies now lying beneath the plane, and the prospect of another one every thirty minutes, the Algerian authorities finally decided to give in. Although they had had their own special forces (colloquially known as the 'Ninjas' because they dressed all in black) on standby, they had decided against using them, fearing a blood-bath. That fear was shared by many of the passengers, who had little faith in the Ninjas' ability to carry out a rescue without massive loss of life.

At 1 a.m. on Boxing Day, the third day of the hijacking, Yahia's demands were finally met. The passenger steps which had prevented the plane from moving were finally taken away, and Flight 8969 was cleared for take-off. No doubt to the intense relief of the Algerian government, the problem was out of their hands. Now the French could deal with it.

The plane's destination wasn't Paris, but Marseilles. Captain Borderie explained why: 'You need approximately twenty tons of fuel to get to Paris, but once you've been stuck on the ground for a couple of days, your reserves go down. You need fuel for the air conditioning, for electricity and for the coffee machines. With two hundred people on board, it goes quickly.' French Interior Minister Charles Pasqua was now a much happier man. Knowing what he did about the real purpose of the hijacking, he didn't want the aircraft to go anywhere near Paris. 'Once it landed in Marseilles to refuel, it was absolutely clear in our minds that the plane wouldn't be going anywhere else,' he told me. Orders were given to the GIGN on standby in Majorca to get to Marseilles as quickly as possible, and to prepare to put their intensive training into practice and storm the plane. They arrived in Marseilles just twenty minutes before the Airbus touched down at 3 o'clock on Boxing Day morning.

Yahia, determined to get to Paris to carry out the planned attack, demanded twenty-seven tons of fuel, three times the amount necessary. The airport authorities played for time while the GIGN got ready. 'We told the terrorists we would bring them some fuel,' said Pasqua, 'but we explained that we had some technical problems, and didn't have enough tankers to transport it. We told them various things to gain time.' The negotiations carried on through the morning and much of the afternoon, with Yahia growing increasingly frustrated and menacing at the lack of progress. 'It's not you who decide or the pilot,' he warned the control tower. 'We are the ones who decide. And you will pay very dearly.'

The protracted delay was necessary while the GIGN worked out where the hostages and the hijackers were located on the plane, and what weapons and explosives the hijackers had. Valuable information was fortuitously provided by an elderly couple whom Yahia agreed to let off the plane. He had been prepared to allow them to disembark in Algiers, but they hadn't wanted to walk over the dead bodies. They came down the steps of the plane at 4.05 p.m., and were immediately debriefed by the GIGN. They were able to give details about the number of terrorists, their weapons and the hierarchy within the group. Yahia and his number two, they said, seemed to spend most of the time in the cockpit.

The French authorities managed to protract the negotiations for a total of thirteen hours. By then Yahia had had enough. 'This is the last chance,' he told the control tower. 'One hour, and then you will have to bear the full responsibility.' If the fuel didn't arrive by a 5 p.m. deadline, he said, they would start killing the hostages. The three dead bodies in Algiers indicated that he meant what he said. As there was no sign of movement from the airport authorities, he probably knew that the hijackers were never going to get to Paris to carry out their mission. Zahida noticed their attitudes change as they realised that martyrdom in Marseilles was the only option left to them: 'They started to read verses from the Koran out loud, and the verses spoke of death. "We shall die. God is waiting for you. We shall die as warriors. We do not fear death."'

With five minutes to go to the 5 p.m. deadline, Zahida was convinced that she was going to die. Most of her fellow passengers probably felt the same. No one inside the plane was aware of what was going on outside. In Algiers the Ninjas had been visible; in Marseilles, the GIGN were not. Concealed out of the line of sight of the aircraft, the assault team was now fully armed and ready to move. One of its officers, Thierry Lévêque, told me what it felt like at that critical time: 'We know the terrorists are heavily armed and that they're likely to use explosives, so we're thinking that as soon as we walk in there, it's going to be fireworks, real combat. It's a good moment. There was emotion and fear, fear that is in your stomach before you go up and meet your adversary. Here you are playing with life and death.' Lévêque's colleague Roland Martin described the final moment before storming the plane. The members of the team piled one hand on top of the other in a pyramid of physical and spiritual solidarity. 'All these hands became one single, powerful hand which had the strength to take on the terrorists. That was it.'

At 5.15 p.m. the GIGN, masked and dressed in black, raced to the plane on a motorised passenger gangway and attacked through the rear and side doors. The stewardess Claude Burgniard remembers, 'They were not human beings. They were machines.' There was a fierce gun battle as the terrified passengers dived for cover between and under the seats. Yahia and two of the other terrorists were shot dead while offering determined resistance. That left one, Yahia's number two, who was also determined to go down as a martyr, with gun blazing. 'Then we had to deal with this warrior,' Roland Martin told me. 'I described him as a warrior because to launch a counter-attack single-handedly against the GIGN meant that he was doing his duty.'

When the noise and smoke cleared, all four terrorists were dead. Ten members of the GIGN were wounded. Miraculously, all the hostages were alive. They had been held prisoner on the plane for fifty-four hours. Their liberation took just twenty minutes. The Eiffel Tower survived too.

There is a fascinating and instructive postscript to the story. Among the political leaders of the Islamic Salvation Front who were arrested in the wake of the cancellation of the multi-party elections was a charismatic young cleric called Ali Belhadj, who had studied at Wahhabi schools* in Saudi Arabia and had risen to become the

---

*Wahhabism is a deeply conservative Islamic movement derived from the teachings of the eighteenth-century theologian Mohammed ibn-al-Wahhab, who preached in what is today known as Saudi Arabia. He advocated returning to the principles of the Prophet Mohammed, and sought to purge Islam of the impurities he believed had become attached to it. Wahhabism has shaped Saudi Arabia.

organisation's number two. He had been one of the prime movers of the demonstrations that had prompted the government to grant elections. I remember seeing remarkable video footage of a vast Islamist rally in Algiers shortly after the arrests in which Ali Belhadj's seven-year-old son Abdelkahar, in full junior Islamic dress, addresses a vast crowd, calling for an Islamic state and the release of his father, who was serving a twelve-year sentence for armed conspiracy against the regime.[7] 'There are a billion Muslims and we don't have a state that rules by God's holy law,' he shouts in the high-pitched voice of a child. 'Isn't that a dishonour and shame on us all?'[8] The crowd roars its approval as the little boy is hoisted aloft by his father's supporters. That powerful image brought vividly home to me the force and potential of political Islam.

We then found some even more remarkable footage that was shot many years later, in 2007. It was in a propaganda video made to launch 'The Al Qaeda Organisation in the Islamic Maghreb'.* There, standing in the woods in combat gear and holding a Kalashnikov, was Adbelkahar Belhadj, no longer the seven-year-old hero fêted at the rally, but now a fully-grown and fully-armed Al Qaeda combatant. The cause lives on, running through the blood of families in Ireland, the Basque country, Palestine, Kashmir and other conflict zones around the world. To its adherents, setbacks like the killing of the four Algerian hijackers make it even stronger.

---

*The Maghreb embraces the Muslim countries of North Africa. In the years after 9/11, some disparate *jihadi* groups, most notably that led by Abu Musab Al-Zarqawi in Iraq, chose to affiliate to Al Qaeda. Zarqawi's group became known as 'Al Qaeda in the Land of the Two Rivers'.

FOUR

Talking to the Interrogators

For the security and intelligence services, talking to terrorists face to face is often the most effective way of countering them. Information and admissions gained during interrogation are vital not only in stopping terrorist attacks and bringing their perpetrators to justice, but in helping to paint a bigger picture of the organisation to which they belong. And there's always the possibility of a bonus: turning the suspect and sending him back to the organisation from which he came in order to provide HUMINT – human intelligence – from within.

The problem is that most terrorist suspects refuse to talk, and many have been trained in Afghan camps by Al Qaeda in counter-interrogation techniques. Time and again FBI agents I talked to emphasised the need to establish a rapport with the suspect that might eventually help to break his resistance. To do so, they said, required experience, patience and persistence – and the additional element of luck. These agents were institutionally and personally opposed to the 'enhanced' interrogation techniques that the George W. Bush administration authorised the CIA to use in the wake of 9/11 to break important terrorist suspects, known as 'High Value Targets' (HVTs). They believed that such methods were not only ineffective, but counter-productive (see pp. 131, 293–4), and that talking to terrorists produced more valuable intelligence than subjecting them to humiliation and physical suffering that was tantamount to torture. The interrogation of the Al Qaeda suicide bomber Mohammed Al-Owhali by the FBI agent Steve Gaudin is a perfect case study.

Al-Owhali miraculously survived the bombing of the US Embassy in the Kenyan capital, Nairobi, in 1998, at the time I was still involved in the Northern Ireland peace process. The story illustrates not only the classic rapport-based interrogation techniques, but the evolution of Al Qaeda and its *modus operandi* through the 1990s.

After the Soviet defeat in 1989, the United States pulled the plug on Afghanistan. America's purpose had been served: the Soviet Union had been humiliated; the West had won. Afghanistan was now left to its own devices. Nation-building didn't feature on the United States' agenda.

Osama Bin Laden returned to Saudi Arabia, a hero and celebrity who had vanquished the Russian infidels and was now ready to put his Afghanistan-acquired military skills and his nascent Al Qaeda organisation at the service of the Saudi royal family. When Saddam Hussein invaded Kuwait in August 1990, Bin Laden offered to summon his army of Afghan veterans to wage *jihad* against the Iraqi interloper. His offer was politely refused by King Fahd, on the grounds that the Kingdom had a better offer from the Americans, backed by their British allies, in a coalition that included Muslim forces from Egypt, Morocco, Kuwait, Oman, United Arab Emirates, Bangladesh and, of course, Saudi Arabia. Bin Laden was thanked, and the hope was expressed that he would continue to serve Saudi Arabia as his family had done so loyally over so many years.[1]

The rejection stung him. Not only was it insulting, but it meant that the infidel Americans would be basing their troops on the soil of Saudi Arabia, home of Islam's most sacred places, Mecca and Medina. By joining the unholy US coalition to drive Saddam out of Kuwait, Wahhabi Saudi Arabia was allying itself with the Great Satan. Bin Laden and a number of Saudi clerics publicly denounced the decision – an act that was tantamount to denouncing the Saudi royal family. The dissident clerics were thrown out of the country, and Bin Laden was given a severe warning. His passport was taken away, but in 1991 he managed to get out of the country thanks to a supportive member of the royal family, on the pretext of attending an Islamic gathering in

Pakistan.[2] He was never to return. The Saudi government froze his financial assets and revoked his citizenship. Bin Laden was now stateless, and Saudi Arabia his enemy, behind only America and Israel.

But Bin Laden wasn't homeless. He had already established a good and mutually beneficial relationship with Sudan's Islamist political leader, Hassan al Turabi, whose National Islamic Front had recently seized power. Turabi got Bin Laden's money and construction expertise to build roads and infrastructure, and in return Bin Laden got a sanctuary and a logistical and training base from which to build and expand Al Qaeda. Before going into exile he had already laid the groundwork by buying up properties in Sudan.[3] Within three years Al Qaeda had achieved global reach by providing equipment, training and finance to other *jihadi* groups around the world, such as the Moro Islamic Liberation Front (MILF) in the Philippines and Jemaah Islamiyah (Islamic Community) in Indonesia and South-East Asia, the group subsequently associated with the Bali bombings of 2002.

But meanwhile, what happened to Afghanistan? After the Soviet withdrawal in 1989 the country, torn apart by ethnic and regional rivalries, descended into a bloody civil war as competing warlords who had formerly been united in the *jihad* against the common enemy, fought amongst themselves for control of the country. The Taliban emerged on top.

Taliban means 'students of Islam'. The Talibs, the students, emerged in 1994 from the refugee camps along the border between Pakistan and Afghanistan. They had been educated in local *madrassas*, Islamic schools that followed a strict interpretation of Islam, obeying to the letter the practice of the Prophet Mohammed in seventh-century Arabia. Most Talibs were Pashtuns, the majority ethnic group that had ruled Afghanistan for over two centuries. Their aim was to restore order to their war-torn country and establish a state governed under strict *sharia* law. They were financed, trained and armed by Pakistan through its intelligence agency, the ISI, which had established many of the necessary contacts when it acted as the conduit for American arms and money during the Afghan *jihad* against the Soviets. Saudi Arabia supported the Talibs too, and financed many of their *madrassas*

– Islamic schools. Pakistan saw its sponsorship of the Taliban as a way of exerting its influence in Afghanistan as a regional counterweight to its traditional enemy India. With remarkable speed, in 1996 the Taliban laid siege to the Afghan capital Kabul, as a prelude to taking over two thirds of the country.

Once in power, the Talibs did what they had said they would, establishing a state under *sharia* law, with its unbending strictures and draconian punishments for transgressors. All the accoutrements of twentieth-century living – radios, televisions, movies and computers – were banned, on the grounds that they diverted the mind from the pure contemplation of Islam. All images of living things were forbidden, including photographs, paintings and sculptures. In what seemed to the West a supreme act of cultural vandalism, the two huge statues of the Buddhas of Bamyan, that had stood carved in a cliff-face since the sixth century, were dynamited and destroyed in 2001 on the orders of the Taliban's leader, Mullah Omar. Men had to wear beards at least a fist's length below the chin. Women had to be dressed in *burqas*, garments that covered the entire body, apart from a mesh around the eyes:[4] the Taliban believed that 'the face of a woman is a source of corruption' for any man not related to her.[5] Anyone who contravened these rulings was severely punished: a public beating for a man whose beard was less than the required length, and a public flogging or even execution for a woman who disobeyed the laws. Women lived in what was tantamount to a fundamentalist Islamic prison. They were not allowed to work, or to go to school beyond the age of eight, and even during those infant years their education was strictly limited to the Koran.

This was the Afghanistan to which Osama Bin Laden returned in 1996, after he was forced to leave Sudan as a result of UN sanctions and American pressure on the regime. Hassan al Turabi had been giving house room not only to Bin Laden but to other Islamist revolutionaries whose targets were North African regimes from Egypt to Libya. The attempted assassination of the Egyptian President Hosni Mubarak in June 1995, when he was visiting Ethiopia, was probably the final straw. The would-be assassins, members of Ayman al-Zawahiri's Egyptian Islamic Jihad, were harboured by Turabi with the help of Bin Laden, and the regime refused to hand them over.[6] As the balance of power in Khartoum shifted, Osama Bin Laden and his Al Qaeda fighters were no longer welcome.

Bin Laden and his increasing number of Al Qaeda footsoldiers were not homeless for long, as Mullah Omar gave them sanctuary in Afghanistan, most of which was now under Taliban control. After all, the Taliban and Bin Laden shared basically the same ideology. Under the protection of the Taliban, Bin Laden was able to set up his own training camps and to oversee camps for other *jihadi* groups that were ideologically, if not always institutionally, affiliated to Al Qaeda. Between 1996 and 2001 Al Qaeda's most devastating attacks were planned by Bin Laden, Zawahiri and Al Qaeda's military committee. The attacks were now directed against America. Despite pressure from America and its ally Saudi Arabia, Mullah Omar refused to hand Bin Laden over. US intelligence estimates that in this critical five-year period between 10,000 and 20,000 fighters trained at Bin Laden-related camps in Afghanistan.[7] With the benefit of hindsight, it is astonishing that the United States stood by and watched this army of *jihadis* passing through the camps at which many of Al Qaeda's operatives were trained prior to carrying out their attacks.

It would be wrong, however, to think that America just sat on its hands at this critical time. It may have done nothing about Afghanistan, but it was beginning to focus its attention elsewhere. The CIA and the FBI were certainly aware of Osama Bin Laden and his involvement with terrorism, but he was thought of as more a financier than an operator. His name had been on the radar since the Afghan *jihad* against the Soviets, and had kept cropping up in theatres as far afield as Bosnia, Kashmir, Mindanao in the Philippines and Tajikistan. Evidence of America's growing concern about him was the setting up of a secret joint CIA/FBI task force to find out more about him and take appropriate action. The unit's codename was 'Alec Station', and it became operative in 1996, at the time Bin Laden moved from Sudan to Afghanistan. It was headed by the CIA officer Mike Scheuer, and to break a bureaucratic logjam over what it should be called, was named after Scheuer's son, which annoyed the bureaucrats.

'We were most concerned about the geographic breadth of his activities, and wanted to find out if Bin Laden was a threat or just another Saudi spendthrift,' Scheuer told me when I met him in Washington DC. 'Once that was determined, we were ordered to undertake covert operations against Bin Laden and Al Qaeda to assist the FBI in securing an indictment in the United States.' More bluntly, Scheuer says the word came down from on high that 'If you find out that Bin Laden is a threat, get rid of him.' But there had been a prohibition on assassinations since President Gerald Ford had issued an executive order in 1976 forbidding them, in the wake of a series of CIA scandals including multiple plans in the 1960s to kill the Cuban President, Fidel Castro. These harebrained schemes ranged from giving him exploding cigars designed to blow his head off, to putting itching powder in his scuba suit and LSD in his mouthpiece to blow his mind and ensure he never reached the surface again.[8]

Thirty years on, the CIA had become more sophisticated. By early 1998 a plan was in place to kidnap Bin Laden from his compound at Karnak in Afghanistan and fly him to the USA to stand trial. A year had been spent in detailed preparations, involving the CIA and US special forces, across several continents. Particular attention was to be paid to Bin Laden's comfort and human rights, Scheuer explained. He was to be seized with the help of human 'assets' on the ground, recruited by the CIA during the Afghan *jihad*, and would then be taken to a waiting aircraft and seated in a specially adapted container on board. 'CIA engineers built a well-padded, ergonomically comfortable, dentist-like chair for him. The shackles had to be padded so there would be no abrasions or bruises on his arms or legs or wherever he was bound.' There was concern about how he was to be silenced, on a temporary as opposed to permanent basis. CIA lawyers discussed the merits of different kinds of duct tape to seal his mouth while he was being seized and spirited away to America. 'The lawyers sat around playing with the tape, trying to figure out which would be least abrasive to his facial hair.' But the highly ambitious and somewhat bizarre plan was vetoed, according to Scheuer, by President Clinton with the support of his Cabinet. Scheuer said the White House deemed it too risky, and there was concern that vital intelligence assets on the ground might be lost in a possible gun battle with Bin Laden's bodyguards – and American lives might be lost too. Bin Laden himself might be killed in the process, with the result that the USA would be accused of assassination. It remains one of the tantalising 'what ifs' of history. By now the frustrated Scheuer was only too aware of the threat posed by Bin Laden and Al Qaeda. In East Africa, that threat was about to be realised.

One of the two suicide bombers chosen by Bin Laden to transform the threat into horrific reality by attacking the US Embassy in Nairobi with a huge truck bomb was called Mohammed Al-Owhali. Over two hundred people died in the devastating blast, most of them Kenyans. Miraculously, Al-Owhali survived, unlike the other suicide bomber, whose *nom de guerre* was Jihad Ali: it was he who detonated the bomb, and he died in the blast. Al-Owhali was arrested and interrogated by the FBI agent Steve Gaudin, and in the end he told Gaudin everything, not just about the attack but about his journey to *jihad*. Gaudin and his colleagues spent ten days talking to the terrorist, building rapport and never laying a finger on him.

The following account is based on what Al-Owhali told Gaudin, and what Gaudin told me. On a warm June morning in Washington DC in 2007 I sat with my producer Janette Ballard for over three hours listening to Gaudin's story before I had to leave to go to another meeting. When I returned, Janette told me that Gaudin had carried on talking for another two hours. This was a pre-interview conversation, with no camera, just notebooks. There's always a concern on such occasions that when it comes to the on-camera interview, the interviewee will not live up to expectations, either through nervousness or reluctance or both. That was not the case with Steve Gaudin as he told me the story of Mohammed Al-Owhali.

* * *

Al-Owhali came from a wealthy Saudi Arabian family. He was born in 1977 in Liverpool, where his father was studying for a Master's degree. Soon afterwards the family returned to Saudi Arabia. As a teenager Al-Owhali became increasingly obsessed with what he saw as the ills America was inflicting upon the Muslim world. He listened to audio tapes of radical clerics, and read magazines like *El Jihad* and books like *The Loving Hours of the Martyrs*. He told Steve Gaudin, 'If you become a martyr, you're wiping away the tears of all the mothers who've lost their children because of United States policy against the Middle East.' He was convinced that America was planning to occupy the Arabian Peninsula, and his mind was set on opposing US influence in the land that was the birthplace of Islam.[9] After high school he spent two years at the Mohammed Bin Saud University in Riyadh, and then decided it was time to answer the call of *jihad*. His father had to sign a special permission for his son to leave the country, as he was too young to be allowed to do so on his own. He didn't tell his father what his real reason for leaving was.

Al-Owhali first tried to fight in Tajikistan, where conflict had erupted between Muslim and secular forces following independence after the break-up of the Soviet Union, but it didn't work out. He then made for Afghanistan, and in 1997 entered basic training at Khaldan camp, near Khost, where he learned how to use light arms while receiving further religious instruction on the theological basis for *jihad*. Khaldan was a general training camp, and was not under the direct auspices of Al Qaeda, although some of its most notorious members initially passed through there. Its graduates included Ahmed Ressam, who planned to blow up Los Angeles International Airport on Millennium Eve 1999; Mohammed Atta, the leader of the 9/11 bombers; Ramzi Youssef, the mastermind of the first attempt to blow up the World Trade Center in New York in 1993;* Richard Reid, the British Muslim convert known as the 'shoe bomber' who tried to blow

---

*Youssef was also involved in the so-called Bojinka plot (Serbian for 'a big bang') in 1995 to blow up a dozen passenger aircraft as they flew from Manila in the Philippines to the USA. He is the nephew of Khalid Sheikh Mohammed, the architect of 9/11.

up an American Airlines flight en route from Paris to Miami in 2001; and Saajid Badat, a British Muslim student who planned to emulate Reid but was arrested on his return to the UK from training in Afghanistan in 2004.

Al-Owhali passed out of Khaldan with flying colours, and as a reward was granted a meeting with Osama Bin Laden – Al Qaeda chose the best and the brightest graduates. Bin Laden impressed upon him the need to pursue *jihad* further, and to strike a blow against America: he would have an opportunity to do so after further advanced training. Al-Owhali took up the offer, and worked his way through other Al Qaeda camps: Jihad Walh near Herat, Al Farouq near Kandahar, and Al Sadeeq near Khost. He was taught how to work with explosives, how to carry out kidnappings and assassinations, and how to hijack a plane. Again he proved a star pupil, and he was granted a further interview with Bin Laden. Now fully trained, he asked to be given a mission. 'Your mission will come in time,' Bin Laden assured him.

But there were more immediate problems in Afghanistan, and for the time being Al-Owhali's desire to fight *jihad* against America was put on hold. The CIA-backed Northern Alliance was fighting to take Kabul and wrest control from the Taliban. Bin Laden gave Al-Owhali permission to head for the front line, and it was there that he struck up a close relationship with Jihad Ali. He told Al-Owhali that fighting alongside the Taliban was good and noble, but that there were bigger tasks they could be carrying out. Without giving any details, he said one such mission was being planned, and asked Al-Owhali if he would like to join him on it. Al-Owhali said he would, and Jihad Ali told him he would be contacted when the time was right. Some time later he got in touch to say the mission was ready to go, and to ask Al-Owhali if he was still up for it. Al-Owhali said he was, although he did not have any idea what it would involve. The details of the mission were a closely guarded secret, and Al-Owhali knew better than to ask questions, although he assumed that his participation had been cleared by Bin Laden.

Al Qaeda provided him with a false Iraqi passport, and instructed him to travel to Pakistan and then fly to Yemen and await further instructions. He hadn't seen his father for a long time, and was tempted to go from Yemen to Saudi Arabia, as he suspected that it might be the last time he set eyes upon him. He decided, however, that the danger was too great, and that he couldn't risk jeopardising the mission, whatever it turned out to be. From Yemen he was instructed to fly on to Nairobi.

By 1997, while the plan to kidnap Bin Laden was on the drawing board, Mike Scheuer and his CIA and FBI colleagues in Alec Station thought they were making progress against Al Qaeda, gradually identifying some of its cells. One of them, in Nairobi, included among its members a Lebanese Muslim convert called Wadi al Hage. He had excellent credentials, having fought alongside Abdullah Azzam in Afghanistan, emigrated to America, where he'd graduated from the University of South-Western Louisiana, then gone on to work as Bin Laden's personal secretary in Sudan. As a naturalised American living in Nairobi, his cover seemed perfect. On 21 August 1997, members of Alec Station's task force raided his house and seized his computer. On it they found a message believed to have been written by the leader of Al Qaeda's Nairobi cell, Haroun Fazul, who believed the enemy was closing in.

> There are many reasons to believe that the cell members in East Africa are in great danger which leaves us no choice but think and work hard to foil the enemy's plans who is working day and night to catch one of us or gather more information about any of us … there is a war on … anybody who is associated with the Hajj [the annual pilgrimage to Mecca, codename for Osama Bin Laden] … is at risk … We are convinced one hundred percent that the Kenyan intelligence are aware about us and our security situation is extremely bad … work hard to return the Caliphate to earth and fight the forces of atheism and dictators who wreak havoc on earth. We the East Africa cell members do not want to know about the operation's plans since we are just implementers.[10]

There wasn't enough evidence to charge Wadi al Hage in Kenya, but soon afterwards the Kenyan authorities told him he was no longer welcome to stay. The following month he flew to America, where he was promptly arrested. At the very least, Alec Station thought it had disrupted an important Al Qaeda cell. But disruption alone wasn't enough. There was a logistical cell based on the coast in Mombasa, through which guns and explosives were smuggled from neighbouring war-torn Somalia. This cell was completely off the CIA's radar.

There were other warning signs that the US Embassy in Nairobi was at risk. At the beginning of 1998 the US Ambassador to Kenya, Prudence Bushnell, had written to Secretary of State Madeleine Albright expressing her concern that the Embassy was vulnerable to terrorist attack. She had previously been given the brush-off by middle-ranking officers at the State Department: 'I never got a reply,' she told me.[11] At around the same time, Lee Reed, the Embassy's security adviser, had warned that the Embassy was dangerously exposed to a potential truck or car bomb attack. He put the details and, prophetically, photos of the most likely point of attack, in a report that he sent to Washington. Ambassador Bushnell became even more concerned after someone walked into the Embassy with a warning. 'The "walk-in" advised us that we were under threat of a truck bomb,' she told me. 'The information was taken and sent back to the CIA, and I was told that the man was a fabricator and therefore we did not need to take heed of what he said.' The warnings could hardly have been clearer had they been posted in flashing neon lights above the Embassy.

Bin Laden was issuing his own warning. In February 1998 he announced the formation of 'The World Islamic Front', in effect an amalgamation of Al Qaeda and Ayman al-Zawahiri's Egyptian Islamic Jihad. Zawahiri had been Bin Laden's closest associate since the assassination of Abdullah Azzam in 1989. Bin Laden now issued a *fatwa* (a holy Islamic edict) declaring war on his enemies, 'Jews and Crusaders' – America and the West. What seems to have been uppermost in his mind at the time was the continuing presence of American forces in Saudi Arabia and the Arabian Peninsula after the first Gulf War of 1991.

He was probably also still smarting from Saudi Arabia's rejection of his offer to help rid Kuwait of Saddam Hussein. The declaration said:

> For over seven years America has occupied the holiest parts of Islamic lands, the Arabian Peninsula, plundering its wealth, dictating to its leaders, humiliating its people, terrorising its neighbours and turning its bases into a spearhead with which to fight the neighbouring Muslim peoples … Religious scholars have agreed that *jihad* is an individual duty when an enemy attacks Muslim countries. On this basis, and in accordance with God's will, we pronounce to all Muslims the following judgement.
>
> To kill the Americans and their allies – *civilians* [my emphasis] and military – is an individual duty incumbent on all Muslims in all countries … so that their armies leave all the territories of Islam, defeated, broken and unable to threaten any Muslim.[12]

The declaration was made at around the time that Alec Station was finalising its plan to kidnap Bin Laden and fly him to America in his ergonomically designed dentist's chair. It would have been the first rendition in the yet-to-be-declared US 'War on Terror'.

On 28 May 1998, three months after Bin Laden's *fatwa*, John Miller, a senior reporter with the US television network ABC News (and later to become the FBI's Executive Director of Public Affairs), secretly interviewed Bin Laden, talking to the man who was soon to be the world's most wanted terrorist. After elaborate security precautions, Miller ended up at an unspecified location somewhere just inside the Afghanistan border. He told me that Bin Laden's arrival was announced with an impressive array of pyrotechnics from fireworks, rockets and tracer rounds fired into the night. It is thought that both Mohammed Al-Owhali and Jihad Ali were there, as they were still in Afghanistan waiting to be given their mission.

Miller had had to submit his questions prior to the interview, and Ayman al-Zawahiri told him the ground rules before he started. Zawahiri said, 'I have very good news for you. Mr Bin Laden has agreed to answer each one of your questions.' 'Excellent,' said Miller.

Then Zawahiri added, 'But we will not be able to translate his answers.' Miller's face fell. 'Well, that's going to make it very difficult. How am I going to ask the follow-up questions?' 'That will not be a problem,' Zawahiri replied. 'There will be *no* follow-up questions.'[13]

The interview took place a week after Alec Station's plan to kidnap Bin Laden was stood down by the White House. Miller's videotape shows Bin Laden looking nervous beforehand, his eyes darting from side to side. 'The worst thieves in the world today and the worst terrorists are the Americans,' he tells Miller during the interview. 'We do not have to differentiate between military or civilian. As far as we are concerned, they are all targets.'[14] Miller had his headline-making scoop in the can. The interview over, he asked Zawahiri when America might expect Bin Laden's war to begin. 'Oh, you will see the result of this *fatwa* in the next several weeks,' Zawahiri replied. Miller thought this was a little unusual, as terrorist groups don't normally spell out when they're going to carry out their operations. 'They're trying to tell us something,' he said to himself. 'Something's about to happen.' Ten weeks later, that 'something' did happen, in a spectacular way.

On the morning of Friday, 7 August 1998, Mohammed Al-Owhali and Jihad Ali drove a Toyota truck laden with 1,600 pounds of high explosives into the centre of Nairobi.[15] Coincidentally or not, the date marked the anniversary of the arrival of American troops on Saudi Arabian soil eight years earlier. The huge bomb was made up of four to five hundred soft-drink-sized cans of TNT, aluminium nitrate and aluminium powder. Jihad Ali was at the wheel. Al-Owhali was carrying a gun and four grenades. Four years earlier in Sudan, Bin Laden had identified the optimum point of attack on the US Embassy in Nairobi from photographs taken by one of his most trusted colleagues. Al Qaeda plans well ahead. The most vulnerable spot was at the back of the building, by the drop-down security barrier where deliveries were made.

Four days before the operation was scheduled, Al-Owhali had been briefed by a cell leader known as 'Saleh' at a house in a middle-class suburb of Nairobi. This was probably when he was informed what the target was. He later told Steve Gaudin that he told Saleh he had reservations about the operation, and was concerned that by attacking the rear of the Embassy, more innocent Kenyans would be killed. 'I said I wanted to be involved in killing Americans and I want to kill them in the United States. I don't want to be part of some little thing. I want to be part of the big attack. I want to attack Americans in America.' 'Listen,' Saleh had replied, 'we have plans to attack inside the United States, but we're not ready yet. First we need to hit American targets outside the US at a number of different points so that we distract them, so they'll be concentrating on things here and there and they'll never see us coming inside.' Al-Owhali was apparently mollified, accepting that the attack on the US Embassy was 'part of a bigger thing'. The 'bigger thing' was to be 9/11.

Al-Owhali told Gaudin that Saleh informed him, 'Your job is to get out of the truck and assault the guards so that they open the drop bar so Jihad Ali can get a little bit closer to the Embassy. And you're both going to be killed in the explosion.'

At the appointed hour, the truck pulled up at the security barrier. Al-Owhali, who was carrying a couple of concealed grenades, jumped out as instructed and ordered the guard to raise the bar so they could drive in. My producer Janette Ballard tracked down the guard, a shy, nervous man called Joash Okindo, who recalled being confronted by Al-Owhali. He said he had been suspicious: 'The truck didn't have a complete registration number. I thought it was delivering a parcel, but there was no relevant information or paperwork.' Al-Owhali 'seemed calm and spoke slowly'. Okindo said he couldn't open the gate, as he didn't have the keys. 'You'll have to go to reception [at the front of the building],' he told Al-Owhali. Thwarted and frustrated, and suddenly realising that he'd left his gun in his jacket in the truck, Al-Owhali began hurling the grenades at random. Watching from the cabin of the truck, Jihad Ali pressed the button. The giant bomb ripped through the Embassy, causing destruction on an unimaginable scale. Over two hundred people were killed, and thousands were injured. Jihad Ali died instantly: his wish to become a *shaheed* had been granted. Al-Owhali, who had shared the same wish, was left bleeding but alive, denied the martyrdom he had craved. It's not clear whether he changed his mind at the last minute or was floored by the explosion. In the confusion, he disappeared into the stunned and screaming crowd. The scene was one of almost biblical devastation, with rescuers, loved ones and relatives crawling like ants over the mountains of debris. Six minutes later, another truck bomb destroyed the US Embassy in the Tanzanian capital Dar es Salaam, killing eleven people and wounding eighty-five. Al Qaeda had struck not just once, but twice. Its message could not have been clearer.

John Miller was on vacation at the time, and was on a fishing boat seventy miles out in the Atlantic north of Montauk, Long Island, when his mobile phone rang. It was the ABC newsroom. They told him the news. His reaction was immediate. 'It's Bin Laden,' he said. Ambassador Prudence Bushnell, who had warned Secretary of State Madeleine Albright about the vulnerability of the Embassy only a few months before, was stunned. 'It was a whack around the head,' she told me. 'A message that we chose not to listen to because we were tone deaf to terrorism at the time.'[16] The attacks were Bin Laden's wake-up call to the world.

Steve Gaudin was on vacation too, and was on a beach on the New Jersey shore when his pager went off. The message was 'Get into the office ASAP.' He didn't have a clue what it was about. He'd taken the security cover off his car radio and left it at home, so he wasn't able to listen to the news as he drove straight to his office in New York, still in bermudas and flip-flops. He was told what had happened and ordered to go home, dress more appropriately, get his passport and pack for either Nairobi or Dar es Salaam. 'I don't even know where Dar es Salaam is,' he confessed, and he'd only dimly heard of Osama Bin Laden. He'd spent his six years in the FBI in upstate New York chasing bank robbers and drug dealers, not terrorists. He was told that as a former military man, his job on the mission was to protect the FBI's advance party, led by Pasquale 'Pat' D'Amuro, with his Heckler & Koch MP5 submachine gun.

The journey to Washington DC by a normal commuter bus, requisitioned at the last moment by New York City Police, seemed to take forever, as the vehicle had a speed limiter which meant that it couldn't go faster than 50 mph. The fact that the FBI team was effectively travelling by public transport was an indication of how hurriedly the task force was put together. The 9,000-mile journey across the Atlantic to Nairobi on a military C5 Hercules transport was hardly more comfortable. Having flown on one myself, from Ascension Island to Angola in 1995, with a British army peace keeping mission, I know what it would have been like. Noisy and smelly, with the toilet behind a curtain of hessian sacking.

When the team arrived at the site of the bombing in Nairobi, they could not believe what they saw. The area was still burning. 'I remember the smell of everything,' Steve told me. 'Burnt gasoline. Burnt bodies. Burnt everything. Rescue crews still trying to help people, regular Kenyan citizens climbing on top of the rubble looking for relatives or just anybody.' A photograph taken at the time shows the team looking on, utterly bewildered. A makeshift operations room was set up, and hundreds of people rang in responding to the FBI's request for information, which had been relayed via the Kenyan government.

After two days, Debbie Doran, a young FBI agent who was manning the phones, told Pat D'Amuro that she'd just received an interesting tip-off. Someone had called from a hotel in Eastleigh, a small town about twenty miles outside Nairobi which had become home to thousands of refugees from the conflict in neighbouring Somalia. The caller, who wanted to remain anonymous, said he was concerned about a stranger who had checked into the hotel, left on the morning of the bombing and returned injured. He had no identity documents, and appeared to have no money. D'Amuro gave Gaudin the scant details scribbled on a piece of paper. 'Go find him,' he said. With an armed Kenyan police escort, Gaudin traced the man he was looking for to a cheap hotel room in Eastleigh. 'It was a JDLR case,' Gaudin told me: 'It Just Doesn't Look Right.' His quarry had over $800 in $100 bills, and he was carrying a casualty record card that showed he had been treated at the M.P. Shah hospital in Nairobi on 7 August, the day of the bombing. He was obviously nervous. 'He had bandages on both his hands, and a massive amount of stitches in the middle of his fore-head, just like the big laces you get in an American football.' He was arrested by the Kenyan police officers and put in the back of the truck. Gaudin immediately began talking to him, trying to build rapport. He assured him that everything would be all right, and gave him some butterscotch sweets that he had in his pocket.

Back at base, the interrogation began. The suspect said his name was Khalid Saleh Selin bin Rashid, and that he had been going to a bank near the Embassy when the bomb went off, and he'd been injured in the blast. It seemed a plausible enough story. But JDLR kicked in. Although he claimed to have been injured in a huge bomb blast, and had been treated for quite serious injuries, there was not a speck of blood on his clothes. Gaudin asked what he had done with the clothes he'd been wearing when the bomb went off. He said he was wearing them, explaining that he was a very clean person and washed his clothes every night before he went to bed. 'That's when the lights really started flashing. Not that he's a bomber or a terrorist, but "This guy's lying. I don't know what you're hiding but you're hiding some-thing."' The suspect's shoes were filthy – clearly he didn't polish them at bedtime when he washed his clothes. Then Gaudin noticed his belt. He smacked the table hard. 'Stand up!' he ordered. The suspect sprang to attention in an instantaneous reaction. Gaudin knew immediately that he had had military training. He told him to take off his belt. As he did so, Gaudin noticed a price tag inside the buckle. The suspect knew the game was up. He sat down, looked at Gaudin and the other interrogator who was with him and said, 'You guys are good. Now I need to pray.' Gaudin's female interpreter had also had a hunch that something was not quite right, pointing out that the suspect spoke classical Arabic. 'This guy is not some poor street vendor,' she said. 'He's been to college, and is very intelligent.'

The man finally told Gaudin his real name. He said he was Mohammed Rashed Daoud Al-Owhali, and he was from Saudi Arabia. He promised that, on condition that he was tried in America, before an American court, he was also willing to tell everything, including the details of his involvement with Osama Bin Laden and

Al Qaeda. 'I had never heard the word "Al Qaeda" until that particular day,' Gaudin told me.

President Clinton, who was embroiled in the Monica Lewinsky affair at the time, responded to the Embassy bombings by authorising retaliatory strikes. Thirteen Tomahawk Cruise missiles were fired at a pharmaceutical plant in Sudan that was suspected of being a secret chemical weapons factory alleged to be part-owned by Bin Laden (the intelligence, however, appears to have been wrong).[17] Sixty-six Tomahawks were also fired at two training camps around Khost in Afghanistan, where Bin Laden was believed to be staying. It seems he had been heading there the night before, but changed his mind at the last minute and decided instead to go to Kabul to visit friends.[18] He must have thought God was on his side that day. Dale Watson, Steve Gaudin's overall boss in charge of the FBI's investigation into the bombings,* was dismissive of Clinton's reaction. 'Bin Laden would say, "Mmmm. Is that the best that they can do for two US embassies simultaneously bombed? A few dozen Cruise missiles into two empty training camps? Let's keep going, because the US is a paper tiger. They're not going to do anything." And in hindsight, we didn't.'

Gaudin's interrogation of Mohammed Al-Owhali lasted ten days, during which the White House deliberated how to respond. I asked Gaudin if the experience had been part of his own learning process, given that he was a novice in the field of counter-terrorism, and had never set eyes on a *jihadi* before, let alone sat down and talked to a terrorist. 'It was a life-changing experience for me,' he said. 'I knew very little about Islam, or what his world was like. There's an old saying: "Don't judge an Indian until you've walked a mile in his moccasins." Well, that's what I was doing, walking in his steps. He was basically teaching me what his religion was like.' The FBI's traditional, rapport-based way of talking to terrorists was paying off. In the later

---

*In July 1998 Watson was made Deputy Assistant Director with responsibility for the FBI's counter-terrorism programme. In this capacity he oversaw the investigation into the bombings of the East African embassies.

stages of the interview, Gaudin asked Al-Owhali how the fighting was going to end. 'It's never going to stop until the United States leaves the Arabian Peninsula, leaves the Arabs alone and stops supporting Israel,' he said.

Mohammed Al-Owhali's wish was granted. He stood trial in a federal courtroom in Manhattan, and on 29 May 2001 was sentenced to life imprisonment, along with three others involved in the bombing of America's East African embassies.* The sentences were passed just over three months before 9/11. On the morning that the two American Airlines planes hit the Twin Towers, Ambassador Prudence Bushnell was eating breakfast in Guatemala when she got a call from a woman colleague. 'Ambassador, turn on the television,' she said. 'The bastards are doing it to us again.' The Ambassador wasn't surprised.

---

*The three others were Wadi al Hage, Mohammed Sadiq Odeh and Kalfan Khamis Mohammed. A fourth man, Ahmed Kalfan Ghailani, was arrested in Pakistan in 2004, and subsequently transferred to Guantánamo Bay. In 2010 he faced over 280 charges of conspiracy and murder, but was convicted by a New York jury on only one – conspiracy to destroy government buildings and property. The admissions he had made as a result of the CIA's 'enhanced interrogation techniques' (see final chapter) were not admissable as evidence in court. Ghailani now faces a minimum sentence of twenty years.

FIVE

Talking to a Convicted Terrorist

Talking to terrorists in gaol isn't easy. It is now almost forty years since I interviewed my first 'terrorist' in prison. It was the late summer of 1971, four months before I was sent to cover the events of Bloody Sunday. The 'terrorist' – as President Nixon called her[1] – in question was Angela Davis, a Marxist revolutionary associated with the radical Black Panther Party, and a former professor at the University of California, from which she'd been fired. She had been on the run, and was high on the FBI's 'Most Wanted' list. She was ultimately arrested and charged with conspiracy in connection with a shootout outside a California courthouse – a charge of which she was acquitted in 1972.[*] At the time I wanted to interview her she had been incarcerated for sixteen months. Via her attorney she had agreed to see me, but the problem was persuading the Sheriff of Marin County gaol, where she was a prisoner, to let me in. It was one of those cases where luck and coincidence played their parts.

Marin County gaol lies in a prosperous, middle-class suburb across the Golden Gate bridge from San Francisco. I drove there on a day of brilliant sunshine, having made an appointment to meet the Sheriff. My heart sank as I walked into his office. He was a bull of a man, who reminded me of Rod Steiger's Police Chief Bill Gillespie in the film *In the Heat of the Night*. My long hair and embarrassing Mexican

---

[*]The shootout took place in 1970 at Marin County courthouse. It followed an attempt to take the judge, the prosecutor and two members of the jury hostage in order to bargain them for the release of Davis's close friend George Jackson, a black revolutionary prisoner.

moustache were unlikely to endear me to him. To say his welcome wasn't exactly warm would be an understatement. 'Whadya want?' he asked curtly. I could see this wasn't going to be easy. Then I noticed a Boy Scout *fleur-de-lis* pinned to the khaki lapel above his Sheriff's star. 'Were you a Scout?' I asked, pointing to the badge. 'Yes. Why, were you?' he replied suspiciously. 'Yes,' I said. He visibly thawed. 'Why, I was in your country in 1957.' Before he could finish I interjected, 'Not at the World Boy Scout Jubilee Jamboree at Sutton Coldfield?' 'Why, yeah. Were you there?' he replied in astonishment, now with a smile on his face. 'Yes. And it rained all the time,' I added. 'Sure did,' he replied. The ice was broken. 'So how can I help?' I told him I would like to film an interview with his most famous, or infamous, prisoner. 'Sure, no problem,' he said. 'When do you want to do it?' He told me that Davis would be sitting behind a bulletproof screen, for security reasons. I said I thought we could handle that. And so I got a world scoop, and talked to my first 'terrorist' in prison.

Talking to convicted Islamist terrorists in gaol requires much more than coincidence and luck. The vast majority don't want to talk, and on the rare occasions when they are prepared to do so, filmed interviews are only possible if the prison authorities allow a camera crew inside. In Britain, filming Islamist prisoners is a no-go area, as it is deemed far too sensitive by Ministry of Justice officials. They fear that publicity will be given to the reality of what is going on inside some of Britain's top-security gaols, like Belmarsh, where hardened *jihadis*, many of them serving life sentences, are reportedly radicalising other Muslim prisoners who have been gaoled for non-terrorist offences.

In Germany, where the authorities are more enlightened, things are different, although to be fair the Germans don't have the same concentration of Islamist prisoners that Britain has. The prisoner I managed to interview was a young Algerian Muslim called Salim Boukhari, who had formerly lived in London. He had become a member of a terrorist cell based in Frankfurt, and was serving a twelve-year sentence for conspiracy to murder following a plot to blow up Strasbourg's Christmas market in December 2000. My interview with him needs to be placed in the context of the rise of Islamist extremism that, as we have seen, manifested itself in Algeria in the early 1990s, culminating in the hijacking of the Air France Airbus in 1994, before spreading to France, and from there to Britain and Germany.

After Yahia, the leader of the Algerian hijackers, had been shot dead in Marseilles by French GIGN commandos, the GIA vowed to avenge the deaths of one of its most senior leaders and his three fellow hijackers. Vengeance was not long in coming. Seven months later, on 25 July 1995, the GIA launched a bombing campaign on the Paris Métro. Ten people were killed and fifty-seven wounded at the Saint Michel-Notre Dame station. The following month an attack on the TGV line north of Lyon involving a pressure cooker packed with explosives was foiled.[2] According to France's legendary anti-terrorist judge Jean-Louis Brugière, there was more to the attacks than mere revenge: 'The GIA decided to make a strategic step in 1994 not only to fight inside Algeria, which is their homeground battlefield, but to export violence outside,' he told me. 'Algeria was only the first base for a much larger strategy to promote *jihad* as a tool to have a worldwide Caliphate in the future, the same [goal] as Al Qaeda.' There were reports that Osama Bin Laden had been in touch with the GIA via emissaries from his sanctuary in Sudan. He saw the GIA as a natural Islamist ally in his evolving global campaign.

Following the 1995 attacks, the French authorities cracked down hard on known and suspected Algerian extremists, with the result that many sought refuge in London, to the increasing exasperation of the French police, intelligence services and judiciary. One of these suspects, Rachid Ramda, who was believed to be the mastermind behind the attack on the Métro, was subsequently arrested by London's Metropolitan Police anti-terrorist officers. It was in his flat that the pro-GIA pamphlet with the cover depicting an exploding Eiffel Tower was found.*

---

*After a long legal battle, Rachid Ramda was finally extradited to France to stand trial for his involvement in the Métro bombing. He was sentenced to life imprisonment in October 2007.

The following year the GIA split. Splits often happen in insurgent groups, for ideological, political, practical or personal reasons (the IRA is a prime example). In 1996 a new insurgent group was born from the splinters of the fractured GIA. Known as the Salafist Group for Call and Combat (Groupe Salafiste pour la Prédication et le Combat – GSPC), it had divorced itself from the GIA because it disagreed with its policy of deliberately targeting civilians. The GSPC's professed aim was to hit military targets only, although the reality was somewhat different.

The architect of the GSPC network which over the next four years stretched from the training camps in Afghanistan to Europe, Canada and the United States is thought to have been an Algerian with many aliases, although he is best known as Abu Doha. He was familiar to those in the *jihadi* cells allegedly connected to him as 'the Doctor'. Doha was one of the many Algerians who sought refuge in London following the French anti-terrorist sweeps after the Métro bombing. London became known as 'Londonistan', and it was during this period that Finsbury Park mosque, under its controversial one-eyed, hook-handed *imam*, Abu Hamza, became notorious as a meeting place for *jihadis*, actual and intentional, from many countries. Abu Doha was one of its more high-profile worshippers. The British intelligence services were aware of the existence of Algerian extremists in London, and kept a watchful eye on them, but as long as there appeared to be no plans to attack targets in the United Kingdom, generally no disruptive action was taken. It seems that at the time, MI5 and the Metropolitan Police's Special Branch did not have the full picture of the extensive international reach of these Algerian cells. The linkages only began to emerge as cells were taken down and the connections between them were gradually established, most notably those that led from Abu Doha in London to related cells in Canada and the USA that were responsible for an abortive plot to blow up Los Angeles International Airport on Millennium Eve. As Assistant Commissioner David Veness, the Metropolitan Police's senior anti-terrorist officer, told me, with the aid of hindsight, 'Perhaps we should have joined up the dots more closely.'[3]

Abu Doha was the alleged mastermind behind GSPC plans to stage a series of spectaculars to mark the arrival of the new millennium. Los Angeles International Airport was the prime target. The bomber designated to carry out the attack was a fellow Algerian called Ahmed Ressam, who had trained with Doha in the Afghan camps in the 1990s. The plot, however, was foiled in mid-December 1999 when Ressam was intercepted while crossing the border from Canada into the USA with the bomb ingredients in the boot of his car. The US indictment of Ressam provides an insight into Doha's alleged role in the GSPC network.

> While in the training camps Ressam had extensive contact with Doha and understood that Doha's responsibilities in the camps were to facilitate the travel of the trainees into the camps as well as their entry into and out of countries in which various terrorist 'operations' were to take or had taken place. Doha would facilitate such travel by obtaining for the terrorists various forms of false identification and travel documents. In addition, Doha was responsible for establishing means of communication among the various cells, including Ressam's Algerian cell, that were associated with various *jihad* training camps in Afghanistan.[4]

Abu Doha was arrested in London on 27 February 2001 as he was about to board a flight to Saudi Arabia with a false passport. He was detained in Belmarsh prison in south-east London for six years on immigration charges, pending deportation to Algeria, as there was not enough evidence to charge him with terrorist offences. The Americans sought his extradition in connection with the Los Angeles Airport plot, but finally had to drop their request when Ahmed Ressam refused to give evidence against him at trial.

The other 'spectacular' allegedly planned by Doha and his network was the plot for a GSPC-related cell in Frankfurt to bomb the Christmas market in Strasbourg in December 2000. This plan was foiled when four Algerians who were members of the cell were arrested. Their alleged leader, thirty-year-old Salim Boukhari, had been based in London.

The more I learned about Boukhari, about his upbringing in Algeria, his time in France and his life in London, the more I wanted to meet him. I discovered that the flat in which he and his family had lived in London was on a sprawling council estate. Finding it wasn't easy. After wandering around asking passers-by if by chance they knew a family called Boukhari and being met by a series of blank faces or shaking heads, I finally had a brighter idea. At the bottom of a sign that bore a map of the estate was the name and telephone number of the caretaker. I rang him on my mobile and asked if he could help. I explained that the Boukhari I was looking for was an Algerian, and apologised for not being able to give him any more information. He paused, then said he thought there was an Arab family living on the first floor of a block of flats further up the road.

When I got to the block I found I couldn't get to the first floor, as a key was needed to unlock the security door. From its location I knew this was unlikely to be the safest of estates. I looked around, eventually found a gate with spikes on the top and managed with some difficulty to edge my way precariously round it. I then started knocking on doors. I drew blanks until someone said they thought an Arab family was living across the landing. That meant knocking on more doors, and getting yet more puzzled looks. At last I struck lucky. A door was opened by a woman dressed in the *niqab*, a black garment that totally covers the entire body except for a slit through which the eyes can be seen. I was a little taken aback at first, as this was not what I had been expecting. I gave my name, but did not mention the BBC, knowing from experience that when people don't want to talk to strangers who arrive on their doorstep, least of all journalists, they simply close the door on them. To my surprise, however, the woman, who confirmed that she was indeed Mrs Boukhari, invited me in. For a strict Muslim woman to let a male stranger into her home when she was alone was exceedingly rare. It was only when I was inside the flat that I realised why I had been allowed inside. It transpired that Mrs Boukhari thought I was from the council or social services, as she had phoned them about a problem and had been told that somebody would be coming to see her. When she discovered that I wasn't that person, she was very upset. She became even more agitated when I told her I was a BBC journalist, and asked if I could talk about her husband in gaol in Germany. Trying to reassure her, I said I would really like to talk about what had happened and how her husband was. To my relief, I was invited into the living room, which was neat and sparsely furnished, with a television in the corner and a pile of toys on the floor among which her son, a toddler, was playing.

Mrs Boukhari remained very suspicious, and was reluctant to talk without her husband's permission. 'If you want to talk about my husband, you should talk to him and not to me,' she said. I explained that that would be difficult, as he was in gaol in Germany, but said I would try. She told me he was being held in Kassel prison, and gave me the name of his solicitor in Frankfurt. We parted amicably, with me apologising profusely for the intrusion. I then wrote a letter to Salim Boukhari, while my colleague Patricia de Mesquita, a fluent German-speaker, got in touch with his solicitor. I heard nothing back from Boukhari but his solicitor told Patricia that he would be happy to meet us in Frankfurt to discuss the possibility of filming an interview with his client. In the end Boukhari agreed to the interview.

I had interviewed 'terrorists' in gaol before, from Angela Davis in 1971 to IRA and Loyalist paramilitary prisoners inside Northern Ireland's Maze prison in 1990. But this would be my first interview with a convicted *jihadi*. However, getting agreement to an interview and getting it on film are not always the same thing. Patricia and I arrived at the prison in Kassel with a film crew and our fingers crossed. Remarkably, Patricia had navigated the shoals of the complex German bureaucracy and persuaded the prison authorities to let us in to film the interview.

I felt slightly queasy as we passed through the prison gates, negotiated security and made our way inside the forbidding, grey stone walls of the gaol. It could have been a film set. We were shown into a small room with one window, a table, a couple of metal chairs and a washbasin in a white-tiled corner. We set up the camera, and waited. After a while a guard came in with Salim Boukhari. An intense-looking man, he wore glasses, had a goatee beard and was dressed in a blue denim prison shirt. I heaved an internal sigh of relief, and thought we were almost there. How wrong could I be? We shook hands, then Boukhari asked, 'What's the camera doing here?' I explained that it was to film the interview he'd agreed to do. 'I never agreed to film an interview,' he said. I felt the ground opening up beneath me at the thought of having to return to London empty-handed after all our high expectations. 'But my understanding was that you had,' I said. 'Your solicitor said you'd agreed, and that's why we're here, and that's what the camera's for.' The guard asked if Boukhari and I would like to go into another room and talk privately. I said that would be a good idea. We then adjourned next door.

In situations like this, the only thing you can do is summon up all your powers of persuasion, and hope they will prove sufficient. I began by asking how he was, and how he was finding life in prison. He said it wasn't too bad, and told me that the other Muslim prisoners had given him a warm welcome when he arrived, bringing him sweets, assorted goodies and other signs to show how pleased they were that he was among them. I explained that I wanted to talk to him about himself and his journey to *jihad*, and why he believed what he did. He was softly-spoken, clearly highly intelligent, articulate and completely self-contained. Again, he did not fit the stereotype of a 'terrorist'. He took some convincing, but at the end of an intense forty-five minutes he finally agreed to do an interview, and we returned to the room where the crew and Patricia were waiting.

I began by asking about his upbringing in Algeria. He said he came from a normal, middle-class family, and that like his brothers and sisters he had been encouraged to study by his parents. His ambition was to become an electrical engineer, and his mother and father were very strict in ensuring that he worked hard enough to achieve this. Boukhari was studying at a time when Algeria was on the brink of its most traumatic period, with the Islamist GIA and the military government locked in the bloody civil war that followed the cancellation of the elections in 1991. I asked if he had any sympathy with the GIA, and whether he had ever considered joining them to take up arms against the government. He said the thought had never entered his head. 'I think they were bad, because the GIA was killing innocent people,' he told me. Despite the seismic political upheaval around him, Boukhari said he wasn't interested in politics at the time, and was not particularly religious. He didn't say his prayers or read the Koran.

When he told his parents that he wanted to go to France to study at university, they tried to dissuade him, saying it would be better for him to stay at home, be guided by them and finish his studies in Algeria. But he was determined to go. When he arrived in France, he found that life there could be hard. 'I thought things would be easy in Europe, but they weren't. In Algeria you don't have to pay anything to study. In France you have to work very hard to pay for it. I had to find work and someone who would help me get a student visa, but it was very difficult.' He didn't feel particularly at home in France. In the wake of the GIA's attack on the Paris Métro in 1995, Algerians were increasingly seen as members of a suspect community. The French police got tough, and Boukhari became fed up with constantly being asked for his papers. When his visa expired he decided he'd had enough of France and the harassment he had found there. Friends had told him that life was better in England, that you didn't need a visa and you could live without forever being asked to produce your documentation.

Boukhari was allowed to come to England on the basis of his French ID document, and tried a variety of occupations, from training as a cook at a college in Richmond to working as a security guard for £200 a week at Sainsbury's Homebase and the Safeway supermarket in Camden Town. He started going to a mosque in Leyton: 'It was a normal mosque. There were no extremists there talking about *jihad*.' Then he had a taste of Finsbury Park mosque, and that may well have been the point at which his radicalisation took root. 'Finsbury Park was "hotter" than Leyton. I felt at home there. They were speaking about *jihad* and what was happening to our brothers in so many countries. The oppression and aggression. It made me think that I had to come back to my religion, so I started studying the Koran and the *hadiths*. I found out so many things that I didn't know in my own country.' Boukhari didn't put names to any of the individuals who were instrumental in his radicalisation, but he did admit the influence they had had on him: 'I found some friends, religious people, who knew more about religion than me and they helped me.'

Boukhari seems to have followed a common path to radicalisation: a lonely figure in a strange and alien world, befriended by clerics and their followers who gave him a sense of belonging and a deeper reason for being. 'I became a different person,' he said. Among those whose sermons and teachings he listened to were Abu Hamza and Abu Qatada, the radical Palestinian/Jordanian cleric who had been granted political asylum in Britain in 1994.* Former Home Secretary David Blunkett once described Qatada as the most significant extremist preacher in the United Kingdom,[5] and like Abu Hamza he became a hate figure in the popular press. Mr Justice Collins, who heard the appeal against Abu Qatada's subsequent detention, described him as 'a truly dangerous individual. We have no doubt that his beliefs are extreme and are indeed a perversion of Islam for the purposes of encouraging violence against non-Muslims and Muslims who are, or have been, supportive of Americans.'[6] I asked Boukhari about Abu Qatada. 'He's a good cleric and I think he's a good man,' he said. As he could have walked out of the interview at any moment, and had been reluctant to do it in the first place, I decided it was advisable not to challenge him at this stage. Nothing I could have said would have made him change his mind about Abu Qatada.

The teachings of his religious mentors persuaded Boukhari that he was part of the *ummah*, the global brotherhood of Muslims, whose sufferings he felt and shared. 'Before, I never thought about it at all, what was happening to our brothers in so many countries, in Bosnia,

---

*Abu Qatada was born in Bethlehem on the West Bank when it was part of Jordan, before its annexation by Israel after the Six Day War of 1967. He was detained in Belmarsh prison and then freed on bail in 2005, but was kept under virtual house arrest – known as a 'control order' – pending deportation to Jordan, which his lawyers have contested.

in Albania, in Chechnya and in the Middle East,' he said. Now he believed he had an obligation to do something about it. 'They [the clerics] give you the proof from the Koran and *hadith* that if you go and help your brothers, you are doing your duty to fight the aggression. To see the Palestinians suffering like this, it's hard. Israel does what it likes and no one is trying to stop them. It isn't fair. All the time, America is helping Israel. America and Israel are the same. There's no difference.' But above all it was the war in Chechnya in the north Caucasus between the Russians and the Muslim *mujahideen*, fighting to establish an Islamic republic in central Asia, that fired Boukhari. He spent hours watching DVDs of Russian atrocities in their satellite fiefdom. 'It hurt me to see people getting slaughtered like this. I wanted to go to Chechnya. It was in my head. This is the *jihad* I wanted to go for, to fight the aggression of the Russians, what they're doing to the Muslims of Chechnya. Some other people might have it in their head to fight the Americans, but that was up to them.'

He told me, 'I thought about it very hard. For a Muslim to help his brothers, you have to train and the only country you could do it in at that time was Afghanistan.' After talking about it to 'two or three good friends', he decided to take the plunge. 'You have to speak with some people who've done the journey before, and they explained how to get there. They showed me the way.' Again, he wouldn't name the individuals who had access to the keys to the Afghan training camps, but he said they were Algerians who lived in London, and insisted that they did not have connections with any particular mosque. It's likely he was guided by Abu Doha's 'Londonistan' network, but this is speculation, and Boukhari himself has never confirmed it. In fact he denied having any links with Doha, and said that although he had heard of him, he had never met him.

He was given a name and a phone number to call when he got to Pakistan. He told me the name was that of Abu Jaffar, the facilitator believed to be answerable to Abu Zubaydah, the senior figure who became a *jihadi* travel agent, vetting volunteers and filtering them into and out of the camps.[7] (See pp. 290–92 for the arrest and interrogation of Abu Zubaydah.) On his arrival in Pakistan in 1998, Boukhari rang Abu Jaffar, who was expecting his call, and told him who he was and who had sent him. He was given traditional Afghan clothes and smuggled across the border with a group of Afghanis. 'I looked just like them, but I didn't have a big beard like them.' But nobody noticed, or appeared to care. Boukhari said that it seemed to him as if he was now entering 'a different world'. 'After living in Europe it was strange, with people walking around with Kalashnikovs.' He says he was taken to a training camp about five kilometres from Jalalabad and kitted out with the necessary equipment. The camp loaned him a Kalashnikov, but to his surprise he found he had to buy the bullets. He was philosophical about it. 'It's business for some Afghan. Over there it's easy to buy stuff like this.' Many of the other trainee *jihadis* were Algerian, as were the instructors, most of whom were veterans of the *jihad* against the Soviets.

He described the routine of a typical day: 'Getting-up time was when it was time for prayers. In summer that was about 3.30 in the morning. In winter it's about 5 or 6 o'clock. After prayers you start training with the Kalashnikov. I'd never fired one before.' He was also instructed in how to use a rocket-propelled grenade: 'It was a bit noisy, but you get used to it.'

Having studied electronics in Algeria, Boukhari was given special training in how to detonate a bomb via remote control. Other trainees were taught how to make bombs, and Boukhari's responsibility was to assemble the electronic devices that would detonate them. He didn't practise on real bombs: 'That's dangerous and expensive if you're not going to use them.' Instead he would test his detonating devices by sending a signal from them that would light up a filament in a lightbulb some distance away. I asked him over what distances the detonators could operate. He said anything between five and twenty kilometres, depending on the device. Boukhari never completed his training, as he fell ill with malaria and was incapacitated for three months. When he was well enough, he returned to England.

He thought he had had enough training to be able to fight, however, and was anxious to go to Chechnya as soon as possible. But he was told that getting into Chechnya was very difficult and dangerous, as the borders were heavily patrolled by the Russians. He would have to wait until a 'line' was open. 'I was disappointed, because that's why I went to train in Afghanistan, to try and help our brothers. But I didn't want to take the risk, to get there and then get arrested by the Russians.' It seemed to me that his disappointment was genuine, and it wasn't a question of a lack of resolve. In 2000 he got married. 'I wanted to have a son or a daughter to leave someone behind me. And now I have a son, thank God,' he said, with a look of happiness mixed with sadness, no doubt thinking of the little boy I'd seen playing on the floor far away on the estate in London where I had met his wife.

How Boukhari came to be involved in a plot to blow up Strasbourg Christmas market remains obscure, as for obvious reasons he wasn't prepared to tell me the whole story, or about the means by which he was drawn in. Again, it may have been through the Abu Doha connection, although there is no evidence to prove it, and Boukhari's lips are sealed. 'Let's leave it,' he advised me. I didn't press the point. All he would tell me was that he had been in touch with an Algerian friend living in Frankfurt whom he'd met in Afghanistan. They were training at different camps, but were being billeted in the same house, and struck up a relationship. The man's name was Aeurobi Beandali, and he was closely associated with the GSPC. According to Boukhari they discussed the plan with the other two members of the cell, Fouhad Sabour and Lamine Maroni, both Algerians who had also trained in Afghanistan, and who like Boukhari had been living in England.

These were four mature men who knew what they were doing, not vulnerable teenagers who had been radicalised and recruited for *jihad*. All of them appear to have left Afghanistan in early 2000. Maroni had been granted asylum in Britain, and had been living in Sheffield. In his statement to the court in Frankfurt when the case came to trial in 2002, Beandali, a former drug dealer, described how he came to meet up with Boukhari again. Beandali had been smuggling army boots and electronic spare parts to the GSPC in Algeria.

Boukhari came to visit me in Frankfurt and told me that he too had been asked to get some stuff for the fight back in Algeria. But I have no idea who asked him to do so. (I didn't know Abu Doha, but it was his London contact.) In December [2000] he suddenly told me how urgent it was to get as much calcium permanganate* as possible as quickly as possible. I asked him what the urgency was.

Boukhari told me he had received strict orders from London to get hold of the chemicals in order to bomb a target in France. He asked me if I would help him and I immediately said no, as I wasn't quite sure how an attack against the French would be of any help to my cause.

He told me it was not an action against the French but for the Palestinians. He didn't have all the details yet but would advise me in due course.

I had to remind myself throughout the interview that Boukhari was not always necessarily telling the truth, and there were probably elements of his story that were self-serving, intended to protect his contacts and conceal the details of his involvement in the plot. This was only to be expected. He claimed the operation was devised in Frankfurt, not London, and that he knew nothing about it until he met the other members of the cell in Germany, as it would have been too risky to discuss it over the phone.

In Germany, Boukhari was tasked with obtaining the chemicals that would provide the basic ingredients for the bomb. He crisscrossed the country visiting chemist shops to do this, since to have visited a series of chemists in any particular city might well have aroused suspicion. He made sure he looked smart, so as not to raise eyebrows when he asked for the chemicals, which he said were for hospitals in Africa. 'I was dressed as a European. Suit. Collar and tie. Very nice. Respectable.' The purchases were made using cloned credit cards: an American Express card later traced to someone in Milan, and a Visa card that belonged to someone in Austria. It's believed that

---

*A chemical oxidising agent that accelerates the burning of combustible material. It is used as a disinfectant and deodoriser in household cleaners, etc.

they were provided by the Abu Doha network in London. Other members of the cell also went on a chemical buying spree, visiting forty-eight different chemists in total and purchasing forty-four pounds of potassium permanganate, acetone, hydrogen peroxide and battery acid, ingredients capable of creating a powerful explosion.[8]

I asked Boukhari what the intended target was. 'I prefer not to answer that question,' he said. He denied that it was the Strasbourg Christmas market, as charged by the prosecution, nor was it the famous Synagogue de la Paix in that city. He did however admit, 'It was a Jewish target, yes.' But he would give no further details. There were many possible targets in Strasbourg, which was home to such a thriving and long-established Jewish community that it was known as the Jerusalem of France. But first the cell had to case the city to work out the best way in and the best escape route after the bomb had been detonated: there were no plans for any of them to become *shaheeds*. It was decided that Boukhari and Sabour would carry out the reconnaissance. They bought a video camera to record their trip, and presumably the target. Making videos of this kind, which was common practice among *jihadis*, had probably been part of their training in Afghanistan.

The famous Christmas market, first established in 1570, was believed to be the target because scenes of its stalls, decorations and sparkling lights formed a central part of the video that the police subsequently seized from the camera, and that was produced as evidence at the trial in 2002. But Boukhari claimed that the market only featured on the video because he and Sabour were changing money in the square at the time, and thought they would take a video of the festive scene and the famous Cathedral of Our Lady that was its centrepiece. He also denied that the cathedral was the target. He said they had had to change money to rent an apartment in Baden Baden, just across the border in Germany, where they planned to assemble the bomb. On the video you hear a *nasheed*, a *jihad* song, being played in the car as they drove into the city. Over the shots of the cathedral you can hear Boukhari saying, 'This is the house of the infidel.' He denies adding, 'And may the pigs rot in Hell.'

Boukhari remains adamant that the Christmas market was not the target. 'I am charged for it so I will say to you, yes, we were going to do the Christmas market. But it wasn't the plan. The plan wasn't to kill people.' His co-accused, Beandali, stated that the market was the target, but Boukhari claimed he only said this as a way of getting his sentence reduced. Whatever the target, Boukhari did admit that he was going to trigger the bomb using the expertise he had gathered in Afghanistan.

I asked him if he was a terrorist. It's a question I've asked more times than I care to remember. I once asked it of an Islamist militant in Lebanon who was surrounded by men with AK-47s. His reaction was a gale of laughter. Boukhari's reply was, 'I'm not a terrorist. I think people see me as a terrorist, but I'm not. I'm a *mujahid*.' I pointed out that the reason most people would probably see him as a terrorist was that he'd learned how to detonate remote-control bombs in Afghanistan, and had been planning to bomb a target in Strasbourg. He made a distinction, saying that he regarded terrorists as those who killed innocent people. 'Religiously this is not correct,' he said. Perhaps he was telling the truth. It is impossible to say, but from my brief acquaintance with him he did not seem to be someone who would deliberately target innocent civilians. He was not a member of Al Qaeda, as he was at pains to point out from the very beginning of the interview. If he had been it would have meant taking the *bayat*, the oath of allegiance to Osama Bin Laden, which he never did. Al Qaeda deliberately targets civilians, and justifies doing so because they are non-believers, *kuffar*, and – so the Al Qaeda *jihadi* justification goes – if they live in Western democracies they vote for governments which either carry out or sanction the killing of Muslims in the lands they invade, whether Iraq or Afghanistan.

None of the members of the cell was aware that they were under surveillance. The first they knew about it was when the German special forces of GSG 9 (Grenzschutzgruppe 9 – Border Guard Group 9) smashed down the door of the apartment in Frankfurt's Sigmund Freud Strasse where they were staying. It's thought that the original tip-off came from a source who was working for French intelligence, since the French probably knew more about the GSPC and GIA from their own bitter experience at the hands of those organisations. As Judge Brugière told me, 'Our great strength in France was to develop human intelligence, and our recruits were able to infiltrate some of the most dangerous, the most secret meeting places, like garages and flats.' It seems that French intelligence tipped off its German counterpart, which in turn tipped off the police. It's also said that British intelligence, probably through its secret listening post at GCHQ in Cheltenham, intercepted a phone call made on Christmas Eve by a member of the cell to Abu Doha in London, and that it was this that triggered GSG 9's intervention. The call was allegedly made to ask Doha to send more money. Boukhari denies making such a call, and points out that no intercept was ever produced in court. This does not prove that the call was never made, since such sensitive telephone intercepts are not admissible in court, although there is an ongoing debate about the wisdom of holding back the potentially crucial information they may provide.*

The police had identified the apartment in which the cell were staying by placing a tracking device in a bag containing weapons that Beandali was transporting to it. Boukhari was asleep in bed when the raid took place. 'I just found them on top of my head. They had big guns in their hands. It was so quick, so fast. I was shocked. How did they know? They didn't hit me. They treated me OK. They just arrested me.' In the flat the police discovered weapons, false IDs, cloned credit cards, mobile phones, an address book and a huge quantity of the chemical ingredients of the high explosive TATP (triacetone triperoxide). They also found a pressure cooker that the prosecution alleged was to provide the shrapnel for the bomb. Boukhari said it was for cooking. The videotape from the Strasbourg reconnaissance was also found, still inside the camera, and there was a piece of paper with Abu Doha's London number scribbled on it.

---

*In her lecture to the Parliamentary Mile End Group on 9 March 2010, the former Director of MI5, Dame Eliza Manningham-Buller, said with regard to the use of telephone intercepts in court: 'I favour [it] in principle, provided some complex procedural issues ... can be satisfactorily resolved.'

The police set about establishing the true identities of the four members of the cell. Salim Boukhari they traced through the British authorities. Beandali, the former Frankfurt drug dealer, they knew from their existing criminal records. They traced Fouhad Sabour via the French, who had investigated him in connection with the Paris Metro attacks in 1995. Lamine Maroni was tracked, with the help of the British, to a flat in Abbeydale Road, Sheffield, where he had been housed as an asylum seeker by a local charity called Safe Haven. When police searched it they came up with nothing, but outside on the roof they found a crumpled-up piece of paper with a list of chemicals written on it. 'That paper was a shopping list for TATP,' a South Yorkshire anti-terrorist officer told me.

The four members of the Frankfurt cell were found guilty of conspiracy to murder, and sentenced on 15 March 2003 after a trial lasting almost a year. Lamine Maroni had to be escorted from the court after repeatedly insulting the jury and shouting that Allah was his sole lawyer. Salim Boukhari got twelve years, Fouhad Sabour and Lamine Maroni eleven years each, and Aeurobi Beandali ten years.

Towards the end of our interview Boukhari told me how much he missed his wife and two-year-old son, whom he had hardly seen. I asked him if, given the pain of separation and the long years in gaol that stretched before him, he regretted what he had done. 'I cannot answer this question,' he said. 'Thanks be to God, I have patience. It's hard, very hard, but I'm surviving.' I finally asked him if he thought the West could win the so-called 'War on Terror'. 'They cannot win this war,' he said. 'They have to stop the aggression. Then this war will be finished. If the aggression continues in the Middle East and other countries, people may end up in gaol but others will come after them.' Would he continue fighting his *jihad*? 'After all that's happened to me, I cannot answer this question.' Somehow I thought he'd already played his part.

As Salim Boukhari and the Frankfurt cell were preparing to attack Strasbourg, Al Qaeda was planning its second lethal strike against America. The bombing of the East African embassies in 1998 had been the first, and Osama Bin Laden made it clear that it would not be the last. 'We are certain that our *ummah* today is able to wage *jihad* against the enemies of Islam and especially against the greatest external enemy, the Crusader-Jewish alliance,' he said. 'Every American is our enemy, whether he fights directly or whether he pays taxes.'[9]

On 12 October 2000, Bin Laden struck again, this time against Americans 'fighting directly', by which he meant military targets. Two suicide bombers in a fishing boat packed with explosives blew a huge hole in the side of the $1 billion US Navy destroyer the USS *Cole* while it was refuelling in Aden harbour, Yemen. Seventeen sailors were killed and over forty injured. The attackers came alongside the ship, made friendly gestures to the unsuspecting crew, and then detonated the explosives. Bin Laden himself chose the target, and personally selected the bombers, Hassan al Khamri and Ibrahim al Thawar. He also provided the money for the operation. To him it was money well spent. The attack was designed not only to prove that he carried out his threats, but to fire angry young Muslims around the world with the notion of *jihad* and show them that the Great Satan was not invulnerable. Bin Laden had ordered a propaganda video to be made of the attack, instructing one of his trusted operatives to film it from an apartment on the shore. The cameraman didn't get there on time, but a video was still made, using television pictures of the gaping hole in the side of the destroyer, and footage of training camps, Bin Laden's speeches and images of the suffering of Muslims in Palestine, Kashmir, Indonesia and Chechnya.[10] President Clinton attacked Al Qaeda, but only with words, promising to hunt down the bombers. 'Justice will prevail,' he said.[11] Dale Watson, who at the time was Assistant Director of the FBI's new Counter-Terrorism Division, was scathing about the White House's response. He had been equally critical after the attacks on the US embassies in Kenya and Tanzania. 'There was no political will,' he told me. 'It was always, "It happened somewhere else. It happened in the port of Yemen. It happened in two embassies in Africa. It did not happen in the heartland [of America]." They really looked the other way.' The USS *Cole* was attacked less than a year before 9/11. It was only a matter of time.

SIX

Anatomy of a Sleeper Cell

By the spring of 2001 the countdown to 9/11 had already begun. In the *jihadi* training camps in Afghanistan Osama Bin Laden was already hinting that something of great moment was about to happen, although he gave no details. Remarkably, a group of young Yemeni Americans were training there at the time, and some of them heard him say it. The FBI pieced together the complex story of these home-grown American would-be *jihadis* after a long investigation that only came to fruition more than a year after 9/11 had happened.

When law-enforcement agencies initially talk to terrorists, they don't always get the confessions their intelligence-gathering leads them to believe are warranted. It is often only persistence and the acquisition of irrefutable intelligence that breaks down the wall of prevarication and lies, and leads the suspects finally to tell the truth. In America this can also be the result of a plea bargain between the defence and the prosecuting authorities, with a deal that leads to the accused receiving a lighter sentence.

The case of a these young Yemeni-American Muslims from just outside Buffalo in upstate New York illustrates the painstaking process of talking to terrorists and bringing them to justice. They had all been to train in Afghanistan, and some of them had actually met Bin Laden. They then returned home to America.

Towards the end of 2000, as Salim Boukhari's cell was plotting to bomb Strasbourg and Al Qaeda was planning its suicide attack on the USS *Cole* in Aden, twenty-eight-year-old Sahim Alwan was one of seven young Muslims in the process of being radicalised in the small town of Lackawanna, a few miles outside Buffalo, 'the City of Good Neighbours'. The others were Jaber Elbaneh, Yassein Taher, Faysal Galab, Shafel Mosed, Mukhtar al-Bakri and Yahya Goba. All were American citizens, most of them born and raised in the United States. Yahya Goba was thought to be the *emir*, the leader of the group. In the spring of 2001, their radicalisation complete, they left for Afghanistan. Jaber Elbaneh never returned home. Those who did became known as 'the Lackawanna Six'.

Lackawanna is barely a town, more a community at the southern end of the huge Meccano-like bridge that spans the fringe of Lake Erie. It used to be known as 'Steel Town', in the days when the mighty mills of Bethlehem Steel provided employment for 20,000 people, many of them immigrants from Yemen who came to find work and make a better life for themselves and their families. Today 'Rust Town' would be more appropriate. The great mills are silent, the tall chimneys dead. The railway tracks that once brought the coal to fire the furnaces that made the steel are overgrown with weeds. Sagebrush blows across the empty yards, and everything seems to be coloured a dusty orangey-brown. It's like an abandoned museum of America's industrial past.

Today Lackawanna is home to around 3,000 Arabs, mainly of Yemeni descent, who live in a small enclave of half a dozen narrow, parallel streets. Now there is little work for them to go to. At the heart of the community is the Alhuda Guidance Mosque, a low brick building which is a magnet for street vendors at Friday prayers. Opposite the mosque is a telegraph pole, at the top of which worshippers are convinced a secret camera is hidden, trained on the mosque to identify those who come and go. This is nothing less than I would expect, given the history of the Lackawanna Six. Houses that may once have been elegant are now in a state of disrepair, with peeling paint and weed-tangled gardens. Men sit on rickety wooden porches and look at you suspiciously as you walk by. There's nothing openly sinister about it, it's just not very friendly. By and large, the media aren't welcome. I heard the same things there that I've heard in other

Muslim communities, from West Yorkshire to North America. There's a feeling that they are targeted, stereotyped and stigmatised as 'terrorists'. But when you make the effort to get to know them, and convince them that you're there to listen and learn, not to condemn, the Muslims of Lackawanna are friendly and, within certain limits, helpful. They hesitate to talk about the 'Six' lest they be tainted by being thought Al Qaeda sympathisers – again, I found the same reluctance in Muslim communities elsewhere. But I was struck by a fundamental difference between American Muslims in Lackawanna and British Muslims in West Yorkshire towns like Bradford, Dewsbury and Halifax. In the latter, there are few outward signs that the communities associate themselves with the country of which they are citizens. The Muslims of Lackawanna are different. They are proud of being American. The Stars and Stripes hangs on porches and flutters on front lawns in the more affluent parts of the Yemeni-American neighbourhood.

A huge American flag also flies outside Lackawanna High School, where four of the Lackawanna Six were students: Sahim Alwan, Shafel Mosed, Mukhtar al-Bakri and Yassein Taher. Most British schools attended by convicted terrorists tend to close their doors to the media, fearing their reputation will be sullied by association with them. Not so Lackawanna High School. I was made welcome, and had no problem in talking about their notorious alumni. Yassein Taher had been voted 'Friendliest Student in Class', was a star of the school's soccer team, and went on to marry one of its cheerleaders, Nicole Frick. None of the teachers had a bad word to say about any of them. All thought they had probably been brainwashed and misled. I was invited to spend Homecoming Day at the school, complete with an American football game and cheerleaders who chanted the team's name and performed gravity-defying acrobatic feats. The day climaxed with the ritual evening prom, with young men in tuxedos and their partners glamorously attired. Throughout the day, I noticed how easily Muslim and non-Muslim students mixed. The thought that four alumni of such an all-American school had trained in an Al Qaeda-related *jihadi* camp was difficult to come to terms with.

Lackawanna is soccer mad, and a visitor from the UK is constantly asked about Manchester United, Liverpool and Chelsea. The community has a thriving after-school soccer club run by Yassein Taher's uncle, Abdul Noman, who came to the town in 1975. The clubhouse, situated in the heart of the Yemeni enclave, also serves as a youth club and social centre, and Abdul acts as social worker and mentor as well as coach. He proudly showed me all the trophies his team had won, lovingly polished and shining on shelves around the pool room. He can't understand how his nephew ended up meeting Osama Bin Laden in a training camp in Afghanistan. 'Those six guys are fools,' he said. 'They made a stupid mistake, but I don't think they could do anything to hurt the United States.' Abdul is as patriotic as they come. When I asked him what the American flag meant to him, his eyes grew moist. 'We cannot forget what America gave us. Freedom and a better life. I've always told my kids, "This is the flag of the country we live in." I made this country my country. I'm gonna live and die here in the United States of America.'[1] He is acutely conscious of the way his community is viewed by others. 'People look at us with suspicion and give us dirty looks, as if we're outsiders and a threat to them. They harass us even during soccer games, but we always kept going forward. We put these things behind us. We have nothing to do with the Lackawanna Six. We are Americans first.'

The longer I spent in Lackawanna, the more I wondered how a group of young Muslims from such an all-American community could have ended up in a *jihadi* training camp. They did so because they were recruited by a twenty-six-year-old Yemeni called Kamal Derwish, who was born in Lackawanna but left at the age of five when his parents went back to Yemen. After his father was killed in a car accident,[2] the young Derwish went to live with relatives in Saudi Arabia, where he was raised and educated in the strict Wahhabi school of Islam. That was probably the beginning of his path to radicalisation and extremism, a path followed by many young Saudi Muslims. Derwish trained in Afghanistan, and is thought to have fought against the Serbs in Bosnia in the mid-1990s. The FBI believe that he became an Al Qaeda leader, and was personally known to Osama Bin Laden. He allegedly became involved in extremist activities in Saudi Arabia, was deported to Yemen, and returned in 1998 to Lackawanna, where his uncle and cousins still lived. He therefore had no problem in settling back into the community from which he had originally come. But Derwish had a mission in mind, most likely on the instructions of Al Qaeda: he was to recruit young Lackawanna Yemenis and send them to the Al Farouq camp in Afghanistan for training. Young Muslims with American passports and American roots would be invaluable to Osama Bin Laden, whether they became active operators themselves or formed a sleeper cell and potential staging post for other Al Qaeda operatives to carry out attacks inside America.

Derwish volunteered to assist at the Alhuda Guidance Mosque, and began giving religious lectures, warning against the evils of popular music, watching television, going to the cinema and clubs, associating with girls and even putting pictures on walls. It was as if he had received the script straight from the hand of Mullah Omar, who was then harbouring Osama Bin Laden in Taliban-run Afghanistan. A charismatic and forceful preacher with an engaging personality, Derwish soon attracted a group of impressionable young Muslims, including Jaber Elbaneh and the Lackawanna Six. Their interest was developed in private study groups, some on a one-to-one basis, that Derwish held at Yahya Goba's apartment. There, in a process that mirrored Salim Boukhari's radicalisation in London, they were shown videos of the sufferings of Muslims from Chechnya to Palestine.

The Buffalo FBI agent Edward 'Ed' Needham, who was to play a key role in bringing the Lackawanna Six to justice, told me about the process of radicalisation. 'The focus was that they should prepare for *jihad*, that it was mandatory and obligatory and that it would absolve themselves of any sins that they had committed, and also help their families absolve themselves of their sins. The commitment was to the whole concept of *jihad*. It ranged from a struggle against non-Muslims to turning the whole world into a Muslim state. There was also a fair amount of excitement and curiosity.' In Derwish's eyes, Yassein Taher's 'sin' of marrying his white cheerleader sweetheart would have needed to be cleansed by *jihad*. The others too, who had lived the lives of normal American teenagers, had plenty of 'sins' to be washed away.

Sahim Alwan quickly got to know Derwish well. He became an eager student both at the mosque and in Derwish's out-of-hours study groups. 'He was very impressive and very articulate. He was very likeable and joked a lot. He was very social,' Alwan said.* 'One of the things he talked about was learning how to prepare for *jihad* in case you do have to go to war. To learn how to use weapons and things like that.'[3]

Derwish was soon well on the way to persuading his would-be *jihadi* students that they had a religious obligation to go to Afghanistan to train. But it seems that they needed one final push, and that was given by a controversial visitor to Lackawanna, a travelling *imam* called Juma al-Dosari, whose previous stop had been preaching at an Islamic centre in Indiana and who is thought to have fought as a teenager in 1989 in the anti-Soviet *jihad* in Afghanistan, and later in Bosnia and Chechnya.[4] Kamal Derwish called him in, probably as part of a predetermined recruitment programme to firm up any waverers and set the seal on their radicalisation. The FBI regarded Dosari as the 'closer' of the deal.

At Friday prayers at Lackawanna's Guidance mosque one week in April 2001, Dosari gave a fiery sermon about the suffering of Muslims in Chechnya, Kosovo and Kashmir, and the obligation of other Muslims to come to the aid of their brothers and sisters. The sermon caused great offence to the president and elders of the mosque, who told Dosari that such sermons weren't welcome, and they didn't want to hear the like again. The president, Mohammed Saleh, a quietly-spoken, moderate *imam*, told me how upset everyone was. 'This mosque is not radical. It's very open to the public, the community and all nationalities. We have no extreme behaviour nor any negative

---

*Although I met Alwan in gaol, he declined to be interviewed. I am therefore relying on an interview conducted by Lowell Bergman for the *New York Times* and PBS's *Frontline* programme.

approaches towards any human beings, whether they are Muslim or non-Muslims.'[5] I believed him. He was shocked by what some of his young worshippers had gone on to do. I spoke to him at the mosque, where he was teaching the Koran to very young children, and then at his home, where I also met his two daughters. They were attractive, intelligent and wonderfully articulate students at Lackawanna High School. A radical word never passed their lips. They too were shocked at what their former classmates had done.

After the clincher from Juma al-Dosari, Kamal Derwish achieved his goal. The first group of young Muslims were ready to go to Afghanistan. But they needed a cover story: they couldn't tell their families they were going to train for *jihad*. They decided they would say that they were going on a religious pilgrimage to Pakistan, organised by the transnational missionary organisation Tablighi Jamaat.[6] Their families were probably delighted that they were striving to find out more about their faith, and shunning sex, drugs and rock 'n' roll. They had no idea that their sons were heading for a *jihadi* training camp.

Sahim Alwan was excited at the prospect. 'It was an adventure. We were gonna learn how to use weapons. That was the exciting part. You're gonna be able to shoot.' He even entertained the possibility of staying in Afghanistan and living there, 'if the Taliban is a really good government, if it's nice'.[7]

The recruits travelled from Lackawanna to Pakistan in two separate groups: the first on 27 April 2001, from New York's JFK airport to Lahore; the second on 14 May, from Toronto, the nearest international airport to Buffalo, to Karachi. They all then flew on to Quetta in Pakistan's Tribal Areas, the gateway to Kandahar across the border in Afghanistan, where Osama Bin Laden was based and the Al Farouq camp was located. Kamal Derwish met them in Pakistan, and Alwan was surprised by how many people Derwish knew when they arrived at a guest house in Quetta. When he asked him about this, Derwish just smiled.[8] The recruits then crossed the border and bedded down in a guest house in Kandahar run by Arabs, with Afghans doing the cooking and cleaning. Alwan remembers picking up a book by Bin

An IRA press conference in Derry in June 1972. Left to right: Martin McGuinness, David O'Connell, Séan MacStíofáin, Seamus Twomey. Few could have imagined that thirty-five years later McGuinness would become Deputy First Minister, under his old adversary the Reverend Ian Paisley, in a devolved Northern Ireland government.

The author and his Thames Television crew come under attack from Loyalists in Lenadoon Avenue, West Belfast, in 1972. They'd been filming the confrontation between Republicans and the British Army that led to the end of the 1972 IRA ceasefire.

Brendan Duddy, codenamed 'the Mountain Climber', at Grianán of Aileach, 'Fortress of the Sun', outside Derry. For almost a quarter of a century he acted as the vital secret conduit between the British government and the leadership of the IRA.

Michael Oatley, the MI6 officer who worked with Brendan Duddy over many years to attempt to bring about a peaceful settlement of the Northern Ireland conflict.

Former enemies Martin McGuinness and Ian Paisley on the steps of Stormont House on 16 July 2007, after being sworn in as Deputy First Minister and First Minister of Northern Ireland's power-sharing Assembly.

The FBI's Pat D'Amuro (centre) and his investigative team looking over the ruins of the US Embassy in Nairobi after it was destroyed by an Al Qaeda suicide bomber on 7 August 1998. Over two hundred people, most of them Kenyans, died in the attack.

Kenyan soldiers searching through the ruins of the US Embassy in Nairobi.

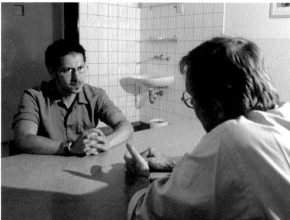

The author interviewing the Algerian Salim Boukhari in gaol in Germany. Boukhari was imprisoned in 2002 for plotting to bomb Strasbourg Christmas market in 2000. He had formerly lived in London.

Al Qaeda's suicide attacks on New York and Washington on 11 September 2001 were intended to deliver a blow that America and the West would never forget.

After the 9/11 attacks, Al Qaeda's leader and founder Osama Bin Laden became the world's most wanted man. On 2 May 2011 he was killed by US special forces whilst hiding in a compound in Abbottabad, Pakistan.

Bin Laden (right) with his closest associate, the
Egyptian leader of Islamic Jihad, Ayman al-Zawahiri.

The Sari Club at Kuta Beach, Bali, after the bombings
of 12 October 2002 that killed 202 people, many of
them young Australian tourists.

On 16 May 2003,
ten suicide bombers
attacked targets in
central Casablanca,
including this restaurant.
Forty-five people died,
including the bombers.

The author with General
Ahmidou Laanigri, the
head of Morocco's
Interior Ministry.

The author in the shanty town of Sidi Moumen, outside
Casablanca, long regarded as a hotbed of militant Islam,
and the home of many of the bombers who attacked the city.

Laden that described the concept of the snake and the need to kill it. 'The head of the snake is America,' Alwan said. 'That was why you had to kill the head to kill the snake. It also focused on how all Muslim governments are hypocrites because they don't follow the example of Islam.' These thoughts chimed with and strengthened what the group had heard from Derwish and al-Dosari back in Lackawanna.

At the guest house the Lackawanna recruits were shown the video about the suicide attack on the USS *Cole* in October the previous year – they were probably among the first to see it, as it had not yet been widely distributed. As a warm-up before their actual military training began, they were subjected to anti-American diatribes and indoctrinated about the value of and need for suicide or 'martyrdom' operations. Alwan remembers thinking to himself, with some degree of understatement, 'This is radical.'[9]

There was a surprise on their fourth day at the guest house, when Osama Bin Laden walked in surrounded by men touting AK-47s.[10] 'He's tall,' Alwan remembers. 'We shook his hand and then he sat down. He asked our names. He didn't speak English. He was calm.' Bin Laden was asked about rumours that there was going to be conflict, and that something big was going to happen. 'He just said that America was threatening us, and we're threatening them.' Alwan recalls Bin Laden saying enigmatically, 'But there are brothers willing to carry their souls in their hands.' This was roughly three months before 9/11. It reminded me of the hint of the forthcoming attack on America's East African embassies that Ayman al-Zawahiri had given to the ABC journalist John Miller after Miller's interview with Bin Laden in May 1998. Alwan was speechless at what he heard. 'I was astonished,' he said. 'I've heard of extremism, but hearing something like this and at first hand [from Bin Laden himself] really is different. At that point I knew I was in the shit. I thought, "Wow, this is real. It's the real stuff."'

The following day, after the sobering meeting with Bin Laden (thought to have been facilitated by Kamal Derwish), an uneasy Alwan shared his thoughts with Jaber Elbaneh. Alwan said that on reflection he didn't think what they were doing was right, and asked

Jaber if he was sure he wanted to stay. 'Jaber liked Kamal Derwish a lot, and was excited about the weapons. His mindset was on joining the fighting against the Northern Alliance. Basically it was, "I want to be a martyr. I want to die."' Alwan then proceeded to the Al Farouq camp for training, still feeling nervous about what he was letting himself in for. Perhaps there was no way out – he had had to hand over his passport for Al Qaeda's safekeeping. He and the others were kept waiting in tents outside the camp for three days before they were finally admitted. Demand for training at Al Farouq was high, and they had to take their place in the queue.

Alwan said that all he did at the camp was learn how to fire an AK-47, but Mukhtar al-Bakri was much more forthcoming. He said he received training in the use of a variety of firearms, from AK-47s to 9mm handguns, M-16 automatic rifles and rocket-propelled grenades, and explosives including TNT, detonators, landmines and Molotov cocktails. [11] He described a typical day at the camp.

> Three o'clock, wake up. Four o'clock, prayer time. Five o'clock, an hour of physical fitness where you run and do push-ups. Six thirty, break- fast. Allowed to take a nap. Eight thirty to eleven thirty, military lecture where you would learn about things like weapons. Thirteen hundred hours, lunch followed by prayer. Clean up the camp. More military lecture about one hour. You were free to sunset, dinner, prayer. [12]

There were discussions about the bombing of the East African embas- sies and Al Qaeda's intention to attack the United States, although no specific details were given. Recruits were fired with the desirability of taking part in 'martyrdom' operations, and encouraged to sign up as suicide bombers when a list was passed around. [13]

While the group was training, Bin Laden paid another surprise visit. His previous appearance at the guest house had been private and personal. This was a big production number. Trainers from Al Farouq were stationed on the hills all around, and one took up position on the top of a mosque. Two 4x4 vehicles arrived and Bin Laden's body- guards piled out. There was wild shooting in the air to herald the arrival of the *Sheikh*. 'They didn't tell us Bin Laden was coming,' said Alwan. 'You just know.' This time Bin Laden wasn't alone – at his side was his deputy, Ayman al-Zawahiri, the leader of Islamic Jihad. Everyone went into the mosque to hear Bin Laden praise the unity of their two organisations and declare their intention to drive the Americans from the holy soil of Saudi Arabia and to make their infidel enemies pay. He spoke of 'forty to fifty men on a mission' who were to carry out an attack on the USA, although no specific details were given. At some stage, al-Bakri had a private meeting with Bin Laden. Although Alwan says they were instructed not to reveal their true identities and the fact that they were US citizens, with vital American passports, it seems highly unlikely that Bin Laden did not know who they were and what their potential use might be. Hence the private meetings. Bin Laden was putting the final stamp of commitment on what Juma al-Dosari and Kamal Derwish had achieved.

But Alwan wasn't happy. He had realised after his meeting with Bin Laden and all that he had seen and heard at the camp that he was getting in too deep. He told the camp commander he wanted to go home, and was told in no uncertain terms to get back to his training. He says he even faked an ankle injury, but it cut no ice. In desperation he went to see Kamal Derwish, who was training in a separate area. Derwish told him that if he tried to leave without permission he would probably be shot, and suggested that he say he was just going to Kandahar to get medical treatment for his ankle. When Alwan's transport, presumably arranged by Derwish, arrived, Jaber Elbaneh asked him where he was going. 'I said, "I'm getting the fuck out of here. I'm leaving." And I left.' Alwan had been in the camp for ten days. Elbaneh and the others carried on training.

When Alwan returned to the guest house in Kandahar he had a surprise: he was asked if he wanted to see Bin Laden again before he left. By this time it seems that Kamal Derwish may have tipped off Bin Laden that Alwan wanted to go home, and advised that he should be allowed to do so. Alwan politely declined the offer of another meeting, but his refusal was not accepted and he found himself once again in the presence of the *Sheikh*. He had already made it clear that he was not prepared to give Bin Laden the *bayat*, the pledge of personal allegiance, and was told not to worry, as he wouldn't be asked to do so. 'You're just going to see him,' he was told. 'He knows you're going back.' Alwan was taken to a big house with a courtyard, and ushered into a room where he found Bin Laden sitting on the floor. They shook hands, and Bin Laden asked him how he was and why he was leaving. 'He seemed very like a really quiet, humble guy. He didn't really look at you. He gazed down.' Alwan explained that he hadn't realised he would be away for so long, despite the fact that he'd only been at the camp for ten days, and that he needed to get back to his wife and children. Bin Laden seemed understanding, and asked if he'd like his passport 'cleaned', with the entry stamps and visa erased. Alwan said it wasn't necessary.

FBI agent Ed Needham told me what he believes happened at that final meeting between Alwan and Bin Laden: 'Bin Laden wanted to know how Islam was doing in America. He wanted to know what Americans thought of suicide missions and martyrdom missions, which was a major focus of the Al Farouq training camp during the time that they were there. The trainers, the indoctrination at the guest houses, the speeches by Bin Laden, focused continually on suicide and martyrdom missions. And Bin Laden wanted to know from Mr Alwan what Americans thought of suicide missions.'[14]

Alwan was told he could leave the following day. Bin Laden stood up, shook his hand and said, 'May God make you successful.' Before he left, one of Bin Laden's men gave Alwan two copies of the USS *Cole* video. One was to be given to a contact in Karachi, from where Alwan was going to fly home. The other, he was told with a smile, he could give to the US government.

How did the FBI find out what seven young Muslims from Lackawanna had done in Afghanistan? In 2003, when their investigation was close to success, I went to Buffalo and Lackawanna to try to put the pieces together.

When the first members of the group went for training in spring 2001, the Buffalo FBI was completely in the dark. Having got the green light from the FBI, without which nothing happens, I met Ed Needham, the only agent there with responsibility for terrorism, in an Italian restaurant in Buffalo. Ed looked like the typical 'G-man': short, neatly cropped hair, dark suit, white shirt, button-down collar, sober tie, dark socks and shiny black shoes. He seemed apprehensive at first. The FBI, like so many government institutions, is suspicious of the media. He was also understandably guarded, as the Lackawanna Six cases were still going through the courts.

Needham had started working in the FBI's counter-terrorism division at FBI headquarters in Washington in 1995, when it was known as the Radical Fundamentalists Unit – the forerunner of Mike Scheuer's Bin Laden unit, Alec Station. He returned to Buffalo in December 1998, and from then until 9/11 ploughed a lonely counter-terrorist furrow there. On 15 June 2001, an anonymous letter arrived at FBI headquarters in Buffalo, and ended up on Needham's desk. His journey was about to begin. Suitably edited, the letter read:

> I am very concern [sic]. I am … Arab American … I cannot give you my name because I fear for my life … two terrorists came to Lackawanna … for recruiting the Yemenite youth … the terrorist group … left to Afghanistan to meet … Bin Laden and stay in his camp for training.

The 'two terrorists' were Kamal Derwish and Juma al-Dosari. Their names appeared in the letter, but they meant little to Needham. It also listed six of the young men who had left for Afghanistan. I asked Needham if he ever found out who wrote the letter. He said he'd rather not answer that. Did he ever talk to the person who wrote it? Same answer. But he obviously had. It turned out that the source was exceptionally well informed, and Needham immediately put out 'lookouts and stops' at airports and border crossings, listing the names of those mentioned in the letter.

A week after the letter was received, Sahim Alwan returned from Karachi. Needham went to see him, and asked where he had been and what he had been doing. Alwan said the trip had been a religious pilgrimage to Pakistan arranged by some people from the Lackawanna mosque, and that he'd come back earlier than the others because he'd missed his family. Needham asked if he'd been to Afghanistan, and to a Bin Laden training camp. 'He said by no means had it anything to do with a training camp and Afghanistan, and that the trip primarily consisted of religious orientation and training.' At this stage Needham had nothing to go on but the anonymous letter.

Three other members of the group – Faysal Galab, Shafel Mosed and Yassein Taher – returned from Lahore a week after Alwan, on 27 June 2001. They all told more or less the same story: they had been on a religious pilgrimage to learn more about Islam. Not to Afghanistan. Not to Bin Laden's training camp. Needham was unconvinced, and used all the technology and facilities at his disposal to put the returnees under surveillance. I said to him that I assumed this meant their phones were tapped and their emails monitored. Again he neither confirmed nor denied it. Yahya Goba, the *emir* of the group, and Mukhtar al-Bakri returned at the beginning of August, but the FBI still had no hard evidence, and only suspicions to pursue. Jaber Elbaneh, the seventh member of the group, was still at large somewhere, and was certainly not in Lackawanna. Needham faced a frustrating problem. He suspected the Six had done what the letter claimed, but he had no way of proving it. Was there was a potential sleeper cell in Lackawanna, about which the FBI could do nothing? All the suspects were American citizens – they couldn't just be locked up without trial.

When Al Qaeda attacked New York and Washington on 11 September 2001, says Ed Needham, 'I knew that things would never be the same again, and that we had to do everything within the realms of the Constitution, laws and policies to never let this happen again. I knew in some form or fashion, whether it be small or large, that it was my job more than ever to contribute to that.'

Alarm bells at the FBI office in Buffalo began to ring even more loudly in the months after 9/11 when telephone intercepts* indicated

---

*The intercepts were most likely made by America's equivalent of Britain's GCHQ, the National Security Agency (NSA). Its vast listening post is based at Fort Meade, Maryland.

that Kamal Derwish, who appears to have vanished after further training in Afghanistan and was now probably back in his native Yemen, was in touch with a senior Al Qaeda figure, Tawfiq bin Attash, the alleged mastermind of the USS *Cole* bombing.* They also suggested that Derwish was checking out how his recruits were faring back at home in Lackawanna. Juma al-Dosari was also back in town, and stayed at Yahya Goba's apartment for around six weeks after 9/11. When he left he told Goba that he was going to fight for the Taliban.

In October 2001 America responded to the attacks on New York and Washington by invading Afghanistan. The invasion, named Operation Enduring Freedom, took place after President George W. Bush had issued an ultimatum to Mullah Omar to hand over Bin Laden. He refused. Taliban and Al Qaeda forces withdrew to the honeycombed cave complex that Bin Laden had helped to build in the Tora Bora mountains, where in December 2001 they made their last stand before melting across the border into Pakistan. It's thought that Bin Laden was there with them, but he was never captured, and simply disappeared, presumably joining his supporters in their flight into the mountain wilderness of Pakistan's Tribal Areas. Juma al-Dosari was also in Tora Bora, prior to crossing the border, where he surrendered to the Pakistani security forces.[15] He was handed over to the Americans, probably at a price, interrogated at Kandahar and then rendered to the Guantánamo Bay prison camp in Cuba that the Americans had opened in January 2002 to hold prisoners, most of them captured in Afghanistan and Pakistan. His interrogation is thought to have provided the CIA and the FBI with valuable information about the Lackawanna recruits he had influenced in the final stages of their radicalisation.

By the spring of 2002, Ed Needham felt that the pieces of the Lackawanna puzzle were beginning to fall into place, but he still lacked the evidence he needed to bring the case to court. He was also beginning to feel the heat from the Director of the FBI, Robert

---

*Attash, otherwise known as 'Khallad', was arrested in Karachi on 29 April 2003, interrogated at a CIA secret site and transferred to Guantánamo Bay in 2006.

Mueller, and indirectly from the White House, where President Bush is said to have requested a daily update on the case. Nerves were taut at the very highest levels of government, as another Al Qaeda attack on the Homeland – the 'second wave' – was feared. Then, in May 2002, Mukhtar al-Bakri left Lackawanna with his family to get married in Bahrain. The NSA continued to monitor the emails of some of his associates and friends. One email of 18 July, sent on al-Bakri's Hotmail account from an internet café in Jeddah, Saudi Arabia, was entitled 'The Big Meal', and mentioned a 'meal that will be very huge. No one will be able to withstand it except those with faith.' The FBI say the recipient was close to the Lackawanna group, but have never revealed the name. The words triggered immediate concern, as they were thought possibly to be code for an imminent attack, with the first anniversary of 9/11 approaching.

Mukhtar al-Bakri was married on 9 September 2002. With scant regard for the nuptials, the local Bahraini police burst in on him and his bride on their wedding night and arrested him. Two days later he was interviewed by two FBI agents. He told them that the 'Big Meal' email referred to some gossip he had heard from an old man in Saudi Arabia who had said there was going to be 'a big bomb', 'a big explosion' that only people with strong faith would be able to withstand. Al-Bakri understood that this meant an attack on Americans in Saudi Arabia.[16] The FBI agents asked him about the trip to the Al Farouq training camp the previous year. They advised him not to lie, and warned that he could be polygraphed. He told them everything. It was the breakthrough Ed Needham had been waiting for. He now had evidence he could use to lever admissions out of the other members of the Lackawanna Six. Al-Bakri was flown back to Buffalo to find that all his former travelling companions had been arrested and charged with giving 'material support to terrorists', a catch-all phrase which at the lowest level can include giving false information to a law officer (which the Lackawanna Six did), while at the higher end it could mean training in a terrorist camp (which, again, the Lackawanna Six did). By now all of them realised that the game was up. Among the articles seized when their houses and apartments were searched were weapons, computers, radical Islamic tapes and a pamphlet on 'Martyrdom'. It was found at the house where Yassein Taher, Lackawanna High School's 'Best Student in Class', lived. It read:

> Martyrdom or self sacrifice operations are those performed by one or more people against enemies far outstripping them in numbers and equipment, with prior knowledge that the operations will almost inevitably lead to death. The form this usually takes nowadays is to wire one's body or a vehicle or a suitcase with explosives and then to enter amongst the conglomeration of the enemy ... to cause the maximum losses in the enemy ranks, taking advantage of the element of surprise and penetration. Naturally the enacter of the operation will usually be the first to die.

In December 2003 all six pleaded guilty to giving material support to terrorists. Sahim Alwan, Mukhtar al-Bakri and Yahya Goba were sentenced to ten years' imprisonment; Yassein Taher and Shafel Mosed to eight; and Faysal Galab to seven. As part of their plea agreement they all agreed to cooperate with the US authorities, and told the FBI everything about their trip to Afghanistan and their training in the Al Farouq camp. Ed Needham and his team talked to terrorists, and finally got the result they had laboured so long to achieve.

After his conviction, Sahim Alwan expressed remorse – genuine or otherwise. 'We knew we made a mistake. I tried to forget about that whole thing. It was so bad. It's a part of my life I wish I could change. You force yourself to forget it.'[17] He then echoed the sentiments that I had heard Yassein Taher's uncle Abdul Noman express: 'America is my country. I was born here. I love my country as much as I love my religion. I want people to see that I'm not a terrorist. I would never hurt any fellow American. I could have been in the [Twin] Towers. My kids could have been on that plane.' I asked Ed Needham if he thought Alwan was being sincere. He said that he believed he was, and pointed out that Alwan, Yahya Goba and Yassein Taher had kept to their part of the plea bargain, and given whatever assistance they could to help the FBI by providing intelligence and testifying in other terrorist cases.* As a reward for their testimonies, Alwan had his sentence reduced by six months and Goba by a year. All the Six have now been released, with the exception of Mukhtar al-Bakri, who is still in gaol at the time of writing.

The question remains, were the Lackawanna Six an Al Qaeda sleeper cell? Certainly that's how the White House and administration officials regarded them. In his State of the Union address on 28 January 2003, President Bush declared: 'We've broken Al Qaeda cells in Hamburg, Milan, Madrid, London, Paris, as well as Buffalo, New York ... We have the terrorists on the run. We're keeping them on the run. One by one the terrorists are learning the meaning of American justice.'[18]

Perhaps significantly, neither Buffalo's US Attorney, Mike Battle, who prosecuted the Six, nor Ed Needham and his colleagues, who put the case together, were prepared to go as far as to label them a sleeper cell. I asked Mike Battle if he really thought they would have returned to Lackawanna, settled down and put everything behind them. 'No, I don't,' he said. 'For them to have gone to the lengths they did, to travel, the contacts they were able to make, the people they were able to meet with, and to come home and not talk about it speaks volumes about what they were in a position to be influenced to do.' I put a similar question to Ed Needham. 'I've never used the term "sleeper cell",' he said. 'They'd trained on automatic weapons, rocket-propelled grenade launchers, plastic explosives, TNT, dynamite, detonators. They had met face to face with the most dangerous man in the world, Osama Bin Laden, and concealed facts about their trip. They were a group that supported Al Qaeda, a network of individuals that were in a position to help Al Qaeda. That could be defined as a "cell".'

In the end, I concluded that perhaps they were a cell, and potentially a very dangerous one had they ever been activated. None of

---

*The trials included that of Ali Hamza al-Bahlul, held at Guantánamo Bay in 2008. Al-Bahlul was Osama Bin Laden's media propaganda chief, and had been involved in the preparation of the USS *Cole* video that Sahim Alwan was asked to take to Karachi. He was sentenced to life imprisonment. Testimony was also given at the trial of the alleged 'dirty bomber' José Padilla (see p. 295).

them ever admitted to it, but that doesn't mean that, had they not been arrested, they would necessarily have rejected any approach from Al Qaeda to assist in some way with an operation inside America, even if only at the level of providing a safe house. But despite strong suspicions, the charge that they were a sleeper cell was never proved. Ed Needham was also convinced that the recruits were not one-offs: 'I think we stopped a network of individuals that could possibly have assisted Al Qaeda in the future. We also stopped at least four other Americans who were going to the Al Farouq camp after the return of the Lackawanna defendants.' These four had already sorted out their passports for their trip. They too had been recruited by Kamal Derwish, whose aim was to set up a regular supply chain of recruits from America to the training camps in Afghanistan.

Kamal Derwish's recruiting days came to a sudden and violent end on 3 November 2002, in the sands of Yemen. He was travelling in a convoy with Qaed Salim Harethi, who was believed to have been closely involved in the bombing of the USS *Cole*, when both were incinerated by a Hellfire missile fired from a CIA pilotless drone. It was one of America's first 'targeted killings' unleashed from high in the sky. Many more were to follow. They were in effect state-authorised assassinations.

And what became of Derwish's recruiting accomplice, 'the Closer', Juma al-Dosari? After his capture in Afghanistan in November 2001 he was allegedly tortured by American personnel during his interrogation in Kandahar. 'They poured boiling liquid on my head and the investigator stubbed his cigarette out on my foot,' he claimed. 'They stripped me of my clothes and lay me flat on the ground. One of the soldiers urinated on my head and my face. After that a soldier brought petrol and injected it into my anus.' He also says that he was given electric shocks with 'a small device like a mobile phone' that was applied to his face, back, limbs and genitals.[19] The Americans deny the allegations, but the abuse al-Dosari says he suffered tallies with only slightly less disturbing claims I heard from other former detainees I later met in Saudi Arabia who had been interrogated by the Americans either at Kandahar or Bagram airbase (see pp. 271–7). In early 2002 al-Dosari was transferred to Guantánamo Bay, where he alleges the abuse continued, and he went on hunger strike in protest.[20] The American authorities denied his claims. On 9 November 2005 the State Department said:

> The US government takes all allegations of abuse seriously. When a credible allegation of improper conduct surfaces, it is reviewed, and when factually warranted, investigated. As a result of the investigation, administrative, disciplinary, or judicial action is taken as appropriate. We have no evidence that substantiates that Mr Al Dosari was the subject of any sexual humiliation.[21]

Juma al-Dosari was finally released without charge on 15 July 2007, and repatriated to Saudi Arabia under the Kingdom's controversial rehabilitation programme (see pp. 272–4).

That leaves only Jaber Elbaneh, who never returned to Lackawanna. Unlike his travelling companions he put his training at the Al Farouq camp into practice, and became a seasoned *jihadi*, securing a place on the FBI's 'Most Wanted Terrorists' list, with a $5 million reward on his head. He was finally arrested in Yemen in late 2002, and sentenced for his involvement in the bombing of the French oil tanker *Limburg* in the Gulf of Aden on 6 October that year: one crew member was killed and twelve were injured. In a near-replica of the attack on the USS *Cole*, a dinghy laden with explosives rammed the side of the ship. But in February 2006 Elbaneh, along with several other Al Qaeda prisoners, escaped Sana'a's top-security gaol through a 220-foot tunnel that conveniently ended up in a mosque.[22] He went on the run, before giving himself up in December 2007.[23] He was never returned to gaol, and according to Ed Needham, who expressed great frustration about his dealings with the Yemeni authorities, his whereabouts and status are unknown. 'Elbaneh is responsible for my hair getting greyer,' Needham told me. The US authorities are still seeking his extradition. Jaber Elbaneh remains the only piece of unfinished business before the FBI's file on the Lackawanna Six can finally be closed. Ed Needham and his colleagues would love to talk to him.

I finally asked Needham how he viewed talking to terrorists. 'There's nothing more important,' he said. 'I've interviewed the Lackawanna Six seventy-five times, and there's nothing I'm more proud of than the intelligence we've gained from debriefing these guys. We've got an unbelievable amount of information about recruitment, training camps and trainers, facilitators, guest houses and the [Al Qaeda] leadership. That's the result of establishing a relationship with them, and treating them fairly and their families properly.' In the case of the Lackawanna Six, talking to terrorists in the end produced results, convictions and cooperation. There was no need for the Bush administration's coercive interrogation techniques, some of which amounted to torture (see final chapter), that were deemed necessary in the wake of 9/11.

SEVEN

One Morning in September

While the Lackawanna Six were training in Afghanistan in the early summer of 2001, with some of them meeting Osama Bin Laden and hearing him talk of 'brothers willing to carry their souls in their hands', these 'brothers' – the nineteen hijackers – were putting the final touches to the mission that culminated so spectacularly on 11 September 2001. The attack was designed to deliver a blow to America that it and the West would never forget. It succeeded.

The leader of the hijackers was an Egyptian, Mohammed Atta, who graduated from Cairo University with a degree in architectural engineering in 1990, and moved in 1992 to Germany, where he remained for most of the rest of the decade, to continue his studies. Friends he made there regarded him as 'charismatic, intelligent and persuasive, albeit intolerant of dissent'.[1] When he arrived in Germany he was not particularly religious, but his radicalisation took root and grew, as with so many other young Muslims in the 1990s, when he saw the suffering of Muslims in Bosnia, Palestine and other parts of the world. His fellow students remember his virulently anti-Semitic and anti-American views, and his polemics against 'infidel' regimes in the Arab world. Within his tight circle of friends he became an advocate of violent *jihad*.[2] These companions, with whom he shared an apartment in Hamburg and attended the Quds mosque in the city, were to become key figures in the 9/11 plot. They included Ramzi Binalshibh from Yemen, and Marwan al Shehhi from the United Arab Emirates.

Eventually they decided to practise what they'd been preaching, and to go and fight in Chechnya against the Russians. But first they needed to train, which is why in November 1999 they left Hamburg for Afghanistan, where they were quickly drawn into Bin Laden's circle and took the *bayat*. Their ambition to wage *jihad* in Chechnya was soon superseded by the far more exciting prospect of fighting on American soil. Bin Laden personally selected Atta and al Shehhi to be key suicide operatives. They were joined by two Saudis born in Mecca, Khalid al Mihdhar and Nawaf al Hazmi, both of whom had already fought in Bosnia. In their enthusiasm to become *shaheeds* al Mihdhar and al Hazmi had already obtained US visas, and Bin Laden ordered them to go to America for pilot training so they could take control of the planes after the hijackings. Binalshibh was unable to acquire an American visa, so he became a key coordinator of the plot, connecting Atta and the other hijackers with Bin Laden, Khalid Sheikh Mohammed and the Al Qaeda leadership in Afghanistan.*

The plot was of course a closely guarded secret, but by the end of 1999 US intelligence suspected something was going on. The NSA intercepted signals which indicated that several members of an 'operational cadre' were planning to travel to Kuala Lumpur, Malaysia, in January 2000, and a CIA desk officer felt that 'something nefarious was afoot'.³ Two of the cadre were subsequently identified as Khalid al Mihdhar and Nawaf al Hazmi. Al Mihdhar was spotted arriving in Kuala Lumpur, and al Hazmi's identity was later confirmed in Bangkok. Both were en route for pilot training in America via South-East Asia, where it was felt they could travel relatively freely, and which served as a more secure departure point for the USA. Although the two were identified by the CIA, the Agency did not register them with the State Department's TIPOFF watchlist, which would have alerted airlines to their presence. And, critically, none of this information was communicated to the FBI, with the result that on 15 January 2000 al Mihdhar and al Hazmi arrived in Los Angeles on their way to begin their pilot training.

---

*Ramzi Binalshibh was arrested following a gun battle with Pakistani security forces in Karachi on 11 September 2002, the first anniversary of 9/11. He was handed over to the Americans and rendered to a secret location, thought to be in Morocco, for interrogation. In 2006 he was transferred to Guantánamo Bay.

It was the first of several intelligence oversights or failures that were to mark the decade after 9/11, although intelligence-gathering can never be 100 per cent perfect. MI5 were unable to put the leader of the 2005 London bombers in the intelligence frame, and American agencies were unable to spot the Nigerian so-called 'underpants bomber' Umar Farouq Abdulmuttalab, who tried to blow up Flight 253 over Detroit on Christmas Day 2009, although his father had warned the American Embassy in Nigeria about his son's extreme religious views. Despite the warning Abdulmuttalab's name was never put on a US 'No-Fly' list, although he was included on a terrorist database.

Neither al Mihdhar nor al Hazmi had any experience of living in the West, and they had been advised by Khalid Sheikh Mohammed, who had studied in America in 1986, obtaining a degree in mechanical engineering at North Carolina State University, to present themselves as newly arrived Saudi students and seek assistance at local mosques.[4] From Los Angeles they moved to San Diego, where they embedded themselves in the local community and signed on with a flying school called the Sorbi Flying Club. A pilot they consulted said they would begin their instruction on small planes, but they told him they wanted to learn how to fly Boeing jets. The pilot was convinced they were either joking or dreaming, and said that no such school existed. Nevertheless, they enrolled and took lessons, surprising their instructors by having no interest in take-offs and landings, only in learning how to handle a plane in the air.[5] Despite what in hindsight were glaring warning signs, no one brought these two recent Saudi arrivals, with very little English and bizarre flying requests, to the attention of the police or the FBI. This was the third intelligence failure. The first was the failure to put them on the flight TIPOFF list, and the second was the CIA not passing on what they knew to the FBI. If any of these steps had been taken, it's conceivable that 9/11 may never have happened.

In the early summer of 2000, Mohammed Atta and Marwan al Shehhi arrived in America and enrolled at Huffman Aviation in Venice, Florida, where they signed up for the Accelerated Pilot Programme.[6] The plot's coordinator, Ramzi Binalshibh, sent them about $10,000 in wire transfers to meet their costs. While the two were doing their pilot training, Bin Laden and his inner circle in Afghanistan were selecting the 'muscle', the hijackers who were to take over the planes. Twelve of them were Saudis, all of them in their twenties, most unmarried and unemployed with only a basic high school education. All of them acquired US visas in Saudi Arabia, then returned to Afghanistan for final training. They were even taught how to butcher a sheep and a camel as part of their instruction in how to use knives on the planes' passengers and crew.[7] However, they were not told the full details of the plot to hijack the planes and fly them into buildings until they set foot in America. There they were joined by the failed pilots Khalid al Mihdhar and Nawaf al Hazmi, who had now become part of the 'muscle'. Everything was in place for the most audacious terrorist plot in history.

At 7.59 on the morning of 11 September 2001 American Airlines Flight 11, a Boeing 767, took off from Boston's Logan Airport for Los Angeles. On board were the leader of the hijackers, Mohammed Atta, and four of the 'muscle', armed with an assortment of knives – subsequent investigations revealed that some of the hijackers had bought Leatherman multi-function knives.[8] The 'muscle' took over the aircraft, possibly killing some of the passengers and crew, and stormed the cabin, probably killing the pilots, enabling Atta to take over the controls. At 8.48 a.m. Flight 11 crashed into the North Tower of New York's World Trade Center, hitting the building between the 95th and 103rd floors.

At 8.14, fifteen minutes after American Airlines Flight 11 had taken off from Boston, United Airlines Flight 175, another Boeing 767, departed from the same airport for Los Angeles. On board were Marwan al Shehhi, Mohammed Atta's flatmate from Hamburg, and four other hijackers. What happened followed a similar pattern to that on board Flight 11, with al Shehhi taking the controls. A flight attendant, Robert Fangman, made an emergency call on a special phone at the back of the plane, and said both pilots had been killed.[9] At 9.03 a.m. Flight 175 crashed into the South Tower of the World Trade Center, fifteen minutes after Flight 11 had hit the North Tower. The South Tower burned for fifty-six minutes, then collapsed at 9.59. The North Tower burned for 100 minutes before collapsing at 10.28.

At 8.20 a third plane, American Airlines Flight 77, a Boeing 757, took off from Washington's Dulles International Airport bound for Los Angeles. On board were Nawaf al Hazmi, Khalid al Mihdhar and two other hijackers, plus the 'pilot', Hani Hanjour. Hanjour had studied in America in the 1990s, when he had obtained a private pilot's licence and subsequently a commercial pilot's certificate from the Federal Aviation Authority. On 8 December 2000 he returned to America from Saudi Arabia to brush up his skills, and trained on a Boeing 737 flight simulator at Pan Am International Flight Academy in Arizona.[10] At 9.37, Flight 77 crashed into the Pentagon, the US military headquarters in Washington.

A fourth plane, United Airlines Flight 93, another Boeing 757, took off from Newark airport, New Jersey, at 8.42, bound for San Francisco. Al Qaeda had deliberately selected transcontinental flights, as they had the maximum amount of fuel on board, and would therefore create the maximum damage on impact. On board Flight 93 were the 'pilot', Ziad Jarrah, plus three hijackers. Jarrah had attended the flight centre in Venice, Florida, where Atta and al Shehhi had also trained. It's still unclear what Flight 93's target was, although it was probably either the White House or the Capitol Building in Washington. Whatever it was, it never got there. The passengers heroically overpowered the hijackers, with the result that at 10.03 the plane crashed in a field in Pennsylvania, eighty miles south of Pittsburgh. All on board were killed. Remarkable and moving mobile-phone messages were sent to some of the passengers' loved ones just before the plane went down. One caller said the passengers took a vote on whether to rush the hijackers. Another passenger, Thomas Burnett, told his wife, 'I know we're all going to die … There's three of us who are going to do something about it.'[11]

Like the rest of the world, it took me some time to grasp the sheer horror of what had happened. This was a terrorist attack on a scale that had never been seen before. Nor had there ever been a terrorist operation of such vaulting ambition, so meticulously planned and carried out with such awesome sophistication. A total of 2,995 people died that day.*[12] 9/11 marked a paradigm shift that would change our perception of terrorism forever. It also marked a turning point in my journey. The task of attempting to understand and report the phenomenon of Al Qaeda was unlike anything I had ever undertaken before.

That almost unbelievable day had huge political and military repercussions, as President Bush declared his 'Global War on Terror' and bluntly promised the nation that Osama Bin Laden would be tracked down and apprehended 'dead or alive'.[13] The events of that September morning would dictate the shape of the world for the next decade and beyond, as America and her allies invaded Afghanistan in Operation Enduring Freedom on 7 October 2001, with the intention of destroying the terrorist training camps and toppling the Taliban, and invaded Iraq in Operation Iraqi Freedom on 20 March 2003, removing Saddam Hussein. The dreadful repercussions of those wars and of 9/11 are still being felt, although to date there has been no subsequent Al Qaeda attack on such a scale. That is largely because plots of potentially similar magnitude, such as the attempt to blow up seven airliners in mid-Atlantic (see Chapter 13), were foiled by the intelligence services of the West and their foreign partners. That does not mean that another 9/11-type spectacular is not being planned. But as the history of the decade since September 2001 clearly shows, Al Qaeda does not have to rely on epoch-changing attacks to make its mark. Bombs in Madrid (2004) and London (2005) sent the same message and left the same bloody mark, as did those on Bali a year after 9/11. The added significance of the bombs on Bali is that they revealed Al Qaeda's close operational connection with regional *jihadi* groups, like South-East Asia's Jemaah Islamiyah, which shared its ideology and which was behind the devastating attacks on the island paradise. The broadening of Al Qaeda's support network and operational range served to increase the pressure on the West's intelligence services and those of its regional partners.

---

*The breakdown of the deaths is as follows: 2,605 in the Twin Towers, 125 at the Pentagon, 265 on the four planes, including the nineteen hijackers. All the victims were civilians except for fifty-five military personnel killed at the Pentagon.

EIGHT

A Warning Not Heeded

Tragically, the story of Al Qaeda is replete with a series of warnings not heeded, partly due to the fact that Western intelligence agencies have never had to deal with anything like this before, and partly in some cases to institutional failure, including a reluctance to share intelligence, and sometimes to incompetence. The bombings of the East African embassies and 9/11 are the most dramatic illustrations of these failures. The attacks on two nightclubs on Bali on 12 October 2002 (see Chapter 9), in which 202 people, eighty-eight of them Australian and twenty-four British, died, are yet another example. Hindsight makes it all too easy to criticise intelligence agencies fighting to stop terrorist attacks, but if warnings are not heeded and lessons not learned, the mistakes may be repeated.

The broad warning about the Bali bombings came from the interrogation by the FBI of a young Canadian Muslim called Mohammed Mansour Jabarah. Jabarah and his associates were planning to attack Western holidaymakers in South-East Asia, whom they referred to as 'white meat'. His story provides an insight not just into Al Qaeda and its senior leadership, but also into the growing range of its operational base.

I managed to obtain a copy of a debriefing of Jabarah's interviews with the FBI that illustrate his remarkable story, which goes far beyond anything experienced by the Lackawanna Six. These interviews, conducted in May 2002, were again the fruit of an intelligence service talking to terrorists. Following his arrest Jabarah had agreed to cooperate with the FBI. Going through the fifty-seven-page document, a distillation of interviews that lasted over twenty-four days, brought to mind the minutes of the IRA's meeting with the British that I read while eating fruitcake and drinking tea in Ireland in the mid-1970s.

As I read, I noticed a double coincidence involving the Lackawanna Six. The first was that although Mohammed Jabarah is Canadian, he had lived only about an hour and a half's drive from Lackawanna, across the border in the small and picturesque town of St Catharines, by the shore of Lake Ontario. The second was that the dates when Jabarah was at the Al Farouq training camp roughly coincided with those when Sahim Alwan was there, in April–May 2001. It seemed likely that Alwan and Jabarah were both present on the occasion when Bin Laden visited the camp and addressed the trainees. Jabarah told the FBI: '[There were] from 100–150 people at the training camp at that time ... UBL [Usama Bin Laden] stated that there were brothers awaiting the call to attack the United States and he asked that everyone pray for them.' It is unlikely that Jabarah and Alwan would have known each other, as in the interests of security all trainees adopted new identities once they had surrendered their passports at the guest houses where they were billeted. But as fellow English-speakers they would probably have been aware of each other. The advantage of both of them to Al Qaeda was that they had 'clean' American and Canadian passports.

I hoped to interview Jabarah's mother, who was still living in St Catharines, but I knew from my experience of meeting Salim Boukhari's wife in London that wives would only talk to strangers with the permission of their husbands. On making enquiries I discovered that Jabarah's father, Mansour, was in Kuwait. I managed to obtain a telephone number, and rang Mr Jabarah. To my relief he said he was happy for me to go and see his wife. He seemed convinced that his son was innocent, a reaction I often encountered when talking to the parents of convicted or suspected terrorists. Many, like some elements of Muslim communities, are in denial. He gave me the number of the family home, and I made the call. Mrs Jabarah agreed to see me. In the depths of the Great Lakes winter I crossed the border at Niagara Falls – the spray from its lower reaches was frozen into stunningly beautiful patterns as the great waters came crashing down.

St Catharines was another hour's drive away along the Queen Elizabeth Way, the freeway that runs from Niagara to Toronto, bordered on either side by flat, prairie-like plains. The town was pretty, its gentrified old quarter of painted wooden houses clearly a tourist and vacation attraction for visitors from Toronto, whose skyline, with its famous 1,800-foot CN Tower, you can see on the misty horizon across Lake Ontario.

The Jabarah family originally came from Kuwait, and had emigrated to Canada in 1994. Their home was located in a middle-class suburban close of detached houses. Mrs Jabarah, a fresh-faced woman in *hijab* and Arab dress, greeted me and invited me in. She was friendly and hospitable in the traditional Arab way. On the low coffee table was a collection of sugary Arab treats waiting for the pot of hot, sweet coffee that Mrs Jabarah set about preparing in the kitchen. Having exchanged pleasantries, and explained who I was and what I was doing, I asked about her son Mohammed. I didn't know at the time that another of her sons, Abdul Rahman, had also gone to Afghanistan and become an Al Qaeda *jihadi*. She said she had no idea what had happened to Mohammed, and was convinced he was innocent of all the charges levelled at him.

We hadn't been talking for long when the door opened and Mrs Jabarah's third son, Abdullah, walked in. He was wearing a jacket or shirt with a Canadian maple-leaf emblem on it. No question, I thought, where his allegiance lay. He was startled when he saw me alone with his mother, and demanded to know who I was. When I said I had spoken to his father, and mentioned the incendiary word 'journalist', he exploded and started verbally attacking me, and the media in general, saying we were all liars and distorters of the truth. I can't have been the first journalist to have beaten a track to his family's door. He then unleashed a tirade against his brother Mohammed, accusing him of dragging the family down and bringing it into disrepute. Having seen the prosperous neighbourhood in which they lived, I could well understand his feelings. He said with bitterness that his girlfriend, who was white, had left him because of his brother. He mellowed a little after I had a chance to get a word in, but when I hesitatingly mentioned the possibility of doing an interview with him and his mother, his reaction was swift and unequivocal. Out of the question. Hadn't they suffered enough at the hands of the media? Did they want the whole world to know of the family's disgrace? I left knowing that there was zero possibility of any interview. Clearly the family was split.

I went to St Catharines' Masjid al Noor mosque, which Mohammed Jabarah had attended, sat cross-legged on the floor and talked to one of the elders. It was a familiar story. Jabarah had been a devout Muslim. The mosque had no extremist tendencies, and on reading Jabarah's interrogation it became clear that his radicalisation started not in his home town, but many thousands of miles away, in Kuwait, at the feet of an extremist cleric in his mid-thirties called Sulaiman Abu Ghaith, who was close to Osama Bin Laden and went on to become one of his spokesmen. Jabarah's Islamic education began in his formative years, before the family emigrated to Canada in 1994. That period covered the beginning of the war in Bosnia that planted the seeds of radicalisation in the hearts and minds of so many young Muslims around the world. Jabarah said he watched videos of ethnic cleansing being carried out by Serbs, and was inspired to go to Bosnia and join the international army of Muslims who had volunteered to fight *jihad* against the Serb enemy. But Abu Ghaith told him he was too young, and should finish his studies first. After emigrating with his family to Canada, Jabarah stayed in touch with his mentor, and visited him in Kuwait during vacations. His older brother Abdul Rahman did the same, and was intent on following the same path to *jihad*.

In the summer of 2000 the two brothers travelled to Afghanistan to train, the trip being financed and organised by Abu Ghaith. Mohammed told his parents that he was going to study at the University of Kuwait. Abdul Rahman had gone ahead, and Mohammed met up with him at a guest house in Jalalabad after a five-hour trek on foot across the border. Both were eager to get their training under way as soon as possible, with a view to fighting *jihad* in Chechnya, Kashmir or the Philippines. They didn't train at the Al Farouq camp, perhaps because there was a waiting list, but ended up at the Libyan-run Abu Yahya camp, thirty-five miles north of Kabul. Mohammed spent fifty days there undergoing initial training, learning about explosives and various weapons, from handguns and rifles to Russian artillery equipment.

At the end of the course, graduates had the choice of going to join the Taliban front line in its battle against the Northern Alliance, or signing up for more advanced courses. Mohammed and Abdul Rahman opted for the latter. This involved two months' training in city warfare, in which they learned about codes, counter-surveillance and forming cells. At the completion of the course in December 2000 Mohammed went north to join the Taliban forces, but found there was little action as winter had set in. He returned to Kandahar, lodging in an Al Qaeda guest house where he said 'there were brochures and pamphlets containing information on all kinds of training courses'.

By this time Mohammed was utterly committed to the cause of *jihad*, and wanted to meet Osama Bin Laden himself. Presumably he was trusted because he was a protégé of Abu Ghaith, had trained in Afghanistan for about six months and had been regarded as a good student on all the courses he had taken. It was as if he'd been an outstanding trainee at Sandhurst and was being honoured with a personal meeting with the academy's commanding officer. One night in March 2001 he was taken to Bin Laden's house in Kandahar, where they talked and had dinner. Mohammed didn't say much about what had passed between them, although he did mention that Bin Laden requested him to ask Abu Ghaith to come to Afghanistan.

Mohammed next enrolled on yet another course, this time on mountain warfare, at the Al Farouq camp. It was there, in April–May 2001, that Sahim Alwan and other members of the Lackawanna Six were present. When Bin Laden came to visit the camp Abu Ghaith was with him, having accepted the *Sheikh*'s invitation to come to Afghanistan. Mohammed thought it was Abu Ghaith's first visit to the country to which he had sent a number of his pupils. The newly arrived cleric didn't disappoint either his host or his pupil, and gave a sermon eulogising Bin Laden, attacking America and assuring his eager audience that Allah would guarantee them success.

As an indication that he was now on the brink of being accepted into the upper echelons of Al Qaeda, Jabarah was invited by Abu Ghaith to move into the Islamic Institute in Kandahar, across the road from where he had been billeted. The two became regular companions, a further sign that Jabarah was now becoming part of the inner circle. Sometime in May 2001, Abu Ghaith invited him to a meeting at Al Qaeda's VIP guest house in Kandahar with Bin Laden and two dozen senior members of the leadership, including Ayman al-Zawahiri and members of its military committee, including its chief, Mohammed Atef,* who Bin Laden later nominated as his successor, and its head of security, Saif al Adel.[1] Both Atef and Adel were connected to Zawahiri's Egyptian Islamic Jihad, the military brains and muscle behind Al Qaeda. Presumably Jabarah did not contribute to this meeting of the most wanted men in the world, but simply observed. He said, 'UBL [Osama Bin Laden] gave a general speech about the upcoming strikes against America. The speech provided no details about the attack but only gave indications that the attack would be severe.' These words echoed the enigmatic threat that Sahim Alwan had heard from Bin Laden's lips a few months earlier, when he spoke of 'brothers willing to carry their souls in their hands'.

Back at the Islamic Institute after the meeting, Abu Ghaith asked Jabarah if he was 'with Al Qaeda', in the sense of being a member. Jabarah said he wasn't. His spiritual mentor told him it was now time for him to make his mind up, and he was finally persuaded to take the fateful step. Another personal meeting with Bin Laden was arranged in May 2001 at which Jabarah swore the *bayat*, promising to fight the enemies of Islam wherever they may be, and to stand by Bin Laden

---

*Mohammed Atef was also known as Abu Hafs al Masri. He was one of Bin Laden's longest-serving lieutenants, going back to the days of the Afghan *jihad* against the Soviets. He was killed in an American bombing raid in November 2001, when the US and its coalition allies set about destroying Afghanistan's *jihadi* training camps.

until death. He shook Bin Laden's hand, but didn't sign any membership form as the *bayat* was regarded as 'a word of honour'. He also put himself at Bin Laden's operational disposal. He spoke good English, had lived in Canada for over six years and had a 'clean' Canadian passport, which was potentially as valuable to Bin Laden as the American passports of the Lackawanna Six. One of Bin Laden's men gave him an English test – Jabarah concluded that his English was better than his examiner's.

Towards the end of July 2001 Jabarah was told he was to travel to Pakistan, but that he needed to see the *Sheikh* first. Bin Laden told him he had been selected for 'an outside mission' because his English was so fluent and he had a 'good' Canadian passport. He didn't tell him what the mission was, but said that in Karachi he was to meet a man called Mukhtar. 'Mukhtar' was a codename for Khalid Sheikh Mohammed (KSM), the mastermind of 9/11 and Al Qaeda's chief operational planner.* He spent three weeks in August 2001 teaching Jabarah 'how to travel on trains and buses, how to book travel tickets and how to conform to local customs when travelling'. When he was satisfied that Jabarah was up to the task, he informed him that he was 'to go to Malaysia to meet with individuals who were planning an operation against the US and Israeli embassies' in Manila, the capital of the Philippines. For security reasons, the fine detail of the plans would never have been mentioned. KSM then went to a bank in Karachi and withdrew $40,000, including $10,000 to cover Jabarah's expenses. Jabarah was told he was to be the paymaster of the operation, and was introduced to the man who was to be in overall control, Riduan Isamuddin, better known as 'Hambali', an Indonesian whom the CIA referred to as 'the Osama Bin Laden of South-East Asia'. The CIA believes that it was Hambali who arranged the meeting in Malaysia in January 2001 between the two 9/11 hijackers who subsequently travelled from there to America. He is alleged to have been the

---

*Khalid Sheikh Mohammed was America's 'highest value' target. On 1 March 2003 he was arrested in Rawalpindi by the ISI, no doubt with CIA assistance, and rendered to Guantánamo. Under interrogations that included repeated waterboarding, he confessed to involvement in a series of Al Qaeda plots.

Operations Chief of Jemaah Islamiyah (JI), the extreme regional Islamist group thought to have been closely affiliated to Al Qaeda. KSM told Jabarah that he must 'complete his travel from Pakistan' before Tuesday, 11 September 2001. Jabarah assumed that there would be 'a very big attack' that day because of what he'd heard Bin Laden say at the meeting in Kandahar.

Jabarah was booked on a flight from Karachi to Kuala Lumpur via Hong Kong on 10 September. He was in Hong Kong when he heard the news of the attack he had heard Bin Laden referring to. Jabarah said he was 'happy with the success of the operation', and that it 'inspired' him to fulfil his own mission. While the airlines of the world assessed the momentous implications of the attacks on New York and Washington, Jabarah spent three nights at a hotel in Hong Kong, before flying on to Kuala Lumpur. He lay low for a few days so as not to attract attention, then went to an internet café to check if there were any email messages related to his mission – Khalid Sheikh Mohammed had advised him to use internet cafés since emails sent from them were more difficult to track. There was a message from KSM telling him to find a man called Ahmed Sahagi, whom Jabarah had met when he was staying with KSM in Karachi, and who, the message said, was staying in the same area.

Sahagi was in his mid-twenties, had been in Afghanistan for five years, and was to be one of the suicide bombers in the planned attack on the embassies in Manila. Jabarah believed Bin Laden personally selected those who were chosen to carry out 'martyrdom' operations (including, as we have seen, Mohammed Al-Owhali and Jihad Ali for the attack on the US Embassy in Nairobi). After checking out several hotels in the neighbourhood, he eventually found Sahagi, who told him he had been with KSM when the planes hit the Twin Towers, and described his reaction. All the video equipment in the apartment had been set to record the news. Initially KSM was disappointed because the first plane hit the North Tower near its top, and he feared that the point of impact was too high to bring it crashing down. However, when the towers collapsed KSM was 'very happy'. Sahagi said the operation had taken two years to plan, and that KSM told him the fourth plane, which crashed in the field in Pennsylvania, had been heading for the White House.

The original targets for the suicide bombings in which Ahmed Sahagi was to become a *shaheed* were to be the US and Israeli embassies in Manila, but when he and Jabarah carried out an on-the-spot recce, they decided that plan should be aborted, as the location of the embassies meant that the bombs would not have maximum impact – the building that housed the US Embassy was situated well away from the road. There was then discussion about a Plan B, and it was decided that embassies in Singapore would make better targets. By this time the various members of the attack cell had assembled and made contact with Jemaah Islamiyah cells in Singapore. Jabarah, who had been given the codename 'Sammy', took a bus to the island state, where he met up with a member of one of the local JI cells. Various potential targets were videoed, including the Bank of America, the Caltex oil company offices, and the Israeli, British and US embassies. It was decided the Israeli and US embassies were the priorities. Each would require a bomb of two tons of TNT mixed with ammonium nitrate and other chemicals. The cell estimated that the whole operation, which involved six huge truck bombs directed at the targets identified during the video recce, would cost around $50,000. As paymaster, Jabarah phoned KSM in Karachi and asked for a further advance. He was told the cash was available, and would be handed over by a courier in $10,000 instalments at a series of meetings.

Around the beginning of December 2001, Jabarah received a message that Hambali was in Kuala Lumpur in Malaysia, and wanted to see him urgently, as he had important information to communicate. Jabarah met him in front of a shopping mall, and they went somewhere more private to talk. He told Jabarah that he had been in Kandahar during the US air strikes, and that Mohammed Atef, Al Qaeda's overall military commander, had been killed. Hambali had been talking to Atef two days before his death, and Atef had made it clear that he wanted the South-East Asia operation carried out as soon as possible, presumably to maximise the ongoing impact of 9/11, and to show that those attacks were not a one-off. Hambali also told

Jabarah that he was concerned that one of the Singaporean contacts had been picked up for questioning, which could put the whole operation in jeopardy.

Hambali's information and instincts were correct. But before the operation could get under way, Singapore's intelligence service, the Internal Security Department (ISD), arrested fifteen members of local JI support cells, including some of those who had helped Jabarah video the potential targets. The video itself, or a copy of it, was also seized. It was innocently labelled 'Sightseeing in Singapore'.

In Singapore I met the Minister for Home Affairs, Wong Kan Seng, who told me about the breaking of the JI cells and the thwarting of the planned attacks. I asked him how the ISD had found out about the plots. He said a Singapore Muslim had told the agency that he had heard of an individual called Aslam who claimed to know members of the Al Qaeda leadership. I assumed the informant was one of the ISD's sources within the Muslim community. 'Our Internal Security Department put Aslam under observation, and over time also found out who his associates and friends were,' said Wong Kan Seng. 'This was just after 9/11. In early October Aslam left Singapore for Pakistan. We watched him and let him go. He was going to join in the fight with the Taliban. One of his earlier claims was that he went to provide humanitarian assistance, but in fact he was there to do more than that. He was captured by the Northern Alliance and admitted [his role] when he was brought back to Singapore.' The Northern Alliance had handed Aslam over to the Americans, who in turn had handed him back to the ISD.

By this time the ISD had all the intelligence it needed to arrest the members of the local JI cells. Under interrogation, they talked about 'Sammy', Jabarah's codename. 'They told us he came here, guided us and helped us conceive of this plan.' I asked about the JI detainees. What kind of people were they? The Minister's answer, as so often, contradicted the stereotype of the terrorist: 'They are not poor, disenfranchised, marginalised people. They have jobs, they are married, they have children and homes which they own. They have secular education in school. They studied English. They didn't go to the *madrassa.*' His description fitted the pattern of so many other young Al Qaeda recruits and the ideology of violent extremism they had embraced: 'They went into this originally in search of religious knowledge to fill a vacuum in their lives. They wanted to know more about religion and about the Koran. Over time they were shown videos of repressions committed against Muslims in other parts of the world. They felt that was a cause they could identify with and join. They get sucked into it and feel it was their duty to do something about it.' He had no doubts about the connection between Jemaah Islamiyah and Al Qaeda. Hambali, he said, was the crucial link. He had written letters of introduction to Al Qaeda to facilitate members of the JI cells in Singapore going to Afghanistan for training. But the real clincher was the discovery of a copy of the video of Jabarah's Singapore recce in the ruins of Mohammed Atef's bombed home near Kabul. 'The Americans found it and handed it over to us,' the Minister said. 'The tape is the direct link, as it was brought to Afghanistan by one of the detainees to show the Al Qaeda leaders what they planned to do in Singapore.'

Because of Hambali's tip-off about the arrests, Jabarah had managed to get out of Singapore before the ISD tracked him down. He ended up in Bangkok, where in January 2002 he had a final meeting with Hambali that was to be of great significance. Two planned Al Qaeda/JI attacks in South-East Asia had been thwarted, but with money and explosives still at his disposal, Hambali was determined to press on. Jabarah said that at their meeting in Bangkok Hambali discussed carrying out further attacks in the region. 'His plan was to conduct small bombings in bars, cafés or nightclubs frequented by Westerners in Thailand, Malaysia, Singapore, Philippines and Indonesia.' Hambali also stated that he had 'one ton of PETN explosive* in Indonesia', but he did not know who would carry out the bombings, or when. Nine months later, on the Indonesian holiday paradise of Bali, two JI suicide bombers launched their attack, targeting the popular tourist area Kuta Beach, on the southern tip of the island.

---

*Pentaerythritol trinitrate, the explosive used by the shoe bomber Richard Reid.

After Mohammed Jabarah left Hambali in Thailand in January 2002 he went to Dubai, where he met up with his brother Abdul Rahman. Both were now high on the FBI's wanted list. Jabarah called Khalid Sheikh Mohammed, who told him to go to neighbouring Oman and arrange a safe house for *jihadis* who were fleeing Afghanistan after the battle of Tora Bora, and were en route to Yemen. Jabarah understood that Bin Laden was considering Yemen as an alternative base to the one he had just lost in Afghanistan as a result of the American invasion, and that Ahmed Sahagi was heading there to set about preparing the way for Al Qaeda. KSM notified Jabarah in an email that he was 'sending fifteen nice girls without papers', and that Jabarah should fix them up with an apartment. It wasn't the most subtle of coded messages. Jabarah's role as interim travel agent didn't last long. He was arrested in Oman, along with Sahagi, on 2 March 2002, and interrogated by the Omani authorities. Officers from the Canadian Secret Intelligence Service (CSIS) then flew over and took him back to Canada, where they interrogated him over several days.

In the end the Canadian prosecuting authorities decided that there was not enough evidence to bring a charge against Jabarah, and at that time they did not have the wider legislation that would have stood a far better chance of securing a conviction. But CSIS was in touch with the US authorities, who were obviously interested in Jabarah, as he had planned attacks on their embassies in Manila and Singapore. A deal was done. Jabarah agreed to hand himself over to the FBI and enter into a cooperation agreement under which he would assist the US Department of Justice and plead guilty to the charges. That led to his twenty-four-day interview with the FBI, in which, as we have seen, he provided 'a considerable amount of valuable intelligence'.[2] The details were passed on by the FBI to Singapore's intelligence agencies in May 2002 – five months before the Bali bombings. I assume they would also have been forwarded to other interested foreign partners. Given that Jabarah had been operating at the highest level of Al Qaeda, having had personal contact with Osama Bin Laden himself, Khalid Sheikh Mohammed and Hambali, it's not unreasonable to think that the warning of future attacks on 'bars, cafés and nightclubs', and the mention of a ton of high explosive in Indonesia, would have suggested Bali in general, and Kuta Beach in particular, as likely points of attack. But the warning was not heeded.

The extent to which Australia was aware of the threat to Bali remains a matter of some dispute. The then Foreign Minister, Alexander Downer, insisted that the country never received any direct warning before the bombings. 'Neither the Americans, nor the British nor us had any specific warnings in relation to Bali, but we had generic warnings about Indonesia, and Bali is part of Indonesia,' he said.[3] Mr Downer was technically right. There was no indication of a specific target on the island, or of the timing of any potential attack. But the intelligence from Jabarah on what Hambali had said should have been sufficiently alarming to put governments in the area on alert, especially the Australian government, large numbers of whose nationals holidayed on Bali, and who were among the 'Westerners' Hambali had referred to. Confusion and controversy would rage over who knew what, and when. Had Australia been made aware of the Jabarah debriefing before the bombing, or not? I thought it reasonable to assume that it had, given that Singapore had received the document two months before the attack. It seems unthinkable that the specific intelligence of what Hambali had said had not been passed on to Australia by either CSIS or the FBI. Even if it hadn't, I would have expected someone to pick up the phone or pass on the word, given the close links between the American and Australian agencies. After all, Australia was America's eyes and ears in that highly combustible part of the world.

As a result of the controversy the Australian Senate conducted an inquiry into what the government knew and did not know.[4] It established that in May–June 2002 the Canadians, in whose custody Jabarah initially was, had forwarded 'some general background' on their detainee to the Australian government, but this made no mention of what Jabarah had said about Hambali's proposed attacks on tourist destinations. The Australian authorities asked for access to Jabarah, who by now had been transferred from CSIS to the FBI's custody, but it was denied. The investigation concluded that Australia received no further information about Jabarah until it was sent the debriefing details 'several weeks' after the bombings. By then it was too late.

The Senate investigation accepted that there had been 'a failure of intelligence', but far from laying the blame at the Australian government's door, or that of any other intelligence agency that was in a position to alert Australia to the threat, it pointed the finger at the Indonesian government, referring to its 'incapacity, or lack of political will ... at that time to fully acknowledge JI's presence on its soil and to act decisively against extremists'. The charge was that Indonesia was in denial. No doubt acting on the intelligence that Jabarah had provided to the FBI, America had issued a warning to its citizens prior to the bombing to avoid Bali's bars, restaurants and nightclubs. In contrast, the Australian Embassy in the Indonesian capital, Jakarta, told its travellers that Bali was 'calm' and tourism was 'normal', although it did add a rider that they 'should observe the same prudence [on Bali] as tourists in other parts of the country'. It was hardly a flashing red light.

Reviewing the evidence, some of which because of its sensitive nature was only disclosed *in camera*, the investigation concluded:

> To terrorists like JI, nursing their potent grievances and looking for suitable soft targets on which to exact their revenge, it is likely ... that Bali (along with other sites) would have been drawn into focus on the terrorists' strategic landscape. In the light of these considerations, the majority of the Committee finds it difficult to agree with the assessment of [intelligence] agency heads that Bali was not any more vulnerable than many, if not most, parts, especially given the fierce anti-Western, *jihad* inspired and self-righteous anger of Indonesia's extremists.

The committee was right when it said that the deaths and injuries suffered by so many Australian citizens were due to 'a failure of intelligence', although it failed to assign blame to any specific intelligence agency or agencies. If the FBI had been prepared to send a detailed précis of Jabarah's interrogation to Singapore some months before the bombings, why hadn't it sent it to Australia? The question has never been satisfactorily answered, and raises doubts about the often proclaimed commitment to international and inter-agency cooperation in the battle against terrorism.

After Jabarah had agreed to cooperate with the FBI he was detained in 'secure FBI housing', where he was allowed to read, watch television and films, make monitored telephone calls to his family, exercise and prepare his own food. Although he wasn't in gaol, he was effectively incarcerated. His behaviour seemed quite normal until he heard that one of his closest childhood friends, Anas al-Kandari, with whom he'd grown up in Kuwait and travelled to Afghanistan in 2000, had been shot dead while attacking a US Marines base in Kuwait.[5] Kandari had only recently returned from Afghanistan, and had left several wills which he asked his mother to open after his death. The family said they described the suffering of the Palestinian people and the massacres committed against them by Israel, and the sufferings of Muslims worldwide. He asked that all his property should be given to the *mujahideen*.[6] Kandari is said to have worshipped at the mosque where Abu Ghaith had often led the prayers before he left for Afghanistan.[7] Jabarah was devastated by the news, and the FBI agents who were monitoring him observed that he changed noticeably. As a precautionary measure they searched his room when he had gone out for a walk,[8] and found two concealed steak knives; a newspaper cutting on Kandari's death alongside which Jabarah had written, 'By Allah I will avenge your death'; a two-page document that he described as his will, in which he asked to be granted 'the highest honors of martyrdom'; a letter to his parents in which he appeared to be saying goodbye; a long letter on *jihad* and 'martyrdom' in which he asked to join fellow 'martyrs', sooner rather than later; and, most worrying of all to the FBI, the names of the agents who were guarding him. The authorities concluded: 'These writings make clear that Jabarah had secretly disavowed cooperation and was affirmatively planning further *jihad* operations, including in all likelihood the murder of government officials in some sort of suicide operation.'[9]

Jabarah had blown it. The FBI was not prepared to give him a second chance. He was tried, and on 7 May 2007 was sentenced to life imprisonment. He was denied the martyrdom he craved. His brother Abdul Rahman, however, did achieve his wish to die as a martyr. He was shot dead on 3 July 2003, during a firefight with Saudi Arabia's anti-terrorist police.

I sometimes wonder if, throughout the long years in gaol that lie ahead of him, Mohammed Mansour Jabarah will be haunted by the Bali bombings and remember that he was an eyewitness to their beginnings at his meeting with Hambali in Bangkok in January 2002. Will he also remember that one of the others present at that meeting was a man known as 'Muklas', who was to become the recruiter and leader of the Bali bombers?

NINE

Bombs on Bali

Visiting the site of a bombing is never easy, even for a journalist with no direct connection to the victims. I've looked at memorials to the dead of Bloody Sunday in Derry, the US Embassy bombing in Kenya, 9/11 in New York, Bali at Kuta Beach, Casablanca in the heart of downtown, Madrid at Atocha station and the London 7/7 bombings. Most of these formal memorials to the dead are simple structures with names inscribed in stone, marble or metal. Some, like the fifty-two stainless-steel pillars in London's Hyde Park, each representing one of the innocent victims of the 7/7 bombings, are elegant and moving in their simplicity.

I've often stood reading the names on these memorials and thinking of what each one means, in terms of a life ripped away or a loved one lost. But the impromptu, *ad hoc* memorials that spring up in the immediate wake of attacks can be more moving and more personal: the mountains of flowers piled outside King's Cross Underground station in London or at the site of the World Trade Center in New York; the photographs and messages left by families and friends. When I visited the site of the Bali bombings in August 2003, ten months after the attack, I saw anger as well as grief in the assorted memorabilia left in the street and at the empty space where Paddy's Bar, one of the suicide bombers' targets, once stood. As I walked slowly along, shading my eyes from the glare of the sun, I read words that were a mixture of defiance and pain scribbled on Australian T-shirts. 'Fuck the Terrorists. Bali. Black October 12 2002. To all our mates. We will never forget you'; 'Brothers in Arms. Together go rest

4 ever as one'; 'Sadly missed but never forgotten. See you in the next life'.

Indonesia, with a population of over two hundred million, is the most populous Muslim nation on earth. Eighty-six per cent of its citizens follow the faith.[1] The island of Bali, however, with a population of only three million, is mainly Hindu.

The chain of events that led to the Bali bombings began in Bangkok in January 2002 when Mohammed Jabarah met Hambali, who talked of targeting 'bars, cafés or nightclubs frequented by Westerners'. Two other key figures were present at that meeting. One was 'Muklas', the heir-apparent to Hambali and the strategic brain behind the bombing. The other was Dr Azahari Husin, the brain behind the bombs themselves. Muklas (his real name is Huda bin Abdul Haq; he is also known as 'Ali Gufron') was an Islamic teacher who had fought in Afghanistan in 1989, in the closing months of the *jihad* against the Soviet Union. It was then that he met Osama Bin Laden. Dr Azahari was an engineer with a PhD in property valuation from the UK's Reading University, who learned how to make bombs in Afghanistan and went on to become Jemaah Islamiyah's most experienced explosives expert. His nickname was 'the Demolition Man'.[2]

To assist with the planning of the Bali bombing, Muklas brought in his two brothers, Amrozi bin Nurhasyim and Ali Imron. The original intention was to carry out the operation on 11 September 2002, to mark the first anniversary of 9/11 and create the maximum impact, but the plans weren't ready, so it was put on hold until the following month.

Amrozi bought the chemicals, and with Dr Azahari made up one of the bombs. Ali Imron also helped, and made up a suicide vest. The main targets were to be Paddy's Bar and the Sari Club, two popular nightclubs in Kuta Beach, the party capital of the island. They were situated opposite each other on Legian Street, Kuta Beach's main drag. The bombers thought they would be full of American tourists, not realising that Kuta Beach was in fact a favourite destination for Australians, particularly backpackers and surfers in search of sunshine and the perfect wave. The attacks were planned for a Saturday night, when the bars and clubs along the strip would be heaving.

Two suicide bombers were selected. Known as 'Iqbal One' and 'Iqbal Two', both had agreed to take part in the 'holy bombing'. Iqbal One was to drive a van packed with explosives to the Sari Club, and Iqbal Two was to carry a bomb in a rucksack into Paddy's Bar. Both clubs would be full of young tourists and backpackers drinking and dancing the night away as midnight approached – in Kuta Beach terms, the night would be young. A third target was also selected, the US Consulate in Denpasar, the island's capital, six miles away. The plan was to detonate this much smaller bomb by remote control, using a mobile phone. It was probably intended to be little more than a calling card to remind the world of one of the reasons for the attacks.

Five days before the operation, the cell travelled to Bali to put everything in place. Amrozi and Ali Imron bought a Yamaha motorbike to ride to the US Consulate to plant the bomb, and Amrozi purchased a white Mitsubishi L300 minivan. Ali Imron planted the bomb at the US Consulate, and then drove Iqbal One and Iqbal Two to Kuta Beach in the minivan, loaded down with a ton of high explosives. At about 11 p.m. he watched Iqbal Two make for Paddy's Bar with the bomb concealed in a backpack. He then got out of the van and told Iqbal One to drive straight to his target. It was at this point that he found out, rather late in the day, that Iqbal One couldn't drive, so he told him to just go straight ahead. Iqbal Two detonated his suicide bomb at five past eleven. The explosion was devastating. The bar was immediately engulfed in flames, causing mayhem and carnage. Those who were able to fled outside in panic, many bleeding from their injuries, and rushed straight into the path of the Mitsubishi which Iqbal One detonated outside the Sari Club less than a minute later. A huge fireball engulfed the area. The bomb left a massive crater five feet deep and twenty feet wide. Leaving the blazing street and the screaming people behind, Ali Imron got on the Yamaha bike, rode to the US Consulate in Denpasar and detonated the bomb there with his Nokia mobile phone. The motorbike was then left outside a mosque. The death toll that night was 202: eighty-eight victims from Australia, thirty-eight from Indonesia, twenty-four from the United Kingdom, and seven from the USA. The other victims came from Europe, Canada, South America and the Far East.

I walked across the piece of waste ground where Paddy's Bar once stood, and thought of what the scene must have been like that night. I had been told that in the immediate aftermath of the bombing the site was cleared and the earth carried out to sea, in accordance with Hindu tradition, which holds that it contains the souls of the dead. The site that had once been so horrific had now returned to normal, with tourists – although in fewer numbers than before the bombings – walking up and down Legian Street in T-shirts and shorts as if nothing had happened. There were only the sad and fading pieces of memorabilia on the walls to remind them of the terrible events of that night. I thought too of the intelligence warnings that had not been heeded. Something the FBI's Pat D'Amuro had told me ran through my mind: 'We had intelligence indicating that Al Qaeda and groups affiliated to [Jemaah Islamiyah] were looking at soft targets. Wherever you have intelligence indicating specific targets, you disseminate that information as quickly as you can.' But the world of intelligence-gathering, and the dissemination of its product, are not perfect. By its very nature, however good information may appear, whether it has been obtained as the result of talking to a terrorist or is the product of electronic or human surveillance, there is never a guarantee that it is 100 per cent accurate. When the IRA bombed Canary Wharf in London's Docklands on 9 February 1996, six months before its historic cessation of hostilities, the shock waves shook Britain's intelligence community, which had thought it had the IRA covered. That attack illustrates the principle that however good the intelligence, there is always the possibility of an attack getting under the wire.

Casting my mind back to the scene that night on Bali, I wondered where on earth an investigation to find those responsible would begin. Indonesia, which had long been in denial about the fact that it had a terrorist problem, was now confronted with the undeniable evidence that it had. Within twenty-four hours a 140-strong team of experienced forensic and investigative officers from the Australian Federal Police (AFP) arrived on Bali. Graham Ashton, the team leader, was undaunted by the formidable mountain he had to climb. 'If you look at the whole picture, you might be overwhelmed by the sheer enormity of it,' he said. 'At the crime scene there was rubble everywhere. The amount of victims at the mortuary far outweighed the amount of space available, and obviously there was still a lot of search and rescue to be done. At that stage there was no indication as to who was responsible.'[3] The AFP Commissioner, Mick Keelty, was equally unfazed as his team set about trying to find the evidence to bring those responsible to justice. 'Terrorism is a crime,' he said. 'At its base is mass murder. The way to investigate terrorism is the way we investigate crime. Once you start chasing down that direct evidence, you are chasing down the terrorists.'[4]

From the beginning the AFP team worked closely with the Bali police, who had never had to deal with anything remotely on this scale before: investigating drug-trafficking and petty theft was their usual routine. For Bali's Chief of Police, General Made Pastika, it was a matter of honour that those who had brought such human and economic devastation to the island should be tracked down to stand trial. When I was in Washington a few months before my trip to Bali in 2003, I had found out that General Pastika was giving a lecture on the bombings at a downtown hotel. I managed to get an invitation, and was impressed by his PowerPoint presentation and his command of his subject. After the lecture I introduced myself, and said I was planning to go to Bali later that summer to make a documentary about the bombings. Could I come and see him? I knew it was best to strike on the spot, experience having taught me how difficult it can be to cut through bureaucracy and get to the person you want to see once you're on location. General Pastika told me to give his office a ring when I arrived. I did, and arranged to meet him at the headquarters of the Bali police.

I sat on a plastic-covered green sofa in a waiting room for what seemed an age until the General had time to see me. It was obvious that this wasn't the FBI or the AFP, but a small rural police force that twenty-first-century technology had simply not reached. On the way to the reception area I'd passed a warren of small offices with creaking ceiling fans in which not a single computer was to be seen. Police officers sat hunched over manual typewriters, laboriously and slowly hammering out reports. Meeting General Pastika in his dark-panelled office, it became clear that while the AFP and other Western intelligence agencies could provide the technology, he and his officers could provide local knowledge and expertise. He was aware of the expectations upon him. 'The pressure came from everywhere,' he told me. 'As a police officer everyone wanted us to uncover the case as soon as possible. I believe no crime is perfect. They must leave evidence we can trace. I was very optimistic.'[5]

The first breakthrough came with the discovery of parts of the mobile phone that had detonated the small bomb at the US Consulate, in which no one had been killed. For the AFP's Graham Ashton, the meticulous detective work had begun. 'We had the serial number of the phone and identified where it was purchased from. They gave witness accounts of the purchasers and so we had identikit pictures of the terrorist team involved in the plot.' Further assistance in assembling the photofits of Amrozi and Ali Imron came when the shop where the abandoned Yamaha motorbike had been purchased was identified. The biggest breakthrough came about three weeks after the bombings, when General Pastika was praying at a Hindu temple. One of his men rang him on his mobile and asked if he was praying for success. If he was, the officer said, his prayers had been answered: they had just located the chassis number of the Mitsubishi van. It had been found on a piece of metal that the blast had hurled onto a nearby roof. The vehicle was traced to Amrozi, who was found and arrested without a struggle. When the police searched his house, they found a ton of potassium chlorate. I asked General Pastika if Amrozi had talked. 'Yes, yes,' he said. 'After twenty-four hours of interrogation, he confessed.' Given the magnitude of the crime he had committed, I imagined that Amrozi's interrogation probably wasn't carried out with kid gloves.

Whatever the methods used in Amrozi's day-long interrogation, he admitted everything, and gave the names of the other members of the cell, including his brothers Muklas and Ali Imron. All were subsequently arrested after being tracked down by mobile-phone-tracing technology provided by the AFP. I asked General Pastika what the bombers were like. 'I was puzzled by Amrozi,' he said. 'How could someone who looked so innocent do such a thing? He just smiled all the time. He wondered how the police caught him, as he believed his crime was perfect.' Did he show any signs of remorse? 'No, not at all. He said that he did his job. He said that his "job" was to kill the *kuffar*, the enemies of the Muslim.' And what about his brother, Ali Imron? 'He's very calm but very cooperative, giving us all the information. He's so proud, telling us how expert he is in making bombs.' And the third brother, Muklas? 'He was much more confident, more serious. He's a very macho man. I did not want to talk to him. I met him and then left. I let a subordinate talk to him. I didn't want to interview him. Even though I try not to be emotional, with this man I couldn't do it. I had to stay away.' The look of disdain on General Pastika's face said it all. To him, the Bali bombers were terrorists, who had deliberately targeted and slaughtered over two hundred innocent civilians.

Iman Samudra, the so-called field commander of the operation, was arrested along with the three brothers. General Pastika talked to him too. 'He had a lot of experience in terrorist activities. He chose the targets and organised all the activities on Bali. He too was surprised that we caught him. He had a new passport and was about to fly abroad. He was so cold-blooded, and very silent. He didn't say much. It was very hard to get his confession.' Did he show any sign of remorse? 'No.'

Following chaotic scenes in court orchestrated by his furious supporters, the alleged spiritual leader of Jemaah Islamiyah, Abu Bakar Bashir, was sentenced to less than three years' imprisonment for being part of an 'evil conspiracy', although all charges directly linking him to the bombings were dropped.[6] But Bashir left no one in any doubt about where his sympathies lay. 'I support Osama Bin Laden's struggle because his is the true struggle to uphold Islam,' he said in a statement following the attacks. 'The terrorists are America and Israel.'[7] Nevertheless, he has consistently denied any involvement with terrorist acts suspected of being associated with Jemaah Islamiyah. In 2006 his conviction was overturned by Indonesia's Supreme Court, and he was released after serving just over a year of his sentence.[8] In 2010 he was arrested again, in connection with his alleged involvement with a new militant Islamist group that takes its name from the troubled territory of Indonesia, 'Al Qaeda in Aceh'.[9]

While they were in gaol, the bombers gave a series of remarkable interviews that provide a chilling insight into their motivation and mentality.[10] Muklas described meeting Osama Bin Laden in Afghanistan. 'We met face to face while we were staying in caves when he was leading the war against Russia. He led the war by himself. He's the one human being I very much adore in this life.'[11] Amrozi talked about the operation. 'The preparation began in September. I bought one ton of potassium chlorate. I already had a ton sitting at home, but that had been ordered by someone else so I couldn't use that. Then I bought the aluminium and sulphur and started sending it to Bali. I sent it on about five buses.' He described making up the suicide vest in a matter-of-fact way: 'It was just a regular vest, assembled to have pockets for the explosives. Anyone could have made it with lots of pockets, just like the ones in the movies.' Iman Samudra attacked America as the fount of all evil. 'When did the enmity start that initiated this fourth crusade? When America invaded the Arab Peninsula. Everyone knows that Israel receives their weapons, equipment and financial support from America. They have attacked Afghanistan and it's been cited that some 200,000 Muslims were killed by thousands of tons of American bombs.' Samudra made it clear that he didn't fear death: 'A death sentence would be welcome, because our acts are based on conviction. It's done purely for our beliefs.'

Ali Imron was the only member of the cell to express any regret. 'If this was a crusade, it shouldn't have been a bloodbath like the Sari Club,' he said. 'They weren't the enemy. They weren't soldiers prepared to go to war and therefore prepared to die. When I was caught, I gave in. I didn't resist. I realise what I've done. I feel guilty. What I did was wrong, and I regret it. I am ashamed.'[12]

Ali Imron was sentenced to life imprisonment because he had shown remorse. Iman Samudra, Muklas and Amrozi were all sentenced to death. Just after midnight on 9 November 2008 they were executed by firing squad on a prison island south of Java. All pleas for clemency were rejected.[13]

On 20 March 2003, just over six months after the Bali bombings, American, British and coalition forces invaded Iraq. America provided 248,000 troops, Britain 45,000 and Australia 2,000. Spain supplied 2,115 troops for non-combat roles like medical support.[14] As I watched the live television coverage of the 'shock and awe' assault, the curtain-raiser to the invasion, with its unremitting aerial bombardment of Baghdad, I thought that it looked like an incredible New Year's Eve firework display. I wondered how many people died, and how the city could ever be put back together again. When would the electricity supply be restored? When would clean water flow once more? How could the pieces of a fractured society be put together again?

To President George W. Bush, 'Operation Iraqi Freedom' meant finishing the business that his father, former President George Bush, had left unfinished at the end of the first Gulf War in 1991 when, having driven Saddam's forces out of Kuwait, the decision was made not to march on Baghdad and remove the dictator. But publicly his son justified the invasion on two counts. He presented it as part of the 'Global War on Terror', alleging that Saddam Hussein was hand in glove with Al Qaeda – which was never the case – and ratcheted the threat up even further by pronouncing that Saddam was harbouring weapons of mass destruction (WMD): 'In Iraq a dictator is building and hiding weapons that could enable him to dominate the Middle East and intimidate the civilised world – and we will not allow it.'[15] But many believed that the real driving force behind the invasion was America's wish to gain control of Iraq's rich oilfields.

Britain's Prime Minister Tony Blair was Bush's staunchest ally, determined to maintain the United Kingdom's 'special relationship' with the United States. On 18 March 2003, two days before the invasion, he left Parliament and the British people in no doubt about his concerns: 'Terrorist groups in possession of WMD, even of a so-called dirty radiological bomb, is now in my judgment a real and present danger.'[16] Perhaps with the appeasement of Hitler in the 1930s in mind, he also made clear his deep personal commitment to act:* 'Of course Iraq is not the only part of this threat. But it is the test of whether we treat the threat seriously. Faced with it, the world should unite ... To fall back into the lassitude of the last twelve years [since the 1991 invasion], to talk, to discuss, to debate but never act, to declare our will but not enforce it, to combine strong language with weak intentions, [is] a worse outcome than never speaking at all.'[17]

Blair faced fierce opposition, not only from within his own Labour Party, of which 139 backbenchers voted against backing the war, but in the country at large. On 15 February 2003, a month before the invasion, around a million people from all walks of life and all social classes marched in London against the war, and there were similarly huge demonstrations around the world on the same day.

Blair remains unrepentant about the invasion of Iraq. In his memoirs, published in 2010, he wrote: 'I can't regret the decision to go to war ... I can say that never did I guess the nightmare that unfolded, and that too is part of the responsibility. The truth is we did not anticipate the role of Al Qaeda or Iran. Whether we should have is another matter; and if we had anticipated, what we would have done about it is another matter as well.'[18]

On 9 April 2003, twenty days after the invasion began, US troops entered Baghdad, and Saddam's regime was toppled. The historic event was marked by an allegedly stage-managed set piece in which a huge statue of the dictator was brought crashing to the ground.

---

*More recently, Blair had intervened in Kosovo in 1999 in support of the NATO mission to protect its two million Muslims from Serbian aggression.

Saddam himself was on the run, and evaded capture for eight months. Following a tip-off, he was finally arrested on 13 December 2003, when he was found hiding in a secret cellar in a farmhouse near his home town of Tikrit. He surrendered, and offered no resistance. He was tried, and was executed by hanging on 30 December 2006. And what of the alleged weapons of mass destruction? The United Nations weapons inspectors under Hans Blix had searched for them before the invasion, with limited cooperation from Saddam, and found little evidence of their existence. Even with Saddam gone, no WMD were ever found. Despite this failure to find any proof for the stated reason for which Britain went to war, Tony Blair subsequently made a defiant defence of his decision to support Bush. Giving evidence to the Chilcot Inquiry into the war in 2010, he said he had 'no regrets' about removing 'the monster' Saddam, and that the world was now a safer place[19] – despite the fact that 'regime change' had never been one of the publicly declared purposes of the invasion. The irony is that Iraq has become Blair's legacy, when it ought to have been Northern Ireland.

One consequence of the invasion was that although America's stated justification for it was Saddam's connection with Al Qaeda – for which there was not a shred of evidence – it gave Bin Laden a cause and a footing in Iraq that he had never had before. Iraq became the new *jihad* for Al Qaeda. American, British and coalition troops were initially welcomed as saviours, coming to liberate Iraq from the tyranny of Saddam's regime. There were cheers and celebrations when his statue in Baghdad was pulled down with the assistance of a US tank-recovery vehicle.[20] But as the months went by, the Western liberators were increasingly seen by many Sunni Iraqis as invaders of a Muslim land.* This transformation reminded me of the way in which the attitude of the Nationalist population of Northern Ireland towards British soldiers changed in the months following their deployment in 1969. The fact that the country's reconstruction proceeded at a snail's pace made some Iraqis yearn for the stability of the Saddam era,

---

*Although Sunnis were the minority Muslim sect in Iraq, they had run the country under Saddam, himself a Sunni, at the expense of the Shia majority.

which though oppressive and bloody at least provided security, water and electricity. American preparations for what was to happen after the invasion had been woefully inadequate. Soldiers unaccustomed to playing the role of peacekeepers found themselves under attack, initially from pro-Saddam Sunni insurgents and then from hundreds of volunteer *jihadis* from the Middle East and Europe, including the United Kingdom, many of whom coalesced under the banner of 'Al Qaeda in Iraq', seeing the Iraqi *jihad* as a call to liberate a Muslim country from a foreign invader. As troops hit back with aerial support that did not always distinguish civilians from the enemy, Iraq became the *jihadi cause célèbre*. The organisation's leader was the Jordanian Abu Musab Al-Zarqawi, who in 2004 had taken the *bayat* to Osama Bin Laden. Zarqawi subsequently alienated much of his support base in Iraq and the wider Arab world by killing Shia Muslims – the majority in Iraq – as well as occupying coalition troops. So concerned was the Al Qaeda leadership that Zawahiri sent him a letter warning him of the counterproductive effect of his targeting fellow Muslims. Zarqawi's bloody rampage came to an abrupt halt in 2006, when he was killed in an American aerial attack. In the end, George W. Bush provided Osama Bin Laden with an opportunity he could hardly have dreamed of, in addition to the *jihad* that was already developing in Afghanistan after the overthrow of the Taliban. America and Britain were now faced with increasingly unpopular wars on two fronts.

The radicalising effect of the invasion of Iraq cannot be overestimated, despite Tony Blair's subsequent insistence that terrorist attacks in Britain had nothing to do with the war, but were motivated by a hatred of the West's freedom and way of life. This assertion was dramatically rebutted in 2010, when the former Director of MI5, Baroness Manningham-Buller, gave evidence to the Chilcot Inquiry and in one of her rare public declarations dismantled Blair's denial of any link between Iraq and terrorist attacks:

Our involvement in Iraq radicalised, for want of a better word, a whole generation of young people, some British citizens – not a whole generation, a few among a generation – who saw our involvement in Iraq, on top of our involvement in Afghanistan, as being an attack on Islam ... there had been an increasing number of British-born individuals living and brought up in this country, some of them third-generation, who were attracted to the ideology of Osama Bin Laden and saw the West's activities in Iraq and Afghanistan as threatening their fellow religionists and the Muslim world.[21]

As part of the evidence to Chilcot, a secret letter that Baroness Manningham-Buller had written to the Home Office on 22 March 2002 was declassified. It stated:

> There is no credible evidence that demonstrates that Iraq was impli-
> cated in planning the 11 September attacks ... We assess that Saddam
> is only likely to order terrorist attacks if he perceives that the survival
> of his regime is threatened.[22]

Another paragraph in the letter warned that South-East Asia was a possible target for terrorist attacks, should they be instigated by Saddam. The identification of the area was right, although the source of the attacks was wrong. Seven months after the invasion of Iraq it was Al Qaeda that struck Bali, not terrorists directed by Saddam Hussein.

Lightning was to strike twice on Bali, with the Iraq war fuelling the second group of bombers' motivation, as their suicide videos subsequently revealed. They attacked in almost the same place, at Kuta Beach once again and at Jimbaran, another holiday playground just down the road. In coordinated attacks on 1 October 2005, twenty people died and 129 were injured. The attacks were carried out by three suicide bombers, all of whom were connected to Jemaah Islamiyah. Dr Azahari, who was still at large, made the bombs. The driving force behind them was Noordin Top, who is also believed to have been involved in the first Bali bombings. 'Noordin Top is more powerful in recruiting and training people, while Azahari is an expert in making bombs,' General Ansyaad Mbai, head of Indonesia's anti-terrorist operations, told me. 'Together they're a very, very good combination.'[23] Top is believed to be the masked figure who appeared in a propaganda video and declared: 'Our enemies are the supporters and accomplices of Bush and Blair, the liars who pursue the infidel and apostate rulers that rule the Muslims and who chase after the *ulemas* [the clerics] and the *mujahideen*. They are the enemy that we target in our attacks.'[24] Despite the rhetoric, fifteen of the dead were Indonesians, and four were Australians. There were no Americans or British.

Before they set out on their mission, the three suicide bombers made their own propaganda video. Their average age was twenty-two, and on the video they all look incredibly young. One of them is smiling, just like Amrozi. The war in Iraq was clearly on his mind. 'Oh, leaders of America and her allies, retreat from Muslim lands or we will bring terror on you,' he says. 'We will not let you live in peace even in your own countries.' The second bomber pronounces, 'True believers be obedient to Allah and never die except as a Muslim. At this moment in time, it is the highest duty of every Muslim to wage *jihad*.' The third has a similar message. 'Oh, Muslim brothers, eliminate the infidels around you.' At the end of the video they appear masked and clad in black, with suicide vests lit up like Christmas trees with flashing coloured lights to indicate that their bombs are primed and ready to go. The bombers were identified when their heads were found separated from their bodies. They had murdered twenty innocent civilians without warning.

I never imagined I would be making a second trip to Bali so soon after my first. The reason was to interview a senior JI commander who had trained several of the first Bali bombers and who was Muklas's brother-in-law. His name was Nasir Abbas, and he had now put terrorism behind him, changed sides and was helping the Indonesian authorities track down those responsible for the second Bali bombings, and some of those involved in the first attacks. He was also helping the government to deradicalise convicted JI members and encourage them to see the error of their ways. Nasir Abbas is a remarkable converted 'terrorist'.

I was not in the best shape for my all-important first encounter with Abbas. The fifteen-hour flight from London to Jakarta is exhausting, and I arrived early in the morning, heavily jetlagged and struggling to cope with the seven-hour time difference. There was no time to snatch even a few hours' sleep before the meeting with Nasir Abbas and two of his now former JI comrades that had been arranged at a restaurant in the countryside outside Jakarta.

Nasir Abbas is a small, intense, slightly nervous man with glasses, in his late thirties. He looks more like an accountant or a junior bank manager than someone who until relatively recently had been one of JI's top commanders, in charge of Mantiki [Region] 3, the JI-designated area responsible for training.* It covers east Malaysia, parts of Indonesia and the Philippines. He was arrested in 2003, interrogated and then persuaded to change sides, or 'turn'. General Ansyaad Mbai has no illusions about his former enemy's past. 'Of course he was a terrorist,' he told me. 'He is a very dangerous man, because he was one of the key figures in JI.'

Abbas told me he first went to Afghanistan to join the anti-Soviet *jihad* in 1987, at the age of eighteen, when he was still a student at an Islamic school in Indonesia. He had read all about the heroic *mujahideen* who were taking on the second most powerful army in the world. In his eyes this was a legitimate *jihad*, sanctioned by the word of the Holy Koran. 'They were defending their homeland and also defending their faith,' he said. 'They were fighting Communism. The Soviet Union wanted to conquer their country. I wanted to help the *mujahideen*.' He was given the opportunity to go and join the *jihad* by the cleric Abdullah Sangkar, one of his mentors, who almost a decade later would found Jemaah Islamiyah.[25] All his expenses were paid, and he arrived in Afghanistan as one of a batch of fourteen Indonesian recruits. He naïvely expected that he would go straight to the front line, but was told that he would have to wait until he was properly

---

*According to Nasir Abbas, Mantiki 1 covered west Malaysia and Singapore. It was known as the 'economic' region. Hambali had been its head, and Muklas, Ali Imron, Amrozi and Dr Azahari were all members. Mantiki 2 was the 'recruitment' region, and covered other parts of Indonesia.

trained. He was promptly enrolled in what he called a 'military acad-emy' on the Pakistan side of the border. This sounds rather grand for what it probably was, a series of simple huts, barracks and classrooms around a dusty parade ground. There he learned a variety of military tactics and skills: how to use small arms and heavy weapons; how to prepare landmines and booby traps. He was also instructed in how to be a good *jihadi*, through a heavy dose of Islamic teaching. He said he studied there for three years, and during his two-month vacations was allowed to experience front-line fighting, where he saw action and death, and came face to face with the bloody reality of war. One of his friends died beside him, cut down by machine-gun bullets. Another stepped on a landmine and died on the way to hospital. Abdullah Azzam came to preach at the 'military academy', and Abbas remem-bered him talking about battlefield ethics. 'He said we cannot kill women and children, and cannot destroy buildings if there is no enemy inside them.' That code of *jihad* remained firmly implanted in his mind.

By 1993 he had graduated from the 'academy' and joined Jemaah Islamiyah. He became a senior instructor in Afghanistan and trained, among many others, some of the Bali bombers, including Ali Imron and Iman Samudra. 'I never taught or trained them to kill innocent people,' he said. 'We taught them to fight people who attacked them, like troops with guns. It's dishonourable if they're killing innocent people.' So, I asked him, he didn't train them to kill tourists on Bali? 'No. I'm ashamed of that. I feel guilty. That's why I try to do what I can to stop any of my friends who want to harm innocent civilians.'

In 1994, JI ordered him to go to the jungles of Mindanao in the southern Philippines and set up a training area, known as Camp Hudaibiya ('Peace Agreement'), where JI members and others could be trained to fight *jihad* in the Philippines and elsewhere. Mindanao is a predominantly Muslim area in a Catholic country, and has long been the seat of an insurgency fighting for independence led by the Moro Islamic Liberation Front* (MILF). Many MILF members were

---

*The Moro are the people who inhabit Mindanao.

trained there, along with *jihadis* from other parts of the world – Dhiren Barot, also known as Issa al Hindi, who was sentenced to forty years' imprisonment in Britain for a series of bomb plots, is believed to have been one of them. Camp Hudaibiya was a military training camp run along strictly structured academic lines. I saw some of the report cards that had been seized when the Philippine army took over the camp: each student's progress and exam results were meticulously recorded in longhand, and marks were given for achievement. I visited the site of Camp Hudaibiya, which had been taken over by the MILF before it was put out of action, and shuddered as I walked into one of the cold, dark concrete bunkers in which captives had been held. Rusty metal plates were still lying on the floor, and through the gloom I could see graffiti and the names of prisoners that had been scrawled on the walls with smoke-blackened sticks.

Abbas told me that in 2001 Abu Bakar Bashir personally appointed him as head of Mantiki 3. I asked if he met Bashir at the time he was promoted. 'Yes, of course,' he said. 'He's my *emir*.' He also said that Bashir stayed at Camp Hudaibiya for 'two or three nights', and attended a passing-out parade of graduates at which Abbas was the 'field commander'. 'He gave a speech as *emir* of Jemaah Islamiyah, and motivated us to keep on with the military training and fight *jihad* to help the [Moro] Muslims who were struggling in the area.'

In the year he was promoted to be head of Mantiki 3, Abbas was shocked by the Al Qaeda attacks on New York and Washington, because they were directed at civilians. 'If this is called a war, what kind of a war is this?' he said. 'If this is a battle, what kind of battle is it? I don't understand. If this is carried out by Muslims and they believe it is *jihad*, I disagree.' The attacks epitomised all that he believed *jihad* should not be. He was unequivocal on the issue. When he was instructed to read out to his men Osama Bin Laden's *fatwa* of 1998 against 'Crusaders and Jews', which authorised the killing of civilians, he refused. In October 2002, when over two hundred civilians were killed in the Bali bombings, he was incandescent at the direction in which some elements of JI were going, elements that had presumably heard and accepted Bin Laden's *fatwa*.

Abbas was on a ferry when he learned about the Bali bomb attacks. His immediate reaction was that JI had to be behind them, as only it had the ability and expertise to carry out such an operation. 'In my heart I suspected that Hambali and his men had done this,' he said. But he wasn't sure until five days later, when he went to visit his sister and had a private talk with his brother-in-law, Muklas. 'He told me that he and his brothers were involved in the Bali bombs and that he and other JI members were under Hambali's command. I felt my initial suspicion was correct.' I asked him if Muklas had expressed any regret about what he had done. He said he hadn't: 'He was proud that the operation had been a success.' He was shocked when he learned that several of his students from his days as a trainer in Afghanistan, including Ali Imron and Iman Samudra, were involved in the bombings. 'I felt sorry. I felt sin because they used their knowledge to kill innocent civilians,' he said. I could see from his expression that he meant it. The seeds had been sown for his increasing disillusionment with the direction JI was taking.

Abbas went on the run, suspecting that as a senior JI commander and Muklas's brother-in-law he would be hunted down, and possibly killed. He evaded capture for six months, but on 18 April 2003 he was arrested at a safe house in a village outside Jakarta. I went with him to the place where his freedom had ended. He warned me to be careful, as he feared there would be supporters of JI around who might not be friendly. If they recognised him, he might never return. He stayed in the car while I went to look at the house, which was clearly empty. I tried the door. It was locked. I peered through the dirty window, and rubbed some of the grime away to get a better view of what was inside. Then a man turned up. I thought it might be trouble. He was holding a large bunch of keys, and I assumed he must be the landlord or someone working for him. Perhaps he thought I might want to buy or rent the empty house, although why anyone would be interested in what was probably a rat- and snake-infested hovel was beyond me. To my surprise, he tried several keys in the lock, then let me in. The place had obviously been abandoned a long time ago. I was told that the reason there had been no takers for the house after Abbas's arrest was that evil spirits lurked inside, and it was in fact pretty spooky.

I did a quick piece to camera to give some flavour and a sense of place to illustrate Abbas's description of what had happened on the day of his arrest. He told me he had been prepared for it, and had instructed his students at Camp Hudaibiya what to do in such circumstances: 'We trained JI members that it is better to be killed than get arrested, as it's more important to die with the information rather than give it to the enemy.' He told me that five police officers had burst into the house. He wasn't armed, but he put up a fight: 'I was hoping that if I attacked them they would use their guns to shoot me, but they didn't.' I was never quite sure if Abbas was telling the story as it really happened, or if he was making some of it up because he'd previously agreed to do a deal with Indonesia's intelligence agencies. I was surprised when he described his interrogation, which was not what I would have expected, given his seniority in JI and his personal and family connections to the Bali bombers. Not a finger was laid on him. No doubt the agencies realised that they had captured a rare, highly placed asset who could provide vital intelligence on JI and help them track down other senior JI commanders.

Abbas told me that all sorts of thoughts ran through his mind as he was being interrogated. '[When I was arrested] I tried to fight to die, but I'm still alive, so this is new and something that God needs me to do.' He soon realised that his interrogators knew more about him than he'd bargained for. They told him that they weren't interested in just arresting Muslims – they wanted to stop the attacks. 'Mr Nasir,' they said, 'we know that you disagree with the Bali bombings.' They then produced a piece of paper written by one of Abbas's former comrades that indicated Abbas's opposition to the attacks. 'I recognised the writing,' he said. 'It was all about me.' The game was up. Abbas decided to tell his interrogators everything. He admitted that he cried as he did so: 'Not loudly. Just a few teardrops.'

Abbas's decision to help his former enemies was potentially life-threatening. The IRA showed no mercy to 'touts' who betrayed its secrets, and Al Qaeda is the same. I asked if he felt like a traitor after so many years of serving JI. 'No,' he said. 'I feel I'm doing the right thing. I never feel I'm a traitor. I'm trying to bring people back to the right paths of Islamic teaching. I want to defend Islam from those who seek to use it to do bad things. If people say I'm a traitor because I join the police, I don't care about that.' I asked if the authorities had paid him any money for his decision to change sides. He assured me they hadn't, but said they helped look after his family and assisted with his children's education. The only tangible sign of gratitude from the authorities was an impressive Panasonic all-terrain laptop of the type that I imagined American and British soldiers would be using in Afghanistan and Iraq. Abbas was clearly very proud of it, and was expert at using it.

When Bali was attacked for the second time, on 1 October 2005, Abbas was the Indonesian security forces' secret weapon, helping not only to track down the bombers but, through his contacts, those who made the bombs and planned the operation – among them some of the JI members who were involved in the first Bali bombings. An intelligence picture of their movements and whereabouts was built up over many months, assembled not just by Abbas's encyclopedic knowledge of JI but by the sophisticated technical means put at Indonesia's disposal by America, Australia and other Western allies.

Once the prime targets had been identified, Indonesia used its other secret weapon, the masked and black-clad officers of its elite counter-terrorist unit known as Detachment 88.* It had been set up in the wake of the 2002 bombings, and was funded and trained by America and its allies, no doubt using the expertise of their special forces. Dr Azahari, the master bombmaker, was shot dead on 9 November 2005 during a raid on the house in which he was hiding. Noordin Top, who was believed to have supplanted Hambali as the leader of Al Qaeda in South-East Asia, was also in the house, but managed to escape and remain on the run for another four years.

---

*The unit is said to have been given this name after a senior police officer at a briefing misheard the initials 'ATA' (Anti-Terrorist Assistance) as 'eighty-eight'. As eight is believed to be a lucky number in Asian culture, the name became permanently attached to the unit.

Hambali himself had been arrested on 12 August 2003 in Thailand, and handed over to the Americans for interrogation and ultimately for detention at Guantánamo Bay.* Noordin Top was eventually tracked down and shot dead on 17 September 2009. He is also believed to have been involved in the original Bali attacks, as well as the bombing of the J.W. Marriott and Ritz Carlton hotels in Jakarta in July 2009, in which nine people died. The Bali slate was finally wiped clean on 10 March 2010 with the killing of Dulmatin, the last main suspect connected to the original Bali bombings. He was known as 'the genius of Jemaah Islamiyah',[26] and had a $10 million price on his head.[27] The Australian Foreign Minister, Alexander Downer, described his death as 'no great loss'.[28]

Before I said goodbye for the last time to Nasir Abbas, I asked if he lived in fear of his life, given that he must be one of JI's prime targets. 'Yes, as a normal human being I do feel worried about that and feel I'm in danger,' he replied. 'But because of my faith, I believe that God will always be with me and covering me.'

The Bali bombings, and Nasir Abbas's role in helping to track down the terrorists who were responsible for them, illustrate how Al Qaeda's operational capacity had begun to change, by increasingly utilising local and regional groups like Jemaah Islamiyah which shared Bin Laden's ideology and readiness to cause mass civilian casualties. The same process was under way in southern Europe and North Africa, where similar *jihadi* groups were beginning to plan operations, although not necessarily under the banner of Al Qaeda. The bombings in Casablanca in 2003 and Madrid in 2004 were calling cards of what I refer to as the 'new' Al Qaeda.

---

*It is thought that his whereabouts were identified following the interrogations of Khalid Sheikh Mohammed (see p. 293).

TEN

Understanding the 'New' Al Qaeda

The 2002 Bali bombings marked a transitional phase in the evolution of Al Qaeda. The East African embassy bombings, the attack on the USS *Cole* and 9/11 were all centrally directed by the organisation. The Bali bombings were a halfway house: the finance came from Al Qaeda via Khalid Sheikh Mohammed and Hambali, but the actual planning and execution of the attacks were carried out by local operatives from Jemaah Islamiyah. In the months and years that followed, many attacks were driven by the same ideology but implemented by local groups with no umbilical connection to Al Qaeda. It was all too easy for the media to stamp them with the Al Qaeda name, and some of the participants even claimed to be Al Qaeda, but this tended to be more rhetoric than reality. That is not to say that 'core' Al Qaeda did not remain a serious threat.

The change in authorship came about for two main reasons. The first was imperative. After the US military and its allies invaded Afghanistan in the wake of 9/11, driving out the Taliban and destroying the *jihadi* training camps, Osama Bin Laden had to adjust to changed circumstances, as he was no longer secure as Mullah Omar's protected guest. The second was opportunistic. Bin Laden saw that Al Qaeda had become a global brand, to which countless Muslims were attracted either through ideological sympathy or a desire to strike back at America and its allies and the regional 'apostate' regimes that supported them. Operations no longer needed to be planned and directed by 'core' Al Qaeda, but could be left to local *jihadi* groups. If they wanted to claim an Al Qaeda connection, that was fine by Bin

Laden, as it would enhance his brand still more. I refer to these changes as bringing about a 'new' Al Qaeda, with a different *modus operandi*. The pivotal years that marked the transition were 2003 and 2004.

On 12 May 2003, nine suicide bombers drove car and truck bombs into four compounds in Riyadh, the Saudi capital, that housed US contractors and other foreign nationals. Thirty-five people were killed, including nine Americans. Over 160 were wounded. One of those believed to have been involved in the attack was Mohammed Jabarah's brother Abdul Rahman, who as we've seen was shot dead two months later in a firefight with Saudi anti-terrorist troops. If Abdul Rahman was involved, the Riyadh bombings, like those on Bali, would be an indication of Al Qaeda's transitional phase, as he, like his brother, had taken the *bayat*, the oath of allegiance to Bin Laden. The attacks however rebounded on Al Qaeda, as the Saudis hit back hard, largely destroying Al Qaeda's infrastructure in the Kingdom.

Later that year, the pattern of the new Al Qaeda began to emerge. On 20 November 2003, suicide bombers attacked the British Consulate and headquarters of the HSBC bank in Istanbul. Thirty-two people were killed, among them three Britons. A local Turkish Islamic group, the Great Eastern Islamic Raiders' Front (IBA-C), claimed responsibility, and included Al Qaeda in its claim.[1] Certainly Al Qaeda was not going to deny this, and the Turkish group does share its ideology. Five days earlier, suicide bombers had attacked two synagogues in Istanbul, killing twenty-five people. But the real major step in the evolution of the new Al Qaeda is illustrated by two attacks carried out by cells in Morocco and Spain.

On 16 May 2003, ten suicide bombers hit targets in the centre of Casablanca, including the Jewish Commercial Centre, the Belgian Consulate and the five-star Hotel Farah. Nine of the bombers became *shaheeds*, the tenth being captured in a Jewish cemetery. The other young bomber who was with him blew himself up there, presumably thinking he would achieve martyrdom among the Jewish gravestones.

General Ahmidou Laanigri, the head of Morocco's powerful Interior Ministry, probably knows more about Al Qaeda and its affiliates' activities on his own home ground than anyone else. I met him at his office at the top of a vertiginous winding staircase in the Interior Ministry in Rabat. Arranging the interview with the General was not straightforward, as he doesn't normally talk to the media. He began by explaining why the bombers had chosen Casablanca, and how they fitted into the wider Al Qaeda picture: 'When Al Qaeda's central hub was dismantled in Afghanistan, orders were given for all *mujahideen* to return home and wage *jihad* back there,' he told me. 'This was when Al Qaeda turned into a fluid, nebulous movement that was international. Certain people saw Osama Bin Laden at that time and were given direct orders and a direct blessing to specifically attack Morocco. They all escaped [after the US invasion of Afghanistan] and fled across the border, mainly returning home in disguise through Iran. They then recruited young people, who were indoctrinated very quickly. They promised them Paradise on earth, and made sure they could be relied upon.' He said that he had received intelligence, presumably from interrogations of suspects, that there had been a high-level secret meeting in Istanbul in 2002 between senior members of the Moroccan Islamic Combatant Group and the Libyan Islamic Fighting Group, at which a decision had been made to attack Casablanca. I later saw a secret Spanish intelligence report that confirmed this Istanbul meeting. It said that the participants 'agreed *jihad* should be waged where the leaders and their supporters actually lived, in Europe and North Africa. Our same informants confirm that the meeting was coordinated by Abu Musab Al-Zarqawi, a terrorist leader affiliated to al Qaeda,* and with the approval and support of Osama Bin Laden.'[2]

Many of the Casablanca bombers came from the shanty town of Sidi Moumen, just outside the city, which is a breeding ground for militant Islam. General Laanigri told me that some of them had been to a local internet café and emailed Mullah Omar in Afghanistan,

---

*Abu Musab Al-Zarqawi is also believed to have taken part in videoed beheadings. He was killed on 7 June 2006 by laser-guided bombs fired from two US aircraft at a house where he was attending a meeting.

presumably via intermediaries, to seek a *fatwa* authorising the attacks.* Laanigri said that evidence his intelligence service had collected when they traced the internet traffic indicated that the bombers had indeed received the *fatwa* they were hoping for.

I decided to go to Sidi Moumen to try to understand the background from which many of the attackers came, and to see if I could meet and talk to any of their families. I knew this wouldn't be easy, and would possibly be dangerous. Less than a year later, my BBC colleague Frank Gardner miraculously survived a gun attack by Saudi militants when he was filming in an extremist area in Riyadh. Frank was severely wounded, and his cameraman, Simon Combers, was shot dead.

Sidi Moumen had a fearsome reputation as an extremists' stronghold. I have been to shanty towns from Brazil to Gaza, and it is always easy to see how they become hotbeds for drugs, crime and terrorism. People who have nothing, have nothing to lose. From a distance, which was the healthy and advisable place to start, Sidi Moumen looked a forbidding place, a vast area of tin shacks and low breeze-block huts that housed over 150,000 people. I was surprised at the number of television aerials and satellite dishes that sprouted in a tangle of wire and metal from their roofs. It was set back two hundred yards from the road, beyond an open space littered with rubbish among which little children played. At the far side, where the waste ground met the first line of shacks, stood a fountain at which people were queuing for water. Someone pointed out a low building standing apart from the rest and said it was the mosque. There was nothing to indicate its function – no minaret or any other identifying marks. I had heard that the Islamist extremist who ran Sidi Moumen, the *capo di tutti capi*, was known as 'the Angel of Death'. He tolerated no deviation from the rigours of seventh-century Islam, and was said to have slit the throat of his own uncle for having an extra-marital affair, and

---

*As an eminent Islamic scholar, Mullah Omar has the authority to issue *fatwas*. There is some disagreement among Islamists as to whether Bin Laden also has the authority to do so. Perhaps the would-be suicide bombers were playing it safe.

to have ordered others to be beheaded or stoned to death for trans-
gressions that ranged from smoking to drinking. I hoped I wouldn't
run into him.

I knew that somewhere in that labyrinth were the families of the
young men who had blown themselves up. I had a few names, but no
addresses; in fact I doubted if there were any such things. Sidi
Moumen was hardly built on a grid pattern with street names and
numbers. We were soon approached by the local police, whose station
stood a healthy distance from the slum, but close enough for it to be
kept under constant observation. They clearly knew who we were,
although we had not given our itinerary or our filming plans to the
Moroccan authorities. That's the way Morocco works. It is the intelligence service's job to be aware of everything. This was a couple of
days after I'd spoken to the all-seeing and all-knowing General
Laanigri, so I assumed that he'd instructed his men to keep an eye on
us, wherever we were. I told the police officers I'd just interviewed
their boss – which they probably knew anyway – and was trying to
find a member of one of the families of the suicide bombers that I
might talk to. They looked sceptical, and warned us that we would be
mad to try to go into Sidi Moumen on our own, but they did offer to
help. One of them said he knew one of the families, and would try to
locate them for us, but that we must be careful. There are times when
you don't want a police escort, and other times when you're grateful
for one. I suspected that on this occasion it might be a mixed blessing,
as the presence of a police officer would perhaps be even less welcome
than that of an English journalist.

We followed him through the maze of alleyways, with water
running down the middle of them and serried ranks of washing
draped from one tin roof to the other. Western T-shirts with designer
logos were occasionally in evidence, along with the ubiquitous jeans
and freshly laundered sheets. I was surprised by how relatively clean
and organised everything seemed. The water, which I would have
expected to look contaminated, appeared clear and clean. The police
officer located the local head man, who took us to the home of the
mother of the bomber who blew himself up in the Jewish cemetery. It

was suggested that I wait outside while they went in to sound things out. After five or ten minutes they emerged and said I could come in, but there was to be no film crew. I entered a low-ceilinged room furnished with a bed and a chair. The walls were bare except for a frame containing verses from the Koran. The bomber's mother was a quiet, dignified woman, simply but neatly dressed, her head of course covered with a scarf. She looked much younger than I had expected. I knew better than to try to shake hands. She invited me to sit down on the edge of the bed.

With the obliging police officer as my interpreter, I explained that I was making a documentary about the Casablanca and Madrid bombings, and asked if I could talk to her about her son. It's always a difficult position to be in, meeting someone like this. Instinctively I wanted to extend my condolences for her loss, but a natural restraint kicked in, triggered by the knowledge of what her son did. I ended up saying something that I hoped was polite but non-judgemental. She told me that she had been relieved when her son had taken to the faith and was going to the mosque with all that entailed, praying five times a day and reading the Holy Koran, and had hoped that his discovery of Islam would keep him away from Sidi Moumen's drug dealers and criminals. Like many parents I met in similar circumstances, from Bradford to Atlanta, whose sons had become involved in Islamist extremism, she was totally unaware of what he had been up to, buoyed by the fond notion that Islam would keep him out of trouble and harm's way.

At the end of our conversation I thanked her, and asked if she would mind if I took a photograph of her. I knew she did not want to be filmed, but I thought that second best would be a still photograph to illustrate the encounter in the documentary. I asked rather hesitantly, as the request seemed intrusive, given the sensitivity of the situation. But she agreed, and we emerged from Sidi Moumen unscathed – and with a slightly-out-of-focus photograph. We weren't going to hang around.

General Laanigri told me he hadn't been surprised that some of the terrorists came from Sidi Moumen, but he hadn't expected that they would be prepared to blow themselves up. He called them 'kamikazes'. As the Jabarah brothers had Abu Ghaith and the Bali bombers had Abu Bakar Bashir, the Moroccan *jihadis* had a spiritual mentor. Mohammed Fizazi was a radical cleric who had trained in Saudi Arabia and returned to Morocco to preach an extreme form of Wahhabism. General Laanigri had no doubt about Fizazi's malign influence on impressionable young minds: 'He is without doubt the most dangerous ideologue in Morocco. He's not only erudite and a very good public speaker, but also very active and has converted many people,' he said. 'He's well connected, well travelled, has an important network of contacts in different countries, from the UK to Germany, Algeria and Saudi Arabia. He is a man who wanted to play a very important ideological role and expand and export violent political Islam.' I asked if Fizazi had given his blessing to the Casablanca bombers. 'It's better than that,' the General said. 'He wrote an article in the weekly magazine *Le Journal*, criticising the bombers' choice of targets, saying that next time they should go for bigger and more obvious symbols of the state, and more populated locations, like Parliament. So not only did he think it was a good idea, but he also told them how to do it better next time.' Fizazi is now serving a thirty-year gaol sentence, having been convicted in August 2003 for preaching radical Islam in mosques and meeting the perpetrators of the suicide attacks.[3]

The General told me that the fanaticism of the bombers became clear when the one surviving kamikaze was interrogated. 'The answer is always the same: "We are doing *Jihad* for the victory of Islam. We are true followers of Islam and those who don't follow it the way we do can be condemned to death." That's a fundamental common trait. "We are right. You are wrong and must die" is a slogan that unifies them. They are proud to defend an Islam that they see as being perverted by the cultural influence of others.' He explained the chilling ideology of Muslims who hold these beliefs, who are known as *takfiris*: 'They decide death or life for whoever doesn't comply with their way of looking at Islam. They have the power to decide upon the fate of someone else. They excommunicate them and eliminate them. They are very dangerous.' Their views are based on a literal interpretation of the words and sayings of the Prophet Mohammed. No deviation is tolerated. Muslims who do not agree are regarded as apostates, and can be killed. *Takfiri* ideology is as simple and brutal as that. Despite their strict adherence to the word and the world of the Prophet, *takfiris* are not bound by normal Muslim conventions if it suits their political and military purpose. They don't have to wear a beard. They can wear Western clothes, smoke and drink alcohol, and even traffic in drugs. This outward lifestyle diverts suspicion and provides a perfect cover for their terrorist activities.

The root of the Moroccan *jihadi* connection is reflected in three brothers from the Benyaish family, all of whom became committed to the cause. Their names were Abdulaziz, Salaheddin and Abdullah. The family lived in Tangier, only a dozen miles across the Strait of Gibraltar from Spain, which is a magnet for the thousands of unemployed young Moroccans living in poverty in shanty towns like Sidi Moumen. General Laanigri knew all about the Benyaish brothers: 'They all started out as drug traffickers, and dabbled a bit with clandestine emigration. They were common-law criminals.' He said they converted to radicalism in the mid-1990s, at the time of the Bosnian war.

Abdullah, the youngest, converted while serving one of his many prison sentences in Spain: 'After two years he came out a changed man, and was the first to go to the [Bosnian] front.' Abdullah was killed in the American bombing of Tora Bora in December 2001.

The second brother, Salaheddin, also fought in Bosnia, where according to Laanigri 'he distinguished himself as a great operational leader'. During the fighting he lost his right eye, and subsequently became known as 'Abu Mughen', 'the One-Eyed One'. He recovered in Spain, then slipped back into Morocco, where he covertly did recces and provided logistics for the *tafkiri* cells that were then being put in place. He is now serving almost twenty years' imprisonment for his role in the Casablanca bombings.[4]

According to Laanigri, the oldest brother, Abdulaziz, was 'by far the cleverest and most cunning of the lot'. He married a French woman, which gave him French nationality and an all-important European passport. 'The key people in the Al Qaeda network are people chosen for their passport, and EU passports are like gold dust. They're people with clear legal status, they work and have European wives and go unnoticed.' Abdulaziz recruited cells for the network and, like his brother, provided logistical support: 'He's the brains, and he's very mobile.' Laanigri's men had him under surveillance, but he slipped through the net the day after the Casablanca bombings. When his home was searched they found an arsenal of weapons, manuals on poisons downloaded from the internet and, most ominously, electronic diagrams on how to make a mobile phone function as a bomb detonator. The explosives used in the Madrid train bombings the following year were detonated by mobile phones. Abdulaziz was later arrested in Spain, sentenced, but then released by the Supreme Court. He then proceeded to fight extradition to Morocco.

Ten months after the Casablanca bombings, on 11 March 2004, terrorists attacked four commuter trains at the height of Madrid's rush hour. Ten bombs were detonated within three minutes of each other in a carefully planned and coordinated attack. One train had already arrived at the city's Atocha station, while the other three were on their way there. One hundred and ninety-one people were killed and almost 2,000 wounded.[5] The bombs were concealed in rucksacks, and were detonated by signals from mobile phones wired in a way similar to that in the diagrams found at Abdulaziz Benyaish's flat. General Laanigri pointed out the contrast between these attacks and the bombings in Casablanca the previous year. 'Madrid was sophisticated,' he said. 'They wanted to be able to harness the technology of remote-controlled detonation in order to spare the bombers or use them more efficiently over time. In this way you don't lose all your footsoldiers, but can use them again later.'

The members of the Madrid cell who carried out a terrorist atrocity unprecedented in Europe were *takfiris* with direct Moroccan connections. The SIM cards for the mobile phones used to trigger the explosives were supplied by a young Moroccan called Jamal Zougam, who had gone to Madrid to live with his mother when he was twelve. He grew up in the Lavapies area of the city, long a byword for poverty, a favoured destination for immigrants and an ethnic melting pot. It's not the sort of place into which you wander alone at night. I found Zougam's mobile-phone shop, and was not surprised to find its metal shutters pulled firmly down.

It was while Zougam was living in Lavapies that he was recruited by Salaheddin Benyaish after he'd returned from Bosnia and was recovering from the wound to his eye. General Laanigri's intelligence service warned their Spanish counterparts about Zougam, whose lifestyle was that of the classic undercover *takfiri*: 'We told them he was a hardened militant. The Spanish placed him under some sort of surveillance. I don't really know what it was, but I don't think that anything much came from it.' France's leading anti-terrorist judge, Jean-Louis Brugière, also tipped off the Spanish. As a result the police searched Zougam's flat, but they found no evidence against him.

Jamal Zougam seemed no more than a tiny fish in an Islamist pond in which many bigger predators swam. In the wake of 9/11, Al Qaeda was the overriding priority for European intelligence agencies – after all, Hamburg had been home to Mohammed Atta, the leader of the hijackers, and Marwan al Shehhi, the pilot of United Airlines Flight 175. Spain was also more concerned about the threat closer to home from the militant Basque separatist organisation ETA, which over four decades had killed more than eight hundred people, many of them politicians and members of the Guardia Civil. But the warning signs were there. Spain had contributed over 2,000 troops to the multinational force in Iraq, and was one of the countries Osama Bin Laden had threatened in an audio tape message on 18 October 2003, a year after the first Bali bombings and five months before Madrid. 'We will go on fighting you and we will carry on martyrdom operations,' he had said. 'We reserve the right to retaliate ... against all countries that take part in this unjust war.' He singled out Britain, Spain, Italy and Australia.[6] The timing of the bombings was no accident: they were intended to send a message three days before Spain's general election.

Jamal Zougam had been part of an extremist group in Spain whose spiritual leader was a radical Madrid cleric known as Abu Dahdah (his real name is Imad Eddin Barakat Yarkas). Abu Dahdah was suspected of being close to Al Qaeda, and to have been responsible for raising money and recruits to fight in Bosnia, Chechnya, Afghanistan and Indonesia. He was also alleged to have met Mohammed Atta, the leader of the 9/11 hijackers, in Tarragona on 16 July 2001, two months before the attacks on New York and Washington – the intelligence services thought this might have been a final planning meeting. Although Atta did meet Ramzi Binalshibh, the external coordinator of the 9/11 attacks, in Spain, there is no conclusive evidence that Abu Dahdah was involved. It was Abu Dahdah, a Balkans veteran himself, who had taken care of the injured Salaheddin Benyaish when he returned from Bosnia. When Abu Dahdah's group was broken up and Abu Dahdah arrested,* Zougam became part of the cell that would bomb Madrid's early-morning commuter trains.

The spiritual leader of the cell was another Moroccan immigrant, Serhane Fakhet. He was one of the crucial connections between the Casablanca and Madrid bombings. His brother-in-law, Mustapha al-Maymouni, was arrested in connection with the Casablanca bombings and sentenced to twenty years in prison. Fakhet was living in Spain on a Spanish government scholarship to study economics at university in Madrid. While doing so he had a variety of jobs, including one with an estate agency where he was regarded as a very good asset and a very stable person. He also worked part-time at Madrid's main mosque, the Islamic Cultural Centre, often referred to as the M-30 mosque because of its proximity to the noisy M-30 motorway. It's a moderate place of worship, and preaches tolerance rather than extremism, but that didn't prevent it from being a meeting place and recruitment pool for potential *jihadis*. It often has 5,000 worshippers for Friday prayers. Jamal Zougam was one of them, as was his mentor Abu Dahdah, whose children attended the mosque's *madrassa*. The recruitment process worked in the now well-established way, with

---

*Abu Dahdah was arrested on 19 November 2001, and protested his innocence of all charges. He was subsequently sentenced to twenty-seven years' imprisonment, later reduced to twelve.

potential young *jihadis* being fired up by videos portraying the suffering of Muslims around the world.

I visited the cultural centre and met its spokesperson, Mohammed al-Affifi, in the cool of the courtyard. The only sound was the tinkling of fountains, and it seemed far away from the roar of the motorway. I asked him about Serhane Fakhet. 'Initially he came here to pray, and later on he began to work on an hourly basis as a bookkeeper in the restaurant that we have. He wasn't very communicative, a man of few words.' Did he ever imagine that Fakhet would be involved in an atrocity like the Madrid bombings? 'Never. It would never have entered my head that a person like him could ever do such a thing. What happened was awful, terrible. It was an earthquake which has shaken Muslims living here in Spain. It has ended the trust that there was between Muslims and Spanish society.'

I asked José Cabanillas Sanchez, Head of Intelligence for the Madrid police, how an outwardly moderate mosque could be a fertile recruiting ground where the Madrid cell could enlist other potential *jihadis*. He replied: 'It provided them with the perfect opportunity to meet other people, get their message out there and see who else was on the same wavelength as them. Then they could arrange to meet up outside, well away from the mosque. So it was the perfect place to recruit. There's nowhere else in Spain where so many Muslims gather together at the same time.'

What the embryo bombing cell lacked was someone with the experience and contacts necessary to supply the explosives, and the wherewithal to pay for them. That crucial figure was a drug dealer and convicted criminal called Jamal Ahmidan, who had been radicalised while serving a prison sentence in Morocco. José Cabanillas Sanchez explained the importance of Ahmidan's role: 'It was an article of faith to Fakhet that following Islam meant carrying out acts of terrorism. The only problem was that he had no idea how to go about it. So it was really fortunate for him that Jamal Ahmidan arrived on the scene at just the right time, because he was a criminal. Ahmidan had the nerve, the experience, the capability and the contacts to successfully carry out an undercover operation right under the noses of the police.'

In Morocco I interviewed Ahmidan's uncle, a gentle and dignified man living in a flat in a poor part of Tangier. Again, as was so often the case with the relatives of alleged terrorists, he could not believe that his nephew was capable of involvement in such an atrocity. He had last seen him before he left Morocco. 'I am angry with those who exploited him, and I'm against all that happened in this catastrophe. He was a victim. When he left, he told me he was going to Ibiza. I don't know what happened.' The way he spoke and the way he looked convinced me that he was telling the truth. I didn't think he was trying to pull the wool over my eyes.

Ahmidan, like Zougam, had seemed something of a Westernised playboy, roaring through the streets of Madrid with a girl on the back of his motorbike. He was a fanatical supporter of Real Madrid, smoked, drank and lived life in the fast lane, travelling around Europe with fifteen different IDs, trafficking ecstasy, cocaine and Moroccan cannabis. It was the perfect cover. No one suspected him of being a *jihadi*. The police knew him only as nightclub drug dealer with an extensive criminal record. Manolo Navarette, who headed the Guardia Civil's investigation into the bombings, told me: 'He was a crook with a clear idea of what he wanted to do. They [the cell] then moved his commitment to crime into the commitment for terrorist activity.' Spain's intelligence agencies never imagined that a small-time drug trafficker would become a suicide bomber. No one, except Ahmidan's closest colleagues in the cell, had any idea that his profits would be used to obtain explosives.

Some of Ahmidan's drug-dealing contacts were located in a mining area in the Asturias region of northern Spain. Mines, explosives, drugs: a combustible mixture ready to be ignited by a corrupt former miner and contacts in the local drug underworld. One of those contacts was also a police informer, who tipped off his handler that Moroccans were in town looking for explosives. But nothing was done. I asked Manolo Navarette why, with the Casablanca bombings still fresh in the mind, the warning sign had not been heeded. He admitted the deficiency: 'Maybe we were focused on an Al Qaeda type of attack, more sophisticated and very well organised. We follow patterns,' he said. 'We were looking at how Al Qaeda was acting outside Spain, in Istanbul, in Bali, in New York.' That was Ahmidan's first lucky break. Then, on New Year's Eve 2003, he shot a drug dealer who hadn't paid his dues. It was hardly keeping a low profile, but Ahmidan got away. That was lucky break number two.

Two weeks before the bombings, the hash-for-cash – drugs-for-explosives – deal was done. Ahmidan handed over eighty kilos of Moroccan hash, and in return took collection of 150 kilos of GOMA-2 dynamite, normally used for blasting quarries, that had been hidden in a cache in the woods. The explosives were driven south in several batches to a secret location outside Madrid. Ahmidan now had his third slice of luck. He was driving south with the GOMA-2 in the boot when he was stopped by the police for speeding. He was given a fine, but the car wasn't searched.

The explosives were destined for a small farmhouse in Morata, several miles outside Madrid, that the cell had rented to use as their bomb-making base. The rental was made by Mustapha Maymouni, the brother-in-law of the estate agent Serhane Fakhet, who arranged the deal. There the cell had yet another lucky break. In the week before the bombing, the Guardia Civil received a phone call from neighbours expressing concern about the comings and goings of strangers at the farmhouse. A police unit was sent to investigate, but did not carry out a search.

In trying to build up a picture of the people and places involved in the lead-up to the bombings, I wanted to locate the farmhouse at Morata. All I had was the name of the village. Finding it wasn't easy, and once found, the farmhouse was even more elusive. I finally managed to come across it by a process of trial and error. It wasn't really a farmhouse, but a rundown bungalow hidden behind a high wire fence covered with green tarpaulin, perhaps to keep unwelcome eyes at bay. The gate was locked, and the place was obviously empty. I managed to find a hole in the fence, and squeezed through. The garden was overgrown with weeds and strewn with rubbish, including some white latex gloves. I wondered if they had been used by the bomb-makers, but thought it unlikely, as I assumed Scenes of Crime

Officers (SCOs) would have been over it with a fine-toothed comb. There was a big concrete hole where a swimming pool or large pond had once been. It clearly hadn't seen any swimmers or pond life for many years. I proceeded cautiously, worried about snakes. The door to the bungalow wasn't locked. Inside were a plastic imitation-leather couch and a table. The room smelled damp and musty. I stood there, thinking of what must have gone on inside and what conversations must have taken place. The kitchen was a mess, as if the occupants had left in a hurry. A large empty bottle of Mecca Cola, the Arab world's answer to Coke, stood on the draining board. I assumed it had been there on the evening before the attack, when the fourteen bombs were made ready and the timer alarms on the mobiles set for 7.40 the following morning. The mobiles would then have been wired to the bombs, the detonators put in place, and the deadly packages carefully placed in fourteen rucksacks.

Early on the morning of the next day, 11 March 2004, the bombers drove off in a white Renault van to the suburban commuter station of Alcalá de Henares, where they unloaded the rucksacks, put them on the trains and then left. They didn't intend to become suicide bombers, at least not yet. At 7.40, or seconds before, the timers on the mobiles were triggered. The carriages of four trains exploded. After visiting the abandoned bomb-factory farmhouse, I stood on the walkway above the platform at Atocha station and tried to imagine the horror that had been unleashed that day, as the carriages exploded in gigantic fireballs. In fact it did not require a great deal of imagination, as the scene had been captured on someone's camera or mobile phone and broadcast around the world.

The following day, two days before the general election, two million people packed the streets of Madrid to condemn the atrocity. The government was briefing journalists that ETA was behind the attacks, but it soon became clear that this wasn't the case. When police searched the van that the bombers had abandoned at Alcalá de Henares, they found detonators and *jihadi* tapes. Such tapes are invariably played before bombers set out either to do a recce or to carry out a bombing mission. Then came proof positive. A TV station received a phone call saying that a video had been left in a litter bin in the park outside the M-30 mosque. It featured the drug dealer Jamal Ahmidan, who described himself as Al Qaeda's military spokesman in Europe. He clearly linked the attack with Iraq: 'We declare our responsibility for what happened in Madrid, a response to your collaboration with the criminals Bush and his allies,' he said. 'This is a response to the crimes that you have caused the world and specifically in Iraq and Afghanistan, and there will be more, if God wills it. You want life and we want death.'

There were seismic repercussions. In the election on 14 March the People's Party government of José María Aznar fell, and the Spanish Socialists of José Luis Zapatero replaced it. One of the first things the new Prime Minister did was to announce that Spanish troops would be brought home from Iraq. On the face of it, this looked like a victory for terrorism, but it wasn't as simple as that. Zapatero had opposed President George W. Bush's foreign policy, and the vast majority of the Spanish electorate was against it too. Perhaps the most that can be said is that the bombings gave the new government the final push in a direction it was already heading.

The intelligence agencies believed that the Madrid bombings were only the beginning of a much wider campaign, hence the decision of the bombers not to become 'martyrs'. Their fears were confirmed three weeks later, when a bomb was found on the high-speed rail line between Madrid and Seville. The same explosives were used as in the Madrid bombings, but this time they failed to detonate. The cell was still at large. Where would they strike next? There had been a vital breakthrough when an unexploded bomb was found in the wreckage in Madrid, still attached to its mobile phone. The nerve-racking job of dismantling it was carried out by a bomb-disposal specialist, whose name cannot be disclosed for security reasons. 'I think all the bombs were probably made by the same person,' he told me. 'I've got to say that, personally, he did a very good job. They were brutally efficient. I didn't cut any wires with wire cutters, as I suspected that the bomb could be booby-trapped. So going very slowly, step by step, I eventually managed to take out the detonator.' He also managed to retrieve the SIM card, which would provide the vital clue to the whereabouts of the cell. It was traced to a batch purchased by Jamal Zougam for his mobile-phone shop in Lavapies. An electronic net was thrown over Madrid in the hope that one of the other SIM cards in the mobiles still being used by the cell would come flashing up. In time it did, and its location was pinpointed to an apartment in the Madrid outer suburb of Leganés.

The building was surrounded by Spanish special forces, who came under machine-gun fire from the apartment.[7] Inside were seven men, including the leaders of the cell, Serhane Fakhet and Jamal Ahmidan. Negotiations got nowhere. Blockaded inside, the cell members were prepared to die: they had dressed in the white robes of martyrdom and shaved their body hair as part of the ritual. Before they blew themselves up, final phone calls were made to relatives. Ahmidan rang his mother in Tangier. His uncle told me what happened. 'He said, "Mum, pray for me. We're all holy warriors and in a minute we're going to be with God." She came here in her car and said, "They are surrounded. They're going to be killed. They're going to be martyrs." And that's what did happen.' The cell detonated their explosives as the police were preparing to storm the apartment. The first officer through the door, Francisco Javier Torrenteras Gadea, was killed instantly. In the ruins, the remnants of a laptop were found which provided valuable data on the cell's contacts and future targets. One of them was the Bernabéu Stadium, home of Ahmidan's beloved Real Madrid. In further raids in Madrid and across Spain more than twenty other suspects were arrested, among them Jamal Zougam. Police also uncovered a wealth of cash, guns and computer files.

On 31 October 2007, twenty-one of the twenty-seven accused, most of them Moroccans, were sentenced to tens of thousands of years in gaol, a purely notional figure, as the maximum term that can legally be served is forty years. Four were acquitted on appeal.[8] Zougam was not one of them: he was sentenced to 43,000 years on ninety-one counts of murder.[9] His telephone days are over.

* * *

Although there is no evidence or intelligence that Al Qaeda directed the attacks on Casablanca and Madrid, at the same time 'core' Al Qaeda was actively giving approval and practical assistance in the planning of other attacks against the background of the war in Iraq. The United Kingdom, President George W. Bush's staunchest ally, was the next target. What was worrying for MI5 and MI6 was that the chain of operational command between *jihadis* in the UK and in Pakistan was strengthened and made more effective by the placing of British Muslim intermediaries in Pakistan to act as links between Al Qaeda's terrorist training areas and *jihadi* cells back in Britain. Two of these individuals, Salahuddin Amin from Luton and Rashid Rauf from Birmingham, would play crucial roles in the deadly plots that were soon to unfold in the UK.

ELEVEN

Terror on the Ground

In the summer of 2003 a group of British *jihadis* was training at an Al Qaeda camp near Malakand in Pakistan's North West Frontier Province. They were planning to bomb Britain, with the approval and facilitation of 'core' Al Qaeda. It is believed that the plot was not generated by 'core' Al Qaeda but by the British would-be *jihadis* themselves, with 'core' Al Qaeda's blessing. The investigation into the cell by MI5 and the Metropolitan Police became known as Operation Crevice.

Initially the group had gone to the Tribal Areas to train for *jihad* in Afghanistan, but Al Qaeda told them that there were already more than enough recruits to fight across the border, and that with their valuable British passports they would be of much greater use attacking targets in the UK. Al Qaeda's strategy was clear from Osama Bin Laden's taped message later that autumn, in which he threatened martyrdom operations against Britain and Spain for supplying troops for the 'unjust war in Iraq'.

The leader of the group was Omar Khyam, a young Muslim from Crawley, a dormitory town that supplies much of the workforce for nearby Gatwick airport. When I went to Crawley to try to find out more about him, I heard only good things, not just from his friends but from teachers at Hazelwick Comprehensive School, where he took his A-levels. Three other members of the cell, Jawad Akbar, Shujah Mahmood and Nabeel Hussain, were also former pupils of the school. It was unusual to find a school willing to talk about and face up to the fact that some of its promising pupils had become involved in terrorism. Normally journalists are stopped at the gates. The head teacher, Gordon Parry, was honest in facing up to a painful reality that bore no relationship to how he remembered his former students: 'My recollections are that they were normal, integrated, responsible members of the school community. They were popular, positive contributors, and there was absolutely no evidence that they had anything other than normal social and academic ambitions for themselves. I don't believe that anybody in school considered them in any way abnormal or extreme.' I asked one of the teachers, Sonia Alder, who taught the young Omar Khyam religious studies, how she regarded him. 'He was polite, always respectful and well behaved. A nice lad. A decent lad. But he wasn't just hard-working. He was also one of the boys, and fitted in very well. He played football for the school, and had lots of friends within the class.'[1] This is not what many would expect the profile of a future *jihadi* to be. How did things change? 'I don't know,' she said. 'I don't think he had those sort of beliefs when he was at school. I think that after he left school, something or somebody got hold of him and changed his mind.'

The something and someone that got hold of Omar Khyam was the extremist Islamist group Al-Muhajiroun, and its controversial leader Sheikh Omar Bakri Mohammed.* It achieved notoriety when it referred to the 9/11 hijackers as 'the Magnificent Nineteen'. Khyam had become involved with Al-Muhajiroun long before then, when he was still at school. Gordon Parry told me that another of Hazelwick's pupils had written in his end-of-school yearbook: 'One of his own ambitions would be to become the next Osama Bin Laden.'[2]

At the time Omar Khyam was a teenager, Omar Bakri Mohammed visited the Crawley area and gathered together a group of young

---

Al muhajiroun in Arabic means 'the emigrants'. The group has had a chequered and controversial history. On 29 April 2003 Asif Hanif, who had attended its study circles, became a suicide bomber, killing three people and injuring fifty-five others when he blew up 'Mike's Place', a bar in Tel Aviv. The British government banned the group in 2005, and prevented Omar Bakri from returning to Britain on the grounds that he was 'not conducive to the public good'. Some alleged members of the group reassembled under different names, the Saviour Sect and Al-Ghurabaa ('the strangers'). They were subsequently banned for 'glorification of terrorism', as was their alleged successor, Islam4UK.

Muslims whom he indoctrinated in a Scout hut in the woods. At one of their meetings in 1997 he told them: 'There is a time when military struggle must take place. *Jihad*. It's called conquering. One day without question, [Britain] is going to be governed by Islam … You must be ready to defend yourselves militarily.'[3] Gordon Parry thinks it was probably Bakri who visited Hazelwick School at around this time to deliver a lecture. The head teacher had had no idea what the young audience was in for: 'After his visit, one or two of the school governors expressed concern that he did represent a very extreme set of politico-religious views that weren't typical of Islam in Crawley.' Mr Parry told me that some of his students who attended local mosques and knew about Bakri expressed similar concerns.

But Omar Khyam was hooked. In 1999 he went to visit relatives in Pakistan, where he made contact with Kashmiri *jihadi* groups. Apparently his family had to drag him back to England to continue his studies. He returned to Pakistan to train for *jihad*, feeding his mother a cover story that he was moving to France to further his education. He came home radicalised and unrecognisable from the student Hazelwick School had known. Back in the UK, Khyam continued moving in *jihadi* circles, and met other like-minded young Muslims, many of them in Al-Muhajiroun's circle. One of them was Hassan Butt, another British-born Muslim, who lived in Manchester and travelled around the country addressing Al-Muhajiroun meetings and spreading the radicalising message. There is photographic and eyewitness evidence that he not only proselytised for Al-Muhajiroun, but played an active part in recruiting for *jihad*.

I met him over a curry and mango juice at a restaurant in Stretford Road in Manchester, which is lined with takeaways and mobile-phone shops, and could easily pass for a street in Islamabad or Lahore. Butt is a confident, articulate young man who was dealing in mobile phones when I met him. He was busy talking on two of them over lunch.

Al-Muhajiroun originally sent Hassan Butt to Pakistan to spread its message there, agitating for the establishment of *sharia* law and the removal of President Pervez Musharraf, whom he regarded as 'a traitor to Islam'. He was also there to channel recruits from Britain and

America to *jihadi* training camps in Pakistan, Kashmir and Afghanistan. 'We had the necessary contacts and links,' he told me. This was the route through which Omar Khyam and other members of the cell recruited around him travelled to an Al Qaeda camp. Butt facilitated travel to the same camp for a young American Muslim called Mohammed Junaid Babar, who was later to be turned, like Nasir Abbas, and would play a key part in Operation Crevice, helping to take down the cell and bring its members to justice.

Hassan Butt had no reason to doubt Babar's commitment to *jihad*. Ironically, his mother had narrowly escaped death in the World Trade Center attack, as he told Butt: 'I remember he said his first concern was whether his mother was OK, after which he was overjoyed with what had actually taken place.'4 While in Pakistan he gave a television interview in which he said: 'My intention is to go to Afghanistan and fight the Americans that have invaded and attacked our Muslim brothers and sisters. There is no negotiation with the Americans. I will kill every American that I see in Afghanistan, and every American I see in Pakistan.'5 This automatically put him on the FBI's radar.

Babar did much more than just give a television interview for propaganda purposes. He spent several months from the summer of 2003 providing a senior Al Qaeda official in South Waziristan with equipment destined for the *jihad* in Afghanistan, from night-vision goggles to waterproof socks. He had also helped to set up the training camp for the British *jihadis*, and supplied the weapons and the aluminium powder and ammonium nitrate that they needed to test explosives. Another key member of Khyam's cell who was training at the camp was Mohammed Momin Kawaja, a computer programmer from Ottawa whose parents originally came from Kashmir, and who was working under contract to the Canadian Ministry of Foreign Affairs. At the camp Khyam and the cell learned how to use an AK-47, experimented with rocket launchers, and mixed the chemicals to make a bomb. But they did not have the technical expertise to detonate it by remote control, and that was where Kawaja came in – he was able to construct the remote-control detonating device: Khyam and his fellow *jihadis* had no intention of becoming suicide bombers.

When the members of the cell returned to their respective homes in the UK, America and Canada they kept in touch by email and text messages. They had no idea that the traffic through the ether was to become part of their undoing.

The British, American and Canadian intelligence services had no specific information that a cell was training and getting ready to bomb Britain, although there were growing fears about the likelihood of such an attack, which had been anticipated since 9/11 and Bin Laden's threats to strike countries allied to the war in Iraq and Afghanistan. In 2004 I asked David Veness, head of the Metropolitan Police's Specialist Operations, about the likelihood of a suicide attack on the UK. His words were prophetic: 'A danger remains that there will be an attack, and I fear it is "when", within the United Kingdom. I think the "if" is academic.'[6]

How was Omar Khyam first identified, and how did Operation Crevice begin? He appeared on MI5's radar because some of its officers had been watching a man in Luton known as 'Q' (his full name is Mohammed Qayum Khan), who was connected to an Islamic centre above a fruit shop in the Pakistani area of the town.[7] MI5's surveillance of him began sometime during the spring or early summer of 2003, when it received intelligence that he was the leader of an 'Al Qaeda facilitation network' in Britain providing financial and logistical support.[8] He was believed to be at the UK end of a pipeline that channelled money, resources and recruits to Pakistan. Omar Khyam's involvement with him only came into the frame early the following year, 2004, when MI5 suspected that he was a courier for the network. It took the Security Service a considerable time to join up the dots; Operation Crevice turned into the largest operation MI5 and the police had ever undertaken. It had a global reach, and involved 45,000 man hours of monitoring and transcribing covertly recorded tapes, and 34,000 man hours of surveillance.[9]

Intelligence indicated that the key contact in Pakistan for the network – far more important than Hassan Butt – was another Muslim from Luton called Salahuddin Amin, who was believed to have been Omar Khyam's *emir* when the cell went to train in Pakistan.

The head of the Metropolitan Police Anti-Terrorist Branch, DAC Peter Clarke, had no doubt about Amin's role: 'Amin was a key facilitator acting as a link between young men in the United Kingdom and Al Qaeda in Pakistan,' he told me.[10]

'Q', Salahuddin Amin's putative *emir* in Britain, was obviously a canny and suspicious operator. When he visited Pakistan he was convinced that he was being watched by the ISI, and he assumed, correctly, when he returned to England that he was being watched by MI5. Deciding that things might be getting a bit hot, he handed over his responsibilities for feeding potential British *jihadis* down the pipeline to the training camps in Pakistan to another man, who in due course, perhaps for similar reasons of personal security, handed them over to Omar Khyam. That was how Khyam came to be 'a person of interest' to MI5 in late January 2004.

Omar Khyam and the other members of the cell left the camp in Pakistan around 5 August 2003, and a fortnight later the Canadian Momin Kawaja sent an email to the Pakistani woman he was planning to marry. He said he had been able 'to join a few brothers and spend time in a *mujahideen* training camp. It was there that we built our spiritual link with Allah, trained in the ways of *jihad* and devoted our lives to the uplifting of the *deen* [the Islamic way of life] and the defence of the *ummah*.'

Back in the UK, Khyam and the rest of the cell were busy too. Khyam had smuggled a quantity of aluminium powder in his suitcase, and he hid it in a biscuit tin by a shed in his mother's back garden in Crawley.[11] The priority was to get hold of enough of the other vital ingredient, ammonium nitrate fertiliser, to make either one huge bomb or several smaller ones. The quantity required would not fit in the boot of a car, so Khyam rented a truck using his own Barclaycard, hardly the act of a sophisticated *jihadi*. On 5 November 2003 another member of the cell, Anthony Garcia, went to place the order with an agricultural merchant in West Sussex called Bodle Brothers. The salesman was a little surprised when Garcia said he wanted six hundred kilograms. 'What's it for?' the salesman asked. Garcia said it was for his allotment. 'That would do twenty allotments, that amount of fertiliser,' the salesman pointed out. 'I'll probably be sharing it with other people who also have allotments,' Garcia replied. He bought the six hundred kilograms for £105.75. 'I hope you're not going around bombing anything with this thing,' the salesman joked as Garcia left. The following week the consignment was driven to a lock-up company called Access Self Storage in Hanwell, west London.

Meanwhile, on the other side of the Atlantic, Momin Kawaja was busy putting the remote-control detonating device together. On 30 November he reported on his progress in an email: 'Things go good. We started at work on the project again. We still need a few weeks, bro. It's not as easy as we thought it would be. Lots of custom electrical work, equipment, but it should be excellent once it's finished.'[12]

MI5 knew nothing about these developments. It was only at the beginning of 2004 that the Security Service began to realise that Khyam was a significant player, and potentially posed a serious threat. He was placed under surveillance, and notes were made on all his associates. The pieces of the intelligence jigsaw gradually came together after cars and flats were bugged and mobiles, texts and emails were monitored. Operation Crevice had now expanded well beyond its beginnings, with the surveillance of 'Q'.

On 13 February 2004 Omar Khyam, now under intensive human and technical surveillance, rang Salahuddin Amin, his contact in Pakistan, on his mobile to tell him that he had six hundred kilograms of explosives, but couldn't remember the recipe for the mixture. Amin was a little put out, as Khyam had been taught this at the Malakand training camp.[13] The message, or an ancillary communication, was picked up by the NSA's formidable listening post at Fort Meade, Maryland. The Americans passed on the warning to the British, and alarm bells began to ring even more loudly. 'Operation Crevice moved into a higher gear,' Peter Clarke told me. The fear was that Khyam's cell might be getting ready for an attack.

A week later, there was a major breakthrough when a member of staff at Access Self Storage in Hanwell rang the police to express concern about a large quantity of ammonium nitrate that was being stored in one of its lock-ups. At this stage the police didn't make the connection with Omar Khyam, as the fertiliser wasn't stored in his name. In the middle of the night, officers gained entry to the lock-up to take a sample of the contents of the huge bag and establish that it was in fact ammonium nitrate. Tests immediately showed that it was, and the trap was set. The contents of the bag were replaced with six hundred kilograms of a substitute, possibly cat litter, and a covert camera was installed to capture anybody who came and went. The police then waited.

On Friday, 20 February, the same day Access Self Storage tipped off the police about the fertiliser, Momin Kawaja flew into Heathrow, where he was met by Omar Khyam. Kawaja had told his mother he was meeting a girl he'd met on the internet. Neither he nor Khyam suspected that Khyam's Suzuki Vitara was being bugged. In the car, Khyam stressed the need for secrecy: 'We don't want to mix too many things together. We only work one thing with one group, because if you start to mix too many people in this life, you get caught.'[14] The two men then went to the Universal and Video internet café in Slough, where Kawaja downloaded pictures of his detonating device and showed them to Khyam.

Two days later, on Sunday, 22 February, a listening device planted in the flat of one of Khyam's associates picked up the first direct reference to a possible target for a terrorist attack. Khyam was talking to Jawad Akbar, another member of the cell. Akbar made a reference to 'the biggest nightclub in central London, where no one can turn round and say, "Oh they were innocent, those slags dancing around"'. Khyam then asked him what he would do if he got a job in a bar 'like the Ministry of Sound'. 'Blow the whole thing up,' Akbar replied. They then discussed other targets. Khyam suggested the public utilities: 'Electricity, gas, stuff like this I'm saying is good. Get the brothers in each and every field. Water. Everything.' There's then an ironic exchange. Khyam suddenly appears to get the jitters and asks Akbar, 'You don't think this place is bugged, do you?' Akbar is dismissive. 'No, I don't think it's bugged, bruv, at all. I don't even think the car's bugged. If they knew about it they wouldn't wait a day, bro. They wouldn't wait a day to arrest me, yeah, or any of us.'[15] But it was only a matter of time. That same evening Kawaja flew back to Canada, where the Canadian intelligence services, who were working closely with the British, kept him under close surveillance.

Three weeks later, on 12 March, Omar Khyam paid a visit to Access Self Storage to check on the ammonium nitrate. He didn't know that the woman on reception was a specialist police officer with the cover name 'Amanda'. By this time the police and MI5 had little doubt that the bag of fertiliser and the intelligence they had been picking up on their bugs were related to the same plot. All they needed was proof. Khyam walked straight into the trap, and was captured on the covert camera in the lock-up as he walked in and examined the bag.

A week later, on 19 March, the bug in Khyam's car picked up another alarming conversation, between Khyam and a fellow conspirator, Waheed Mahmood. Large sections of the audio tapes are very indistinct, but it is evident that they were discussing another possible target, the giant Bluewater shopping centre to the east of London. 'Bluewater's only an hour [away],' said Mahmood. 'Might as well do one to see what it's like. Do one tomorrow if you wanted to. I don't know how big it would be because we haven't tested it. We know it's going to work, *insh'allah* [God willing]. Tomorrow. Do one tomorrow.' DAC Peter Clarke summed up his reaction: 'You can imagine what a large bomb would do to Bluewater on a day when it's crowded with shoppers. Totally indiscriminate, completely deadly, absolutely devastating. And that's what they were thinking in terms of. It just confirmed to us that we were dealing with a very serious plot indeed.'[16] If there was any doubt that the conspirators would not shrink from slaughtering innocent civilians, it would have evaporated when they were heard referring to the Madrid bombings of 6 March 2004 as 'fantissimo' and 'absolutely beautiful'.

When the police discovered that Omar Khyam had bought a ticket to fly to Pakistan on 6 April, they decided they could not risk waiting any longer, fearing that he was preparing to get out of the country after an attack. On 29 March the green light was given, and the cell was taken down. The Canadians moved first, arresting Momin Kawaja at his home in Ottawa. They wanted to make sure he wasn't alerted by the arrests in the UK, which would have given him the opportunity to destroy any evidence. When the police searched his house they found a radio frequency transmitter, receiver boards, a grenade launcher, a Norinco M-14 assault rifle, 640 rounds of ammunition and $10,000 Canadian in cash.

The UK arrests were meticulously coordinated for 06.00 hours the following morning, so no member of the cell could tip off the others. Jawad Akbar was arrested at 05.58; Anthony Garcia at 06.05; Omar Khyam at 06.08, in room 440 of the Holiday Inn in Horley; and Waheed Mahmood at 06.10. Two other suspects were also arrested: Nabeel Hussein at 05.58, and Shujah Mahmood at 06.11. At the same time armed police wearing body armour also visited Salahuddin Amin's sister, Fauzia, in Luton. 'At 6 o'clock there was this really loud knock on the door,' she told me. 'I kept on asking them, "What is the reason that you are here?" and one of the forensic officers said, "Watch the TV and you'll know."' She did, and soon found out.

The arrests in England and Canada had repercussions in Pakistan. Two days later Salahuddin Amin gave himself up, and volunteered to meet the ISI at the home of a well-connected uncle. He said he wanted 'to clear the allegations they were making against me', but failed to convince them, and was arrested. He was held and interrogated for ten months by the ISI, during which he alleges he was severely tortured: 'I felt as if my skin was being ripped apart,' he said.[17] He claims he was repeatedly beaten and abused, constantly humiliated and threatened with an electric drill. He says his interrogators threatened to 'make a second hole' in his bottom. 'They were doing this to break me. I started saying to them that I would agree with whatever they would want me to.'[18] He said that after the torture he was visited on several occasions by MI5 officers and questioned about his activities and contacts with Omar Khyam's cell and others.

I had long talks with Amin's solicitor and his uncle, who had facilitated the handover to the ISI, and concluded that much of what he alleged about being tortured may well have been true. The ISI have a fearsome reputation. I also asked DAC Peter Clarke what he thought of Amin's claims. 'I have no reason to believe or disbelieve him,' he said. 'I have no knowledge as to what happened to him when he was in Pakistan.' So was he denying the possibility that Amin could have been tortured? 'I'm neither confirming nor denying, because I simply do not know,' he replied. Did he or anybody else in Britain ask the ISI what they had done to Amin? 'I haven't been in contact with the ISI,' he said. An anonymous senior officer from the ISI's Counter-Terrorist Unit whom I interviewed in Pakistan flatly denied that torture was used. I suspected he was never going to say anything else.

When Salahuddin Amin was released from custody in Pakistan he was free to return to England, and Peter Clarke's officers from the Anti-Terrorist Branch were waiting for him when his plane landed. He was taken to west London's Paddington Green high-security police station, and interviewed again. In the police video of the interview which was played at the subsequent court case, Amin, with his lawyer at his side, seems perfectly relaxed and cooperative. He talks about the Malakand training camp, and how Omar Khyam and the others had been taught to use ammonium nitrate to make a bomb. He says that Khyam had told him that 'they wanted to get explosive training to do something in the UK', although he adds, 'I didn't know what their intention was.'[19] He later said that his Pakistani interrogators had told him that if he came clean and told everything to the British police when he returned to the UK, everything would be all right. It wasn't: Amin was arrested and charged.

Meanwhile, Mohammed Junaid Babar, who had helped set up the Malakand training camp, had returned to New York, where he was working for a taxi company. He was detained by the FBI on 6 April 2004, taken to a hotel and questioned, and was formally arrested a few days later. Like the Canadian *jihadi* Mohammed Jabarah, who'd met Hambali in Bangkok before the Bali bombings, he cut a deal with the FBI, agreeing to plead guilty and cooperate with the authorities, including giving evidence against his former associates in Omar

Khyam's cell. FBI agents spent most of the rest of the year debriefing him, getting the most minute details of who he had met and what he and they had done. Once again, talking to terrorists paid dividends, as Babar became the Al Qaeda supergrass to end all supergrasses.

Babar was flown to Britain to give evidence against his former 'brothers' at their trial at the Old Bailey. It was to prove crucial. I spent many days in the hot courtroom in the summer of 2006 watching him do so. He was controlled, calm and credible. The trial lasted thirteen long months, and the jury was out for a nailbiting twenty-seven days. The verdict finally came on 30 April 2007. Five members of the cell were convicted: Omar Khyam, Salahuddin Amin, Jawad Akbar, Waheed Mahmood and Anthony Garcia. All were sentenced to life imprisonment. Shujah Mahmood and Nabeel Hussain, Khyam's fellow alumni of Hazelwick School, were found not guilty on all charges.

Following the successful conclusion of Operation Crevice, DAC Peter Clarke issued a statement on behalf of the Metropolitan Police:

> This case marked a new stage in our understanding of the threat posed by Al Qaeda to this country. The investigation showed the links that these men had with Al Qaeda in Pakistan … This was not a group of youthful idealists. They were trained, dedicated, ruthless terrorists who were obviously planning to carry out an attack against the British public … At the time it was the largest counter-terrorism operation ever seen in the UK. The success was achieved through close cooperation and sharing of intelligence between the UK, the USA, Canada and Pakistan.[20]

Mohammed Junaid Babar had delivered on his part of his bargain with the FBI, and he would do the same in Canada at the trial of Momin Kawaja. On 12 March 2009 Kawaja was sentenced in Ottawa's Superior Court to ten and a half years in prison – in addition to the five years he'd already served since his arrest – for financing and facilitating terrorism. Babar is now living under the FBI's Witness Protection Scheme. I tried to get him to agree to an interview, but he didn't want to know. According to the US Justice Department he still has to be sentenced, and is expected to give evidence in other *jihadi* trials – as some members of the Lackawanna Six have done.

There was one piece of crucial information that Babar provided but which at the time meant nothing to his FBI debriefers or to the MI5 officers to whom it was passed on. While listing the names of those who had trained at the Malakand camp with Omar Khyam, Babar said that there was one who was called 'Ibrahim'. He didn't know his real name. It subsequently turned out that 'Ibrahim' was Mohammed Saddique Khan (MSK), who went on to become the leader of the cell that bombed London on 7 July 2005. It was only much later, when Babar saw a newspaper photograph taken from Khan's suicide video broadcast after the attacks, that he realised who 'Ibrahim' was. By then it was too late.

Omar Khyam remained in touch with Mohammed Saddique Khan after they returned to England. The fact that MI5 failed to recognise the significance of this connection represented a serious intelligence failure. MI5 was under great pressure at the time, and came across around 4,000 contacts as a result of Operation Crevice alone. Nor did it have the increased resources and personnel that it was later given in the wake of the 7 July 2005 bombings. How did the intelligence failure happen, and could it have been avoided?

During their surveillance of Omar Khyam and the Crevice conspirators, MI5 officers had come across MSK and one of the other 7/7 bombers, Shehzad Tanweer, although they didn't know who they were, or recognise the serious terrorist threat they were to pose. At one stage a bug in Khyam's Vitara had even recorded Khyam talking to MSK. He was simply thought to be someone on the periphery of Khyam's group, and from the tenor of the bugged conversation it was assumed that his connection was related to financial fraud, not to terrorism. Shehzad Tanweer was also in the car with Khyam and MSK.

On 2 February 2004, only a few days after surveillance on Omar Khyam had been activated, MSK and Shehzad Tanweer were seen in Khyam's company, although their identities were not known. In the hours that followed a significant lead emerged that, as we will see, was not fully followed up at the time. MI5 considered the suspects to be of sufficient interest to warrant Security Service officers following MSK's Honda up the M1 to their homes in West Yorkshire.

In the controversy that raged after the attacks on London,* when it was disclosed that MI5 had come across and 'housed' two of the bombers, MI5 said that they had never been under its definition of 'surveillance'. It was all a question of semantics. Tailing suspects nearly two hundred miles up the motorway and noting addresses at the end did not qualify as 'surveillance' in MI5's book. MI5 said that MSK and Tanweer had cropped up on the periphery of other investigations,[21] but had not been judged to be serious enough 'players', and crucially there was no indication at the time that they were planning an attack in the United Kingdom.

I took a personal interest in the controversy, as I had had sight of the MI5 surveillance log of the officers who followed MSK and Tanweer up the M1 on 2 February 2004. The log indicated that they had stopped off at Toddington services to fill up with petrol. When MSK went inside, he was covertly photographed near the Burger King outlet. The photograph is indistinct, and wouldn't meet identity-parade standards, but he can be roughly identified. (MSK had been covertly photographed earlier by undercover West Yorkshire Police officers in 2001 while taking part in an Outward Bound-style exercise with other Muslim 'brothers'. It was not known who he was at the time.) The MI5 team then followed the car for another 150 miles up the M1 and watched MSK drop two of his passengers off at Lodge Lane and Tempest Road in the Leeds area. One of them was thought to be Shehzad Tanweer. The MI5 log notes the addresses. MSK was then followed to Dewsbury, where he left the Honda outside the house where he was living with his wife, Hasina Patel. Again the address was recorded in the Security Service log.

---

*The details of what MI5, the Metropolitan Police and West Yorkshire Police did and did not know about MSK and Shehzad Tanweer *before* the 7/7 attacks is complicated. It is covered at great length in the hundred-page report of the Parliamentary Intelligence and Security Committee, 'Could 7/7 Have Been Prevented?' It concluded that MI5's decisions were not at fault. See Epilogue for update on 7/7 inquest coroner's report.

The question that puzzled me was, what happened immediately afterwards? If MI5 itself hadn't followed up the leads because MSK and Tanweer weren't deemed to be priority targets, one would have assumed that it would have asked West Yorkshire Police's Special Branch to take an interest, keep an eye on the suspects and report back, given their observed connections with a potential terrorist like Omar Khyam. That seemed the obvious thing to do, given the pressure MI5 was under at the time, with so many other emerging terrorist cases and multiple suspects to watch. There were fifty-five suspects in Operation Crevice – in addition to the 4,000 'contacts' – and MI5 had dozens of other cases on its radar, most of them requiring intensive surveillance.[22]

I had got to know the West Yorkshire Police well over the years. I had met its former Chief Constable, Colin Sampson, a man of great probity, while investigating the Stalker affair in the late 1980s.* I also knew one of his successors, the late Colin Cramphorn, whom I'd met in Northern Ireland when he was Sir Ronnie Flanagan's Deputy Chief Constable. We shared an interest in Irish and Islamist terrorism, and occasionally met over tea and sandwiches at police headquarters in Wakefield. I also knew some of Mr Cramphorn's senior officers. I started to make enquiries. Had MI5 informed West Yorkshire Special Branch or West Yorkshire Police shortly after following the suspects up the M1 and 'housing' them in West Yorkshire's patch? The answer was no. I asked the question of several senior officers, and got the same response. I found it difficult to believe, but I didn't think they would lie to me and betray a trust that had been built up over nearly twenty years. It was a sensitive subject.

Further confirmation that my concerns were justified came a couple of years later, when I was talking on another matter to a very senior officer in the West Yorkshire Police, who for the first time

---

*John Stalker, the Deputy Chief Constable of Greater Manchester Police, was asked to investigate the so-called 'shoot to kill' incidents in Northern Ireland in the early 1980s, but was suspended from the inquiry in controversial circumstances. Colin Sampson was asked to investigate Stalker's conduct, and then took over the inquiry. See my book *Stalker: The Search for the Truth.*

volunteered the information, without any prompting from me, that MI5 had never told the force about following MSK and Tanweer up the M1 to their homes in the heart of West Yorkshire. It was later further revealed in the Parliamentary Intelligence and Security Committee (ISC) report, 'Could 7/7 Have Been Prevented?' – referrred to in detail in the following paragraph – that on 28 February 2004 a Metropolitan Police Service (MPS) surveillance team followed the same Honda Civic with the same suspects to two of the same locations in the Leeds area, Tempest Road and Lodge Lane, to which the MI5 team had tracked them almost three weeks earlier. The following day, the Metropolian Police ran a check on the Honda and found that it was registered to 'Sidique Khan'. As we are about to see, ownership had been transferred from his wife. Again, there's no indication that West Yorkshire Special Branch were informed of the MPS surveillance operation. At the time of 'Operation Crevice', again according to the ISC report, information supplied to West Yorkshire appears to have been on a 'need to know' basis – meaning that the recipients were not necessarily told 'the full details and background'. Although it's using hindsight, the question remains, might 7/7 have been prevented if West Yorkshire Police Special Branch had been given the full picture from the very beginning?

When the ISC later investigated the intelligence available on MSK before the 7/7 bombings, it became clear what had happened and what had not. The ISC reported that MI5 had initially checked out the Honda's registration, and traced it to Hasina Patel of 10 Thornhill Park, Dewsbury. On 16 February 2004, two weeks after following the Honda up the M1, MI5 asked West Yorkshire Police to check out her name and address against their databases 'to enable us to fully identify any potential associates of Khyam'. The ISC report concluded: 'Nothing significant was found and, with no evidence to justify further action, none was taken.'[23] It notes that there was 'no record of a written response to this request'.[24] It was only later discovered that Hasina Patel was the wife of MSK, whom she'd married in October 2001. So MI5 had informed West Yorkshire Police in general terms, but crucially had not apparently gone into detail about the surveillance operation up the M1, or their concern about the connections of the unidentified men in the Honda with their main target in Operation Crevice, Omar Khyam.

The reason for the lack of detailed communication between MI5 and West Yorkshire Special Branch is provided in the ISC report. Local Special Branches were only told what they needed to know, and no more. Circumstances only changed if the police received a 'cluster' message of secure communications from MI5. The ISC report defines a 'cluster' as a secure form of communication used by MI5 and the police that contains operational intelligence and requests for information checks to be carried out. In this case, West Yorkshire Police received the registration of the Honda but no operational detail about why the enquiry was being made. The Chief Constable of West Yorkshire Police, Sir Norman Bettison, told the ISC Committee:

> In fact there was an unwritten protocol that we did not act; we in a sense did not get out of bed until we had received a cluster message or unless there had been a very high-level conversation between somebody at Thames House [MI5 headquarters] and the head of the Special Branch ... The Met SB ... and other Special Branches operated independently.

West Yorkshire Police was only given detailed intelligence – perhaps of the 'cluster' variety – about Mohammed Saddique Khan on 8 June 2004 – that's over four months after MI5 had first followed his Honda up the M1 and almost two months after Omar Khyam and his cell were arrested on 30 March. It was an institutional failure. It could be argued that four months would hardly make any difference, but it should be borne in mind that by then the Crevice cell had already been arrested, which probably meant that MSK and Tanweer had been alerted and gone to ground.

After MI5 initially declined to share detailed intelligence with West Yorkshire Police and ask its Special Branch to follow up the leads, a series of regional counter-terrorist centres (CTUs) – with hubs initially in London, the West Midlands, Greater Manchester and West

Yorkshire – were set up in which MI5 officers and police officers worked side by side and shared intelligence. Although these CTUs had been on the drawing board for some time, their final implementation after the July bombings underlined the pressing need for the different arms of the intelligence services to work more closely together. In the case of Operation Crevice this had not happened. One UK Chief Constable told me that before the London bombings, MI5 officers were based at his headquarters but their doors were kept firmly locked. After 7/7, he said, the doors were always open and there was a free flow of intelligence that there had not been before. The lesson was learned, but, it could be argued with hindsight, at terrible cost.*

---

*More light was shed when Lady Justice Hallett, the coroner at the inquest into the 7/7 bombings, heard evidence early in 2011 on what intelligence MI5 had on MSK before the London attacks, and what action was taken upon it. The Security Service had argued that if its evidence was heard in public, national security would be put at risk, but the High Court ruled that it should be heard in open court. The Home Office did not appeal. See Epilogue.

TWELVE

Clean Skins

At lunchtime on the day before the 7/7 bombers struck, I happened to be passing Trafalgar Square, which was packed with thousands of people waiting to hear the result of London's bid to host the 2012 Olympic Games. There were wild scenes of jubilation when it was announced that the city had won. As I stood in the warm summer sunshine, I couldn't help thinking that an event like this was wide open for a terrorist attack. I'd just finished recording the commentary for my documentary on the Madrid bombings in an edit suite close by, so terrorism was fresh in my mind. I remembered what DAC David Veness had told me some time before, that an attack on the United Kingdom was a question of 'when', not 'if'. I never imagined that my fears would become dreadful reality the following day.

In Luton, Thursday, 7 July 2005 dawned grey and wet. At 7.21 a.m., CCTV cameras at the town's railway station picked up four figures with rucksacks on their way to the London platform. They were Mohammed Saddique Khan and three other members of his cell, Shehzad Tanweer, Germaine Lindsay and Hasib Hussein, on their way to catch the early commuter train to the capital. All were 'clean skins', individuals not known or suspected by the intelligence services. (Although MI5 had come across Khan and Tanweer the previous year, they had failed to connect them to the operational planning of any terrorist plot.) Three were British-born Muslims of Pakistani origin. Lindsay, a convert to Islam, had been born in Jamaica. Khan, Tanweer and Hussein had come down from Yorkshire: Khan from Dewsbury, and Tanweer and Hussein from the Beeston area of Leeds. On their way down the M1 they'd stopped off at Woodall services and bought petrol, bottled water, Ginster's cheese-and-onion slices and Walkers Sensations crisps. Lindsay had driven from Aylesbury in Buckinghamshire and had met up with the other three at Luton. Their rucksacks were packed with explosives.

After their train arrived at King's Cross they headed for the Underground. At around 8.50, three of them detonated their bombs, as arranged. Tanweer's exploded first, on the Circle Line between Aldgate and Liverpool Street, then Khan's, at Edgware Road station, and Lindsay's on the Piccadilly Line between Russell Square and King's Cross.[1] At 9.47 there was a fourth explosion, on a number 30 double-decker bus in Tavistock Place, near King's Cross station. The bomb was detonated by Hasib Hussein, the youngest member of the cell. It's speculated that he may have intended to take the Northern Line from King's Cross, but when he found that it wasn't operating that morning, he left the Underground along with thousands of other evacuated passengers after the three 8.50 bombs had gone off. He then took the bus, and detonated his bomb on board. Photographs of the mangled wreckage are among the indelible images of that day. Fifty-two people died in the attacks, and over seven hundred were injured. All four bombers were also killed. It was the biggest attack on London since the Blitz.

I got up early that morning to finish off some work and walk my dog, Josh. It may have been raining in Luton, but where I lived outside London the sun was shining brightly. Before I left home for work I needed to ring my office to let my colleagues know roughly what time I would be in. I was a little puzzled when I couldn't get through. I didn't think much of it, assuming that there must be a fault on the line. I got into the car and headed for the motorway into London just after 9 o'clock, to avoid the worst of the rush hour. I didn't switch on the car radio, as I'd heard the news just before leaving. Half an hour or so later I read a flashing sign on the gantry above the motorway advising motorists to avoid central London, as there had been an incident. I immediately switched on the news, and my mobile started to ring. That evening I scribbled a brief entry in my diary:

The nightmare has come true. Terrorists attacked London in the rush hour this morning. Over 30 dead. What a contrast to the euphoria of yesterday. Almost certainly AQ. What price 'The Power of Nightmares'?

The Power of Nightmares was a Bafta-award-winning documentary series made by my colleague Adam Curtis that had been transmitted around the same time as my second series on Islamist extremism, *The New Al Qaeda*, which included the documentary on the Madrid bombings. Adam's documentaries were brilliant, but I disagreed with their thesis: that the terrorist threat had been hugely exaggerated by governments as an excuse to curb civil liberties and increase control over their citizens. I believed the threat was real, and not hype. The carnage that morning proved it.

The families of the four suicide bombers were devastated. None had imagined that their husbands and sons would ever contemplate massacring their fellow citizens. All four were known to be deeply religious, praying five times a day, but so did many of the UK's 1.6 million Muslims, and they didn't become terrorists.

Mohammed Saddique Khan was respected in his community and by the parents of the children with special needs whom he taught as a classroom assistant at Hillside Primary School in Beeston.[2] 'The children loved him and looked up to him,' one mother said. 'He showed a lot of enthusiasm in the classroom, and knew how to get the best out of the children. I could not believe it when I heard he had been involved in this. He must have been leading a double life.'[3] The thirty-year-old Khan came from a moderate and respectable family background, and to outsiders appeared to be comfortable being a British Asian. He had many non-Muslim friends who called him 'Sid', a nickname with which he seemed comfortable. The only outward clue to his radicalisation was his association with the Iqra bookshop in Beeston, which was also a study centre with a reputation for radical Salafist* teaching.[4] In 2002 he married Hasina Patel, an Indian

---

*Salafis want to return Islam to its purest, fundamentalist form, as practised in the time of the Prophet Mohammed in the seventh century AD. Wahhabism has broadly the same aim. As a general rule, all Wahhabis are Salafists but not all Salafists are Wahhabis.

Muslim, whose mother Farina had once received an invitation to a garden party at Buckingham Palace in recognition of her community work. Khan and Hasina had met at Leeds Metropolitan university in 1997,[5] and later married for love, not because their parents had arranged it according to Pakistani Muslim custom. 'He was a good family man,' Hasina, wearing a *burqa*, told Sky News on the second anniversary of 7/7.[6] They had a young daughter who Khan adored. When police searched his home after the attacks they found a video in which he is saying goodbye to the little girl. Although it is moving it is also deeply disturbing, and leaves no doubt as to his commitment to what he was about to do. 'I just so much wanted to be with you,' he tells her in a broad Yorkshire accent, 'but I have to do this for our future and it will be for the best, *insh'allah*, in the long run ... And I'm doing what I'm doing for the sake of Islam, not, you know, for materialistic or worldly benefits.'[7]

As Khan was making his preparations to bomb London, Hasina was heavily pregnant with their second child: she miscarried on the day of the bombings. When she heard about the attacks, and then of her husband's involvement in them, she was shocked. 'I can't believe that people can do that kind of thing. How can you be so calculated and cold and not have any emotions ... I think he was probably misled and brainwashed by the wrong people ... If someone had done that to my daughter, I would never forgive them.' The question that confronted Khan's family and friends, and the nation at large, was why a young British-born Muslim from a good background and a stable family would commit such a heinous crime. The answer was given in the video he'd previously recorded, probably while training in Pakistan, and that was transmitted after the attacks. Echoing the bombers of Bali and Madrid, he blamed British and American foreign policy in Iraq, Afghanistan and Palestine, although the words themselves were not mentioned in his diatribe:

Your democratically elected governments continuously perpetuate atrocities against my people all over the world. And your support of them makes you directly responsible, just as I am directly responsible

Attacks on four crowded commuter trains in Madrid on 11 March 2004 left 191 people dead and almost two thousand injured.

A surveillance camera captures three of the four London bombers (left to right), Shehzad Tanweer, Germaine Lindsay and Mohammed Saddique Khan, as they enter Luton station on a practice run for their journey to the capital on the morning of 7 July 2005.

Hasib Husain, the fourth bomber, aged eighteen, detonated his bomb on the number 30 bus in Tavistock Square.

In 2006 the author travelled
to the mountainous interior of
Brazil to meet Matazinhos
and Maria, the parents of Jean
Charles de Menezes, who was
shot dead by Metropolitan
Police firearms officers at
Stockwell Underground
station on 22 July 2005 after
being mistakenly identified as
a terrorist suspect.

Abu Hamza, the radical *imam*
of Finsbury Park mosque in
London, became a hate figure
in the British popular press.
His fiery sermons played their
part in radicalising many
young British Muslims.

Sheikh Omar Bakri Mohammed, the leader of the extreme Islamist group Al-Muhajiroun, who attempted to recruit British Muslims as *jihadis*.

Sheikh Abdullah al-Faisal arriving at Bow Street magistrates' court in 2002, prior to his trial the following year. Found guilty of inciting murder and stirring up racial hatred, he was sentenced to nine years in prison.

The bleak top-security Belmarsh prison in south-east London, where many of Britain's convicted terrorists and terrorist suspects are held.

The radical preacher Abu Qatada, who was imprisoned in 2006.

Suspected Al Qaeda and Taliban detainees at Guantánamo
Bay. Human-rights abuses at Guantánamo and elsewhere
have provided Al Qaeda with powerful propaganda.

Mohammed al-Awfi, one of fourteen Saudi Arabians, known as 'Batch Ten', who were repatriated from Guantánamo in November 2007. He alleges that he was tortured by the Americans while he was being held in Afghanistan.

The radical American-Yemeni cleric Anwar Al-Awlaki, who was believed to have helped radicalise the American Muslim army officer Major Nidal Malik Hasan, who in November 2009 shot dead thirteen of his colleagues at Fort Hood in Texas. He was also said to have influenced Umar Farouq Abdulmuttalab, a young Nigerian who had studied in London and who tried to blow up a passenger plane over Detroit on Christmas Day 2009.

A computer printer cartridge containing the explosive PETN (pentaerythritol tetranitrate) that was found in a cargo plane bound from Yemen to Chicago in October 2010.

A pilotless 'drone', of the type increasingly used by the CIA to target suspected terrorists in Afghanistan and the border regions of Pakistan.

for protecting and avenging my Muslim brothers and sisters. Until we feel security you will be our targets and until you stop the bombing, gassing, imprisonment and torture of my people we will not stop this fight. We are at war and I am a soldier. Now you too will taste the reality of this situation.[8]

Shehzad Tanweer, aged twenty-two, was described by friends as 'a nice lad' who could 'get on with anyone'. His family was firmly rooted in West Yorkshire, where his father ran a fish-and-chip shop in Beeston. An uncle said his nephew was 'proud to be British and had everything to live for. His parents were loving and supportive.'[9] He was a sports science graduate who loved cricket and athletics, and had a bedroom full of trophies he had won. He too was associated with the Iqra bookshop, where he worked. Again, his family and friends could not believe that he would ever contemplate becoming involved in mass murder. He also made a video that was broadcast on the Al-Jazeera Arab network on the first anniversary of 7/7. This time Iraq, Afghanistan and Palestine were mentioned, as was Chechnya. Tanweer proclaimed that non-Muslims in Britain deserved the attacks because they had voted for a government that 'continues to oppress our mothers, children, brothers and sisters in Palestine, Afghanistan, Iraq and Chechnya':

What you have witnessed now is only the beginning of a string of attacks that will continue and become stronger until you pull your forces out of Afghanistan and Iraq. And until you stop your financial and military support to America and Israel.[10]

Hasib Hussein, at eighteen the youngest of the attackers, who blew up the number 30 bus, was sporty too, with a passionate love of football and cricket: he played cricket for his local team, and had ambitions to become a professional. He was a quiet boy who lived at home as part of 'a very nice family'.[11] He left school in 2003, with seven GCSEs. In his last year he went on a pilgrimage to Mecca and then travelled to Pakistan, returning to Beeston bearded and wearing Islamic robes, and newly equipped with radical ideas. He wrote 'Al Qaeda. No Limits' on his religious textbook, spoke openly about the 9/11 bombers being 'martyrs',[12] and told teachers he wanted to be an *imam* when he left school.[13] Two days after the bombings his mother rang the police, anxious because her son had gone to London and had not been heard of since. He'd said he'd gone to visit friends, and she was desperately worried that he might have been caught up in the bombings. His elder brother even drove to London to try to find him. The family only discovered what had happened when his driving licence and cash cards were found in the wreckage of the bus.[14]

The nineteen-year-old Germaine Lindsay was described to me by one of his fellow converts as 'very friendly, pleasant, smiling and calm'.[15] He displayed some of the factors that are common in some, but by no means all, young *jihadis*: a fractured family background, vulnerability, insecurity and alienation from mainstream society. He was born in Jamaica, and never knew his father, who left shortly after he was born. He was brought up by his mother Maryam, who moved to England in 1986. She subsequently returned to the Caribbean, and a BBC colleague, Cheryl Varley, spent several days talking to her at her home in Grenada in February 2006 as part of her research for a planned BBC drama documentary on the lives of the 7/7 bombers. The following account is based on Cheryl's notes.

Maryam said she converted to Islam in 2000, and Germaine three days afterwards, when he was fifteen. He then changed his name to Abdullah Shaheed Jamal. The name Shaheed, 'martyr', was to prove prophetic. Maryam was an educated woman who took a degree in social work as a mature student. She was ambitious for her son, who she said was very bright. She arranged piano lessons for him – he played Beethoven.[16] He also expressed his feelings in poetry and words, some of which she quoted: 'Our Muslim brothers and sisters are being slaughtered, raped, murdered and their lands taken away and we are sitting at home watching television as if we don't care.' According to Maryam, the turning point in Germaine's life came a fortnight after his conversion, when mother and son went to a lecture in Bradford given by the fiery extremist cleric Sheikh Abdullah al-Faisal. In his sermons, which were recorded and sold in Islamic bookshops, he is heard declaring that 'the way forward is the bullet', and telling Muslim women to raise their children 'with *jihad* mentality'.

Abdullah al-Faisal's exhortation to young mothers rang a bell when I came across a document entitled 'Sister's Role in Jihad'. It is available on the internet, but the document I saw had been seized during a police raid on a Muslim terrorist suspect's house in the north of England. The suspect was married with a young family, and I was taken aback when I read it, not only because of what it said but because it had been found in a family home.

Raising Mujahid [warrior] children

This is probably the most important role women can play in Jihad …
The key is to start instilling these values in them while they are babies.
Don't wait until they are seven to start for it may be too late by then.

Tell children bedtime stories of Shuhadaa [martyrdom] and Mujahideen … If you cannot eliminate the television completely, then at least use it to show children videos that will instil in them the love of Allah, the love of Islam, the love of the Mujahideen.

… it is a good idea to start your children young in terms of introducing them (through safe toys) to target shooting. Make it very clear who their target should be.

… Show them the pictures of the Mujahideen and encourage them to become like these people at the least. These activities can be done with children even as young as a couple of years or even younger. Don't underestimate the lasting effect of what those little ears and eyes take in during the first few years of life. No child is ever too young to be started off on Jihad training in one form or another.

It had never occurred to me that the indoctrination of *jihad* began at such a young age. But perhaps I shouldn't have been surprised. I thought of the Jesuits' adage, 'Give me a child until he is seven, and I will give you the man.' Just substitute '*jihadi*' for 'man'. I later wondered if the document had inspired England's most biting satirist, Chris Morris, to include a scene in his controversial 2010 film *Four Lions* in which a *jihadi* father tells his son a bedtime story about an Islamic warrior. I had noticed Morris sitting in the public gallery of the Old Bailey observing the trial of the Operation Crevice accused, and had a chat with him in the canteen afterwards. I asked if he was considering taking his satirical knife to the subject of *jihad*. He smiled and said he might be.

Sheikh Abdullah al-Faisal promised Paradise in return for the martyrdom that 'Sister's Role in Jihad' encouraged children to embrace. Maryam believes that Germaine was attracted to Faisal because he was black, a Christian convert to Islam and, like him, came from Jamaica. After the lecture the young Lindsay went up and talked to him. That, Maryam believes, was the beginning of his road to *jihad*. Faisal was subsequently charged with inciting the killing of Jews, Americans and Hindus, and sentenced to nine years' imprisonment, of which he served four years. On his release in 2007 he was deported from Britain.[17]

Lindsay probably became even more vulnerable when his mother left for America to live with a man, leaving her teenage son living alone in a flat in a back street opposite a mosque in Huddersfield.[18] Alyas Karmani, a Salafist social worker who mentors young Muslims released from prison, met Lindsay when he was sixteen. Alyas is as charismatic as any fiery preacher, but endeavours to turn impressionable young Muslims away from any ideas they may be entertaining about violent *jihad*. He has street cred by the bucketload. I talked to him over a game of pool in a large Portakabin in Bradford that was a favourite haunt for young Muslims. On video machines that flashed around the fringes of the room, players tried their hand at everything from Formula One to Penalty Shootouts.

Alyas was humiliating me on the green baize table until he unintentionally potted the black and forfeited the match. He remembered Lindsay well. 'When I met him, he was alone and really the Muslim community was his family.' He knew of Lindsay's fractured family background, and said that the absence of a paternal relationship was something he often came across: 'When I ask nine of out ten of the young men I work with, "Tell me about the relationship with your father," most of them say, "Well, I don't really have much of a relationship with my father." So as a result an individual has a gap in their life in terms of who their role model is, and they search for a father figure, and in particular a senior male role model. Sometimes extremist recruiters seem to play that particular role. Unless they find someone who can channel them down a very positive way and give them a sense of purpose and guidance, they are really prone to a whole range of extreme radicalisation.' Germaine Lindsay's role model became Sheikh Abdullah al-Faisal, whose study circles he is thought to have attended. It's through them that he is believed to have met Mohammed Saddique Khan.

Maryam does not appear to have had much idea about how radical her son was becoming. Perhaps, like so many parents, she was relieved that he was becoming involved in his faith and hoped it would keep him out of trouble and away from sex, drugs and drink and the material temptations of the world. She said however that 'he didn't sound his usual self' when she spoke to him on the phone from America two days before 7/7. 'It felt like he was preoccupied, as if he were planning something.' By then there was another woman in Germaine Lindsay's life. He had married a Muslim convert, Samantha Lewthwaite, and they'd had a son called Abdullah, who in July 2005 was nearly eighteen months old. Lindsay had changed his appearance, and now wore a 'hoodie' instead of traditional Islamic dress. The couple had moved from Huddersfield to Aylesbury in Buckinghamshire, and Samantha was expecting her second baby. She had no idea what her husband was involved in. She did not see him on the morning of 7 July before he silently left for Luton. 'He kissed the child goodbye and then crept off. I found he'd left the keys on the table downstairs. He obviously had no use for them.'[19]

When Samantha heard about the bombings, she thought Germaine was praying at the mosque. The discovery that he was one of the bombers left her devastated. 'How these people could have turned him and poisoned his mind is dreadful. He was an innocent, naïve and simple man. I suppose he must have been an ideal candidate.'[20] I suspected that she genuinely had no idea about Germaine's terrorist involvement, any more than Mohammed Saddique Khan's wife had. But in the end, however vulnerable and socially damaged Lindsay may have been, he was still responsible for his own actions. Vulnerability and social dislocation are no excuse for murdering twenty-six innocent civilians. Alyas Karmani, who had befriended the young Lindsay, was equally shattered. 'I really don't understand it. It baffles me completely,' he told me. He also wondered, at a personal level, how he could have let this happen, given his earlier relationship with Lindsay. I asked him if he felt guilty. There was a long pause. Clearly the question hurt, and brought back memories. He avoided giving a direct answer: 'I can really say that I did all I could to support him during the two years that I knew him. Maybe I didn't support him well enough, so he slipped through the net.' Tragically Sheikh Abdullah al-Faisal's message proved stronger than Alyas' guidance.

On 21 July 2005, two weeks after the 7/7 attacks, Islamist bombers targeted London's transport system again. But this time they failed. Due to a technical fault in the bombs' composition, the detonators exploded but the bombs did not. Bombs of this type need organic material to make them effective: the 7/7 bombers had used black pepper, whereas the 21/7 cell used chapatti flour.[21] As with 7/7, there were three explosions on the Underground system – at Shepherd's Bush, Warren Street and Oval stations – and a fourth on a bus, in Shoreditch. The Metropolitan Police said the intention was to cause large-scale loss of life. This time the bombers were not home-grown terrorists, but fugitives from the strife-torn Horn of Africa. All were 'clean skins'.

Muktar Ibrahim, the leader of the cell, who tried to detonate his bomb on the bus, arrived from Eritrea in 1990 and eventually gained a British passport. He was one of the many young Muslims who attended Finsbury Park mosque and was fired by the sermons of Abu Hamza. Yassin Omar, whose bomb failed to go off at Warren Street tube station, also arrived in the UK in the 1990s, from Somalia.[22] He too frequented Finsbury Park mosque.[23] Ramzi Mohammed was another Somali, who arrived in Britain in 1998 and also became a devotee of Finsbury Park mosque. Before he departed to carry out his bombing mission at Oval station, he left a suicide note in which he wrote: 'My family, don't cry for [me]. But instead rejoice in happiness and love. What I have done [is] for the sake of Allah for he loves those who fight in his sake.' He told his sons: 'Be good Muslims ... and you shall see me again in Paradise, God willing.'[24] Hussein Osman, who launched the attempted attack at Shepherd's Bush station, was born in Ethiopia and came to Britain in the late 1990s as an asylum seeker, pretending that he was from Somalia.

By 29 July, all four main suspects had been arrested in what the Metropolitan Police Commissioner Sir Ian Blair called 'the largest investigation that the Met has ever mounted'.[25] CCTV on the Underground and on the bus helped identify the bombers. Ramzi Mohammed and Muktar Ibrahim were arrested on the Peabody Estate in North Kensington after a siege of several hours. Stun grenades and teargas forced them to come out onto the balcony of the flat and give themselves up.[26] Remarkable video footage shows them stripped to their underpants, Ibrahim with his hands in the air as a sign of surrender and Mohammed wiping the teargas from his eyes. On 11 July 2007, all four were sentenced to a minimum of forty years' imprisonment for conspiracy to murder.

There were strong suspicions that the 7/7 and 21/7 attacks were connected. This wasn't just because in both cases the bombs' main ingredient was hydrogen peroxide hair bleach. There were also coincidences in the travel patterns of individuals from the two groups: Muktar Ibrahim was in Pakistan at around the same time as Mohammed Saddique Khan. When Mr Justice Fulford passed sentence on the members of the 21/7 cell, he clearly linked the two attacks:

I have no doubt that they were both part of an al-Qaeda-inspired and controlled sequence of attacks. This was a viable, indeed a very nearly successful, attempt at mass murder. It was long in the planning and came soon after July 7. It was designed for maximum impact … Though the prosecution during this trial have not attempted to demonstrate a direct link between the carnage of July 7 and the joint crime of these four defendants, which was nearly a carbon copy of that event exactly two weeks later, nonetheless, what happened on July 7 2005 is of considerable relevance. It demonstrates the lethal effect of this plan had it succeeded. It is clear that at least fifty people would have died, hundreds of people would have been wounded, thousands would have had their lives permanently damaged, disfigured or otherwise, whether they were Christian, Muslim, Jewish, Hindu, Sikh, Buddhist, agnostic or atheist. The family and friends of the dead and the injured, the hundreds, indeed thousands, captured underground in terrifying circumstances – the smoke, the screams of the wounded and the dying – this each defendant knew. They planned this, they prepared for it. They had spent many hours making viable bombs. After 7/7 each defendant knew exactly what the result would be. Having heard the scientific evidence, I consider that this plan came very close to succeeding. If the detonators had been slightly more powerful or the hydrogen peroxide slightly more concentrated, then each bomb would have exploded.[27]

There was a tragic footnote to the events of 21/7 as a result of the Metropolitan Police's controversial policy to deal with the threat of a suicide bomb attack in London. The policy was known as Operation Kratos, the ancient Greek word for might, power or strength. Given what happened, it became known in some quarters outside the Met as a 'shoot to kill' policy. The day after the 21 July attempted bombings it was implemented to lethal effect when the Met's specialist firearms unit, known as CO19, shot dead a totally innocent twenty-seven-year-old Brazilian man.

Jean Charles de Menezes had arrived in Britain three years earlier on a six-month visitor's visa. After its expiry he applied to stay on as a student, and was granted permission to remain for another year. Precisely what his status was after that is unclear, but the Foreign

Secretary, Jack Straw, stated that he believed Menezes was living in the UK legally. He was shot seven times in the head by two undercover officers from the elite unit as he sat in a carriage deep underground at Stockwell tube station. He wasn't carrying a rucksack, nor was he wearing a bulky jacket that might have concealed a suicide belt. It was a disastrous case of mistaken identity. The officers thought he was the would-be 21/7 bomber Hussein Osman, who had been identified from CCTV pictures at Shepherd's Bush station the previous day. Osman had abandoned his rucksack when he fled the station, and police had found a gym membership card inside it that gave his address in a block of flats in Scotia Road, Tulse Hill, in south London. As it happened, Jean Charles de Menezes was living in the same block. The flats were put under surveillance, and when Jean emerged to go to work on the morning after the abortive bombings, the surveillance teams thought he was Hussein Osman, and followed him. There was only a very slight similarity in appearance, but the teams never stopped him to check his identity. The inquest into his death revealed a disturbing series of intelligence failures and lost opportunities for the surveillance teams to check who it was that they were following. On 12 December 2008 the coroner, Sir Michael Wright, told the jury that based on the evidence, they could not return a verdict of unlawful killing. They returned an open verdict.

I investigated the shooting of Jean Charles de Menezes for a BBC1 *Panorama* special called *Stockwell: Countdown to Killing*, screened in March 2006. As part of my research for the programme, producer Howard Bradburn and I travelled to the mountainous interior of Brazil to talk to Jean's parents, Matazinhos and Maria, to try to find out what their son was like, and why he had come to London.[28] They are unassuming, dignified people who live on a small farmstead at the end of a thickly wooded valley an hour's drive from the village of Gonzaga, where Jean now lies buried. Spanning the dirt road at the entrance to Gonzaga is a sign that reads 'Land of Jean Charles de Menezes. Victim of terrorism in London. Here we value life.'

It had been a long, hot and dusty journey that ended up with Howard and me spending the night at a hotel inhabited by assorted creepy-crawlies that might have come straight out of a Hollywood B-movie, complete with spluttering neon sign outside. I had initially made contact with Jean's parents through relatives in London. Maria and Matazinhos's livelihood comes from chickens and from two dozen cows that graze in the fields on the hillside. Maria does her main cooking in a makeshift bamboo hut in the back yard, where with boundless energy she hammers coffee beans with a giant wooden pestle. No coffee machine here. Time has passed Gonzaga and the valley by, and there is little there to offer the young: no work and no future. 'Jean couldn't earn a decent wage because people here are poor,' Maria told me through a relative who spoke English. 'He struggled to pay for his clothes, his shoes, his food, to survive. We saw him struggling, but we couldn't help him.' That was why he went to London. Matazinhos told me that before he left, Jean had made them a promise: 'I'll send you everything I earn from my job in London, to help you pay the landlord and survive. And after I have been working there for a few years, I'll come back to Brazil and live here.' Seven shots to the head in a London tube train meant that he was never able to keep that promise.

Jean's family were determined that those responsible for his death should be brought to justice and pay the penalty for what they see as cold-blooded murder. The Metropolitan Police Commissioner, Sir Ian Blair, was top of the list. 'He is the person who is most responsible for what has happened,' Jean's cousin in London, Patricia, told me. 'It was a series of errors which began at the top and then ended up with an officer killing my cousin. I think that all of them, without exception, should be prosecuted. They judged my cousin, and sentenced him, all in the space of a moment.' Patricia's sentiments are echoed by Jean's parents. 'No other mother should ever have to endure the kind of pain that I am going through,' said Maria, with tears welling up in her eyes. 'It is like an illness that I will suffer from for the rest of my life. Nothing will cure this pain.' I could well understand the anger and frustration of Jean Charles's family. I would have been surprised had there been a prosecution, because while there were serious failures on the part of Metropolitan Police firearms and surveillance officers, they did occur in a climate of heightened nervousness and fear.

Stockwell was a double tragedy – above all for the de Menezes family, of course, but also for the Metropolitan Police, whose officers believed they were trying to protect London just two weeks after the 7 July bombings. If the suspect had been another suicide bomber, the officers who ran the operation, and those who carried it out, would probably have been decorated. In an agreed settlement, the de Menezes family received a sum of money believed to be around £100,000, and their substantial legal costs were also paid.

Hussein Osman, for whom Jean Charles de Menezes was mistaken, was, like the other 21/7 would-be bombers, a 'clean skin'. After the perpetrators of those attempted attacks had been convicted and sentenced, I met another potential 'clean skin'. I will call him 'Kasim'. I don't propose to give any dates, as to do so might risk compromising him.

Kasim, like Germaine Lindsay, absorbed Sheikh Abdullah al-Faisal's teachings, and as a result only narrowly escaped with his life. Through a series of contacts I had heard about him and his remarkable story, and I finally managed to meet him in a hotel room some distance from London. We sat and talked over tea, biscuits and sparkling water. He wore Western dress – jeans and a baseball cap. Significantly, he had no beard. It took time to gain his confidence, as he knew he could be putting his life at risk by talking to me. At first he didn't seem comfortable: he fidgeted in his chair and spent most of the time looking down at the floor when he was talking. Sometimes it was difficult to make out what he said. When I told him I would like to hear what had happened to him, and why, he was in no rush to make such a potentially life-threatening decision. He said he would think about it, and be in touch.

I met Kasim again some months later in Blackpool, on a filthy day with pouring rain. The sky was as dark as the sea. The baseball cap was pulled well down over his eyes as we walked along the wet sand between the great iron stanchions of the Central Pier and talked. He was far more relaxed than he had been in the hotel room, and much less monosyllabic. He had clearly decided to take the plunge.

He told me he hadn't come from a deprived area or a poor family. His parents were middle-class Pakistanis, and reasonably well off. 'We're just like a normal secular family,' he said. 'My parents pray on Fridays, but not five times a day. My father doesn't have a beard and my mother doesn't wear the *hijab*.' There was a copy of the Koran in the house, but in the original Arabic, not in an English translation. Kasim could read Arabic, but not understand it. I thought of the little Muslim boys and girls I'd often seen in the UK and Pakistan, sitting cross-legged on the floor repeating the Arabic verses by rote and rocking back and forth in time with the hypnotic rhythm of the words. I often wondered how much they understood of the verses they were reciting.

Kasim's parents had problems: 'They've always had fights. It wasn't very peaceful. It made me a quiet kind of person, more reserved.' I thought of Germaine Lindsay's fractured home background, and what Alyas Karmani had said about dislocated families. Kasim rebelled, dating girls, going clubbing, drinking alcohol and smoking cannabis, but never told his parents. They would have been furious had they found out. He said they would probably have placed him under curfew.

9/11 changed everything for him. 'It was the catalyst. It gave me the hunger to learn more about Islam. Up to that point I didn't have a clue. I never even knew the basics.' He became determined to find out more about the nature and meaning of *jihad*. He started by exploring different schools of Islam, beginning with the most moderate, Sufism, through which he hoped to acquire the 'peacefulness' that he believed would give him guaranteed entry to Paradise. His overriding desire was to ensure that he enjoyed the sublime pleasures of Paradise, and was not condemned to burn in the eternal fires of Hell. That ambition was to govern everything he did on his journey of spiritual discovery. 'I realised that there were seventy-three different sects in Islam, and only one was going to Paradise, and the rest were going to Hellfire.' He wanted to make sure he bought the right ticket. He finally found what he thought he was looking for at a Saudi Wahhabi mosque: 'I felt more peaceful there than anywhere else.' But crucially, as in so many other cases, it wasn't a particular mosque that marked the first step on Kasim's road to radicalisation, but an encounter with an individual who became his spiritual guide and personal mentor. It was this man who filled Kasim's head with the notion that *jihad* was the key to the gates of Paradise. He would not tell me who his mentor was, as he did not wish to break any confidences.

The role of this spiritual guide was clearly pivotal, as it was in the cases of most of the *jihadis* I have studied – from Sheikh Omar Bakri's influence on Crevice's Omar Khyam to that of Sheikh Abdullah al-Faisal on the 7/7 bomber Germaine Lindsay. Kasim's mentor introduced him to Abdullah al-Faisal's inflammatory sermons, and gradually Kasim fell under the radical cleric's spell, spending hours listening to tapes of his speeches. 'Sheikh Abdullah was very charismatic and he had a very great effect on me,' he said. 'He was very forthright in his opinions and about what was happening to Muslims around the world, how they were powerless and oppressed and how they were getting killed. He said the value of a Muslim life wasn't great. He was well educated and had spent a lot of time in Saudi Arabia. He wasn't self-taught but had learned from the religious teachers there.' Faisal's message of *jihad* and the promise of Paradise for 'martyrs' struck home.

By the time of the 7/7 London bombings, Kasim thought he had found the right path, and regarded the deaths of fifty-two innocent civilians as the will of Allah, and those of the four bombers as martyrdom. He does not appear to have had any moral qualms or questions about an attack that went against all the teaching of Abdullah Azzam, the Father of *Jihad*. Islamist extremists were calling the attack 'legitimate' *jihad*, and Kasim does not seem to have taken issue with them. But the bombings did affect him in a different way. They made him more conscious of the fact that he was a Muslim, and after 7/7 he felt that people tended to see him, and countless other Muslims, in a different light. Working in an office environment he began to feel 'insecure' and the 'odd man out'.

Kasim had grown a beard well before 7/7. 'It was because I was getting stronger in my faith, and I realised that as a Muslim you should grow a beard. It was something that I wanted to do to get closer to God.' He never used public transport, but drove to work, and therefore never experienced at first hand the humiliation many young Muslims felt in the aftermath of the bombings: he told me about one of his friends who had got on a bus with a rucksack, and the driver had told him he had to leave it at the front and not take it with him to the back. 'Afterwards there was so much negative publicity in the media about Muslims. Anyone with a beard was targeted. If everyone is attacking you, you become stronger and you probably do things you wouldn't think of doing before.' No doubt thousands of young Muslims all over the United Kingdom felt the same.

The aftermath of 7/7 convinced Kasim that he had had enough of living in Britain, where he now felt Muslims weren't welcome. He decided to move to a Muslim country, where most men wore beards and taking a bag or rucksack on board a bus or train did not raise an eyebrow. There, he believed, he and his family would feel more comfortable and at home: 'I was engrossed in my faith, and wanted to bring up my kids in an environment where they were more influenced by Islam than the normal life of British teenagers.'

The July 2005 bombings, and the suspicion and prejudice that sprang from them, encouraged Kasim to try to meet actual *jihadis* and see the reality for himself: 'I wanted to find out the motives of these people, and why they were prepared to sacrifice everything.' Would he go to Paradise if he became a *jihadi* and a *shaheed*? Via a route and contacts he would not disclose, he managed to make it to the Tribal Areas of Pakistan, where he met up with a group of Pakistani *jihadis*. He knew how dangerous this was, but it was a risk he was prepared to take: 'You need a contact. It's the only way you can get there. If they think you're a spy, they'd kill you.' He moved into a guest house where the *jihadis* were quartered, and was impressed by what he saw: 'They were all active. They would cross the border into Afghanistan regularly and carry out attacks.' He had long discussions about *jihad* well into the night, and was surprised to find that his housemates' views went far beyond those he was formulating himself: 'My philosophy was to fight what I believed *jihad* meant, against those who were invading Muslim lands.' But these *jihadis* had far greater ambitions: 'They said they were fighting *jihad* in Afghanistan primarily to get rid of foreign forces and then the ultimate goal was to establish the Islamic Caliphate (in this context, an Islamic government) there under *sharia* law. Once that was achieved they would turn to Pakistan and other Muslim countries. Afghanistan was just the beginning of their long-term plan.' This made Kasim uncomfortable. His idea of *jihad* was to get rid of the foreign invader, and that was it.

Kasim's discussions and cross-border incursions came to a dramatic and violent end at midnight one night. He had just gone to bed, and was falling asleep. 'I was semi-conscious. I thought I was dreaming. I never knew where I was. I tried to move, but I couldn't. The house had collapsed, and rubble was all on top of me. When I opened my eyes, there was blood everywhere. People were running about shouting and screaming. It's something I will never get over.' The guest house had been hit by a missile fired from a US pilotless drone. About a dozen *jihadis* were killed in the attack, but Kasim miraculously survived. Covered in blood, he was carried to a car and taken to a hospital where injured people were coming in 'every five minutes'. Kasim spent several months there recovering from his serious wounds, which gave him plenty of time to think about *jihad*. The seeds of doubt that had been sown during his conversations at the guest house were probably accelerated by his terrifying close encounter with death.

While Kasim was recuperating, word reached Arab Al Qaeda leaders in Waziristan, on the Pakistani side of the border, that there was someone in hospital with a British passport. He was told that they would like to meet him when he was fit to leave. 'I thought it was a good idea to go and see what they were like, and find out more about their interpretation of *jihad*.' When he was discharged from hospital he journeyed north, and met some of the senior members of Al Qaeda's External Operations Headquarters. They told him they didn't need volunteers to fight in Afghanistan, as they already had plenty. What they wanted him to do was team up with other 'foreigners' who were in the area and carry out operations in Britain and Europe. He assumed these 'foreigners' were British. But by now this wasn't the kind of *jihad* Kasim had in mind, and he told his hosts as much. 'I felt it was the wrong thing to do, morally and religiously. Killing women and children was against the principles of Islam.'

The Al Qaeda leadership told him to stay, and to spend some time thinking about it. His British passport and cover were precious commodities, and Kasim would have been the perfect 'clean skin'. He did think about it – perhaps not having much option – but his answer was still a nervous 'no'. 'I said it was something I was really against, and I didn't want to be part of that kind of thing. It was something that I never considered being part of *jihad*.' At this stage one might have expected Kasim to have ended up with a bullet in his head, IRA style. But surprisingly Al Qaeda let him go back to his family, perhaps thinking he might be of some use to them further down the line. Although it may be difficult to accept, Al Qaeda does have a religious moral code that does not allow it to force a Muslim to do something against his will, especially, perhaps, when it comes to the life or death of the individual concerned. In the case of Kasim, this code was respected.

Kasim now realises that he took the wrong path, but has since seen the light. That is why he was prepared to talk to me. 'It was a life-changing experience. I've now changed my views about Islam. I got influenced by the wrong people. You shouldn't listen to voices like that of Sheikh Abdullah al-Faisal and other extremists, because if you do you'll be led astray from true Islam, and that means going to Hellfire.' I asked him if he thought he would now go to Paradise. 'I hope so,' he said as the rain stopped, darkness fell and Blackpool's illuminations came on.

Kasim thought better of becoming a *jihadi*, but other fellow Muslims and British citizens did not. They were now even more determined to find ways of penetrating the tightening net of security thrown up in the wake of the 7/7 bombings – in particular at airports. Al Qaeda was devising ever more devious ways to get bombs on board aircraft.

THIRTEEN

Terror in the Skies

If Operation Crevice was the largest counter-terrorist operation ever mounted by MI5 and the British police, the subsequent surveillance operation to stop seven aircraft being blown up mid-Atlantic or over American cities was even larger. It was codenamed Operation Overt, but the way in which it was carried out was anything but.

In January 2006, six months after the 7/7 bombings, Osama Bin Laden broke a long silence and issued an audio tape in which he threatened more attacks against America and its coalition allies:

> My message to you is about the war in Iraq and Afghanistan and the way to end it … the *mujahideen*, praise be to God, have managed to breach all the security measures adopted by the unjust nations of the coalition time and again. The evidence of this is the bombings you have seen in the capitals of the most important European countries of this aggressive coalition … Operations are under preparation and you will see them on your own ground once they are finished, God willing.[1]

The preparations for the airlines plot, intended to hit Britain and America with the impact of 9/11, began later in 2006. It was conceived and generated by 'core' Al Qaeda, and intended to be implemented by home-grown British *jihadi* recruits. Aircraft had long been a favoured Al Qaeda target, from Khalid Sheikh Mohammed's Bojinka plot in 1995 to the shoe bomber Richard Reid in December 2001. The attacks on New York and Washington were of a different order, with aircraft being used as missiles. After 9/11, security at airports was greatly intensified and security on board also tightened, with cockpit doors being firmly locked so hijackers could not seize the controls. The *mujahideen* had to find ever more ingenious methods, in Bin Laden's words, 'to breach all the security measures'. The solution they adopted was liquid bombs that could pass through airport security undetected.

The plot never came to fruition, because it was foiled by the British intelligence agencies working closely with their American counterparts. As Philip Mudd, a veteran CIA analyst later seconded to the FBI, told me in Washington, 'This was in the upper echelons of plots that I have seen in the seven years of post-9/11 plotting. I would put it at the Manchester United level. The group, I thought, was sophisticated, driven, patient and operationally secure. I think they would have executed it had they had the chance.' According to Mudd's FBI colleague Arthur 'Art' Cummings, the consequences would have been seismic. 'If [the aircraft] were blips on the radar screen that disappeared in the sky, I'm sure there would be serious economic loss to the airline industry,' he told me. 'If they blew up in American cities or over American cities it would have been catastrophic.'[2]

Operation Overt seems to have begun life in a similar way to Operation Crevice. After the 7 July 2005 attacks on London, in addition to the establishment of regional counter-terrorist units the intelligence services were given a massive increase in human and technical resources to enable them to expand surveillance on the estimated one thousand Islamist extremists living in the UK. A particular individual living in east London, whom I cannot name for legal reasons, was one of them. As with Operation Crevice, surveillance officers were also noting and watching some of his associates. That appears to be how the airlines plot came into the frame. Two young Muslims from Walthamstow in east London, associates of the targeted suspect, had attracted particular interest. They were called Abdullah Ahmed Ali Khan (I will refer to him as Ahmed Ali) and Tanvir Hussain. Ahmed Ali turned out to be the ringleader of the cell, and Hussain his number two.

Walthamstow is a potential breeding ground for extremism, as most of the families of its more than 30,000 Muslims originally came from Kashmir. To them the notion of *jihad* is nothing new, given the conflict in their homeland.* Hanif Kadir knows the area and its people well. He runs the Active Change Foundation, based on a youth centre, mosque, *madrassa* and gym in the London borough of Waltham Forest. The foundation's aim is to divert young Muslims from the lure of extremism. Hanif knows how powerful the pull can be, as he himself once flirted with extremism, and had gone out to Afghanistan with the intention of fighting *jihad*. Sitting cross-legged on the carpet in the mosque upstairs in the centre, he told me why: 'My intention was to help the innocent civilians and the victims caught in the conflict, but also to get involved in the *jihad* because of seeing Western fighters dropping bombs on innocent civilians.' But when he saw the reality of what *jihad* involved he thought better of it, and returned to the UK to propagate the exact opposite message. His first-hand experience of *jihad* gives him the street cred he needs to enable him to relate to young Muslims who may be tempted to follow a similar path.

I asked if he was surprised that young Muslims in this part of London were being radicalised. 'Waltham Forest is one of those areas where radicalisation and recruitment take place,' he said, 'but I would say that it wouldn't take much to radicalise any young person in Waltham Forest.' So how can it be stopped? He told me that a change in Western foreign policy would make a huge difference: 'If we look around the world today, at Iraq, Afghanistan, Palestine, Chechnya, and Kashmir, it doesn't take much to frustrate any young person, especially a young Muslim.' This was the message I had heard so often before, which flew in the face of former Prime Minister Tony Blair's assertion that Islamist domestic terrorism had nothing to do with UK foreign policy. 'This terrorism isn't our fault. We didn't cause it,' he told the Labour Party conference in September 2006. 'It's not the consequence of foreign policy.'[3]

---

*The disputed and divided territory of Kashmir is one of the world's most dangerous flashpoints, with the two nuclear powers of India and Pakistan both claiming it as theirs. The dispute has spawned several Pakistani-supported *jihadi* groups fighting what they regard as Indian occupation of Muslim territory. The most notable are Laskar-e-Toyeba and Harkut-ul-Mujahideen. They are broadly supported by Al Qaeda, and are regarded as part of the *jihadi* brotherhood.

Several of those involved in the airlines plot had attended Hanif's youth centre and gym, a room at the top of the building where, unlike most gyms, the patrons, being Muslim, work out and pump iron without the continuous thump, thump of Western music. The only 'music' allowed is recorded recitals of verses from the Koran. *Jihadi* rap is banned. When Hanif showed me around, I attracted suspicious looks from Muslim 'brothers' working out. Hanif knew Ahmed Ali, Tanvir Hussain and some of the other airline plotters well. 'They were very good guys. The reason why the community felt shocked is because a lot of people knew them and regarded them as very decent, upstanding, humble kids. You would not ever imagine that these guys would do such a thing.' Gordon Parry, the headmaster of Hazelwick School in Crawley, had said much the same about his former students who had gone on to be among the Operation Crevice plotters.

We were filming outside a house in Waltham Forest, a flat in which had been used by the plotters as a bomb factory, when a man called Mark Hough came up and asked what we were doing. When we told him, he said he was a teacher at Aveling Park School, where Ahmed Ali and Tanvir Hussain had been pupils. He had known both of them, and had taught Ahmed Ali GCSE Religious Studies. He, like most of the community, had been surprised and shocked when he discovered what they had been involved in. I went to talk to him at his home on a warm summer morning. 'They were both just normal boys, really,' he said. 'Ahmed Ali was a very good sportsman, and a bit of a lad. He was bright, devout and committed, and didn't hide his political views in class discussions. He thought the way the Taliban were running Afghanistan was to be admired, and we used to have interesting debates about the role of women and *sharia* law.' When I asked if he had been concerned that Ahmed Ali expressed such strong support for the Taliban, he said his extreme views had to be put in context: 'He was a boy who could have gone off the rails, but became a very devout Muslim and regularly went to pray at a house mosque at lunchtime on Fridays. He used to come back with proofs of the existence of God and the experiences of Muslims in different parts of the world. What he said in school did seem to fit in with what he later said in court [about wanting to become a *jihadi* at the age of fifteen].'

In 2003 Ahmed Ali went to Pakistan, through a charity called the Islamic Medical Association, to help refugees from the war across the border in Afghanistan. He was 'shocked' by what he saw, and came to believe that charity work was not enough, and the root cause of the suffering needed to be tackled. To Ahmed Ali, that root cause was Western foreign policy. It is thought that he learned his bomb-making skills while he was in Pakistan. He was there at the same time as the 7/7 bombers Mohammed Saddique Khan and Shehzad Tanweer, and some of the East African *jihadis* who tried unsuccessfully to emulate them two weeks later.[4]

The intelligence services began to identify other members of the cell as they watched Ahmed Ali playing tennis in a local park. As in Operation Crevice, they noted who he was playing with and who he was talking to. One particular individual attracted their attention when they saw him talking to Ahmed Ali in the middle of a wide-open space in the park, well out of earshot of any covert long-distance microphone. They realised that the cell extended far beyond Walthamstow when they followed this man to the town of High Wycombe in Buckinghamshire, thirty miles away. His name was Assad Sarwar, and Ahmed Ali had met him in Pakistan. He turned out to be the person charged with getting hold of the chemicals for the bomb.

Gradually the intelligence services put the pieces of the jigsaw together. They concluded that there were probably eight members in the cell. Keeping tabs on all of them stretched resources to the limit, given, as had been the case with Operation Crevice, that there were other totally unrelated plots in gestation at the same time, and other suspects who had to be monitored. 'At one point there were twenty-seven surveillance teams from the Metropolitan Police and the Security Service engaged,' the head of the police side of Operation Overt, Commander John McDowall, told me. 'To my knowledge that is far in excess of any other policing operation I'm aware of.' The teams watched Ahmed Ali buying half a dozen storage jars in Tesco's, and Assad Sarwar travelling far and wide buying hydrogen peroxide from a variety of outlets so as not to arouse suspicion. He was also seen buying syringes and plastic bottles of Lucozade, Oasis and other popular soft drinks. The syringes were to be used to remove the contents from the bottles and replace them with the explosive chemical mix, without the need to break the seals on the bottles' caps. Meanwhile Ahmed Ali and Tanvir Hussain were videoed showing an interest in disposable cameras. These were intended to provide the electrical charge to the detonators, which were concealed in hollowed-out batteries inside the soft-drinks bottles.

The methodology of the plotters was revealed after surveillance teams followed Ahmed Ali and Tanvir Hussain to the second-floor flat at 386 Forest Road, Walthamstow, which the conspirators had bought for £138,000 in cash and which turned out to be the bomb factory. As the surveillance teams monitored the comings and goings of all those who went through the door, concern about what might be going on inside mounted. It was decided that the only way to find out was to utilise a secret unit known as the 'Creep', and its officers made a covert entry in the middle of the night. The 'Creepers' found and filmed batteries, drinks bottles and glass flasks for measuring chemicals. A tiny video camera with a live feed was concealed in the flat to monitor what was going on inside, as was a listening device to pick up conversations. Those watching the monitors were amused when they heard Cliff Richard's 'Summer Holiday' playing on the radio as the live video transmission showed Ahmed Ali and Tanvir Hussain making up the bombs. They were seen inserting syringes in the base of the bottles, sucking out the contents and then replacing them with the hydrogen peroxide mixture that Assad Sarwar was mixing in High Wycombe. They would then use them to add colouring to make the liquid in the bottles look like the brand on the label. The bug in the flat picked up a key conversation between Ahmed Ali and Tanvir Hussain:

TANVIR HUSSAIN: It's ready. Waiting for the HP [hydrogen peroxide].

AHMED ALI: He [Assad Sarwar] has to boil it down.

TANVIR HUSSAIN: He's got it, yeah.

AHMED ALI: Enough for the mission.

The intelligence services now knew how the bombs were being constructed, but they didn't know what the targets were until they watched Ahmed Ali downloading airline timetables in an internet shop and writing down flight times that he saved on a memory stick. He seemed to be especially interested in the North American carriers United, American and Air Canada. The listening device the 'Creepers' had secretly installed then picked up him and Tanvir Hussain discussing flights, in particular favourite destinations for British tourists: Washington, Philadelphia, Los Angeles, Miami and Texas.

Towards the end of July 2006 the bug picked up the recording of the suicide videos that the would-be *shaheeds* were making for transmission after the planes had exploded. Ahmed Ali's was the first:

I was over the moon that Allah has given me the opportunity to lead this blessed operation. We Muslims are people of honour. We are brave. We're not cowards. Enough is enough. We've warned you so many times, get out of our lands, leave us alone. Sheikh Osama warned you many times to leave our lands or you will be destroyed, and now the time has come. You have nothing to expect but floods of martyrdom operations, volcanoes of anger and revenge.

Tanvir Hussain was equally threatening:

For many years, I dreamt of doing this, but I didn't have any chance … I didn't have any means. You know, I only wish I could do this again, come back and do this again and again until people come to their senses and realise, you know, 'Don't mess with the Muslims.'

By the first week of August, the intelligence services were on red alert. No tickets had been bought for flights, but things seemed to be moving swiftly in the direction of an attack. John McDowall told me how tense the situation was becoming: 'We wanted to apprehend these people safely and to disrupt and prevent the attack taking place. As things began to increase in pace, the pressure on us to act grew.'[5] The operation is an illustration of the difficult dilemma the police and the intelligence services often face: whether to intervene early to prevent the execution of a plot, or to wait and gain more intelligence on individuals, their movements and communications. In the end it's a matter of judging the risks.

On Monday, 7 August, MI5 and the Home Secretary, John Reid, decided it was time to alert the Cabinet about the imminent danger to air travel. The Transport Secretary, Douglas Alexander, was on holiday on the Isle of Mull in Scotland, and was surprised to receive a phone call from the Permanent Secretary, the senior civil servant at his department, telling him that an MI5 officer would be coming up to brief him. Alexander met him the following day on the jetty overlooking the Isle of Iona, and took him back to his holiday cottage, where he received a full briefing. That same day, Prime Minister Tony Blair left the country for his summer holiday at Cliff Richard's villa in Barbados. The next day, Wednesday, 9 August, the Ministry of Defence sent a helicopter to bring Douglas Alexander back to London, where he was briefed by the Director General of the Security Service, Eliza Manningham-Buller: 'She said there was an alleged plot to bring down a number of aircraft over the Atlantic, that surveillance of the suspects was under way and that there was to be a judgement made by the police as to the right time to take executive action against the suspects.' Alexander later asked a senior police officer precisely what 'executive action' was. 'That just means kicking down the doors, going in and getting them,' he was told.[6]

The day Douglas Alexander was being briefed by Eliza Manningham-Buller, another suicide video was being recorded in the bomb factory. The covertly recorded 'warm-up' provides an insight into the mundane way in which such videos are made before their intended posthumous transmission. Ahmed Ali can be heard coaching Umar Islam, another member of the cell from High Wycombe. He, like the 7/7 bomber Germaine Lindsay, was a West Indian convert. Listening to the recording of the conversation that was played in court, it struck me as incongruously down-to-earth, even bordering on the farcical, given its subject matter.

AHMED ALI: Relax. Don't try and speak posh English. Speak normal English that you normally speak.

UMAR ISLAM: Mm.

AHMED ALI: When you mention Allah, do that [points finger]. When you're making a point. You're warning the *kuffar* [the infidels]. Give a bit of aggression, yeah, a bit loudly if you want …

UMAR ISLAM: Ah, OK, I see … Got any water?

AHMED ALI: I haven't got any water.

UMAR ISLAM: Ah, don't worry … It's not gonna be long, sorry. You not worried?

AHMED ALI: Tell me when you're ready.

[Umar Islam is then heard whispering, rehearsing his lines.]

AHMED ALI: When you're ready, yeah … I put my hand down, you start.

[An electronic beep is heard, signalling the beginning of the recording.]

UMAR ISLAM: You're too busy watching *Home and Away* and *EastEnders*, caring about the World Cup [and] drinking alcohol to care about anything … This is a warning to the non-believers that if they do not leave our lands, there are many more like us and many more like me ready to strike until the law of Allah is established on this earth. I say to you disbelievers that as you bomb, you will be bombed. As you kill, you will be killed. And if you want to kill our women and children, then the same thing will happen to you. This is not a joke.

Commander John McDowall's fears were heightened not just by this latest video, but by an indication that the plotters were considering testing their 'soft-drink' bottles to see if they could get through airport security: 'We believed that a dry run was about to take place, and some sort of travel would be undertaken by one of those involved in the plot towards the end of that week … it's not inconceivable that this may have actually involved some form of detonation or some device being used. Potentially the dry run may have even involved an attack, and that was clearly far too great a risk for us to run.'[7]

But what finally triggered the decision to move to 'executive action' was a related event in Pakistan. On Wednesday evening there was news that the alleged key link between Ahmed Ali's cell in Walthamstow and High Wycombe, and Al Qaeda in Pakistan, had been tracked down and arrested. His name was Rashid Rauf, the son of a successful baker and devout Muslim from Birmingham. Rauf had fled the UK in 2002 following the stabbing to death of his uncle, thought to be over a family matter, for which he was the prime suspect. He had radical connections in Pakistan, as his wife was related to Maulana Masood Azhar, the founder of Jaish-e-Mohammed (the Army of Mohammed), the militant group based in Pakistani-administered Kashmir committed to wresting the whole of the divided region from Indian control. It is believed that Rauf, who was thought to be directly connected to 'core' Al Qaeda, met Ahmed Ali and Tanvir Hussain while they were in Pakistan, and became their key contact.

The arrest of Rauf, who was being monitored by the ISI with the CIA's help,* raised fears that it would prompt Ahmed Ali and his co-conspirators either to move or to destroy evidence like the suicide videos and the stock of hydrogen peroxide, and go to ground. It was a risk none of the intelligence agencies was prepared to take. Executive action was authorised. The police didn't have to knock down Ahmed Ali's door, as he was saying his evening prayers with Assad Sarwar in the car park outside Walthamstow Town Hall. When officers searched Ahmed Ali they found the memory stick with flight times and a notebook containing a 'to do' list that included Lucozade, drink bottles, batteries and HP (hydrogen peroxide). In Sarwar's car they found even more incriminating evidence: the camcorder that had just been used

---

*The Americans suspected Rauf of being a key Al Qaeda operative whose activities threatened the US as well as the UK. He was arrested on a bus heading for the town of Multan, the gateway to the Tribal Areas that border Afghanistan.

to record Umar Islam's video, with the still-warm tape inside. All the main suspects were arrested. Police found the other suicide videos in Sarwar's garage in High Wycombe, and later uncovered a suitcase full of bomb-making equipment that Sarwar had buried in nearby woods.

In the immediate aftermath of the arrests, the terrorist threat level that is constantly monitored by MI5 was raised to 'critical', meaning 'an attack is expected imminently'.[8] Fearing that the plot or some elements of it might already be under way, dozens of flights from Heathrow and Gatwick were suspended, causing unprecedented chaos at all British airports. Security measures were intensified, with passengers being forbidden to take any hand baggage or liquids through security. The authorities did all they could to reassure a nervous and sometimes doubting public that such drastic measures were necessary. The Metropolitan Police Commissioner, Sir Paul Stephenson, said, 'We are confident that we have disrupted a plan by terrorists to cause untold death and destruction and to commit, quite frankly, mass murder.' Home Secretary John Reid echoed his sentiments, saying that had the attack gone ahead it would have caused loss of life on 'an unprecedented scale'.[9]

Before the conspirators could be brought to trial, there was an astonishing development in Pakistan. In December 2007, Rashid Rauf escaped from custody. He had been in court in connection with other terrorist charges, and was being driven back to prison under escort. On the way, prisoner and escorts stopped off for a bite to eat on the road at a fast-food outlet. Rauf asked if he could pop into the nearby mosque to pray. When his escorts said he could, he went into the mosque, ran out of the back door and promptly disappeared. It was like something out of the Keystone Kops. I asked CIA and FBI analyst Philip Mudd how he reacted to Rauf's Houdini-like escape. 'I can't say I was surprised. I was angry and disappointed. I have no doubt Rashid Rauf will be caught again, and I look forward to that day. He will go down.' Almost a year later, in November 2008, Rauf was reportedly killed by a missile fired from a US pilotless drone.

The prosecution of Ahmed Ali and seven of his associates began on 3 April 2008 at Woolwich Crown Court, and lasted almost eighteen months. The court is adjacent to Belmarsh prison, where many of Britain's convicted terrorists and terrorist suspects have been held, including Abu Hamza, Dhiren Barot* and Muktar Ibrahim. It's an epic journey to get there by public transport. The court and the prison stand isolated in a windy and barren wasteland, surrounded by a few rundown industrial premises. The final test in reaching the destination is a long walk from the station to the security gate, along an overgrown footpath that appears never-ending. Just before the halfway stage there's a van selling bacon sandwiches and tea, an oasis on a cold, wet, windy morning. I made the pilgrimage many times, often leaving home before 6 o'clock in the morning. I would sit at the back of the modern courtroom, watching judge and jury and the accused, who sat in a row behind a screen. Most of them were neatly dressed in suits, and some wore ties. They didn't look like a group of *jihadis* who had been prepared to blow themselves up, bring down planes and murder their passengers and crews. Ahmed Ali, Tanvir Hussain, Assad Sarwar and Umar Islam pleaded guilty to conspiracy to cause explosions; and Ibrahim Savant, Arafat Khan and Waheed Zaman to conspiracy to commit a public nuisance. Not one of them admitted targeting planes. The only defendant who did not enter a guilty plea was Mohammed Gulzar, a friend of Rashid Rauf's from Birmingham who, like Rauf, had fled Britain in 2002 shortly after the murder of Rauf's uncle. The defence had claimed that the 'martyrdom' videos were simply part of a propaganda exercise to heighten public awareness of the wars in Iraq and Afghanistan, and that they were going to be posted on the internet after a small explosion at Heathrow airport that was not designed to hurt anyone. I remember raising my eyebrows in disbelief as I sat at the back of the hot courtroom, thinking this was a good one for the fairies.

---

*Dhiren Barot, aka Issa al-Hindi, was a British Muslim believed to have been tasked by Osama Bin Laden, via Khalid Sheikh Mohammed, to recce financial targets in New York and Washington with a view to blowing them up. The plot was aborted following 9/11. He was subsequently charged and sentenced to life in 2006 over plots to attack targets in Britain.

On 8 November 2008 the jury delivered its verdict. It wasn't convinced that the purpose of the plot was to bring down aircraft. The furthest it felt able to go was to find Ahmed Ali, Tanvir Hussain and Assad Sarwar guilty of planning to murder persons unknown. It acquitted Mohammed Gulzar, but could not reach a verdict on the other four defendants. There was incredulity at Thames House, MI5's headquarters, Scotland Yard and Downing Street. But the Crown Prosecution Service (CPS) was determined to press ahead, and ordered a retrial. The prosecution opened its case on 3 March 2009, producing fresh evidence in the form of coded emails between Ahmed Ali and Sarwar and an unnamed person in Pakistan, believed to be Rashid Rauf. The following is a sample of some of the exchanges.[10]

18 July 2006, Ahmed Ali to Pakistan:

There are a few lads wanna join up. I have about four lads.

19 July 2006, Sarwar to Pakistan:

Hi ☺ Got some good news that will bring a big smile to your face ... I have some nice files that you will love. It will give you wet dreams after you see it ha ha ha. I have 15 suppliers to give Calvin Klein aftershave. One box of 50 is only £175.

The 'files' are believed to be the 'martyrdom' videos and the 'aftershave' the hydrogen peroxide.

During the week leading up to the arrests on 6 August 2006 there was an exchange between Ahmed Ali and, it is believed, Rashid Rauf about surveillance, coded in the emails as a 'skin infection'.

31 July 2006, Pakistan to Ahmed Ali:

How is the skin infection you were telling me about? Has it got worse or is the cream working?

3 August 2006, Ahmed Ali to Pakistan:

Listen, it's confirmed, I have fever. Sometimes when I go out in the sun to meet people, I feel hot … by the way I set up my music shop now. I only need to sort out the opening time. I need stock.

4 August 2006, Pakistan to Ahmed Ali:

Do you think you can still open the shop with this skin problem? Is it only minor or can you still sort out an opening time without the skin problem worsening?

6 August 2006, Ahmed Ali to Pakistan:

I will still open the shop. I don't think it's so bad that I can't work. But if I feel really ill, I'll let you know. I also have to arrange for the printers to be picked up and stored … I have done all my prep, all I have to do is sort out opening timetable and bookings.

The 'printers' are believed to be the bombs.

Three days later, Ahmed Ali and the others were arrested. On 7 September 2009, following a majority direction from the judge, the jury reached their verdict after deliberating for fifty-four hours and eleven minutes.[11] Ahmed Ali, Assad Sarwar and Tanvir Hussain were found guilty of plotting to blow up aircraft with liquid bombs. Ahmed Ali was sentenced to life with a minimum of forty years, Sarwar to life with a minimum of thirty-six years, and Hussain to life with a minimum of thirty-two years. Umar Islam, who had made the final video on the day of the arrests, was sentenced to life with a minimum of twenty-two years. An additional defendant, Donald Stewart-Whyte, a convert to Islam from High Wycombe, was acquitted of the main charges but pleaded guilty to firearms possession. Ibrahim Savant, Arafat Khan and Waheed Zaman, who had originally pleaded guilty to conspiracy to cause a public nuisance, faced another retrial, charged with conspiracy to murder. On 8 July 2010 they were found guilty at Woolwich Crown Court and sentenced to life in prison, with a minimum of twenty years before they will be eligible for release. Justice, in the eyes of the police and the intelligence services who had invested so much time and effort in thwarting the plot, had finally been done. The persistence of the CPS was vindicated too.

Coincidentally, in early 2010 I met Donald Stewart-Whyte when I was buying a new printer cartridge in a large stationery outlet outside London. He was wearing overalls with the logo of the stationery chain, and had a large bushy beard. He recognised me from *Generation Jihad*, the BBC TV series I'd made that had recently been transmitted. I didn't recognise him until he introduced himself. He said he thought the series was 'quite good', and told me that if I bought two cartridges I would get a 20 per cent discount on one of them. It was a strange encounter. I asked him if he would be happy to meet and talk some time. He gave me his mobile number, and told me to give him a ring. I did, but he never replied. Perhaps he'd taken advice from his solicitor, and decided that it was a conversation best not to pursue.

The verdicts that were finally reached on the airline plotters silenced those sceptics who believed that the plot had been a fantasy fabricated by the state. Hanif Kadir, who knew many of the accused, was desperately sad. 'It's a huge waste of young people who have their whole life to look forward to,' he told me. 'They've lost their youth and their future. It's a shame for the community, it's a shame for other Muslims, and it should never have happened.' But it did.

The airlines plot was devised in Pakistan through the auspices of Rashid Rauf and his links with 'core' Al Qaeda, with a view to attacking British and North American aircraft. The plot was self-contained, with no wider operational links. But around the same time, other operations with global connections were being discussed and planned by networks in the UK, Europe, the USA, Canada and Pakistan. All these networks were linked via the internet, which by the end of the first decade of the twenty-first century had become Al Qaeda's ally in cyberspace.

FOURTEEN

Jihad.com

In the infinite and unregulated domain of the internet, terrorists talk to each other, recruiting, radicalising, training and plotting. That's Jihad.com. But it works both ways. For *jihadis* there is a downside too. Often the intelligence services monitor their conversations, listening in via the NSA in Maryland and GCHQ at Cheltenham. The electronic product of terrorists talking to terrorists is frequently used as evidence to help bring cells down and forestall their plots. The process is dramatically illustrated by the complex *jihadi* global network, spanning three continents, that I investigated in 2009–10.

Luck and coincidence are occasionally useful allies, and they can appear when least expected. For several months I had been trying to interview Sabir Khan, the father of Aabid Khan, a twenty-three-year-old *jihadi* from Bradford who was sentenced to twelve years' imprisonment in 2008 at Blackfriars Crown Court, London, for possessing articles for a purpose connected with terrorism and making a record of information likely to be useful in terrorism.

Aabid Khan was notorious as the 'Mr Fixit' at the centre of a global internet network. Through the ether he was recruiting young Muslims and arranging training in camps in Pakistan via his connections with the militant Kashmiri *jihadi* groups Jaish-e-Mohammed and Laskar-e-Toyeba (LeT), both of which had close connections to Al Qaeda. Laskar-e-Toyeba carried out the attacks on Mumbai that began on 26 November 2008, targeting the Taj Mahal Palace hotel, Mumbai's main railway station, a café and a Jewish centre. At least 175 people were killed and over three hundred injured in the attacks, which lasted three days.

Detective Superintendent Steve Fear, who investigated the UK section of Khan's global network for West Yorkshire Police, summed up Khan's role for me: 'Khan was a talent-spotter, a facilitator with the trust of Al Qaeda.' He described him as an internet predator, seducing vulnerable young Muslims just as paedophiles groom young children. Khan also acted as Al Qaeda's travel agent, with access to Pakistan's *jihadi* training camps. At his trial the judge said that the hoard of terrorist material seized by the police and amassed for the case was among the 'largest and most extensive ever discovered, providing vast, precise information and instruction as to how to carry out terrorist activity … the most chilling find was a folder demonstrating in careful, methodical and lethal detail the step by step instructions of how to make a suicide bomber's vest or belt packed with ball bearings and explosives'.[1] Khan was a serious and dangerous player.

Talking to convicted terrorists is difficult at the best of times, as most of them, like Aabid Khan, are in gaol, and as has been noted, the Ministry of Justice will not allow journalists to interview them, perhaps fearful that they may emerge with embarrassing stories of growing radicalisation in Britain's top-security gaols. There is no doubt that this is happening, although on what scale it's difficult to assess. After being sentenced, Aabid Khan was incarcerated in Belmarsh. When I chatted to Donald Stewart-Whyte in the stationery outlet in early 2010 he had just been released from Belmarsh, and he described how young Muslims were being radicalised on the wings by hardened *jihadis* convicted of terrorist offences.

Given the near-impossibility of talking to *jihadis* behind bars, the second best way to try to get some insight into the kind of people they are is to talk to their families. That's not easy either. I wanted to interview Aabid Khan's father, Sabir Khan, for a number of reasons. What was Aabid like? Had Sabir had any idea what his son was up to? How did he feel about what had happened to him? I understood that Sabir had served as a soldier in Northern Ireland in the early 1970s, although I didn't know in what capacity, and had then been politically active in anti-racist campaigns in Bradford in the spring and early summer of 1981, when violent race riots were erupting in Brixton, Birmingham, Leeds and Liverpool. Infamously, Sabir Khan was one of the 'Bradford Twelve' who were arrested in 1981 and charged with conspiracy and possession of explosives. All were acquitted the following year, on the grounds that the explosives were for self-defence in the face of possible attack by extremist right-wing skinhead gangs. I wanted to talk to Sabir about the way in which Asian political consciousness had changed over the years: from the early politicisation of the 'Bradford Twelve', the seeds of radicalisation planted by the Salman Rushdie affair in 1989* and the evolution of militant Islam in the wake of Bosnia, 9/11 and 7/7. I knew it wasn't going to be straightforward. Sabir had caused a commotion at his son's trial in 2008 when he had yelled at the judge and shouted about 'anti-Muslim terror laws'. Security officers were ordered to remove him, and then outside the court he reportedly punched a reporter who tried to ask him a question.[2] The omens didn't look good.

My BBC colleague Mobeen Azhar spoke to Sabir on several occasions to see if he would consider doing an interview. A young Muslim with a ponytail and bags of street cred, Mobeen was more likely to make progress with Sabir and his community than I was, being a non-Muslim BBC reporter. But in the end even Mobeen hit a brick wall. Sabir did not want to do an interview. I knew that somehow I had to persuade him to talk. In such circumstances, the reporter's last resort is the cold-call knock on the door. It's something I've never relished, but will resort to when all else fails. I've done it many times, and always get an empty feeling in the pit of my stomach as I approach the door. Once the door is knocked or the bell is rung, you're committed. There's no turning back.

First we had to find out where Sabir lived, as he had moved since Mobeen first met him. Having finally located his new address, a

---

*Rushdie's controversial novel *The Satanic Verses*, published in 1988, was regarded as blasphemous by some sections of the Muslim community. In 1989 there were demonstrations and book burnings following a *fatwa* by Iran's Ayatollah Khomeini condemning Rushdie to death. The Rushdie affair played a significant part in the growing radicalisation of some young Muslims.

terraced house on a busy main road leading out of Bradford, we went along. I rang the bell, but there was no reply. Inside, nothing stirred. We appeared to have drawn a blank. We went round the back of the house, into a rubbish-strewn alleyway, to see if there was any movement at the rear, where the kitchen was. There wasn't. We decided we'd have to try again next time we were in Bradford. Perhaps then we might have more luck.

A few weeks later we arrived on Sabir's doorstep again, having parked the car some distance away so as to make our presence less obvious. Again Mobeen and I walked up the steps and I rang the bell. This time the curtains twitched in the window by the door. There was someone inside. I rang again, but there was no sign of anyone coming to the door. When I bent down to look through the letterbox it was clear that there was somebody at home. At that very moment a car pulled up outside, and Sabir Khan got out. He'd seen me looking through his letterbox. 'Oh dear,' I thought, remembering what I'd read had allegedly happened to the reporter outside Blackfriars Crown Court. Possible explanations flashed through my mind, but within seconds a visibly angry Sabir was staring into my face. Who was I? What was I doing peering through his letterbox? Both of which were legitimate questions. I started to explain, in the hope of mollifying him. Suddenly, to my amazement, his tone of voice changed and he asked, 'Haven't I seen you on the telly?' I replied that perhaps he had, and immediately pressed the Northern Ireland button. Perhaps he'd seen one of the documentaries I'd made about the conflict there? Hadn't he served in Northern Ireland too? His mood changed instantly, and he said we'd better come inside for a cup of tea. Once we were through the door, I knew there was everything to play for.

We were introduced to his wife, who promptly, according to custom, left the kitchen and went to join the children in another room. Sabir made tea and brought out some sweet biscuits. I then began to explain who I was, and what I was hoping to do. I said I wanted to get his side of the story – which I genuinely did – and to reflect his feelings about what had happened to his son. It soon became clear that Sabir had not the slightest idea about what Aabid

had been up to. He was convinced that his son was completely innocent, and the victim of a 'set-up' by the British state, which was out
to get Muslims. I didn't feel it was the right time to argue the contrary.
After talking for the best part of an hour, and having established a
seemingly good rapport with Sabir, I found myself almost begging
him to agree to an interview. It's with some embarrassment that I
remember saying, 'Sabir, you've just got to do it.' To my surprise, he
asked, 'When?' I said, 'Now,' as we had a film crew in Bradford already
set up and waiting to do another interview. He agreed, and we drove
off to the café where the crew and producer Fatima Salaria were
waiting. I'd asked Mobeen to ring ahead and inform Fatima that
there'd been a sudden change of plan. I still couldn't believe it had
happened.

Sabir talked about growing up as a Pakistani in Bradford. It put
things in context. 'I remember the National Front coming to our
school and attacking us with their bovver boots. They called us "wogs"
and "niggers". It was really hurtful when somebody calls you that with
no reason at all. I couldn't do much, because they were big kids and I
was only four feet tall,' he said. 'In the end they got chased away by the
teachers. They actually fought them and ran them out of school.' I
asked him about being charged as a member of the 'Bradford Twelve'.
He said that although he hadn't been involved in making petrol
bombs, he had expected to go down for a long time, as IRA men
facing similar charges at the time had. He told me he had been a
bystander at the controversial riots that blazed briefly but intensely in
Bradford in July 2001, two months before 9/11. The riots were triggered as a result of an anticipated march by white extremists, but
ended up as a confrontation between young Asians and the police.
Over three hundred people were arrested, and more than three
hundred police officers injured. Sabir said he was standing behind the
police lines, and watched a BMW garage being set on fire. He had no
truck with the rioters, which I thought was a good indication of what
he thought about violence. 'I saw it all on both sides. It was senseless
damage. It was very vicious and very bad. It was no good.' Watching
his face as he said it, I believed he was telling the truth.

Then I asked him about his son. He said Aabid was just a normal boy who liked cricket and football and supported 'Man U'. They had a good relationship: 'We were like friends, and we could talk to each other. My father used to say, "I know your state of mind and what you're thinking from the first step you take inside the house." It was the same thing with Aabid.' I asked about Aabid's political views, having learned that he had become fascinated with extreme Islam at the age of twelve. Sabir said it was a subject they never discussed. Yes, there was a computer at home, but Aabid only used it to play games. Clearly Sabir was either in denial or was totally in the dark about his son's other life. Perhaps it was a bit of both. His own political activism against racism many years earlier was very different from the radical *jihadism* embraced by his son, and I could find no evidence that he had influenced Aabid in any way. I finally asked Sabir that question I've asked so many times: 'Was he a terrorist?' Sabir looked disgusted at the suggestion. 'No,' he said, as if shocked by the question. 'Aabid is a good person. I know. He's my son. He hasn't a bad bone in his body.' Did he think Aabid was capable of organising *jihadi* training in Pakistan? Again, he was dismissive: 'No, he couldn't kill a fly.' I pointed out that we weren't talking about killing flies. 'No, it's impossible,' he said. 'You had better people doing that. Aabid is a nobody.' But Aabid Khan was anything but a nobody, according to the evidence presented at his trial, on which he was convicted. I found it difficult to believe that Sabir had no inkling of what his son was up to. He must have known something about Aabid's increasing devotion to his faith, but possibly he had no idea of the steps that he had taken beyond that on the road to *jihad*.

I also knocked on the door of the Bradford home of Aabid's co-accused, Sultan Mohammed, who was sentenced to twelve years' imprisonment at the same trial. His mother was a gentle, middle-class woman who, like so many such parents, appeared to have no idea of her son's secret life. She too would have known he had become more devout, like Aabid Khan, and probably welcomed his increasingly close embrace of Islam; but, like Khan's father, she probably had no idea of what he had become involved in.

The third person who had been on trial at Blackfriars was eighteen-year-old Hammaad Munshi from Dewsbury, who was sentenced to two years in a young offenders' institution for making a record of information likely to be of use to terrorists. Munshi was a sixteen-year-old pupil at Westborough High School when he was arrested on his way home from school after taking his GCSE examinations. He was carrying two bags of ball bearings of the type used in suicide bombings. He had been groomed and recruited online by Aabid Khan. His family was devastated by the news. His grandfather, Sheikh Yacoub Munshi, is a highly respected Islamic scholar known far beyond Dewsbury. I met members of the family on several occasions, and they declined to talk. They said Hammaad had suffered enough, and had paid the price for what he had done. Unlike Sabir Khan, they did not believe he was innocent. Police had searched the family's terraced house and seized Hammaad's computer. On it they found a number of incriminating documents, including details of how to make a submachine gun and to manufacture napalm. In his bedroom they found several pages of notes, written in a spidery hand, apparently expressing the wish for 'martyrdom':

> The reason I have gone so early into the house of war is because of the beautiful act of fighting in putting Allah's word high above all … I do not want to stay in this country in Dar al-Kuffar [the House of the Unbelievers] in seclusion and in the shackles of the worldly fitnah [disbelief] as death can come anytime and I would not want to be the person the hadith is talking about, 'one who has not participated …'

Judge Timothy Pontius convicted Munshi as charged, but gave him a much lighter sentence than those he meted out to Aabid Khan and Sultan Mohammed. He took more than his age into account:

> In the light of the evidence, I have no doubt at all that you, amongst others of similar immaturity and vulnerability, fell under the spell of fanatical extremists, and your co-defendant, Aabid Khan, in particular. They took advantage of your youthful naïvety in order to indoctrinate

you with pernicious and warped ideas masquerading as altruistic religious zeal. Were it not for Aabid Khan's malign influence, I doubt this offence would ever have been committed.[3]

At eighteen, Hammaad Munshi became Britain's youngest ever convicted terrorist. His grandfather, Yacoub Munshi, put out a statement on behalf of the family:

All of us feel there are lessons to be learnt, not only for us, but also for the whole Muslim community in this country. This case demonstrates how a young impressionable teenager can be groomed so easily through the internet to associate with those whose views run contrary to true Muslim beliefs and values.[4]

There is, of course, a fundamental difference between the case of Hammaad Munshi, whose only crime was to download *jihadi* material and express the wish to become part of a *jihadi* cell, and at the other extreme the crime committed by Mohammed al-Owhali, the would-be suicide bomber who survived the attack on the US Embassy in Nairobi that resulted in the deaths of over two hundred people. They are at different ends of the scale, and the sentences they received reflect that: Al-Owhali got life without parole. Was Hammaad Munshi a terrorist? No – but he had the potential to become one, hence the conviction and the sentence, Judge Pontius's rationale probably being, with the 7/7 attacks in mind, *pour décourager les autres*. However difficult such judgements may be, a democracy has to defend itself while striking the delicate balance between liberty and security.

Over four thousand miles away, on the other side of the Atlantic, a family in Atlanta, Georgia, was going through similar agonies of disbelief on discovering that their son was a terrorist. Professor Syed Ahmed teaches computer science at North Georgia College and State University. He is a gentle and slightly shy man, with sadness in his eyes. The family came to America from Pakistan in the mid-1990s, when his son, Syed Haris Ahmed, was twelve. Haris is now serving thirteen years in a prison in Los Angeles for giving material support to terrorism, the charge on which the Lackawanna Six were convicted. 'It was the worst shock that I could imagine,' Professor Ahmed haltingly told me. 'The worst thing that could have happened to me as a father. It was just like somebody took all the blood from my body, and there was no life left in me.' The recollection was visibly painful.

My journey to meet Professor Ahmed was long and uncertain. As in so many cases, I never took the eventual attainment of my goal for granted. Occasionally simply talking to someone on the telephone is enough to secure an interview, but more often than not when painful emotions and sensitivities are involved, only a face-to-face meeting will tip the balance. Not many families are prepared to bare their souls to the media when their sons are convicted terrorists. Professor Ahmed finally agreed to cooperate in the hope that other parents might learn from his story: 'I would give parents this message: don't trust your son, or your daughter, when they are in their chat rooms, or talking to their friends, [be aware] they may be being misled. If they're angry, try to find out why they are angry, and explain that Islam does not allow killing anybody, a Muslim or a non-Muslim.'

I had first spoken to Professor Ahmed on the telephone, and told him what I was doing. I said I was planning to come to Atlanta with my producer, Leo Telling, and wondered if it would be possible for us to meet. He sounded abrupt and seemed reluctant, but said I should give him a call when I arrived. I put down the phone knowing that there was no guarantee even of a meeting, let alone an interview. It was a long way to go on the off chance. Nevertheless, Leo and I flew to Atlanta and checked into the Holiday Inn, along with a large army of well-fed baseball fans and their wives who had come to watch the Atlanta Braves play in the stadium just down the road. The hotel was not one to make a jetlagged heart sing after a long journey from London. It must have changed little since the 1996 Atlanta Olympics, and was in desperate need of a makeover.

The following evening, Leo and I made our way to an Islamic centre on the other side of town to meet Professor Ahmed and the family of Haris's Atlanta co-accused, Ehsanul Sadequee, who was born in America in 1986, after his family had emigrated from Bangladesh. We were surprised when we arrived to find a dozen or so people sitting around a long table, all of them relatives of the two accused. They were to be our interrogators over Cokes and pizza. Professor Ahmed seemed lost in the crowd, and was silent during most of the meeting.

Our most formidable inquisitor turned out to be Ehsanul Sadequee's sister Sonali, a college student who was deeply mistrustful of the media and its motivations. Little that Leo or I could say was likely to convince her that we should be allowed to talk to her imprisoned brother. I even mentioned that I had once interviewed her heroine, Angela Davis, but it seemed to cut little ice. All interviews were off until the trials were over, we were told. I thought Professor Ahmed was on the verge of agreeing to be filmed while we were in Atlanta, but felt he couldn't break ranks. His parting words were that he would think about an interview at some time in the future. We left Atlanta feeling down, hoping that it hadn't been an entirely wasted expensive journey. But at least we'd made contact, and we kept our fingers crossed that it would be an investment for the future.

Several months later, when the trials were over and both Syed Haris Ahmed and Ehsanul Sadequee had been found guilty, we returned to Atlanta. To my enormous relief, Professor Ahmed agreed to an interview. We drove for an hour and a half across the green Georgia flatlands north of Atlanta, and finally found the Professor's house tucked away in the gently rolling hills off the freeway. The setting was straight out of a Norman Rockwell painting: each house neatly painted in white and pastel shades, with an unfenced lawn, a double garage and a wooden veranda. Few people would have believed that a convicted terrorist had come from this picturesque and secluded American idyll. The Professor's wife and two daughters were nowhere to be seen. Presumably they had thought it best – or the Professor had thought it best – that they should not be around. Leo set up the camera in the neat, well-ordered kitchen while the Professor made some tea with sweet Carnation condensed milk in the familiar tin that you find everywhere in Pakistan.

We then sat and talked. The Professor said they were just an ordinary, middle-class, moderate family. They prayed five times a day, fasted during the month of Ramadan, and paid the *zakat*, the obligatory tax that is one of the Five Pillars of Islam, by which the family endeavours to abide. Their local mosque is twenty-four miles from where they live. The Professor said what I had heard many times before from parents who had found themselves in a similar situation. Haris was a good son, who only wanted to find out more about his faith. He was just like other teenagers, and loved sitting in front of the television. 'He liked the Disney Channel, and would watch cartoons like *Mickey Mouse* and *Donald Duck*. I would say to him, "You're grown up, why are you watching cartoons?" and he would say, "Because I like them."' Haris never discussed sensitive issues like *jihad* with his father, and there was no outward indication that he was thinking in that direction. None of the family was aware of the websites and chat rooms he was accessing on the computer in his bedroom. The only clue came one day when his mother went in and found Haris at the computer in tears. He had been looking at images of the suffering of Muslims in Palestine, Iraq and Afghanistan, and was crying because he felt he could not do anything to help them. His father told him it was not a good idea to store such images, as they might give people the wrong impression. He asked Haris to delete them, and deleted some himself just to make sure. I asked him if, as a father, he had been worried about the direction in which his son might be heading. He said he wasn't: 'I thought, this is just a young person being a little bit emotional, more attached to the teachings of Islam that say Muslims are obliged to help each other. If you cannot fight by hand you should feel the pain in your heart.' And if the Professor had known then what he knew now? 'I would have been more cautious, more like a friend and father to him, and tried to discuss it, and that would have prevented what happened. It was the internet that portrayed the way in which you can help your brothers.' And that wasn't just by giving aid.

Professor Ahmed has no doubt that Haris was radicalised via the internet. His co-accused, Ehsanul Sadequee, was radicalised in the same way. Like Haris, he too had been in contact with Aabid Khan 4,000 miles away in Bradford. Mark Giuliano, the FBI agent in charge of investigating the Atlanta cell, attests to the power of the internet as an instrument of radicalisation. 'It's absolutely incredible, and almost scary in a number of different arenas,' he told me. 'Number one: what is accessible now on the internet and how easy it is to learn how to make an explosive device. Number two: how easy it is to find these *jihadi* forums and people who are willing to radicalise or help radicalise individuals. And number three: how it flattens out the world and simplifies the ability to make those contacts.'

Although his father had no idea about Haris's clandestine life as a web-surfing would-be *jihadi*, the FBI had. Mark Giuliano and his team were growing increasingly concerned. 'We had information from an informant in Atlanta that there were two individuals who were attending a local mosque and a local college and calling themselves "the Taliban Brothers",' he said. 'They were really radicalised, and were attempting to do something, to plot something.' 'The Taliban Brothers' turned out to be Syed Haris Ahmed and Ehsanul Sadequee. Giuliano and his investigators subsequently discovered an email that Sadequee had written back in 2001 saying that he wanted to go to Afghanistan to fight for the Taliban. 'Here you have a player who's willing to go and actually commit *jihad*,' said Giuliano.

The FBI placed Haris Ahmed under round-the-clock surveillance, seven days a week, monitoring all his movements from his flat to the campus of Georgia Institute of Technology ('Georgia Tech'), where he was studying mechanical engineering. The emails he sent from the departmental computers and the websites he accessed were all noted by investigators. After 9/11 America was taking no chances. Giuliano was worried by what the evolving intelligence picture was beginning to show: 'He was definitely doing a lot of research that concerned us, researching bombs and bomb-making materials and how to defeat FBI surveillance.'

One of the things Professor Ahmed had not known at the time was the purpose of three significant journeys made by his son, the first two with Ehsanul Sadequee. The first was in March 2005, when they took a Greyhound bus to Toronto. The Professor thought they were going to see a relative and friends, but in fact their intention was to meet up with the cell that had been established there, and that had been in contact with Aabid Khan in Bradford. The fact that Aabid Khan himself was present at the meeting indicated that the network was not confined to the internet. At the time the FBI knew nothing about the meeting, but the Canadian Secret Intelligence Service (CSIS) and the Royal Canadian Mounted Police (RCMP) did, as they had been monitoring the Toronto cell amidst growing concern that it posed a serious terrorist threat. CSIS subsequently informed Mark Giuliano and the FBI about the meeting, as Giuliano told me: 'They were getting together to continue to plot a pretty large terrorist event, whether it be in the US, whether it be in Europe, whether it be in Canada. We know there was some operational plan going on.' But neither the Canadians nor the Americans knew what it was. It seems that Haris Ahmed and Sadequee were told by Aabid Khan that if they wanted to go to Pakistan for training, they would have to prove their credentials. Proving their credentials was the purpose of the second journey.

The following month, April 2005, Haris asked his father if he could borrow the family truck to go to Washington DC with his friend Sadequee to do some sightseeing during the spring break from Georgia Tech. The Professor only later found out that he had also taken the family video camera. He had done so because the purpose of the trip was to video potential terrorist targets in the nation's capital, and then email them to Aabid Khan and other contacts in the network to show that they were serious about wanting to fight *jihad*. In Washington they filmed famous landmarks like the Capitol building and the Pentagon, but they also filmed one particular location that was decidedly not on the tourist trail: an oil-storage depot next to a busy freeway about fifty miles south of Washington. Exploding oil tanks would have caused chaos and probably multiple deaths. The video, the duo's calling card, achieved the desired effect, and arrangements were made for Haris to meet Aabid Khan in Pakistan, with a view to getting into a training camp. He told his father he wanted to go to Pakistan to get a proper Islamic education.

Professor Ahmed argued that he would be far better off finishing his studies at college before he went to Pakistan, but Haris was adamant that he wanted to go, and his father finally gave in. As Mark Giuliano told me, all didn't go quite according to plan when Haris arrived in Pakistan: 'We understand that Khan looked at him as a liability, that he came dressed in combat gear and was really kind of loud, not a low-key individual. Khan thought he'd bring scrutiny from either Pakistani or US law enforcement, and potentially hurt Khan.' Haris never got as far as the camp, but returned to Atlanta and continued his studies at Georgia Tech. The day before he arrived home, Ehsanul Sadequee left for Bangladesh, not knowing that his every movement and email activity were being monitored by the FBI. Hidden in the lining of his suitcase were an encrypted CD, a map of Washington including the targets he and Haris had cased, and a scrap of paper with Khan's mobile phone number in Pakistan.[5]

Back in Atlanta, Haris was disappointed by his failure in Pakistan, but remained as committed as ever, telling Sadequee that he was determined to try again. Sadequee, however, had more ambitious plans involving another part of the network, again connected to Aabid Khan in Bradford. An eighteen-year-old Bosnian called Mirsad Bektasevic had established a cell in Sarajevo which he called 'Al Qaeda in Northern Europe'. His self-appointed codename was 'Maximus', after the hero played by Russell Crowe in Ridley Scott's film *Gladiator*. Bektasevic's plan was to base the cell's operational hub in Sweden, where his mother had moved as a refugee from the Bosnian war. Sadequee had been in contact with Bektasevic over the internet, and intended to join the cell. Soon after arriving in Bangladesh he had applied for a visa for Sweden. In Sarajevo, Bektasevic had acquired an arsenal of weapons, which he had been able to assemble with relative ease, given the munitions legacy of the Balkans war, and recorded a video in which, masked and armed, he announced the birth of 'Al

Qaeda in Northern Europe' with the words, 'Here are the brothers preparing for the attacks ... these weapons are going to be used against the countries whose soldiers are in Iraq, Afghanistan.' Standing alongside him in the video was another masked man, twenty-year-old Abdulkadir Cesur. But Bektasevic never got beyond threats, as following a tip-off to the Bosnian intelligence service he was arrested on 19 October 2005. He was caught red-handed with part of his arsenal of weapons, including a ready-primed suicide belt and twenty kilograms of plastic explosive. Sadequee had been in email and telephone contact with him three days before his arrest, discussing the explosives and the making of the video. Bektasevic was sentenced in 2007 to fifteen years in prison, and Cesur to thirteen.

We tried to get in touch with Bektasevic in gaol in Sweden, but he said he was not prepared to do an interview unless we paid him – which of course the BBC could not do. Our only hope was to try to see him in the hope of persuading him, but he refused that too. Our hopes were raised, however, when Abdulkadir Cesur, who was in gaol in Bosnia-Herzegovina, said he would see us. We arrived at the prison after a long, hot drive from Sarajevo, and were admitted with little formality. It felt like a sleepy prison in a sleepy little town. The administration was surprisingly relaxed, and security was less than rigorous. We were shown into a bare room with one grime-stained window, a metal table and chairs and a metal cupboard, and waited there for some time until Cesur was escorted in. He was very relaxed, and was wearing jeans and a casual shirt. It reminded me of meeting Salim Boukhari in the German gaol. Like Boukhari he was articulate and not at all threatening, very unlike what most people would expect a 'terrorist' to be. We told him what we wanted to talk about, and said we hoped he might be prepared to give us an interview. He had clearly thought about it beforehand, and replied that he didn't want to talk. We left empty-handed.

It was as a result of the arrest of Bektasevic that the intelligence agencies were able to complete the picture of the network. His mobile-phone records showed that he'd been in touch with a *jihadi* based in London's Shepherd's Bush called Younis Tsouli, whose internet *nom de guerre* was tauntingly 'Irhabi 007', Arabic for 'Terrorist 007'. Tsouli in turn had been in touch with Aabid Khan in Bradford, and he had also been the recipient of the video that Ehsanul Sadequee and Haris Ahmed had made in Washington DC to establish their credentials. He was arrested three days after Bektasevic. It was some time before the British authorities appreciated the full significance of 'Terrorist 007', who had also been responsible for disseminating *jihadi* videos sent by 'Al Qaeda in Iraq', including horrific scenes of beheadings. In 2007 Bektasevic was sentenced to fifteen years and four months for conspiracy to murder and cause explosions.

One piece of the jigsaw, however, was still missing. What was the Toronto cell plotting? CSIS and the RCMP had it under tight surveillance, but as yet they did not know what its targets were. The surveillance included not only every technical and electronic device at their disposal, but two key 'moles' who had infiltrated the cell. Moles inside a cell are pure gold for the intelligence agencies, and as a rule, for reasons of security and self-preservation, they don't talk to the outside world. One of the CSIS moles was a remarkable exception who was prepared to testify in court against his former terrorist accomplices.

Mubin Shaikh is small, voluble, charismatic and cocky. Most people would think he must be out of his mind to talk openly to the media. It's difficult to take him seriously at first, with his dark glasses, bush hat and khaki combat jacket, almost as if he were dressed to play himself in a movie. His astonishing story would scarcely be credible had it not been confirmed both by the acceptance of his evidence in court and by the intelligence services that handled him. Mubin was largely instrumental in bringing members of the cell to justice, and he was rewarded for his services. He told me he was initially paid $1,000 Canadian a month by CSIS for acting as a consultant, and then transferred to the RCMP, where he negotiated a lump sum of $77,000 Canadian with an option to renew the contract. After he'd delivered what had been hoped for, he told me he requested a further $2.6 million Canadian for his services. Tax free. The intelligence services confirmed that he had been paid an awful lot of money, but it was, they suggested, a bargain, considering the loss of life and property that would have ensued had the plot gone ahead. I told Mubin I thought he had to be joking when he told me about the amounts. He said he wasn't, and insisted he hadn't done what he did for the money, but purely because of 'my conviction that terrorism is against Islam': 'It's no joke. It's my life. I have to think about the safety of my family, to get them out of the country as soon as possible if needs be, to get plane tickets and find a place to live and stuff like that. Whether they pay me or not, I will still be there and commit to the evidence that I collected and that I've testified to in court. I've earned my money.' I wondered why he had opted not to go into a witness protection programme, given that he must now be a marked man. 'You're going to cut your friends and family off, and go somewhere else to start a new life. I can't just up and leave.'

Mubin wasn't a terrorist who was turned from the inside, but was recruited from the world outside to infiltrate the cell. It happened as the result of a remarkable coincidence. He grew up in the same apartment block as his fellow Canadian Momin Kawaja. When he heard that Kawaja had been arrested and charged in connection with the British plot thwarted by Operation Crevice, he says he was shocked, and rang CSIS to see if there had been some mistake. CSIS asked to see him. They were impressed by his story, and saw his potential as someone who could speak the extremists' language and understood their ideology. They were not going to pass up the opportunity of getting someone like Mubin on their side, and recruited him.

The Toronto cell was led by Fahim Ahmad and Zakaria Amara, who were bitterly opposed to the presence of Canadian troops in Afghanistan and believed that terrorist attacks on Canadian soil would force their withdrawal. Fahim Ahmad, the cell leader, had been present at the Toronto meeting in March 2005 attended by Haris Ahmed, Ehsanul Sadequee and Aabid Khan. Mubin's credentials were as attractive to Ahmad and Amara as they had been to CSIS. He was a devout Muslim who had turned from drugs to Allah. He told me that as a teenager he had enjoyed 'sex, drugs and rock 'n' roll': 'It was a good time, but I felt empty.' He had spent his honeymoon in Mecca and Medina,[6] and had once toyed with the idea of fighting *jihad* himself. He had also spent five years as an army cadet, and knew about military procedures and weaponry, which were exactly the skills Ahmad and Amara were looking for.

Once he was inside the cell, Mubin was tasked with organising a training camp for potential *jihadis* far away in the woods at Washago, a two-hour drive north of Toronto. He took us there, and we were almost bitten to death by mosquitoes, as it was the height of summer. The training had taken place in the depths of the freezing Canadian winter, and Fahim Ahmad had fired the campers with a rousing speech about *jihad* which was recorded on video. He said they must band together and sacrifice whatever was needed to defeat Western civilisation: 'It doesn't matter what trials you face. It doesn't matter what comes your way. Our mission's greater. Whether we get arrested, whether we get killed or tortured, our mission's greater than just individuals.'[7] Mubin showed the potential recruits how to use weapons and organised paintballing sessions to practise military manoeuvres. To call it a training camp is an exaggeration: it was more a bonding session, such as the 7/7 and 21/7 bombers had taken part in prior to their attacks on London, in the mountains of north Wales and the Lake District.

At some stage after the camp the cell split, supposedly as a result of tactical disagreements. Fahim Ahmad seemed to be on a fantasy trip: a bug in his car recorded him saying, 'Hey, wanna be part of the group that goes up to Parliament, man, cut off some heads? We go and kill everybody.'[8] Mubin told me Ahmad's plan was to storm the Canadian Parliament building in Ottawa, take hostages and threaten to behead one politician every hour, including the Prime Minister, unless Canada agreed to withdraw its troops from Afghanistan. Zakaria Amara had more conventional terrorist plans: to make three truck bombs, detonate two of them in downtown Toronto outside CSIS headquarters and the stock exchange, and the third at an unspecified military base outside the city. Another bug recorded Ahmad talking about the bombings before the cell split: 'They're probably expecting what happened in London … Our thing is much, much greater on scale … You do it once and make sure they never recover again.'[9]

Amara carried on with the plan after the split of the cell. He set about acquiring 1.5 tons of ammonium nitrate and two gallons of nitric acid. Trucks were rented from U-Haul and money was paid for a lock-up where the cell could store the bomb-making chemicals. What the cell didn't know was that CSIS and the RCMP were watching and recording their every move. The cell got hold of the ammonium nitrate, but the police did exactly what the Met had done in Operation Crevice, covertly substituting it with a similar substance that would not arouse suspicion. Nor did the cell know that they had arranged to rent the lock-up from an undercover police officer who was posing as the owner. When they delivered the supposed ammonium nitrate to the lock-up, a reception party was waiting for them, in the form of heavily armed anti-terrorist police wearing balaclavas and clad all in black. A video camera had been secreted in the U-Haul truck, so the arrests were captured on film. The Toronto cell was smashed.

Gradually the net closed on the global network that had emanated from Aabid Khan in Bradford. Zakaria Amara, Fahim Ahmad and sixteen other suspects were arrested on 2–3 June 2006. Collectively they were known as the 'Toronto 18', and became a *cause célèbre*. Charges were stayed on seven, two were found guilty, and seven pleaded guilty, including Amara and Ahmad. Amara was sentenced to life imprisonment in 2009, the longest sentence meted out under Canada's post-9/11 anti-terrorist legislation. A week before his sentence he publicly apologised for his actions and renounced extremism. The following year, Ahmad received the same sentence. At both trials the defence argued that their clients had been entrapped by Mubin Shaikh, but the judge dismissed the plea. The case was finally closed on 23 June 2010, when the two remaining accused were found guilty of knowingly participating in a terrorist group.

The other dominos quickly fell following the Toronto arrests on 2–3 June 2006. Aabid Khan was detained at Manchester airport on 6 June as he was returning from Pakistan with a wealth of incriminating terrorist material on his laptop, including a reference to the sixteen-year-old schoolboy from Dewsbury, Hammaad Munshi. Munshi was arrested the following day. The intelligence agencies had known nothing about him until then. The network spanning three continents had finally been wound up.

Syed Haris Ahmed had been arrested in Atlanta on 23 March 2006, and on 20 April 2006 Ehsanul Sadequee was detained by the FBI in Bangladesh and controversially rendered to face trial in America. Professor Ahmed and his wife broke down in tears when they heard about the arrest of their son. The Professor said he thought it would never happen to his family. He felt guilty, and regretted never having discussed things with Haris. He believed that if he had, 'I would have saved him and the family from all this trouble. He would have listened to me more than the websites, and he would be a normal person working for his degree, being a source of help to the family and to himself.' He concluded by expressing the wish that no other family should go through what he and his family had.

Haris Ahmed was convicted on 9 June 2009 of conspiring with Ehsanul Sadequee to give material support for terrorism in the USA and abroad, and was sentenced to thirteen years in gaol. Sadequee was sentenced to seventeen years for supporting terrorists and a foreign terrorist organisation. In court he defended himself, and displayed no repentance. 'I submit to no one's authority but the authority of God,' he told the judge.[10] Haris Ahmed, however, did show remorse. Violence, he said, 'is not helping Islam. It's not Islamic. Killing random people, this is not the way.'[11] From prison he wrote a letter to his family in which he expressed his regret in moving detail. It also illustrates a journey to *jihad* that has probably been replicated in the cases of many other young Muslims around the world.

Dear All,
Assalam Alaykum wa Rahmatullah [Peace, Mercy and Blessings be with you]

I'm sorry for getting you all through this mess … Sorry for the heart break I caused you, Ammi and Baba [Mother and Father]. I want to say a bit of my side of the story too. I am not blaming others. I know I am fully responsible for my actions.

Never got a serious or even mediocre Islamic education, or for that matter even secular one at home. I would say that I had zero information about Islam. But I still had curiosity. Thus I turned to the only source of knowledge about Islam available to me, that is the internet. I remember in the early beginning I would sometimes type 'Islam' in the search engine and read whatever sites came up. So there I was, having no background in Islamic knowledge, going through loads of information, mostly opinions of other people about their understanding of Islam. I could not detect authentic from unauthentic, mainstream [Islam]. Reading that stuff on line, had me convinced that most people in the mosques were little short of hypocrites or ignorant.

And coming from Pakistan I knew that the situation in Muslim countries was not very good. Knew that injustices were being committed. Was naturally angry over the plight of my people. No doubt would have liked to help in any way. So with all that it's no surprise if I may get swayed by some extreme propaganda. I had no access to any imam or person with religious knowledge at that time. Then came the Iraq war. The propaganda that was snail's pace became full throttle now.

So looking back at it all I will say I learned a few things, one is that parents are the guardian and nurturers of the children. They should not just provide food and shelter but also be the provider of religious and worldly knowledge.

Always wanted to be part of something larger than myself or immediate family. Was never a fan of a lifestyle that involved 9–5 job then going home. Didn't really want a whole life spent on a mundane corporate job then retirement. I was seeking a purpose in life. And that desire to belong … and desire to get to Paradise seemed to combine in the path I took.

Ammi, Baba, I'm sorry for not being the son I should have been [and to my sisters] I'm sorry for not being the brother I should have been.

Astaghfirullah wa atubu ilaih [May God forgive me my mistakes]
With love and sorrow
Yours Haris

As part of their sentences, Haris Ahmed and Ehsanul Sadequee were given thirty years' probation (in addition to their custodial sentences), during which time they were forbidden to use the internet.

The two young Muslims from Atlanta were convicted as the result of painstaking detective work by the FBI and its partner agencies, and convicted by due process. But in the decade since 9/11, hundreds of 'enemy combatants', as they became known, captured in the so-called 'War on Terror', were detained without trial in America's prison camp at Guantánamo Bay in Cuba. Many alleged that they had been tortured at secret CIA 'black sites' before being rendered to Guantánamo, where they were subjected to further ill-treatment. Guantánamo Bay and torture became an indelible stain on America's reputation as the upholder of freedom, human rights and due process of law. Both did it incalculable moral damage in the eyes of much of the world.

FIFTEEN

Talking to the Victims of Torture

In my long journey from the IRA to Al Qaeda, the torture and ill-treatment of terrorist suspects during interrogation is one of the most difficult and sensitive areas I have had to cover. When, if ever, is it justified? Does the end, even in the cause of protecting life, ever justify the means? If torturing or ill-treating a terrorist suspect produces information that leads to the prevention of a horrific atrocity, does that vindicate its use? The classic scenario – which is highly unlikely ever actually to occur – is the imperative to extract vital information from a suspect who has intelligence about an attack that is about to take place. Hundreds of lives may be lost, and he is believed to know the location of the bomb. It's the so-called 'ticking time-bomb' favoured by Hollywood and by American TV series like *24*. Is torture justified in circumstances where the interrogators believe it is the only way of eliciting life-saving intelligence? I would hate to have to make that decision. Is there any guarantee that the intelligence provided as a result of such extreme measures would be reliable? Should torture or any kind of ill-treatment be outlawed in a civilised society? This is a difficult moral and political question that admits of no easy answers. One senior British civil servant with great experience of countering terrorism told me he believed the prohibition had to be absolute, even if it meant that lives would be lost.

Specific examples I have described in the course of this book indicate that persistent, non-coercive interrogation – talking to terrorists, not torturing them – can produce the desired results without a finger being laid on the suspect. In evidence I would cite Steve Gaudin's interrogation of Mohammed Al-Owhali after his attack on the US Embassy in Nairobi (see pp. 80–92) and the FBI's interrogation of Mohammed Jabarah that led the warning of a possible attack on Bali (see pp. 138–49).

For the journalist, the subject is a minefield. If you report allegations of ill-treatment made by 'terrorists' and their supporters, are you giving succour to the 'enemy'? If you don't, are you being complicit with the state in turning a blind eye to practices which are not only morally questionable, but illegal?

These were the dilemmas I faced when investigating the ill-treatment of IRA and Loyalist terrorist suspects in Northern Ireland during the late 1970s. At the time, which was at the height of the so-called Troubles, Labour government Ministers were making it clear that they believed reporting terrorism left no room for objectivity and neutrality. I disagreed, feeling that the issue was being personalised by politicians who were blaming the messengers for bringing unwelcome and disturbing news. In the late 1970s I remember going to see a very senior officer in the Royal Ulster Constabulary to try to establish the truth about what was going on in the interrogation centres under his command, euphemistically known as 'holding centres'. I was taken aback when he produced from the top drawer of his desk an article I had written about allegations of ill-treatment for *Index on Censorship*, in which I concluded that serious abuses had taken place.[1] In the course of my research I had met two doctors, Dr Robert Irwin at Castlereagh and Dr Denis Elliott at Gough Barracks, Armagh, who regularly examined suspects after their interrogations. They had told me of their grave concerns about the way in which the suspects appeared to have been treated. They believed that some of the marks on their bodies were not self-inflicted, which was one of the explanations the police invariably gave. I felt under attack from the authorities, the clear implication being that I had a personal political agenda. Nothing could have been further from the truth. I felt vindicated when in 1978 Amnesty International published the results of its own investigations into the allegations of ill-treatment at the RUC's interrogation centres, which concluded: 'Maltreatment has taken place with sufficient frequency to warrant a public inquiry to investigate it.'[2] There was never any public inquiry.

When I reflect on Amnesty's conclusions, I realise how relatively minor the ill-treatment was when compared to the 'enhanced interrogation techniques', culminating in waterboarding, that the Bush administration authorised in the wake of 9/11. In Northern Ireland, terrorist suspects were physically assaulted, had their fingers and wrists bent backwards and were made to stand spreadeagled against a wall with their feet apart for long periods of time. Although the IRA and Sinn Féin cried 'torture', I never regarded it as such. I did however believe that it constituted 'inhuman and degrading treatment' – a level below 'torture'. All these practices, whether torture or not, were designed to cause pain and elicit information. Some proved to be counter-productive, as when judges in the province's Diplock courts threw out admissions of guilt that they deemed had been extracted as a result of 'torture, inhuman or degrading treatment'. Such practices, however, were always denied by the Royal Ulster Constabulary and the government, which supported its officers, who were under great pressure in the province, in the interests of keeping up morale.

Of course the situation in Northern Ireland was different from that faced by America and the West in the wake of 9/11. Almost as many people died on that single day as in the first twenty, most violent, years of the Troubles.[3] A desperate situation, the Bush administration would argue, required desperate measures. The most desperate measure of all was the establishment of America's prison camp at Guantánamo Bay in Cuba, where terrorist suspects were held indefinitely, initially without trial or access to any lawyer, and interrogated. The facility was set up in January 2002, after Al Qaeda and Taliban fighters fled Afghanistan following the American invasion in October 2001, many of them subsequently escaping the US aerial bombardment of Al Qaeda's Tora Bora mountain stronghold. The problem for the USA was what to do with the hundreds of 'enemy combatants' trapped on the battlefield or fleeing from it. The British had a similar problem following the introduction of internment without trial in Northern Ireland in 1971. They set up the

'Long Kesh' prison camp. The Americans set up Guantánamo Bay. Both administrations steadfastly refused to give the inmates prisoner-of-war status. Guantánamo was chosen because although the Americans had had that small enclave of the island on permanent lease from Cuba since 1903 – they used it as a naval base – it was nevertheless not US sovereign territory. This meant, conveniently, that US law did not apply on its soil.[4]

The first of an estimated six hundred prisoners touched down at Guantánamo on 11 January 2002, chained and shackled and soon to be clad in the orange jumpsuits that were to become synonymous with the camp. As they arrived, US Secretary of Defense Donald Rumsfeld ominously declared that they had 'no rights under the Geneva Convention'.[5] Many of the new detainees and those who followed had been interrogated at US interrogation centres at Bagram airbase and Kandahar before they were flown from Afghanistan to Guantánamo, or interrogated at CIA 'black sites' where they were subjected to the 'enhanced interrogation techniques' that were authorised by the Bush administration on 1 August 2002. To the White House these techniques, which ranged from sleep deprivation to waterboarding (I will detail them in the final chapter), did not constitute torture, but in the eyes of the rest of the world they almost certainly did. Once such practices had been given the imprimatur of the United States government, it was only a matter of time before other totally unauthorised and even more extreme practices were used not just at Guantánamo but at interrogation centres in Afghanistan. The effect was corrosive.

Mohammed al-Awfi was one of those on the receiving end, although he wasn't subjected to the 'enhanced techniques'. He was one of fourteen Saudi Arabians, known as 'Batch Ten', who were repatriated from Guantánamo Bay in November 2007, as the Bush administration came under increasing pressure from its allies, of which Saudi Arabia was one of the most important, to release some of the detainees.[6] With a total of over 120 detainees, Saudi Arabia had the highest number. Yemen had over a hundred, and Afghanistan only slightly fewer.[7] Perhaps it wasn't surprising that Saudi Arabia came out top of the list, given that fifteen of the nineteen 9/11 hijackers came from the desert Kingdom. To the Americans, Mohammed al-Awfi was known as prisoner number 333.

At various stages during his incarceration, each prisoner's case was reviewed at Guantánamo by a Combat Status Review Tribunal to see if he fulfilled the criterion for 'enemy combatant status', defined as 'an individual who was part of or supporting the Taliban or Al Qaeda forces, or associated forces that are engaged in hostilities against the United States or its coalition partners. This includes any person who committed a belligerent act or has directly supported hostilities in aid of enemy armed forces.'[8] It was a catch-all definition.

In September 2004 the tribunal conducted an assessment of Mohammed al-Awfi's case and confirmed its previous findings: it stated that he was 'associated with Al Qaeda … was a *mujahideen* fighter at Kandahar … [and] had participated in military operations against the United States'. It also alleged that his name had been found on a document recovered at a former residence of Osama Bin Laden in Kandahar.[9]

Saudi Arabia's Ministry of the Interior videoed Mohammed al-Awfi and the other thirteen returnees of 'Batch Ten' on their flight home from Guantánamo in November 2007. Al-Awfi is clearly in pain, and has to be helped onto the plane. During the flight he can be seen being given medical attention, and on touchdown in Saudi Arabia he is put in a wheelchair and lowered onto the tarmac on a mechanical hoist. The Ministry made the video for propaganda purposes, to show its citizens and the world how Saudi Arabia treats its prodigal children, in contrast to the way they had been treated by the Americans. The former detainees who made up 'Batch Ten' were destined to join other former Guantánamo prisoners and others with terrorist convictions in the Interior Ministry's controversial terrorist re-education programme. It had been established in 2004, with its name reflecting its philosophy and purpose: Prevention. Rehabilitation. After Care (PRAC). The programme bears the name of its creator, Prince Mohammed Bin Nayef, the Deputy Interior Minister responsible for Saudi Arabia's fight against terrorism.

Underlying the programme's philosophy is the premise that Saudi Arabia's former terrorists are not criminals, but victims of a deviant ideology. Reformation, the programme believes, is therefore possible after a period of re-education and reorientation under the supervision of trained psychologists and religious scholars. The process lasts as long as it takes, anything from a few months to a year or more, until the point is reached where the 'beneficiaries' can be released back into society, where their progress and behaviour remain strictly monitored by mentors from the programme. The Saudis claim an 80–90 per cent success rate. They say that 107 former Guantánamo detainees were released after going through the programme, as were another 105 former terrorists arrested in Saudi Arabia. Seven were still in the programme, these being the most difficult to deprogramme and rehabilitate. Fourteen were still at Guantánamo awaiting repatriation. Five had been rearrested and returned to prison. Ten absconded to Yemen. One of the absconders was Mohammed al-Awfi.

Al-Awfi spent several difficult months going through the programme as a less than model 'beneficiary'. After a few months he left and disappeared across the border to Yemen, where he joined Al Qaeda. It's probably more accurate to say that he 'rejoined', since it's unlikely that a stranger with no Al Qaeda connections would be invited to join, fresh from the Saudi government's rehabilitation programme – he would almost certainly have been taken for a spy and killed. Al-Awfi didn't simply join Al Qaeda, he rocketed straight to the top leadership level. Remarkably, he appeared in a propaganda video released on 23 January 2009 announcing the amalgamation of Al Qaeda in Saudi Arabia and Al Qaeda in Yemen to form the 'Al Qaeda Organisation in the Arabian Peninsula' (AQAP). Although the marriage was forced, due to the heavy losses suffered by Al Qaeda cells in Saudi Arabia, it was carried out with the blessing of Ayman al-Zawahiri.

Al-Awfi appears in the launch video in combat fatigues with a grenade launcher on his back and a bandolier across his chest. He bears the grand title 'Field Commander'. Three other men appear with him. One of them, Said al-Shiri, Guantánamo prisoner number 372, had also been part of 'Batch Ten', and like al-Awfi was a fugitive from the rehabilitation programme, which had failed to work for either *jihadi*. He also had an imposing title: 'Secretary General'. The two other *mujahideen* in the video are Al Qaeda's 'Commander' in Yemen, Nasir al-Wahishi, and its 'Military Major', Qasim al-Rimi. Al-Shiri spits defiance at the camera: 'We are performing *jihad* ... our imprisonment has only increased our persistence ... we will serve as a buttress for the *jihad* to expand from the [Arabian] Peninsula to Palestine, Somalia, Iraq, Afghanistan and all the Muslim countries ... there is no power and no strength save in Allah.'[10]

Al-Awfi also attacked the rehabilitation programme, with defiant eyes, wagging his finger at the camera – perhaps an indication of how successful the programme was, and how great a threat it posed to Al Qaeda: 'We warn our imprisoned brothers to avoid the programme administered by the ignorant oppressor, [Prince] Mohammed Bin Nayef and his criminal helpers ... to persuade us to stray from Islam and our path ... Praise be to Allah for blessing us with the chance to leave their putrid authority.'[11]

Then, in February 2009, something remarkable happened. Mohammed al-Awfi, for whatever reason, decided to cast off his combat fatigues, bandolier and grenade launcher and give himself up to the Saudis. I was in Saudi Arabia at the time, making a film about the rehabilitation programme for my series *Generation Jihad*.* Having seen the video, I could hardly believe this turn of events. I was told by the Ministry of the Interior that al-Awfi's wife's phone calls had been monitored, and she had been heard telling him to get back home as he had responsibilities to her and the children. Al Qaeda's 'Field Commander' promptly obeyed. An unlikely story, I thought, a Muslim woman ordering her husband about like that: it's usually the other way round. A more likely reason, I was told by others, was that the Saudis used a threat to al-Awfi's family to pressurise him into

---

*In the end we edited the Saudi filming for BBC2's *Newsnight* programme when Al Qaeda in Yemen suddenly hit the headlines following an attempt by a young Nigerian former London University student, Umar Farouq Abdulmuttalab, to blow up a plane over Detroit on Christmas Day 2009.

returning. Whatever the reason, he gave himself up and confessed the error of his ways. He was now back in gaol.

I knew that it would be a coup to secure an interview with him. We were finally given the green light on the day before producer Leo Telling and I were due to leave Saudi Arabia. It seemed too good to be true. We drove for about forty-five dusty minutes to Riyadh's top-security prison, al-Ha'ir, on the fringe of the ever-encroaching desert that the sprawling outskirts of the city struggle to keep at bay. I sat in the car, nervously wondering if it was going to be for real and al-Awfi would be delivered as promised. The prison looked like something out of *Beau Geste*, sitting in the middle of nowhere, among the sand dunes and nothingness. The walls and watchtowers that surrounded it seemed to stretch far off into the horizon. After being told not to film anything on the way in, we were escorted to a special compound in the middle of the complex and introduced to various military offi-cials who ran the gaol. There then followed the traditional courtesy banquet which greets visitors almost anywhere in Saudi Arabia, and for which the schedule has to allow at least an hour. This one had Krispy Kreme donuts on the menu. But there was still no sign of al-Awfi.

It was clear that we were in the VIP reception area, where honoured guests could also stay overnight. The huge tiled and polished entrance hall was filled with ornate couches and cushions. Illuminated pictures of Saudi Arabia adorned the walls and an assortment of crystal chan-deliers hung from the ceiling. Finally we were taken to see al-Awfi's quarters. Not for Al Qaeda's former 'Field Commander' a bleak Guantánamo cell, but a five-star, self-contained apartment with lounge, giant flat-screen television and bedroom with huge double bed. We were told his family was welcome to visit. We repaired down-stairs to the reception area where Leo had been told to set up the camera.

Then al-Awfi came in. I didn't recognise him at first. He looked nothing like the shattered, dishevelled figure I'd seen in the Al Qaeda video. He wasn't in shackles, handcuffed or in prison uniform. There didn't even appear to be a guard with him. His beard was neatly trimmed and he was dressed in a traditional, pristine white cotton *thobe*, with a Saudi red-and-white-chequered *keffiyeh* round his head. We introduced ourselves and shook hands. After a few pleasantries and time for Leo to sort out a recalcitrant camera – technical gremlins always seem to appear at the most inconvenient moments – the interview began, and al-Awfi told me his story.

He said he had worked at the Al Shumaisy hospital in Riyadh, but had left to fight *jihad* in Chechnya, angered by Russia's 'atrocities, torture, rape, kidnapping of women, theft, and destruction of homes'. He didn't tell his family he was going, and they only found out after he had left. He said he did go to Chechnya, but then decided he needed to be properly trained, so he travelled to Afghanistan. This was just a few months before 9/11. I put it to him that the Americans at Guantánamo had alleged in his Combatant Status Review that he had trained at the Al Farouq camp, where he was taught to use weapons, grenades and explosives, and that he had fought with the *mujahideen* around Kandahar. Was that true? He was non-committal, but denied that he had ever fought with the Taliban. The Americans had also said that when he was arrested he was carrying $12,000, destined for a charity called Al Wafa, which they alleged was a cover for supplying money to the *mujahideen*. He admitted carrying the money, but said it was to help refugees.

Al-Awfi told me that he never completed his training in Afghanistan, as after the American invasion everyone was ordered to leave in whatever way they could. He said he escaped to Pakistan, where he was arrested by the army and then handed over to the police,[12] who he claimed sold him to the Americans for $5,000. It wasn't the first time I'd heard about such transactions. I asked how he could possibly have known his sale price. 'We were in the airport when the money was handed over, and we heard them mentioning the amount,' he said. He was then flown back from Pakistan to the US airbase at Bagram.

I remembered the Saudis' video of 'Batch Ten' returning from Guantánamo, and how al-Awfi had clearly been suffering from some painful injuries. I asked him what had happened. He said when he arrived at Bagram the Americans were throwing people onto the runway. 'They lifted me very high while I was completely tied up and then dropped me onto the airstrip which was asphalt. They did this to me three times. My screams were clear for all to hear. I fainted, and didn't regain consciousness until I was inside Bagram. That's how my back pains started.'

He said he was detained at Bagram for four days, and then transferred to Kandahar for interrogation. That was where he said the torture began. He alleges he was given electric shocks: 'They put sensors on your testicles, similar to the ones you attach to the heart. They do it to try and extract as many confessions as possible.' He described some other details of his treatment. 'They used to make you as naked as the day you were born and then assaulted your genitals and your honour directly or indirectly. They know that for Muslims honour and dignity are very important. They put you on a chair with a hole in the seat, pull your testicles through the gap and then beat them with a metal rod. They'd tie up your penis and make you drink salty water to make you urinate without being able to until they make you scream. Even if you're a hero and very courageous, you will not be able to bear it for more than half an hour, and then you will have to confess.' I asked why I should believe his allegations. 'Everyone knows what the Americans did, and President Obama is now talking about torture. We cannot lie to the world about the fact that American soldiers or the FBI or CIA or anti-terrorism squads have used torture in order to extract statements.' President George W. Bush has denied that America ever used torture.[13] It all depends on the definition, and as we will see (p. 292), the Bush administration changed the definition to suit its purposes.

My instinctive reaction as I listened to Mohammed al-Awfi's disturbing allegations was that they were probably exaggerated, and that claims of this type were being deliberately disseminated by former detainees as anti-American propaganda. However, after accessing a wealth of formerly top-secret CIA and FBI documents in America covering the interrogation of detainees, primarily at Guantánamo and unidentified CIA 'black sites' overseas (see pp. 287–90), I was not so sure. Already, in 2008, it had become clear how widespread abuses were from the report of the Senate Armed Services Committee into the treatment of detainees. One of the senior members of the committee was Senator John McCain, who subsequently ran as the Republican presidential candidate against Barack Obama, and who had himself been tortured when held as a prisoner-of-war in Vietnam. The investigation concluded:

> The abuses at Abu Ghraib [in Iraq], GTMO [Guantánamo] and elsewhere cannot be chalked up to the actions of a few bad apples. Attempts by senior officials to pass the buck to low-ranking soldiers while avoiding any responsibility for abuses are unconscionable. The message from top officials was clear; it was acceptable to use degrading and abusive techniques against detainees. Our investigation is an effort to set the record straight on this chapter in our history that has so damaged America's standing and our security. America needs to own up to its mistakes so that we can rebuild some of the goodwill that we have lost.[14]

The Senators found that these abuses at other sites were 'influenced' by Secretary of Defense Donald Rumsfeld's decision on 2 December 2002 to approve 'aggressive interrogation techniques at GTMO'. As will become clear in the next chapter, other *unauthorised* interrogation techniques were also used, above and beyond the already extreme practices that had been approved by the Bush administration. The chilling mood music of the time seemed to be that 'anything goes'. On reflection, I suspected that there was probably more than a grain of truth in the torture allegations made by al-Awfi and other former detainees I met in Saudi Arabia after their repatriation.

I asked al-Awfi how he had been treated during his seven years at Guantánamo. He said the psychological suffering was worse than the physical torture. Eventually, he said, it all became one. 'The situation was terrible. I was naked without clothes. Sometimes they would make you sit for twenty-four or thirty-six hours in the interrogation room with extremely cold air conditioning. [Sometimes] they would pour water on your head and all over you. If you wanted to go to the toilet, they wouldn't let you go and you'd have to do it where you were. Everything they did was in order to aid the interrogators. They didn't let us sleep. In the end you give yourself up or else you lie and confess to things you didn't do in order to stop the torture.' He described the psychological torture: 'They would insult your religion and mock your prayers. You would go into a room and find a line of Korans lying on the floor and the interrogator would then walk over them. A woman would come in and menstruate on the Korans in front of your eyes. All these extreme psychological pressures were practised against the brothers in Guantánamo.'

The Senate Armed Services Committee report and other subsequent investigations by the CIA and FBI Inspectors General confirm these kinds of practices (see final chapter). One infamous case documented in the FBI Inspector General's report is that of Mohammed al-Qahtani, who was captured by the Pakistani security forces on 15 December 2001 as he was trying to enter Pakistan from Afghanistan. He was handed over to the Americans, and rendered to Guantánamo two months later. At first he told his FBI and military interrogators that he had gone to Afghanistan to buy and sell falcons. Not surprisingly, this wasn't believed. It soon transpired, as a result of other inquiries into the 11 September attacks, that al-Qahtani had been refused entry to America at Orlando airport, Florida, in August 2001 – the month before 9/11, and subsequent investigations seemed to link him to the plot. At Guantánamo he was initially interrogated by a Muslim FBI agent who spoke Arabic and who, according to al-Qahtani, treated him well. Then the military took over. The FBI's Inspector General concluded that they used the following practices to try to break him:

- Tying a dog leash to the detainee's chain, walking him round the room and leading him through a series of dog tricks
- Repeatedly pouring water on his head
- Twenty-hour interrogations
- Stripping him naked in the presence of a female
- Holding him down while a female interrogator straddled the detainee

- Women's underwear placed over his head and bra placed over his clothing
- Female interrogator massaging his back and neck
- Describing his mother and sister as whores
- Showing him pictures of scantily clad women
- Discussing his repressed homosexual tendencies
- Male interrogator dancing with him
- Telling him that people would tell other detainees that he got aroused when male guards searched him[15]

In December 2002 al-Qahtani was hospitalised as a result of the treatment he had received. At the time, neither the FBI nor the US Department of Justice was aware of the techniques that were being used. As we will see in the concluding chapter, the FBI refused to have any involvement in such practices.

I remained curious as to why Mohammed al-Awfi had left the Saudis' rehabilitation programme. He said it was because the memories of what he had suffered at the hands of the Americans at Bagram, Kandahar and Guantánamo were far more potent than anything he learned from the programme. And what were the circumstances under which he had taken part in the Al Qaeda video? 'The Al Qaeda leadership put pressure on me, and ordered me to appear. It took them two weeks to persuade me. I was given a photocopy of the full text of what they wanted me to say. They said I must say all this [about the rehabilitation programme] for political reasons. I recited the words against my will, but as I had been ordered to do it, I executed the order.' He said the filming took from 8 o'clock one evening until 2 o'clock the following morning, 'because every time we stopped there were comments'. His description reminded me of Ahmed Ali coaching Umar Islam on what to say in the propaganda video uncovered by Operation Crevice.

At the end of the interview I felt that there was no possibility that al-Awfi would return to his previous existence as an Al Qaeda *jihadi*. Even if he had wanted to, his captors would not have let him. He said he was now a changed man: 'I realise I had a deviant ideology, and this is not just a mood or a whim. I am now a happier and more relaxed person. I've gone through an experience in my life and realise that I had taken the wrong course. I came back, thanks be to God, and things are well.' I wondered if he was reciting a script again, this time written by the Saudi Ministry of the Interior. But he seemed to mean what he said. He concluded with a thought that stuck in my mind: 'I advise everyone not to deal with extremism by the use of force. Force doesn't speak to force. There must be another method.'

I thanked him, shook hands, and said goodbye. As he walked away, I thought how lucky he was to be alive. His fellow member of 'Batch Ten', Said al-Shiri, who had shared a starring role in the video, was still alive too, somewhere in Yemen. He is now thought to be Al Qaeda in the Arabian Peninsula's number two. I wondered how long he would survive.

Whatever the reasons for Mohammed al-Awfi's change of heart, he was a valuable asset to the Saudis. They drained him of every scrap of intelligence while he was staying in the relative luxury of the VIP suite inside the prison. There was no need for torture. As it turned out later that year, his interrogators had good reason to be concerned about Al Qaeda along Saudi Arabia's southern border. In August 2009 a suicide bomber tried to assassinate Prince Mohammed Bin Nayef, the founder of the rehabilitation programme.[16] The bomber, believed to be connected to Al Qaeda in the Arabian Peninsula, died, but the Prince was only slightly wounded. In November an American Muslim army officer, Major Nidal Malik Hasan, based at Fort Hood in Texas, shot dead thirteen of his colleagues. He was later found to have received religious instruction by email from a radical US cleric, Anwar Al-Awlaki, who had returned to live in his native Yemen and taped sermons encouraging *jihad* against the USA. The following month, Umar Farouq Abdulmuttalab, a young Nigerian who had studied in London and then trained in Yemen, tried to blow up Northwest Airlines Flight 253 over Detroit on Christmas Day 2009. There were almost three hundred people on board. The explosives were hidden in his underpants, the same method used, it is believed, by the suicide bomber who tried to assassinate Prince Mohammed Bin Nayef. Abdulmuttalab too was believed to have been influenced by Al-Awlaki. As a result, in April 2010 the Obama administration reportedly authorised the CIA to carry out a search-and-destroy mission to remove the troublesome cleric. They believed he was now not just a firebrand, but an active member of Al Qaeda.[17] The instrument most likely to despatch him would be a missile fired from a pilotless drone, as it had been in so many other CIA targeted killings. One of the earliest victims, also in Yemen, had been Kamal Derwish, the recruiter of the Lackawanna Six, incinerated in the desert by a Hellfire missile.

Mohammed al-Awfi's allegations of torture mirrored accounts I heard from other former Guantánamo detainees in Saudi Arabia. Khalid Al-Bawardi was also on the flight with al-Awfi and other members of 'Batch Ten' when they were flown back to Riyadh in November 2007. Khalid, prisoner number 68, had spent six and a half years in Guantánamo.

I visited him at his home in a poor suburb of Riyadh, the kind of area in which Frank Gardner had been wounded and his cameraman shot dead. It was obvious that we would have to be careful. Khalid lived in a modest little house with his wife and two sons, Bawardi, aged nine, and Said, aged twelve. He brought them into a simply furnished room and proudly introduced them. They were dressed in Persil-white *thobes*, and were impeccably polite and confident. When Khalid had left for Afghanistan, Said was three years old and Bawardi was one. I could only imagine what he must have thought during those long, dark years in Guantánamo, and what the reunion must have been like when he returned.

Khalid had spent about five months in the rehabilitation programme, successfully graduating from it a year before I met him. He said he was eternally grateful: 'It changed my nature and way of thinking, both as a person and in my ideas.' His ambition as a teenager had been to become a professional footballer, and he had signed up with the youth section of Riyadh's Saudi Crescent club. Like Aabid

Khan from Bradford, Manchester United was his favourite team, along with Chelsea and Barcelona. He told me the anti-Soviet *jihad* in Afghanistan in the 1980s had had 'a huge impact' on him. Three weeks before 9/11 he went to Afghanistan to train at the Al Farouq camp, as he felt obliged to help his 'brothers' in Chechnya. He told his parents he was going on holiday to Dubai: 'I thought that I would just go and do some *jihad* for a month or so and then come back.' Like Mohammed al-Awfi's, his training was cut short by the American invasion. He took refuge in the Tora Bora mountains where Osama Bin Laden was holed up, and spent a week or so there under American aerial bombardment. He then headed for Pakistan, where he was picked up in the great sweep that followed the US invasion of Afghanistan. He was handed over to the Americans and flown to Kandahar for interrogation. There he alleges he was tortured. His Combatant Status Review at Guantánamo states that his name had been found on a list in an Al Qaeda safe house in Karachi; that he had been active on behalf of Tablighi Jamaat, which the Americans claimed was 'being used as cover to mask travel and activities of terrorists including Al Qaeda';[18] that he had been in charge of digging bunkers in Tora Bora; and that he had been arrested in Pakistan with a group of thirty Al Qaeda suspects. Khalid disputes most of these allegations.

He described the treatment to which he alleges he and other detainees were subjected at Kandahar: 'They took our clothes off using scissors and took pictures of us completely naked. When they called you up for interrogation, they would cover your face and a soldier would push your head. There was then some torture and beat-ings.' He said he couldn't see the people who were interrogating him, or what was being done to him, because he was hooded. He thought he was subjected to electric-shock treatment: 'They put something on my foot and I felt electricity in my body.' I asked if he was tortured at Guantánamo. He said he wasn't, but 'Guantánamo in itself was torture. I didn't know what my fate was going to be. Life and death were equal to me. I was just thinking about each day. I didn't think about the future'.

I asked what his plans were now. At the time I spoke to him he was working at the Riyadh Chamber of Commerce, in a job that the rehabilitation programme had helped find for him as part of its comprehensive after-care service. He said he had enrolled in a computer course, and when he completed that he planned to attend English classes. 'After I will continue my studies and embark on a PhD, God willing!' And his message to others? 'I don't want kids to fall into the same trap and be fooled as I was fooled. Al Qaeda gives the wrong message. Islam is a peaceful religion, and not what Al Qaeda represents.' Thinking of his little boys, Bawardi and Said, I felt that his experience would ensure that there was little danger of their going through what he had been through. I left feeling cheered.

The Saudi rehabilitation centre has become a must on the itinerary of visiting foreign dignitaries, who are presented with a memorial trophy and Prince Nayef mug on their departure as a souvenir. Mine is in the kitchen cupboard. I was given a tour of the compounds that make up the centre. It had the appearance of a faded 1950s British holiday camp, or a recreational bolthole for Soviet workers. Still, it was infinitely superior to any prison I had ever seen, and I had no doubt which option the inmates would go for. There were no cells, high perimeter walls or watchtowers.

I watched the 'beneficiaries' playing football with the staff: 'guards' seems too strong a word. I hardly saw any member of staff with a weapon. Inmates were free to come and go as they pleased, as long as they remained within the confines of the compounds. I was shown the indoor swimming pool, empty of water at the time, its walls decorated with the brightly-coloured artwork of several of the centre's alumni. I thought how much the inmates must have wished the pool to be full, given the intense heat of the day, with any inch of shade at a premium. I was taken around the classrooms where the 'beneficiaries' were encouraged to discover the 'right path' of Islam and reject the warped ideology of Al Qaeda. I saw the art room, and looked at the work displayed on its walls. Sunshine and flowers were a favourite theme, perhaps not surprisingly after six or seven years locked in Guantánamo.

It was at the centre that I met my most hardened former *jihadi*. He was a member of the last batch that had arrived from Guantánamo: the later the batch, the harder the cases. At first those who ran the programme were reluctant to let me meet any of the most recent arrivals, who were kept separate from the rest. I found it difficult to understand why. Perhaps it was felt that they weren't 'on message' enough to talk to a visiting journalist. It was finally agreed that I could meet one of them, although it was made clear to me that the authorities had had a lot of persuading to do. There were two conditions: I wasn't to name him or film him.

I was surprised when he refused to shake my hand, and did not look at me at any time during our conversation. I assumed it was because he thought I was an infidel. He said he was twenty-five, and had gone to Afghanistan for humanitarian reasons, to help get people away from the American bombings. He alleged that after the US invasion the Afghans sold him to the Americans for about $400: Saudis, he said, were at a premium after 9/11. He was taken to Kandahar, where he claimed he was shackled and hooded, and deprived of sleep. He was not allowed to pray, and once when he was getting ready to try to do so, a SWAT team arrived with dogs to prevent him. He alleges that he was subjected to electric shocks, and drew a simple diagram in my notebook to show how. He couldn't see what was happening, but he could feel it and hear a buzzing sound. He said he was tied up with his hands above his head, and that if he tried to sleep someone would spit in his face.

Guantánamo, he told me, was just as bad, but in a different way. When he arrived, he claimed one of the guards told him, 'We're going to take you to another gaol to be fucked and go to Hell.' He says he was left naked, and his buttocks were beaten to humiliate him. Humiliation was the standard torture: 'The guards would throw the Koran into a bucket of shit. They would let you take your pants down and then watch you do your toilet. We were allowed a shower once a week, and you had to strip in front of a woman. Then they'd laugh at us.' I asked him if he was a terrorist. 'No, I'm a Muslim,' he said. 'The terrorists are the Jews, because of what they're doing in Palestine. I didn't kill any women, children or innocent people. That's what the Israelis are doing in Gaza and the US in Iraq.' Interview over. As he left, he warned me that if I changed a word of what he had said, he would sue me.

Before I left Saudi Arabia, I spoke to a very senior official in the Ministry of the Interior who had helped facilitate my interview with Mohammed al-Awfi. I asked if he believed it was true that his American allies had tortured suspects at Bagram, Kandahar and Guantánamo. He said that he did. I reminded myself that the Saudis didn't always treat their detainees with the gentlest of touches. And what about the electric shocks? He said he believed that had happened too. I too was inclined to believe it. I remembered the notorious photograph of a hooded detainee clad in black at Abu Ghraib, standing on a box with electrodes attached to his body. Although the picture was later revealed to have been faked, it spoke volumes about what was generally happening, and the culture and attitudes that lay behind it.

But that image only hinted at the abuses that were being perpetrated at Abu Ghraib and elsewhere in Iraq – as they were at Guantánamo, Bagram and Kandahar. In October 2010 the whistle-blower website WikiLeaks published 400,000 US documents relating to the Iraq war, a number of which described abuses committed against detainees by the Iraqi security forces. They revealed that coalition troops were ordered not to investigate these abuses unless they directly involved members of coalition forces. The reports invariably ended with the conclusion 'No further investigation.'[19]

The contamination that had begun with the Bush administration's authorisation of aggressive interrogation techniques in 2002 had spread. Nowhere was this more apparent or more corrosive than in the setting up of CIA 'black sites' in unspecified parts of the world, where Al Qaeda 'High Value Targets' were subjected to the euphemistically named 'enhanced interrogation techniques'.

SIXTEEN

Journey to the Dark Side

My journey with producer Mike Rudin to Guantánamo Bay, Cuba, around four hundred miles off the coast of Florida, on Air Sunshine's twin-propped plane was considerably more comfortable than the one experienced by the hundreds of detainees who were rendered there from Afghanistan, Pakistan and many other countries in the months and years that followed 9/11. Flying over a necklace of atolls surrounded by crystal-clear waters, I had a view denied to the early detainees who were flown, shackled and hooded, to an unknown destination where they were to be detained without charge, and in some cases subjected to officially documented human-rights abuses that many would regard as torture – as we will see later in this chapter. The first detainees from Afghanistan and Pakistan were initially imprisoned in 'Camp X Ray', originally constructed to house Haitian refugees in the early 1990s. Looking down on it from a hill above the valley in which it nestles I was reminded of Long Kesh in Northern Ireland. Camp X Ray is now, like Long Kesh, an abandoned historical relic. Its razor-wired perimeter fence and rickety wooden watchtowers are now overgrown with weeds and home to snakes, banana rats and giant iguanas.

Guantánamo today is very different. By the beginning of 2011, only 173 detainees remained, and the infamous orange jumpsuits that for so many years symbolised the camp are no longer in evidence. Many of the detainees are now 'compliant' with prison rules, and have accordingly been rewarded with privileges and much-improved living conditions. But being 'compliant' does not necessarily mean that their ideology has changed. On the contrary, it's likely that the experience of being locked up in Guantánamo for years on end has only hardened it. Most of the remaining detainees are regarded as the 'hard core', the hardest of them being High Value Detainees like Abu Zubaydah and Khalid Sheikh Mohammed, the mastermind of 9/11. Like IRA and Loyalist prisoners in the Maze, the detainees have a command structure and are organised on military lines, as, like the IRA, they see themselves as carrying on the fight in prison. The guards have no illusions about the kind of individuals they are dealing with. The remaining detainees are difficult to repatriate, as some of their countries of origin – in particular Yemen, which as we saw in the previous chapter has its own growing problem with Al Qaeda – are not keen to have them back. That's one of the reasons President Obama has not been able to fulfil the promise he made on entering office to close down Guantánamo. Although Guantánamo's notorious reputation still remains, living conditions and the treatment of prisoners are immeasurably better than they were, as America endeavours to learn the lessons and repair the prison camp's fearsome legacy, which has provided Al Qaeda with such a propaganda field day.

The stain of Guantánamo, the shocking images from Abu Ghraib,* the allegations of torture and the curbing of civil liberties are the political dark side of the decade since 9/11. All were the direct or indirect product of Al Qaeda's assault on the West. Governments in the firing line justified their responses in the name of defending democracy and protecting the freedoms that Al Qaeda seeks to destroy, but in the process they handed the enemy incalculable propaganda opportunities. I watched these abuses in the decade since 9/11 as I had over three decades in Northern Ireland. Such are the dilemmas that governments inevitably face in countering terrorism, as the British found in fighting the IRA. I reported how Bloody Sunday, internment without trial and the abuse of detainees – all measures

---

*The images of the abuse of prisoners by their American custodians at Abu Ghraib prison in Iraq shook the world. Among other things, they depict naked and hooded prisoners being beset by unmuzzled dogs and being sexually humiliated by women gaolers. A selection of the photographs can be found on http://www.antiwar.com/news/?articleid=8560.

designed to crush the IRA – in fact had the opposite effect, and only succeeded in creating more support for it. The reality of terrorist atrocities and the ruthlessness of their perpetrators are sometimes lost in the propaganda war that is the offspring of violent conflict. Like many journalists, I often felt I was in the middle, trying to sort truth from propaganda. From time to time I found myself being attacked by both sides, which I took to mean that perhaps I might be getting things about right.

Governments usually respond to allegations of abuse either by denying that they exist or dismissing them as 'one-offs' or due to the 'bad apple' syndrome. That was how the British authorities responded to my investigations into abuses during interrogation in Northern Ireland in the late 1970s. Smoking guns, like conspiracy theories, are eagerly hunted by journalists, but are seldom found. They lie hidden, locked in government vaults, perhaps, as in Britain, destined to outlive even the thirty-year rule after which most government documents are publicly released. But there is the odd, glaring exception. Very occasionally 'smoking guns' are prised from government, ironically by officials acting at the state's behest. An example is the secret memorandum revealed by Lord Saville's Inquiry into Bloody Sunday, in which Major General Robert Ford warned that to restore law and order it might be necessary 'to shoot selected ringleaders amongst the Derry Young Hooligans after clear warnings have been issued'.

WikiLeaks has now challenged the culture of secrecy. Apart from the disturbing images from Abu Ghraib, nothing shocked me so much as reading the Bush administration's 'top secret' memoranda authorising the CIA to carry out 'enhanced interrogation techniques' on selected terrorist suspects. The original documents date from 2002. Crucially, they show that these abuses were institutionalised, something that in the normal course of reporting terrorism it is impossible to establish. Their controversial release in 2010 was ordered by President Obama, who wished to herald a new beginning by closing Guantánamo within a year of coming into office, and bringing out into the open what the CIA and its contractors had been authorised to do in America's name. The release of the 'torture' memos was head-line news. Seldom can the most sensitive and secret inner workings of an intelligence agency have been so exposed to public scrutiny. Success in gathering intelligence from the interrogation of detainees can determine whether a war will be won or lost. In the eyes of the Bush administration, the end clearly justified the means. The war had to be won.

The authorisation of the techniques was made on 1 August 2002, following the capture earlier that year of Abu Zubaydah at a safe house in Faisalabad, in Pakistan. At the time he was thought to be one of Al Qaeda's most senior commanders. His arrest and subsequent interrogation have to be seen in the context of the time. New York and Washington had been assaulted only six months earlier, and America feared a second wave of attacks. President Bush had pledged to hunt down the perpetrators, and implied he would be happy to take Osama Bin Laden dead or alive.[1] Now the United States had what it believed was one of the key Al Qaeda suspects in its hands. According to the CIA, Zubaydah had not only been the arbiter of deciding who was admitted to Afghanistan's training camps, but 'has been involved in every major terrorist operation carried out by Al Qaeda ... [and was] one of the planners of the September 11 attacks. Prior to his capture he was engaged in planning future terrorist attacks against US inter-ests.'[2] However, the CIA later took the modified view that, although important, Abu Zubaydah was not as significant a detainee as they had believed him to be. His psychological profile indicated that he was utterly committed to *jihad*, had an 'unabated desire to kill Americans and Jews', and was convinced that the global victory of Islam was inevitable. Most ominously, his profile stated that he was believed to have written Al Qaeda's manual on how to resist interrogation, and was therefore likely to 'draw upon his vast knowledge of interrogation techniques to cope with the interrogation'.[3] The CIA believed he had knowledge of networks inside the United States, and of forthcoming attacks on America and its interests overseas. The problem was that he displayed 'no signs of willingness to disclose further information'. Feeling that more coercive techniques were needed to get him to talk, the CIA asked the US Department of Justice to authorise an 'increased pressure phase'.[4] The 2002 memorandum set out why it believed these measures were necessary: '… based on his treatment so far, Zubaydah has come to expect that no physical harm will be done to him. By using these techniques in increasing intensity and in rapid succession, the goal would be to dislodge this expectation.'

'Increased pressure' included the following:

FACIAL SLAP OR INSULT SLAP. To induce shock, surprise and/or humiliation.

WALLING. A flexible, false wall constructed. Interrogator pulls individual forward and then quickly and firmly pushes him back into wall. Loud sound at impact. Creates shock and surprise.

CRAMPED CONFINEMENT. Individual put in darkened box. Dimensions restrict movement. Maximum duration in larger space, eighteen hours. In smaller space, two hours.

Zubaydah was known to have a fear of insects. Approval was given to put one in the 'darkened box' with him. He was told it had a sting, but in fact it was harmless – it was probably a caterpillar. Other techniques included the abdominal slap, wall standing to induce muscle fatigue, extended sleep deprivation, dietary manipulation, standing naked for long periods wearing only a nappy, 'white noise', constant light and dousing with cold water.[5] Together these were known as 'enhanced interrogation techniques'. It was the last of them that was the most contentious and traumatic.

WATERBOARDING. Individual bound securely to inclined bench approximately four feet by seven with feet elevated. Cloth placed over forehead and eyes. Cold water applied to cloth from 12 to 24 inches above using canteen cup or small watering can with spout. Cloth lowered until covers nose and mouth. Airflow restricted for 20–40 seconds. Induces sensation of drowning. Maximum time being strapped to waterboard, two hours. Maximum time for one application 20 mins.[6]

Zubaydah was waterboarded eighty-three times during his interrogation in August 2002.[7] It is difficult to see how waterboarding of this intensity does not amount to torture, but the US government argued that it 'is not physically painful'.[8]

The American government denied that any of these techniques amounted to torture as defined in Section 18 of the United States Code 2340A, which governs the use of torture outside the USA, and which defines 'torture' as the intention to inflict 'severe physical or mental pain or suffering'.[9] The Bush administration's lawyers then refined the definition by adding that the pain and suffering had to be 'prolonged'. The US government was dancing on the head of a pin. The use of the 'enhanced techniques' was forbidden on American soil or against American citizens. They were used in the CIA's overseas 'black sites', to which High Value Targets were rendered. Their locations have never been revealed, but it is thought that they included Thailand, Poland and elsewhere in central Europe. The administration also defended the techniques by pointing out that between 1992 and 2001 they had been used on over 25,000 American military personnel undergoing Survival, Evasion, Resistance and Escape ('SERE') training, and 'very few complaints had been made'.[10] Waterboarding, it is understood, had been used 'thousands of times' in the SERE programme '(*albeit in a somewhat different way* [my emphasis])'.[11] The government also gave the assurance that medical assistance was always to hand. I doubt if any of the SERE candidates had been waterboarded eighty-three times.

To put it in context, waterboarding could only be used in very special circumstances beyond those necessary for the general application of the 'enhanced techniques'. These required 'credible intelligence that a terrorist attack is imminent ... and credible indicators that the subject has actionable intelligence that can prevent, disrupt or delay this attack'. The CIA also had to be convinced that other techniques were unlikely to elicit the information '*within the perceived time limit for preventing the attack* [emphasis in memorandum]'.[12]

Besides Abu Zubaydah, waterboarding was only used as a technique of last resort on two other High Value Targets who were believed to have information about imminent attacks on America or her interests overseas. One was Abdul Rahim Al-Nashiri, the alleged head of Al Qaeda operations in the Arabian Peninsula and the alleged chief planner of the suicide bombing of the USS *Cole* in Yemen in 2000. Al-Nashiri was waterboarded only once, on day twelve of his interrogation. He had started to talk on day one. The other was the highest of the High Value Targets, Khalid Sheikh Mohammed, who had been arrested in Rawalpindi, Pakistan, on 1 March 2003. Before the application of the enhanced techniques he refused to give any answers to questions about future attacks, simply replying, 'Soon, you will know.' The enhanced techniques were applied in the first month of his detention. He was waterboarded 183 times. In the end, after determined resistance, he sang. The CIA reported that he finally talked about the 'second wave' he had planned, in which Jemaah Islamiyah operatives in South-East Asia, known as the Garuba cell,* were ready to 'crash a hijacked airliner' into a building in Los Angeles.[13] The Agency said that information he provided as a result of interrogations using the enhanced techniques also ultimately led to the arrest of Hambali, the financier of the 2002 Bali bombings, and concluded that it 'has been the key reason why Al Qaeda has failed to launch a spectacular attack on the West since 11 September 2001'. The passage appears in the Justice Department memorandum of 30 May 2005. Presumably the Madrid bombings of March 2004 did not constitute 'a spectacular attack on the West', and applying the same criteria, nor did the London bombings five weeks after the date of the memorandum.

But however readily critics of the techniques may dispute their effectiveness – as well as their legality and morality – there are strong indications that they did produce results. For example, the intelligence that MI5 received from the CIA about Dhiren Barot, who had been plotting car-bomb and other attacks in the UK, came from the

---

*Intelligence from KSM led to other arrests that in the end identified the Garuba cell.

interrogation of Khalid Sheikh Mohammed. At his trial Barot pleaded guilty and, as already noted, is serving a life sentence in Britain.

Although few people outside the tight circle of the Bush White House and the CIA knew anything about waterboarding and the other 'enhanced techniques' that were finally revealed on President Obama's instructions, the FBI was very much aware of them, and took strong exception to their use. Ali Soufan was one of the Bureau's most experienced interrogators of Al Qaeda suspects, with the added advantage of being a practising Muslim. I initially met him when he was working in the FBI's New York office, where he had investigated the bombing of the USS *Cole*, all the main perpetrators of which, including its alleged planner, Abdul Rahim Al-Nashiri, were arrested. Soufan told me how he conducted interrogations. Sometimes he would kneel and pray with suspects at the appropriate times of the day. 'We have our own style of building rapport and talking to these individuals, building on common sense and frank discussions,' he said. 'It's a longer process, and we do it step by step and eventually they know that we are not that evil after all.'

He said that the FBI's technique wasn't to apply thumbscrews, as it 'doesn't believe in that'. I asked him why Al Qaeda suspects agreed to talk. 'Everybody talks for their own reasons,' he told me. 'A drug dealer gives you a confession sometimes, admitting his role in a drug deal, and an organised crime Capo will admit his role in money laundering. Interviewing an Al Qaeda guy or a terrorist is no different. Some of them don't talk, and some of them do. Those who don't talk usually eventually end up doing so. We've a track record of interviewing these individuals and obtaining very crucial intelligence, confessions that were extremely instrumental in our targeting of the group.'

Although Ali Soufan didn't tell me at the time, since such matters were highly classified, it later became clear that he had conducted his interrogation of Abu Zubaydah using the non-coercive methods he described. That was before Zubaydah was subjected to the enhanced techniques in August 2002, and waterboarded eighty-three times. The FBI's traditional methods, Soufan says, produced 'important actionable intelligence', including most crucially the information, which

Zubaydah volunteered without being asked, that Khalid Sheikh Mohammed was the architect of 9/11. Zubaydah's interrogation by the FBI also provided intelligence that José Padilla, a Puerto Rican US citizen, was allegedly planning to attack America with a 'dirty bomb'.* The British-based Ethiopian former asylum seeker Binyam Mohammed was believed to be associated with Padilla, which might explain why he was later allegedly subjected to horrific treatment during interrogation. Soufan said that the acquisition of such significant intelligence proved that traditional non-coercive interrogation methods can be successful in identifying operatives, uncovering plots and saving lives. In particular he takes strong exception to the US government's claim that it was the CIA's enhanced techniques used on Abu Zubaydah that produced the intelligence about Khalid Sheikh Mohammed and José Padilla, when in fact it had already been obtained through traditional methods of talking to terrorists.

Soufan reported his concerns about the use of the enhanced techniques to his FBI boss, Pat D'Amuro, who had led the investigation into the bombing of the American Embassy in Nairobi. D'Amuro told him, 'We don't do that,' and immediately took him off the team conducting the interrogations, with the approval of FBI Director Robert Mueller. Soufan also points out an additional institutional problem: the disagreements between the CIA and the FBI only reinforced the barriers in intelligence-sharing that had resulted in the intelligence failures of 9/11.

The CIA Inspector General's report – formerly top secret – that investigated the Agency's interrogation techniques revealed that some CIA officers and their contractors used methods that went far beyond those that had been authorised. There was the staging of a mock execution:

---

*After having spent three years in military detention in America as an 'enemy combatant', Padilla was not charged with any specific plot. On 22 January 2008 he was sentenced to seventeen years' imprisonment for giving material support for terrorism.

[Name redacted] offered to fire a handgun outside the interrogation room while the debriefer was interviewing a detainee who was thought to be withholding information. [Name redacted] staged the incident, which included screaming and yelling outside the cell by other CIA officers and [redacted] guards. When the guards moved the detainee from the interrogation room, they passed a guard who was dressed as a hooded detainee, lying motionless on the ground, and made to appear as if he had been shot to death … Reportedly a detainee who witnessed the 'body' in the aftermath of the ruse 'sang like a bird'.[14]

The High Value Target Abdul Rahim Al-Nashiri, the alleged mastermind of the suicide attack on the USS *Cole*, was not only intimidated by the firing of a handgun but was threatened with an electric drill:

… the debriefer entered the cell where Al-Nashiri sat shackled and racked the handgun once or twice to Al-Nashiri's head. On what was probably the same day, the debriefer used a power drill to frighten Al-Nashiri … [he] entered the detainee's cell and revved the drill while the detainee stood naked and hooded. The debriefer did not touch Al-Nashiri with the power drill.[15]

Despite the clamour from some quarters that the CIA officers responsible for administering these techniques should be prosecuted, Ali Soufan believes that to do so would be a mistake. He says that his CIA colleagues who baulked at the techniques were instructed to continue. 'Almost all the Agency officials I worked with were good people who felt as I did about the use of enhanced techniques: it is un-American, ineffective and harmful to our national security.' Above all he believes it is in America's national security interest 'to regain our position as the world's foremost defenders of human rights'.[16]

Clearly there were CIA officers who agreed. The CIA Inspector General's report noted that at the time – around 2002–03 – there were officers who expressed deep concern about the techniques being used, and feared the consequences both for themselves and the CIA:

One officer expressed concern that one day Agency officers would wind up on some 'wanted list' to appear before the World Court for war crimes stemming from activities ... Another said, 'Ten years from now we're going to be sorry we're doing this ... [but] it has to be done.'[17]

During the course of this review, a number of Agency officers expressed unsolicited concern about the possibility of recrimination or legal action resulting from their participation in the CTC [Counter-Terrorism Center] program ... that a human rights group might pursue them ... Additionally they feared that the Agency would not stand behind them if this occurred.[18]

The Inspector General also heard of wider concerns expressed at the time:

Officers are concerned that future public revelation of the CTC program is inevitable and will seriously damage Agency officers' personal reputations as well as the reputation and effectiveness of the Agency itself.

... The Agency faces potentially serious long-term political and legal challenges as a result of the CTC Detention and Interrogation Program, particularly in its use of EITs [enhanced interrogation techniques] and the inability of the US government to decide what it will ultimately do with terrorists detained by the Agency.[19]

President Obama's courageous opening of this Pandora's Box was attacked as foolhardy and dangerous by members of the Bush administration. The President also decreed that no CIA officer would be prosecuted. Karl Rove, President Bush's senior adviser and Deputy Chief of Staff, known as 'Bush's Brain', said he was 'proud we used techniques that broke the will of these terrorists. I'm proud that we kept the world safer than it was.' He insisted that waterboarding wasn't torture.

In his book *Decision Points*, President Bush defends his authorisation of the use of enhanced interrogation techniques:

I would have preferred that we got the information another way. But the choice between security and values was real. Had I not authorised the waterboarding of senior Al Qaeda leaders, I would have had to accept the greater risk that the country would be attacked. In the wake of 9/11 that was a risk I was unwilling to take.[20]

Such remarkable openness about interrogation and the obtaining of intelligence from it has not been replicated in the United Kingdom. Unlike Americans, British citizens have not been given chapter and verse about the initial rules for interrogation by MI5 and MI6 officers in the aftermath of 9/11, although the government later published modified guidelines. MI5 and MI6 are adamant that they do not torture or ill-treat suspects. The former Director of MI5, Dame Eliza Manningham-Buller, says she only discovered that the CIA had water-boarded Khalid Sheikh Mohammed 183 times when she had retired after thirty-three years in the Security Service – although she acknowledged that she had been aware that waterboarding was one of the techniques used.[21] 'I abhor torture and the threat of it,' she said, but added that she recognised the reality that 'we live in a dangerous world and have to talk to those whose behaviour is very different from our own'.[22] The current Director of MI5, Jonathan Evans, insists that its principles are clear: 'I can say quite clearly that the Security Service does not torture people, nor do we collude in torture or solicit others to torture people on our behalf. That is a very clear and long-established principle.'[23] And, in a rare public statement, the head of MI6, John Sawers, said, 'Torture is illegal and abhorrent under any circumstances, and we have nothing whatever to do with it.'[24] But there are growing concerns that there may have been instances where British intelligence services allegedly turned a blind eye to the ill-treatment of detainees in Pakistan and elsewhere. On 6 July 2010 the Prime Minister, David Cameron, announced that there would be a 'fully independent' inquiry into claims that the UK Security Services had been complicit in the torture of terror suspects. He told the House of Commons:

For the past few years the reputation of our security services has been overshadowed by allegations about their involvement in the treatment of detainees held by other countries. Some of those detainees allege they were mistreated by those countries. Other allegations have also been made about the UK's involvement in the rendition of detainees in the aftermath of 9/11. These allegations are not proven, but today we do face a totally unacceptable situation. Our services are paralysed by paperwork as they try to defend themselves in lengthy court cases with uncertain rules.[25]

The 'lengthy court cases' he was referring to include claims for compensation by Binyam Mohammed and five other former Guantánamo detainees: Bisher al-Rawi, Jamil El-Banna, Richard Belmar, Omar Deghayes and Martin Mubanga. They are claiming compensation for the government's complicity in detention, torture, illegal rendition and other mistreatment. Others convicted of terrorism offences, including Salahuddin Amin and Rangzeib Ahmed, are also taking legal action.*

The inquiry announced by the Prime Minister was to be chaired by the former Appeal Court judge Sir Peter Gibson. Civil liberties groups questioned the likely 'independence' of such an inquiry, fearing a conflict of interest as Sir Peter also serves as the Intelligence Services Commissioner overseeing MI5 and MI6. David Cameron said he hoped the inquiry would start by the end of 2010, after outstanding court actions involving some complainants had been either mediated or resolved. He then made private visits to the headquarters of MI5 and MI6 to explain to staff why he believed the inquiry was necessary, and how it was in their interests that there should be one. In late 2010 the court actions were resolved when the government agreed to

---

*Rangzeib Ahmed, who was born in Rochdale, was sentenced to life imprisonment in December 2008 for being a member of Al Qaeda and directing a terrorist organisation. He alleged that while being interrogated by the ISI in Pakistan, his fingernails were pulled out. An MI5 officer had gone out to Pakistan to interview him. The question is whether his fingernails were allegedly pulled out before or after the MI5 officer's visit. His appeal was heard in December 2010 and failed.

compensate the complainants with an undisclosed overall sum believed to amount to several million pounds.

In the United Kingdom the issue has focused on the alleged torture of Binyam Mohammed, whom Abu Zubaydah associated with José Padilla. Binyam Mohammed was detained at Guantánamo for seven years. His is a landmark case that has caused fierce controversy. The crucial question is whether MI5 knew how he had been treated by the Pakistanis before it sent out one of its officers to interview him. Did MI5 turn a blind eye? The case is important because it raises the highly sensitive matter of MI5's knowledge of, and alleged complicity in, the alleged torture and ill-treatment of a terrorist suspect.

Binyam Mohammed was born in Ethiopia and lived in America for two years before coming to Britain as an asylum seeker in 1994. During his seven-year detention in Guantánamo he told the Americans about his time in London.[26] He said that in 1998 he began to frequent Regent's Park mosque, the largest and most proselytising in the capital, where an Islamist with ties to the Algerian militant group the GSPC was a regular preacher. He then became involved with Tablighi Jamaat, which the Americans believe has connections with Al Qaeda and Pakistani terrorist organisations. Towards the end of 2000 he began watching videos of *jihad* in Bosnia, Chechnya and Afghanistan. In June 2001 he travelled to Afghanistan. He was arrested in Karachi on 10 April 2002.

What the American authorities who conducted his Combatant Status Reviews at Guantánamo alleged has not been widely reported.[27] They say that on arriving in Pakistan he travelled to the Al Farouq camp in Afghanistan, where he received forty days' training in handling light arms and explosives (he would have been there at roughly the same time as Mohammed Jabarah and the Lackawanna Six). Binyam Mohammed admitted to his Personal Representative at Guantánamo that this was true, but said that he had taken the military training with a view to going to fight in Chechnya, which was not illegal.[28] He said that the rest of the allegations made against him by the Americans at Guantánamo were false, and had been extracted as the result of torture – he claimed they were 'rubbish and made under duress'.

The intelligence the Americans say he provided consisted of the following details: that he had suggested attacking US subway trains to senior Al Qaeda leaders; that he had met the shoe bomber Richard Reid at another camp; that he travelled to Karachi, where he received further explosives training from a senior Al Qaeda operative; that he had encountered the alleged 'dirty bomber' José Padilla in Afghanistan, and together they had met one of Osama Bin Laden's closest associates (probably Abu Zubaydah); that he was directed to travel to the USA to assist in terrorist operations; that he admitted being a member of Al Qaeda; and that he planned to use a 'dirty bomb' to carry out a terrorist attack in America. The US government insisted that these statements made at Guantánamo were 'voluntary and un-coerced'.[29] Most of this intelligence was extracted over a long period of time by the Pakistanis, Americans and Moroccans.* Binyam Mohammed insists that the admissions were false, and were made as the result of torture.

The alleged abuse began at the hands of the Pakistanis three weeks after his arrest in Karachi on 10 April 2002, as he was trying to leave the country on a false passport. He was interviewed by FBI agents who, he says, left the room when the Pakistanis came in. He says he was hung up by a leather strap, beaten with a belt and subjected to a mock execution. Understandably, MI5 wanted to interview Mohammed about his activities and contacts in London, and consulted the Americans. In their reply they said they had developed a 'new interrogation strategy' that had been 'designed by an expert interviewer'. The contents of that classified communication, presumably from the CIA, were only revealed six years later, on 6 May 2008, when Binyam Mohammed's legal team began proceedings against the then Foreign Secretary David Miliband. They were seeking evidence to assist Binyam Mohammed's defence, as he was about to be charged as 'an unlawful enemy combatant' before a Guantánamo Military Commission with terrorist offences that potentially carried the death

---

*It seems that the Pakistanis carried out the alleged ill-treatment following his arrest in Karachi, but did not conduct the interviews, which were done by FBI agents.

penalty. The British government did all it could to prevent disclosure of the classified documents, arguing that it would jeopardise its intelligence-sharing relationship with the United States. On 16 October 2009 the Court of Appeal ruled that the redacted seven paragraphs of the Americans' communication to MI5 should be unredacted, and therefore placed on the public record.

The paragraphs revealed that the Americans told MI5 that in Pakistan Binyam Mohammed 'had been intentionally subjected to continuous sleep deprivation', the effects of which were carefully observed; that 'threats and inducements were made to him [and his] fears of being removed from United States custody and "disappearing" were played upon'; that 'the stress brought about by these deliberate tactics was increased by his being shackled in his interviews'; and that as a result it was clear that 'the interviews were having a marked effect upon him and causing him significant mental stress and suffering'.[30]

On 15 May 2002 an MI5 officer, referred to in court only as 'Witness B', went out to Pakistan to interview Binyam Mohammed. The key question with regard to alleged British complicity in torture and ill-treatment is whether Witness B was aware of or read the American communication about the treatment Binyam Mohammed had received in Karachi, either before he travelled to Pakistan or when he was there. In the course of the protracted legal proceedings, Witness B gave evidence *in camera*. Under cross-examination he denied that he had seen the US communication, and was imprecise in his answers. Lord Justice Thomas and Mr Justice Lloyd Jones concluded:

> Our finding after the hearing was that the probability is that Witness B read the reports either before he left for Karachi or before he conducted the interview. Since the hearing we have been provided with the documents ... which show a briefing document was prepared for sending to him.
>
> If ... Witness B had not read them prior to going to Karachi or after arrival at Karachi and prior to the interview, we have no doubt that other persons within the SyS [Security Service], including persons

more senior to Witness B, must have read the reports and must have appreciated what they said about BM's detention and treatment at Karachi. Those officers should have drawn to the attention of Witness B these matters either before or after the interview. It is now clear that the reports were studied by other desk officers.

In the light of Witness B's continued involvement with BM and the importance attached to BM by the SyS, it is inconceivable that he did not carefully read the materials after his return.[31]

The matter became the subject of a criminal investigation by the Metropolitan Police. If it was shown that Witness B knew of how Binyam Mohammed had been treated before he conducted the interview in Karachi, then technically he would be guilty of a criminal offence. On 17 November 2010, the Director of Public Prosecutions, Keir Starmer QC, advised the police that there was insufficient evidence to prosecute the MI5 officer.

After his interrogation in Karachi and the visit by MI5's Witness B, the Pakistanis handed Binyam Mohammed over to the Americans. On 22 July 2002 the CIA rendered him to Morocco from Islamabad on a Gulfstream V jet. He was held there and interrogated for about eighteen months.

On 30 September 2002 MI5 held a case conference about him with their American counterparts at MI5 headquarters, Thames House in London. On 5 November MI5 sent the CIA a list of questions it would like to be put to him. The communication concluded: 'We would appreciate the opportunity to pose further questions, dependent on answers given to the above.' MI5 insists it did not know where Binyam Mohammed was at the time, or how he was being treated. It appears that the CIA would not tell MI5 where he was, which is standard CIA procedure. As a result of the court actions, it later emerged that Witness B visited Morocco once in November 2002 and twice in February 2003. It was never established why he had gone or what he had done there, as the trips only came to light after he had given his evidence. It is possible that he was visiting another prisoner with UK connections who was being detained in Morocco.

It was in Morocco that the almost medieval treatment alleged by Binyam Mohammed is claimed to have occurred. The most graphic and independent description of his ordeal is contained in Judge Gladys Kessler's summing up in an indirectly related US court case.[32] Crucially, Judge Kessler noted that 'The [US] government does not challenge the evidence of Binyam Mohammed's abuse.' She says he detailed how his Moroccan interrogators took 'some kind of doctor's scalpel' and cut both sides of his chest. One of them then held his penis in his hand 'and began to make cuts all over his private parts'. He estimated that they cut him thirty to forty times over two hours: 'There was blood all over.' Doctors then gave him some cream. He says this treatment continued once a month for the eighteen months that he was in captivity in Morocco, and that his captors told him what to tell his interrogators so the torture would cease. In the end Binyam Mohammed agreed to do as he was told.

In January 2004 he was put on a CIA plane and flown to a 'prison of darkness' in Kabul. He says that he was stripped before he got on board, and a female soldier who had been instructed to photograph him 'expressed horror at the scars on his penis'. In Kabul, he says he was chained to the floor in complete darkness and bombarded with loud music. His American interrogators wanted him to repeat what they told him to say, including an admission about his involvement in the alleged 'dirty bomb' plot with José Padilla. This is Judge Kessler's uncompromising conclusion:

Binyam Mohammed's lengthy and brutal experience in detention weighs heavily with this court. [His] trauma lasted for two long years. During that time he was physically and psychologically tortured. His genitals were mutilated. He was deprived of sleep and food. He was summarily transported from one foreign prison to another. Captors held him in stress positions for days at a time. He was forced to listen to piercingly loud music and the screams of other prisoners while locked in a pitch-black cell. All the while he was forced to inculpate himself and others in various plots to imperil Americans.[33]

In the British courts, the prolonged legal saga over the disclosure of crucial documents climaxed with a searing verdict from the three most senior judges in the land, the Lord Chief Justice, the Master of the Rolls and the President of the Queen's Bench Division. They expressed their discomfort at the way in which they believed Binyam Mohammed had been treated by the Americans on the evidence of the CIA's communication to MI5: being shackled, suffering sleep deprivation, threats, inducements and fear of 'disappearing'. They said that this 'could easily be contended to be at the very least cruel, inhuman and degrading treatment of Binyam Mohammed by the United States authorities'. It would also, they said, have been in breach of the undertaking that the British government gave in 1972 following allegations of ill-treatment in Northern Ireland at the time of internment the previous year. Their Lordships did not comment on the Moroccan allegations. The most damning comment came from the Master of the Rolls, Lord Neuberger. In paragraph 168, originally redacted under pressure from the government's leading lawyer, Jonathan Sumption QC, and then reinstated, he wrote:

> ... as the evidence in this case showed, at least some SyS officials appear to have a dubious record when it comes to human rights and coercive techniques, and indeed when it comes to frankness about the UK's involvement with the mistreatment of Mr Mohammed by US officials ... Not only is there an obvious reason for distrusting any UK government assurance, based on SyS advice and information, because of previous 'form', but the Foreign Office and the SyS have an interest in the suppression of such information.[34]

There are still many questions to be answered, and there is no doubt that the inquiry under Sir Peter Gibson will address them, not just with regard to Binyam Mohammed, but to other British victims of alleged torture and the alleged complicity of the British government in it.

* * *

At the time of writing the 'war' against Al Qaeda has all the makings of a stalemate, reminiscent of the later stages of the 'war' against the IRA in the late 1980s and early 1990s. The IRA was not defeated, nor were the Brits. A clear outcome was never on the cards. By that time the IRA had been thoroughly penetrated by British intelligence, and covert and electronic surveillance had severely limited the IRA's ability to operate. Nevertheless, the IRA was still able to strike with devastating effect, attacking targets in the financial heart of the City of London and causing millions of pounds' worth of damage, while still killing soldiers and policemen in Northern Ireland. Such was the background to the secret talks with the IRA that finally brought an end to the conflict in a historic compromise.

In the decade since 9/11, Al Qaeda's leadership has been severely degraded by the concerted efforts of America and its allies, whether by the arrest and interrogation of High Value Targets like Abu Zubaydah, Abdul Rahim Al-Nashiri and Khalid Sheikh Mohammed, or as the result of multiple strikes from the sky by American pilotless drone aircraft, such as the attack that 'Kasim' so miraculously survived.*

Since coming to office, President Obama has authorised over 160 drone strikes – almost four times as many as the forty-three sanctioned by President Bush. Over 90 per cent were directed against suspected Al Qaeda and Taliban targets in North Waziristan. It's estimated that in total the strikes have killed between 1,300 and 2,000 individuals. Around 75 per cent are thought to have been 'militants' – among them a number of senior Al Qaeda commanders. The remaining 25 per cent were[35] civilians. In 2008 the CIA Director, General Michael Hayden, declared: 'By making a safe haven feel less safe, we keep Al Qaeda guessing. We make them doubt their allies, question their methods, their plans, [and] even their priorities.'[36] But there's a downside to the drone attacks. Extensive collateral damage (the deaths of innocent civilians) again helps fuel Al Qaeda's propaganda machine, which is why by 2010 drone attacks had become more focused. In October 2010 one attack in which two missiles were fired

---

*The new Epilogue covers the subsequent killing of Osama Bin Laden.

at a house in North Waziristan was reported to have killed eight 'militants', among them four German nationals believed to have been training there. There were no reports of collateral damage. The US State Department subsequently issued a warning that cells might be planning Mumbai-style attacks on European capitals. The warning appeared to have been prophetic when two months later, on 11 December 2010, Taimour Abdulwahab al-Abdaly, an Iraqi-born Swedish citizen, blew himself up after failing to mount a mass-casualty car-bomb attack in Stockholm as Christmas shoppers were thronging its city centre. It was thought that he may have been radicalised in Luton, home to Salahuddin Amin and other *jihadis*, when he was studying at a local university.

However badly it has been hit, 'core' Al Qaeda still exists, planning and plotting somewhere in the mountains between Pakistan and Afghanistan, apparently not penetrated by US or allied intelligence agencies. Nevertheless, by the end of 2010, President Obama remained upbeat about progress in the war against Al Qaeda, not least because of the success of the increasing number of drone strikes. 'Today Al Qaeda's senior leadership in the border region is under more pressure than at any point since they fled Afghanistan nine years ago,' he said. 'Senior leaders have been killed. It's harder for them to recruit ... It's harder for them to plot and launch attacks. In short, Al Qaeda is hunkered down.' [37]

Al Qaeda's footsoldiers and supporters too have been badly hit, and have been brought to justice through due process in Britain, the USA, Canada, Europe, South-East Asia and many other parts of the world. But the organisation still has the capacity to strike, and given the increasingly fluid nature of its structure, with cells operating independently without any direct link to 'core' Al Qaeda, it is becoming more and more difficult to identify and interdict every plot, however encouraging the track record to date.

The West is facing an increasingly resourceful enemy whose attacks now emanate from bases other than those in Pakistan, most notably Yemen. Yemen was where the 2009 Christmas Day underpants bomber, Umar Farouq Abdulmuttalab, was trained, and is a source of ever-growing worry for Western intelligence agencies. As we saw earlier in the book, in 2003 the Canadian *jihadi* Mohammed Jabarah was tasked by Khalid Sheikh Mohammed to begin preparations to build a new base in Yemen following the rout of Al Qaeda in Afghanistan after the US invasion after 9/11. That base has effectively been constructed through Al Qaeda's surrogate Al Qaeda in the Arabian Peninsula (AQAP) – better known as Al Qaeda in Yemen. On 29 October 2010 explosive devices were found in the holds of two cargo planes – one UPS, the other FedEx – bound for Chicago. Originating from Yemen, they were concealed in laser printer cartridges, and contained PETN (pentaerythritol tetranitrate), the deadly explosive, difficult to detect at airport security checks, used by Umar Farouq Abdulmuttalab and the shoe bomber Richard Reid. One package contained a mobile-phone SIM card, the other a timer. Both, it was assumed, were to be used to detonate the bombs. The packages were addressed to two synagogues in Chicago. One was detected when the UPS flight touched down in Dubai, the other when the FedEx plane landed at the UK's East Midlands Airport. The British Home Secretary, Theresa May, said: 'The target of the device may have been an aircraft and, had it detonated, the aircraft could have been brought down.'[38] The tip-off came from Saudi intelligence, whose connections with Yemen, as we have seen in the case of the Al Qaeda defector Mohammed al-Awfi, are extremely close.

Despite the interception or disruption of these increasingly sophisticated plots, the ultimate nightmare for the intelligence agencies of the West remains that Al Qaeda is planning another 9/11-type 'spectacular', possibly involving a nuclear, chemical or biological weapon. The MI6 Chief, Sir John Sawers, recognises that Al Qaeda is a resourceful and dangerous enemy: 'Al Qaeda has ambitious goals. Weakening the power of the West. Toppling moderate Islamic regimes. Seizing the Holy Places of Islam to give them moral authority. Taking control of the Arab world's oil resources. They're unlikely to achieve these goals, but they remain set on trying, and are ready to use extreme violence … Whatever the cause or causes of so-called Islamic terrorism, there is little prospect of it fading away soon.'[39]

Faced with terrorist conflicts, states have four options. They can defeat the terrorists, be defeated by them, or talk to them and reach a compromise. To some that means entering the dark side and engaging with those who may have blood on their hands. The final option is to accept that the conflict will continue indefinitely, without any clear outcome, at an ever greater cost in lives, resources and money. So what do we do? Do we talk to Al Qaeda, however unthinkable that currently appears to be? Talking to the IRA was once regarded as unthinkable too, but in the end it was the only way to end the conflict. Talking to the Taliban as a way of ending the interminable and unwinnable conflict in Afghanistan was also off-limits for a long time, but that is no longer the case.

President Obama has recognised that the Afghan war cannot be won by military means alone. Britain's most senior soldier, General Sir David Richards, the Chief of the Defence Staff and an Afghan veteran himself, agrees, as he told the BBC's Andrew Marr: 'In every insurgency in history there has been a point at which you negotiate with what is left of the opposition ... You can't defeat the Taliban or Al Qaeda militarily ... I don't think you can probably defeat an idea.'[40] The former United Nations envoy to Afghanistan, Karl Eide, began the process of putting out secret feelers to senior figures in the Taliban leadership in 2009.[41] These contacts were, he said, 'in the early stages ... talks about talks'. Those with whom he dealt, he believed, had the authority of the Quetta Shura, a body not unlike the IRA's Army Council, to engage in dialogue. He had no doubt that it had the approval of the Taliban's overall leader, Mullah Omar: 'I find it unthinkable that such contact would take place without his knowledge and without his acceptance.' Two British diplomats, Michael Semple and Mervyn Patterson, both Afghan experts, were expelled from Afghanistan in 2007 by President Hamid Karzai's government for trying to make contact with elements of the Taliban in Helmand province, where the majority of the approaching 400 British soldiers who have been killed in Afghanistan to date have died.[42] Answering questions about the expulsions in the House of Commons, the then Prime Minister Gordon Brown said, 'We are isolating and eliminating the leadership of the Taliban. We are not negotiating with them.'[43] Successive British Prime Ministers said the same thing about the IRA at various times over more than twenty years. The prerequisite of any talks is that both sides pile on the military pressure to achieve the strongest political hand in negotiations. The British and the IRA both did the same in the lead-up to the secret back channel talks via Brendan Duddy, Michael Oatley and 'Robert' in the early 1990s.

Tentative support for the possibility – it remains no more than that at this stage – of talking to Al Qaeda has been given by two senior British figures with intimate experience of Northern Ireland. Sir Hugh Orde, former Chief Constable of the Police Service of Northern Ireland, who in that capacity and during his previous service with the Metropolitan Police spent thirty years fighting the IRA, chose his words carefully. He implied that talking to Al Qaeda was not unthinkable, and said that he could not remember any terrorist campaign in history that had ended without negotiation: 'What fixes it is talking and engaging and judging when the conditions are right for that to take place. Is that a naïve statement? I don't think it is. It is the reality of what we face.'[44] It was almost another way of expressing General Sir David Richards' sentiments. Jonathan Powell, who was Prime Minister Tony Blair's Chief of Staff from 1995 to 2007, and was instrumental in helping bring the IRA to the negotiating table, has also intimated that talking to Al Qaeda is not out of the question. He said that experience convinced him it was essential to keep a line of communication open even with one's most bitter enemies: 'There's nothing to say to Al Qaeda, and they've got nothing to say to us at the moment, but at some stage you're going to have to come to a political solution as well as a security solution. And that means you need the ability to talk. If I was in government now I would want to have been talking to Hamas, I would be wanting to communicate with the Taliban and I would want to find a channel to Al Qaeda.'[45] At present, talking with Hamas does not figure in the Middle East peace process, an omission that recent history would suggest is an error.

Orde's and Powell's carefully worded views were backed by Lord West, Security Minister in the Brown government: 'To say that there should be no link at all through any … back route would be silly,' he said, but stressed that it had to be done 'on a very careful, secret level really to find out what they're up to'.[46] A Foreign Office spokesman dismissed the idea: 'It is inconceivable that Her Majesty's government would ever seek to reach a mutually acceptable accommodation with a terrorist organisation like Al Qaeda.'[47] That does not rule out the use of intermediaries, be they officials or intelligence officers. This of course assumes that there would be indications that Al Qaeda was interested in dialogue. At the moment there are none: Al Qaeda is more interested in killing than talking. Nevertheless, the notion of dialogue at some stage should not automatically be dismissed.*

But what is there to talk about? The idea that it is impossible to negotiate with Al Qaeda itself is both dangerous and misleading. Bin Laden had an agenda, albeit of a different order to that of any other terrorist leader in history. Interestingly, reading his communications over the years, the historic Muslim aspiration of the global Caliphate of the *Ummah* barely merits a mention. Time and again he sets out his agenda and sends his message to an America that he says has deaf ears: end the occupation of Muslim lands, notably Iraq and Afghanistan; withdraw from Saudi Arabia, the land of Islam's most sacred sites at Mecca and Medina, 'polluted' by the American presence following the stationing of US troops there for Operation Desert Storm in 1991; end support for the apostate regimes in the Middle East and elsewhere, with Saudi Arabia top of the list; and, most crucially of all, end American support for Israel.

The theme that runs through most of Bin Laden's communications is Palestine. His first message, delivered on 29 December 1994, during his time in Sudan, was about 'The Betrayal of Palestine'. In it he described 'these poor men, women and children who have nowhere to go', and reminded Muslims of their legal duty 'to motivate our *ummah* to *jihad* so that Palestine may be completely liberated and returned to Islamic sovereignty'.[48] One of his more recent messages,

---

*See conclusion of Epilogue for updated quote from Baroness Manningham-Buller on talking to the Taliban and Al Qaeda.

on 24 January 2010, colloquially referred to as 'Osama to Obama', begins by praising 'the heroic warrior, Umar Farouq Abdulmutallab' for his alleged attack a month earlier on the Northwest Airlines flight above Detroit on Christmas Day 2009. Bin Laden said the message was 'confirmation of the previous messages sent by the heroes of the September 11', and concluded with the familiar message about Palestine: 'America will never dream of security unless we will have it in reality in Palestine. God willing, our raids on you will continue as long as your support to the Israelis will continue.'[49]

Given the above, it would be erroneous to suggest that there is nothing to talk to Al Qaeda about. Forget the Caliphate – that is the ultimate aspiration, as a united Ireland was for the IRA. In any talks, the issue would probably be parked, as it was in the negotiations in Northern Ireland. But elements of the rest of Bin Laden's agenda could be up for discussion. The declared intention of America and the West is to withdraw gradually from Iraq and Afghanistan – a process that is currently under way – and many US troops have already left Saudi Arabia. With President Obama in the White House, Palestine could be the issue that begins to unlock Al Qaeda, with Bin Laden able to claim a victory of sorts as American support for Israel is reduced. Of course all this is pure speculation. At the time of writing further progress seems unlikely in the foreseeable future, given that talks between Obama and the Israeli Prime Minister, Binyamin Netanyahu, have run into the sand. I list the options simply to illustrate that however difficult the issues, there is something to talk about.

There would still be the question of who to negotiate with, given the way in which Al Qaeda has evolved into a global phenomenon with many disparate affiliates, not all of them directly linked to the core leadership, although they all broadly share Osama Bin Laden's ideology. If Bin Laden's Al Qaeda successors were to embrace some kind of dialogue with the West, there are two possible scenarios: either these loosely linked affiliates would go along with the initiative, or they would dissociate themselves and split – as the dissidents did from the IRA.

The problem, however, remains that at its heart Al Qaeda is a millennialist entity, for which *jihad* and the martyrdom of its adherents represent victory in themselves. One has only to read Khalid Sheikh Mohammed's response in Guantánamo to the accusations levelled against him and four other senior Al Qaeda figures by America to see how irreducible his position is. It contains no hint of compromise:

> Our religion is a religion of fear and terror to the enemies of God: the Jews, Christians and pagans. With God's willing, we are terrorists to the bone … We fight you and destroy you and terrorise you. The Jihad in God's cause is a great duty in our religion. We have news for you. You will be greatly defeated in Afghanistan and Iraq and that America will fall, politically, militarily and economically. Your end is very near and your fall will be just as the fall of the Towers on the blessed 9/11 day.[50]

It is signed 'The 9/11 Shura Council'.

I thought of what Khalid Sheikh Mohammed's fellow *jihadi* and Guantánamo detainee Mohammed al-Awfi told me in his luxury prison accommodation in Saudi Arabia: 'I advise everyone not to deal with extremism by the use of force. Force doesn't speak to force. There must be another method.' I wondered, at the end of my journey from the IRA to Al Qaeda, if either side would pay heed to his words.

EPILOGUE

I always thought that one morning I would wake up and hear on the radio that Osama Bin Laden had been captured or killed. I assumed that the news would be of his death, and not his capture. I couldn't envisage that the Most Wanted Man in the World, who had evaded detection for ten years since 9/11 – and thirteen since the bombings of the US embassies in Kenya and Tanzania – would ever be taken alive. I reflected on the enormous problems that the capture and interrogation of Khalid Sheikh Mohammed had caused, from the controversy surrounding his waterboarding to the contentious issue of putting him on trial. Those problems would pale into insignificance compared to those of keeping Bin Laden in custody and then bringing him to justice before a civilian or military court. The Obama administration's stated mission for its special forces was to 'kill or capture'. Killing Bin Laden and burying him at sea may have seemed the simpler and more expedient option.

On the morning of Monday, 2 May 2011, I switched on Radio 4's *Today* programme and heard the news. Bin Laden had been shot dead in Pakistan the previous night by US Navy Seals.* He had been living in a compound in the quiet hill town of Abbottabad, barely forty miles from Islamabad. So much for the notion that the leader and founder of Al Qaeda was holed up in a remote cave somewhere in the mountains along the border between Pakistan and Afghanistan.

---

* The name is an acronym for Sea, Air and Land.

The operation was the stuff of a Hollywood movie. Bin Laden was even codenamed 'Geronimo'.* Two US special forces Black Hawk helicopters with a team of two dozen Navy Seals on board had secretly flown under Pakistan's radar from Afghanistan and stormed the compound where Bin Laden and some of his family were thought to be staying. Initial reports suggested that Bin Laden had been living in the lap of luxury in a million-dollar villa, and was killed while resisting arrest, using his wife as a human shield. This account was false, and was soon corrected. Bin Laden was unarmed, and didn't use his wife as a shield. He was killed with two shots – one to the chest and one to the head.

President Obama had personally authorised the mission, in preference to a drone attack that would have risked politically devastating 'collateral damage' in Pakistan. Bin Laden's body was flown to an aircraft carrier in the Arabian Sea, washed according to Muslim custom, wrapped in a white sheet and consigned to the deep.

There were scenes of wild rejoicing outside the White House and at the site of the World Trade Center in New York. To millions of Americans, 9/11 had been avenged. In the words of President Obama, 'justice' had been done. He had fulfilled the promise of his predecessor, George W. Bush, that Bin Laden would be taken 'dead or alive'. Publicly Obama reacted with quiet dignity and a notable absence of any hint of triumphalism, fully aware of the impact his words and demeanour would have on the Muslim world he had so assiduously courted since his inauguration. When he laid a simple wreath at the World Trade Center a few days later, the President was eloquent by his silence.

It soon became clear, when images of the compound were subsequently released, that far from living in the lap of luxury, Bin Laden spent his final days in humble circumstances. One video seized by the Navy Seals showed an ageing Bin Laden wrapped in a blanket

---

* Geronimo was the nineteenth-century native American who resisted America's seizure and occupation of Apache lands. After a long hunt, he finally surrendered in 1886 and became a US prisoner of war. He died in 1909.

watching archive coverage of himself on an old television set in the corner of a sparsely furnished room. He looked more like an elderly resident in a retirement home than the World's Most Wanted Man.

But many questions remained. It transpired that Bin Laden had been living in the compound for around five years. Was it conceivable that he could do so without detection in a garrison town that was a cross between Aldershot and Sandhurst, and in a location that was less than a mile from Pakistan's top military academy? Is it credible that some elements of Pakistan's intelligence agency, the ISI, knew nothing about this compound? Did the military never bother to check who was living behind its high walls, topped with barbed wire? Wasn't it strange that the compound had no internet or telephone connection? Could such a complex and daring operation really have been carried out without the covert compliance of elements of the ISI? Pakistan continued to deny all knowledge of where Bin Laden had been living, and fiercely rejected accusations of collusion.

It was talking to terrorists that finally led to the death of Osama Bin Laden. The CIA said the initial intelligence came as a result of the Enhanced Interrogation Techniques (EITs) that were applied at the Agency's secret 'black sites'. The vital snippets of information came separately and at different stages from three high-ranking Al Qaeda suspects, all of whom were subjected to the controversial EITs. The first came from Khalid Sheikh Mohammed (KSM), who had been arrested in Pakistan in 2003. He mentioned a courier whose *nom de guerre* turned out to be Abu Ahmed al Kuwaiti. KSM said that he knew him, but that he had no connections with Al Qaeda. The CIA didn't believe him. The second piece of intelligence came from another senior Al Qaeda suspect, Hassan Ghul, who had been captured in northern Iraq in 2004. He told his CIA interrogators that the courier (Abu Ahmed al Kuwaiti) was crucial to Al Qaeda,[1] and was close to Abu Faraj Al-Libbi, who had replaced KSM as Al Qaeda's operational head. According to a declassified US Department of Justice memorandum of 30 May 2005, Ghul was subjected to the following EITs: attention grasp, walling, facial hold, facial slap, wall standing, stress positions and sleep deprivation.[2] The third piece of confirmatory intelligence on the courier came from Abu Faraj Al-Libbi himself, who had been captured in Pakistan by the ISI in 2005 and also interrogated at a CIA 'black site'. He wasn't waterboarded. At some stage Al-Libbi had lived in Abbottabad.

It was several years before the CIA and other US intelligence agencies were finally able to track down Abu Ahmed al Kuwaiti, through electronic intercepts and other covert methods. He eventually and inadvertently led the CIA to Bin Laden's compound in August 2010. Al Kuwaiti was there, and was shot dead when the Navy Seals attacked nine months later.

To the advocates and supporters of the EITs, the revelation that the intelligence they produced finally led to the tracking down and killing of Bin Laden was the ultimate vindication of their use. José Rodriguez,* head of the CIA's Counter-Terrorism Center from 2002 to 2005, under President George W. Bush, said: 'Information provided by KSM and Al-Libbi about Bin Laden's courier was the lead information that eventually led to the location of [Bin Laden's] compound and the operation that led to his death.'[3] The Obama White House challenged Rodriguez's view, pointing out that the success of the operation was 'the result of years of painstaking work by our intelligence community that drew from multiple sources'.[4] President Obama had been opposed to the use of the Enhanced Interrogation Techniques, and regarded waterboarding as torture.

Perhaps we will never know precisely how the complex intelligence jigsaw was put together – which gives conspiracy theorists a field day. Apart from the White House's own response, the most convincing refutation of their theories was a defiant statement, attributed to Al Qaeda's General Command, issued on 3 May 2011. Its unequivocal message was that Sheikh Osama was dead. Not surprisingly, Al Qaeda's account of the manner of his death is very different from that given by the White House:

---

* In 2005 Rodriguez authorised the destruction of the videotapes of the interrogations of Abu Zubaydah (see p.290) and Abdul Rahim Al-Nashiri (see p.293) that had been carried out under the EITs at one of the CIA's 'black sites', believed to have been in Thailand. Five years later the US Justice Department decided that Rodriguez would not be prosecuted.

… his determination never wavered and his strength was never weakened. He instead stood up to them, face-to-face like a high mountain.
He continued to fight the kind of battles that he was accustomed to …
until he received the bullets of deception and non-belief to surrender
his soul to its Creator …

If the Americans succeeded in killing Osama, that is no shame or
disgrace. Are not men and heroes killed but on the battlefields? But can
the Americans, with their media, agents, tools, soldiers, and apparatus
kill what Sheikh Osama lived and died for? Alas! The Sheikh did not
found an organisation that lives with his life and dies with his death.[5]

Al Qaeda's message concluded with a threat:

The soldiers of Islam, whether in groups or individually, will not
relent, despair, surrender, or weaken and will continue to plan until
you are afflicted with a catastrophe that turns your children's hair grey
prematurely.[6]

Nothing in the statement came as any surprise. Al Qaeda inevitably
depicted its leader going down fighting, meeting the heroic death of
a *mujahideen* martyr.

Less than a fortnight after Bin Laden's killing, two suicide bombers
attacked a training academy for Pakistan's Frontier Constabulary
troops, killing eighty people, most of them young recruits. The
Pakistani Taliban said it was the first revenge attack for the killing of
Bin Laden.[7] The question, as yet unanswered, is whether Al Qaeda is
in a position to carry out its broader threat. It is a threat that should
not be taken lightly. Osama Bin Laden is dead, but the organisation
he founded in Afghanistan in August 1988 at the height of the anti-
Soviet *jihad* (see p.56), and the groups around the world subsequently
affiliated to it, are not. They are no doubt fiercely committed to avenging his death, and will do all they can to make the threat a reality. But
there is no guarantee that they will succeed. As former CIA Director
General Michael Hayden told me, another terrorist 'spectacular' like
9/11 is unlikely to take place, given the huge advances in intelligence

in the decade since then. That intelligence has been improved even more with the unprecedented treasure trove of intelligence material that the Navy Seals brought back with them from their raid on Bin Laden's compound. It included computer hard drives, DVDs, videos, memory sticks and even Bin Laden's own handwritten journal. According to the White House, evidence recovered during the raid indicates that during the years in which Bin Laden was being hunted he was more than just a figurehead for Al Qaeda, as had generally been thought. It appears that he remained the Chief Executive Officer who was still running the organisation.

The CIA subsequently published its own obituary of the quarry it had pursued so relentlessly over so many years:

> The death of Usama Bin Ladin marks the single greatest victory in the US-led campaign to disrupt, dismantle, and defeat al-Qa'ida. It is a major and essential step in bringing about the terrorist organization's eventual dissolution.
>
> Bin Ladin was al-Qa'ida's founder and only *amir*, or commander, in its 22-year history. He was largely responsible for the organization's mystique, its ability to raise money and attract new recruits, and its focus on the United States as a target for terrorist attacks. As the only al-Qa'ida leader whose authority was universally respected, he also maintained the group's cohesion.
>
> Although al-Qa'ida may not fragment immediately, the loss of Bin Ladin puts the deadly organization on a path of decline that will be difficult to reverse.[8]

Following the death of Bin Laden, America and its allies kept up the military pressure on Al Qaeda. On 3 June 2011, a drone strike killed Ilyas Kashmiri, thought to be a senior Al Qaeda leader who was one of several in line to take over the succession. He was taking tea in an orchard in South Waziristan at the time.[9] Three days later, Al Qaeda's leader in East Africa, Fazul Abdullah Mohammed, was shot dead by Somali forces at a checkpoint in Mogadishu.[10] He was suspected of having played a key role in the 1998 bombings of the US embassies in

East Africa, and there was a $5 million price on his head. US Secretary of State Hillary Clinton hailed his death as a 'significant blow' to Al Qaeda.[11] The years ahead will show whether the CIA's prognosis was correct. Bin Laden's successor, his previous second in command Ayman al-Zawahiri, whose appointment was announced by Al Qaeda on 16 June 2011, is now top of the Agency's hit list. In President Obama's televised address to the nation on 22 June 2011, whose main focus was the planned withdrawal of the majority of US troops from Afghanistan by 2014, he referred to the implications of the death of Bin Laden.

> The information that we recovered from bin Laden's compound shows al Qaeda under enormous strain. Bin Laden expressed concern that al Qaeda has been unable to effectively replace senior terrorists that have been killed, and that al Qaeda has failed in its effort to portray America as a nation at war with Islam – thereby draining more widespread support. Al Qaeda remains dangerous, and we must be vigilant against attacks. But we have put al Qaeda on a path to defeat, and we will not relent until the job is done.[12]

Five days after the raid on Bin Laden's compound, Lady Justice Hallett published the findings of her inquest into the 7/7 London bombings. Over a third of her report deals with the alleged failure of MI5 to identify the leader of the 7/7 cell, Mohammed Saddique Khan, and his accomplice Shehzad Tanweer as potential terrorists. The remainder deals with the rescue operation, about which she took remarkable and harrowing testimony from many of the victims and members of the emergency services. One of the witnesses at the inquest was the Chief of Staff to the Security Service's Director General, Jonathan Evans. He was simply referred to as 'Witness G'. His presence in court was the result of Lady Justice Hallett's insistence that he appear, in the face of initial opposition from MI5 and the Home Secretary, Theresa May, on the grounds that such public testimony might prejudice national security.

Lady Justice Hallett's report exonerates MI5 from any overall culpability, and concludes: '… there is simply no evidence at all that the Security Service knew of, and therefore failed to prevent, the bombings on 7/7'.[13] 'Witness G' expressed 'profound regret' that the Security Service had been unable to prevent the bombings. The coroner paid tribute to MI5's work 'in preventing many acts of terrorism in the UK and the inconspicuous success they have had, the precise details of which can never be made public'.[14] Nevertheless, she did forensically identify some failings on the part of MI5. Although, as we have seen previously (pp.205–10), Khan and Tanweer eventually became known to MI5, they were believed to be criminals involved in financial fraud, not potential terrorists intent on bombing the United Kingdom. But Lady Justice Hallett did introduce a degree of scepticism into her findings: '[Khan and Tanweer] were plainly more than minor criminals. They had a number of highly suspicious meetings with a known attack planner [Omar Khyam – the principal suspect in Operation Crevice], at a time when his plans were coming to fruition … Also there was reason to believe they may be leaving for Pakistan intending to become involved in extremist activity there.'[15] She recognised the enormous pressure under which the Security Service was working, with limited resources, so that it was impossible to cover every suspect who appeared on its radar.

She reserved her most stringent criticism for the way in which MI5 handled the surveillance photographs its officers had taken of Khan and Tanweer on 2 February 2004, when they stopped off at Toddington services on their journey up the M1 (see p.206). Contrary to what I had originally believed, having seen the photograph produced during the Crevice trial, the image of Mohammed Saddique Khan was not 'indistinct and wouldn't meet identity-parade standards' (see p.206). On the contrary, in the original surveillance photographs provided to the inquest by MI5, Khan can be credibly identified, as can Tanweer – although not quite so clearly. In fact the inquest revealed, again contrary to what I had thought, that the Toddington services photograph of Khan was never shown to the FBI's 'supergrass', Mohammed Junaid Babar, who knew him from their meeting in Pakistan in connection with the *jihadi* training camp attended by the Crevice plotters. The only photograph Babar was shown was a hazy version of that of Tanweer. It shows him looking rather like a bank robber with a nylon stocking over his head. As Lady Justice Hallett noted, 'the photograph had been cropped in such a way as to render [Tanweer] virtually unidentifiable. A photograph of [Khan], cut in half, was not shown to Babar at all, and thus Babar had no opportunity to identify him. "Witness G" was unable to explain why the photograph [of Khan] was not shown ... He agreed that the photographs could have been provided in a better condition.'[16] She described the photographs as 'dreadful'.[17] How and why they came to be in this condition remains inexplicable. However, she concluded that it was not a fatal error, as other photos of Khan and Tanweer were subsequently shown to Babar and he failed to identify either of them. She hoped that in future MI5's procedures would be improved 'to ensure that "human sources" who are asked to view photographs are shown copies of the best possible quality, consistent with operational sensitivities'.[18]

There is one surprising omission in the coroner's report. It contains no mention of MI5 not immediately informing West Yorkshire Police Special Branch that its officers had followed Khan and Tanweer up the M1 to Leeds on 2 February 2004. (Admittedly, their identities were not known at the time.) The consequence was that West Yorkshire Special Branch was never asked to put the suspects under surveillance, despite the fact that they were clearly associated with the Crevice cell. This omission would seem to have been even more puzzling eighteen days later, on 20 February 2004, when the intelligence services discovered that the Crevice cell had purchased six hundred kilos of fertiliser to make bombs, and had stored the consignment in a lock-up near London.

Finally, a postscript to *Talking to Terrorists*. After I'd finished writing the book, I interviewed Baroness Manningham-Buller, who as Eliza Manningham-Buller was the Director General of the Security Service from 2002 to 2007, for my BBC2 series *The Secret War on Terror*.[19]

Coincidentally, we had both covered the Irish conflict, Al Qaeda and Islamist extremism over the same period from the 1970s onwards, although obviously from a completely different angle. She spoke movingly about the day of the 7/7 bombings. 'It wasn't really until I got home that evening pretty late that I felt weepy about it, because obviously there'd been appalling human tragedy that day. My reaction was a feeling of great defeat and disappointment that this had happened. I also thought that it was likely that we'd be blamed at some stage – which indeed happened.'[20]

One of the most remarkable parts of the interview came at the very end, when we were discussing the implications of the Northern Ireland peace process and the part that 'talking to terrorists' had played in it. We raised the subject of whether the principle should be applied to the Taliban and Al Qaeda.

By the beginning of 2011, almost a decade after the overthrow of the Taliban, it was clear that America and its NATO allies were putting out feelers to the insurgents via intermediaries, as had initially happened at the beginning of the Northern Ireland peace process (see Chapter 1). In Afghanistan, as in Northern Ireland, there was a military stalemate. In February 2011, Secretary of State Hillary Clinton set out America's roadmap for peace in Afghanistan, given that 'we will never kill enough insurgents to end this war outright'.[21] She offered a heavily qualified olive branch to the Taliban, laying out 'unambiguous red lines' for reconciliation with the enemy:

> They must renounce violence. They must abandon their alliance with
> Al Qaeda. And they must abide by the constitution of Afghanistan.
> Those are necessary outcomes of any negotiation. This is the price for
> reaching a political resolution and bringing an end to the military
> actions that are targeting their leadership and decimating their
> ranks.[22]

The 'political solution' envisaged by Mrs Clinton and the Obama administration was to be overseen and orchestrated by the Afghan President, Hamid Karzai. America insisted it had to be an Afghan solution for the Afghan people, with Western-trained Afghan army and police taking over responsibility for security. The preconditions of renouncing violence and becoming part of the political process were not dissimilar to those that had been laid out to the IRA by the British. Mrs Clinton recognised, as had the British at the beginning of the secret talks that led to the peace process, that 'talking to terrorists' would not be easy: 'I know that reconciling with an adversary that can be as brutal as the Taliban sounds distasteful, even unimaginable. Diplomacy would be easy if we only had to talk to our friends. But that is not how one makes peace.'[23] Her sentiments were later echoed by US Defense Secretary, Robert Gates, who said that it was inevitable that as wars concluded, 'peace is made between people who have been killing each other'. On 18 June 2011, President Karzai made the first public announcement of what had been suspected for some considerable time: that 'foreign military and especially the US itself' were involved in peace talks with the Taliban.[24] Ten days later the Taliban launched an audacious attack on the Intercontinental hotel in Kabul, as if making it clear that if there were to be negotiations, its leaders would be entering them from a position of strength – just as the IRA had done prior to negotiations with the British. Around 20 Afghans were reportedly killed in the attack plus three suspected suicide bombers.[25]

Talking to the Taliban is one thing. Talking to Al Qaeda is very different. The Afghan Taliban has a purely national aim. Although it broadly supports Al Qaeda, its priority is to remove foreign forces from Afghanistan, turn back the clock and return to the power it was forced to relinquish following the US invasion in the wake of 9/11. But turning back the clock to pre-9/11 is not an option in any Afghan peace process. If the insurgency is to end and a new political arrangement be put in place, as in Northern Ireland, it has to be the result of compromise. A significant part of any deal would probably be America's agreement to release Taliban prisoners incarcerated at Guantánamo Bay, just as IRA and Loyalist prisoners were released from the Maze prison as part of the Good Friday Agreement. With the withdrawal of American and British troops from Afghanistan anticipated in 2014, there is not a lot of time left for 'talking to terrorists'. Time may be on the Taliban's side.

So is talking to Al Qaeda pure fantasy? I put the question to Baroness Manningham-Buller at the end of my interview. Her answer was not what I expected. 'I would hope that people are trying to do so,' she said. 'It's always better to talk to the people who are attacking you than attacking them, if you can. I don't know whether they are [talking to Al Qaeda], but I would hope that people are trying to reach out to the Taliban, to people on the edges of Al Qaeda, to talk to them.' I asked if she thought that the Taliban and Al Qaeda would listen. 'I don't know,' she replied. 'It doesn't mean to say it's not worth trying.'[26] Talking to terrorists, after the application of intense military pressure, may in the end be the only way forward.

ACKNOWLEDGEMENTS

In writing this book about a journey spanning almost forty years, there are more people I would like to thank than space allows. They include many of my colleagues from Thames Television – where I reported for *This Week* for almost ten years and was first thrown into the deep end of the Irish conflict – and at the BBC, on *Panorama* and elsewhere, where I spent the next thirty years reporting on the impact of terrorism and political violence, and other issues too.

In particular I need to thank my literary agent, Sheila Ableman, who in the gentlest and most charming way persistently encouraged me to write this book, telling me that my putting pen to paper – or fingers to laptop – should not end with Ireland, but should record my work in trying to understand and give perspective to Al Qaeda in the defining decade since 9/11. I am also indebted to Sheila for teaming me with Martin Redfern of HarperPress, who is the most thorough and painstaking editor any author could wish for. The effort needed to bring the manuscript up to his exacting standard was worth it. Thanks also to Robert Lacey who so meticulously copy edited the manuscript and made sense of my scribbles, amendments, references and footnotes, and to Sarah Hopper for her diligent pursuit of pictures. Also to Malcolm Balen who read the manuscript on behalf of the BBC. And to Irene Barrett who so assiduously read every word and improved many of them by helping me find *le mot juste*. I'm grateful too for the support of Clive Edwards and senior colleagues at the BBC who gave me leave of absence for almost six months in order to write the book.

Most of all, I must thank all those individuals from all sides, including the police, security and intelligence agencies – domestic and international – whom I have met over the years, and without whose trust and confidence I could not have made this journey. Brendan Duddy and his family, without whom the first chapter could not have been written, are the perfect example of the trust that has been built up over many years.

Writing this book was a remarkably pleasurable experience, not least because I was able to do so while enjoying the generous hospitality of dear friends, Irene Barrett in Greece, Nigel and Tina Lewis in Spain and Caroline and Marcello Manzo in Sicily, where I was able to unwind after finishing the book. Nor must I forget Philip Mudd, whom I interviewed at his farmhouse in America's beautiful Shenandoah Valley, where I was able to put the final full stop.

I would like to thank my sons, Ben and Sam, and their wives, Aniela and Emily, and my brother John and his wife Thelma, all of whom have been towers of support and encouragement, as have special friends and neighbours who often watered and fed me at the end of a long day at the laptop.

And finally to add thanks to Essie Cousins, Sophie Goulden and their team for overseeing the update of the paperback as well as to Geraldine Beare who so skilfully indexed the manuscript.

Peter Taylor
July 2011

NOTES

One: Talking to the IRA

1 I use the Anglicised version, Rory O'Brady, as opposed to the Gaelic, Ruairí Ó Brádaigh.
2 Taylor, *Provos*, p.31.
3 The quotations from Brendan Duddy are taken from the interview I did for BBC2's *The Secret Peacemaker*, 26 March 2008.
4 *Provos*, p.87. This remarkable memorandum became a public document as a result of the Saville Inquiry into the events of that day.
5 Taylor, *Provos*, p.96.
6 Bew and Gillespie, *Northern Ireland: A Chronology of the Troubles 1968–1999*, p.54.
7 Taylor, *Brits*, p.163.
8 Ibid., p.164.
9 Ibid., p.168.
10 Ibid., p.177.
11 Ibid., p.179.
12 Ibid., p.180.
13 Ibid., p.195.
14 Bew and Gillespie, p.193.
15 Ibid., p.464.
16 Taylor, *Brits*, p.233.
17 Hamill, *Pig in the Middle*.
18 Taylor, *Brits*, p.234.
19 Ibid.
20 Taylor, *Loyalists*.
21 Ibid.
22 Ibid., pp.313–14.

23 Ibid., p.316.

24 Ibid., p.317.

25 Powell, *Great Hatred, Little Room*, p.71.

26 Taylor, *Brits*, p.321.

27 Ibid.

28 Ibid., p.322.

29 Ibid., p.323.

30 Ibid., p.324.

31 Ibid., p.325.

32 Ibid., p.326.

33 Bew and Gillespie, pp.280, 277.

34 Taylor, *Brits*, p.326.

35 Virgil, *Aeneid*, Book 1, lines 203–4. Translated by author. The original Latin is '*Forsan et haec olim meminisse iuvabit. Per varios casus, per tot discrimina rerum.*'

Two: From the IRA to Al Qaeda

1 http://en.wikipedia.org/wiki/Belfast_Agreement.

2 http://www.dailymail.co.uk/news/article-526074/Hardliner-Paisley-81-quit-Ulster-First-Minister-career-spanning-decades.html.

3 Ibid.

4 Randal, *Osama*, pp.53–4.

5 Corbin, *The Base*, p.19.

6 Wright, *The Looming Tower*, p.130.

7 Scheuer, *Through Our Enemies' Eyes*, p.92.

8 Ibid., p.93.

9 Wright, p.79.

10 Ibid., p.127.

11 Bergen, *The Osama Bin Laden I Know*, pp.74ff.

Three: Talking to Hijack Victims

1 Evans and Phillips, *Algeria*, p.102.

2 The *intifada* was initially the first violent uprising of young Palestinians on the Israeli-occupied West Bank between 1987 and 1993.

3 Evans and Phillips, p.104.

4 Ibid., p.105.

5 http://uk.reuters.com/article/idUKAHM54533720070605

6 http://globaljihad.net/view_page.asp?id=1696
7 http://news.bbc.co.uk/1/hi/programmes/age_of_terror/7371008.stm. Article by the author.
8 Ibid.

Four: Talking to the Interrogators

1 Lacey, *Inside the Kingdom*, p.150.
2 9/11 Commission Report, p.57.
3 Ibid.
4 http://www.islamfortoday.com/taleban11.htm
5 http://en.wikipedia.org/wiki/Taliban_treatment_of_women
6 9/11 Commission Report, p.62.
7 Ibid., p.67.
8 http://www.neatorama.com/2010/02/23/the-craziest-cia-plots-to-kill-castro/
9 John Willman, *Financial Times*, 29 November 2001.
10 http://www.pbs.org/wgbh/pages/frontline/shows/binladen/upclose/computer.html
11 *Age of Terror: War on the West*, BBC2, 6 May 2008.
12 Lawrence, *Messages to the World: The Statements of Osama Bin Laden*, pp.58ff.
13 *Age of Terror: War on the West*.
14 Ibid.
15 Wright, p.270.
16 Ibid.
17 Ibid., p.282.
18 Ibid., p.283.

Five: Talking to a Convicted Terrorist

1 http://www.depauw.edu/news/index.asp?id=11770.
2 Evans and Phillips, p.212.
3 *Al Qaeda: The Third World War. The Hidden Enemy*, BBC2, 9 February 2004.
4 USA v Abu Doha. Southern District Court of New York, 2 July 2001. Web reference: news.findlaw.com/hdocs/docs/abudoha/usabudoha70201cmpt.pdf.
5 http://news.bbc.co.uk/1/hi/uk/4141594.stm.

6 http://www.guardian.co.uk/uk/2009/feb/18/abu-qatada-profile.

7 9/11 Commission Report, pp.59, 169.

8 *Observer*, 21 April 2002.

9 Lawrence. Interview with Al-Jazeera, December 1998, pp.70, 80.

10 9/11 Commission Report, p.191.

11 http://www.msnbc.msn.com/id/24449741

Six: Anatomy of a Sleeper Cell

1 *Al Qaeda: The Third World War. The Hunt for America's Sleeper Cells*,
   BBC2, 16 February 2004.

2 http://www.pbs.org/wgbh/pages/frontline/shows/sleeper/inside/
   derwish.html

3 Ibid.

4 Guantánamo Combatant Status Review Board, Juma al-Dosari,
   14 September 2004.

5 *Al Qaeda: The Third World War. The Hunt for America's Sleeper Cells*.

6 Tablighi Jamaat means the Society for Spreading the Faith. It is very
   powerful, influential and well-financed. It was founded in 1926 and is
   an offshoot of the Deobandi movement, which believes that Islamic
   societies have fallen behind the West because they have deviated from
   the original, unadulterated teachings of the Prophet and been tainted
   by the immorality and decadence of the West.

7 http://www.pbs.org/wgbh/pages/frontline/shows/sleeper/interviews/
   alwan.html.

8 Matthew Purdy and Lowell Bergman, 'Unclear Danger. Inside the
   Lackawanna Terror Case', *New York Times*, 12 October 2003. The article
   was written in conjunction with PBS's *Frontline* programme, which
   covered the story in detail.

9 http://www.pbs.org/wgbh/pages/frontline/shows/sleeper/interviews/
   alwan.html.

10 Department of Justice press release, 17 December 2003.

11 Department of Justice press release, 3 December 2003.

12 Taken from Mukhtar al-Bakri's statement to the FBI in Bahrain on 13
   September 2002.

13 Ibid.

14 *Al Qaeda: The Third World War. The Hunt for America's Sleeper Cells*.

15 Combat Status Review Board. Ibid.

16 Mukhtar al-Bakri's statement to the FBI.

17 http://www.pbs.org/wgbh/pages/frontline/shows/sleeper/interviews/alwan.html.
18 http://www.pbs.org/wgbh/pages/frontline/shows/sleeper/inside/cron.html.
19 Worthington, *The Guantánamo Files*, p.97.
20 Ibid., p.241.
21 http://en.wikipedia.org/wiki/Juma_al-Dossary.
22 http://en.wikinews.org/wiki/Masterminds_of_USS_Cole_and_Limburg_bombings_escape_from_Yemeni_prison.
23 http://mypetjawa.mu.nu/archives/191400.php.

Seven: One Morning in September

1 9/11 Commission Report, p.161.
2 Ibid.
3 Ibid., p.181.
4 Ibid., p.216.
5 Ibid., p.222.
6 Ibid., p.224.
7 Ibid., p.236.
8 http://news.bbc.co.uk/hi/english/static/in_depth/americas/2001/day_of_terror/the_four_hijacks/flight_11.stm.
9 Ibid.; http://en.wikipedia.org/wiki/United_Airlines_Flight_175#calls.
10 9/11 Commission Report, pp.223–4.
11 http://news.bbc.co.uk/hi/english/static/in_depth/americas/2001/day_of_terror/the_four_hijacks/flight_93.stm.
12 http://en.wikipedia.org/wiki/September_11_attacks#cite_note-42.
13 http://911research.wtc7.net/disinfo/alibis/bush.html.

Eight: A Warning Not Heeded

1 Wright, pp.131–3.
2 US District Court, Southern District of New York, United States of America v Mohammed Mansour Jabarah, 1 June 2007.
3 http://www.encyclopedia.com/doc/1P1-69608741.html.
4 Foreign Affairs, Defence and Trade References Committee, *Bali 2002: Security Threats to Australians in South-East Asia*, August 2004.
5 Bell, *The Martyr's Oath*.
6 *Arab Times*, 10 October 2002.

7 Ibid.

8 US District Court, Southern District of New York, op. cit.

9 Ibid.

Nine: Bombs on Bali

1 *The Economist*, 22 May 2010.

2 http://en.wikipedia.org/wiki/Azahari_Husin.

3 *The Third World War – Al Qaeda: Breeding Ground*, BBC2, 2004.

4 Ibid.

5 Ibid.

6 http://www.cfr.org/publication/10219

7 Ibid.

8 http://www.nytimes.com/2006/12/22/world/asia/22indo.html?_r=1.

9 http://www.guardian.co.uk/world/2010/aug/09/abu-bakar-bashir-arrested-terrorist-group.

10 *The Third World War – Al Qaeda: Breeding Ground*.

11 Ibid.

12 Ibid.

13 http://www.timesonline.co.uk/tol/news/world/asia/article5114539.ece.

14 Figure provided by Spanish Embassy in London.

15 http://news.bbc.co.uk/1/hi/world/middle_east/737483.stm.

16 http://www.guardian.co.uk/politics/2003/mar/18/foreignpolicy.iraq1.

17 Ibid.

18 *Guardian*, 1 September 2010.

19 http://news.bbc.co.uk/1/hi/8485694.stm.

20 http://en.wikipedia.org/wiki/Media_coverage_of_the_Iraq_War.

21 http://www.iraqinquiry.org.uk/media/48051/letter-manninghambuller-gieve.pdf.

22 http://www.iraqinquiry.org.uk/media/48331/20100720am-manningham-buller.pdf.

23 Ibid.

24 *The New Al Qaeda: Turning the Terrorists*, BBC2.

25 Abdullah Sangkar died in 1999, and was succeeded as leader of JI by Abu Bakar Bashir. The two clerics were closely associated, since they set up Pandok Ngruki, a religious boarding school, known as a *pesantren* or *pandok*, in Solo, central Java. Ngruki is the name of the village where it is situated. It has been referred to as the Ivy League college for JI recruits. Its notorious alumni are said to include Hambali and the three

Bali bomber brothers, Muklas, Ali Imron and Amrozi. http://en.wikipedia.org/wiki/Al-Mukmin_Islamic_school.

26 http://news.bbc.co.uk/2/hi/8559054.stm.

27 http://www.reuters.com/article/idUSTRE62H13F20100318.

28 Ibid.

Ten: Understanding the 'New' Al Qaeda

1 http://news.bbc.co.uk/2/hi/europe/3222608.stm.

2 *The New Al Qaeda: The Drug Dealer, the Estate Agent and the Telephone Man*, BBC2, 1 August 2005.

3 http://www.globaljihad.net/view_page.asp?id=390.

4 http://www.nytimes.com/2004/03/28/world/a-long-fuse-links-tangier-to-bombings-in-madrid.html?pagewanted=al.

5 http://news.bbc.co.uk/1/shared/spl/hi/guides/457000/457031/html/default.stm.

6 http://english.aljazeera.net/news/middleeast/2010/01/2010124123232335456.html.

7 http://www.lawrencewright.com/art-madrid.html.

8 http://news.bbc.co.uk/1/hi/world/europe/4899544.stm.

9 http://news.bbc.co.uk/1/hi/world/europe/7070827.stm.

Eleven: Terror on the Ground

1 *Real Spooks*, *Panorama*, BBC1, 30 April 2007.

2 Ibid.

3 Jon Ronson documentary, *The Tottenham Ayatollah*, Channel 4, 8 April 1997.

4 *Real Spooks*.

5 Jon Gilbert, 'The Supergrass I Helped Create', *The Times*, 3 May 2007.

6 *The Third World War. Al Qaeda. Breeding Ground*.

7 Intelligence and Security Committee, 'Could 7/7 Have Been Prevented? Review of the Intelligence on the London Terrorist Attacks on 7 July 2005', HMSO Cm 7617, May 2009.

8 Ibid.

9 Ibid.

10 *Real Spooks*.

11 Ibid.

12 Ibid.

13 Ibid.
14 Ibid.
15 Ibid.
16 Ibid.
17 Ian Cobain, *Guardian*, 29 April 2008.
18 Ibid.
19 *Real Spooks*.
20 http://cms.met.police.uk/news/convictions/terrorism/operation_crevice_mps_statement.
21 Intelligence and Security Committee, Cm 7617.
22 Ibid.
23 Ibid.
24 Ibid.

Twelve: Clean Skins

1 Factual references from Intelligence and Security Committee, 'Report into the London Terrorist Attacks on 7 July 2005', HMSO Cm 6785, May 2006.
2 http://www.dailymail.co.uk/news/article-355621/Suicide-bomber-profile-The-family-man.html.
3 Ibid.
4 http://www.timesonline.co.uk/tol/news/uk/crime/article6188502.ece.
5 http://www.prospectmagazine.co.uk/2007/06/mybrotherthebomber/.
6 http://www.skynewstranscripts.co.uk/transcript.asp?id=393.
7 http://news.bbc.co.uk/1/hi/7364628.
8 European Strategic Intelligence and Security Centre (ESISC). Background Analysis 07/07/2006.
9 http://news.bbc.co.uk/1/hi/uk/4762313.stm.
10 Ibid.
11 http://news.bbc.co.uk/1/hi/uk/4762263.stm.
12 Ibid.
13 Ibid.
14 http://www.independent.co.uk/news/uk/crime/hasib-hussain-the-boy-who-grew-up-to-bomb-the-no-30-bus-498746.html.
15 *Generation Jihad*, BBC2, 8 February 2010.
16 Notes of interview with Maryam Lindsay.
17 http://news.bbc.co.uk/1/hi/uk/6692243.stm.
18 http://news.bbc.co.uk/1/hi/uk/4762591.stm.

19 http://news.bbc.co.uk/1/hi/uk/4273804.stm.
20 Ibid.
21 www.timesonline.co.uk/tol/news/uk/article2058495.ece.
22 http://news.bbc.co.uk/1/hi/email_news/6634901.stm.
23 http://news.bbc.co.uk/1/hi/uk/6634917.stm.
24 http://news.bbc.co.uk/1/hi/uk/6634955.stm.
25 http://en.wikipedia.org/wiki/21_July_2005_London_
   bombings#Explosions_on_the_underground.
26 http://www.smh.com.au/news/world/dramatic-police-raid-adds-to-
   terrorist-haul/2005/07/30/1122144059913.html.
27 Ibid.
28 http://www.guardian.co.uk/uk/2006/mar/08/menezes.july7.

Thirteen: Terror in the Skies

1 http://news.bbc.co.uk/1/hi/4628932.stm.
2 *Terror in the Skies*, *Panorama*, BBC, 9 September 2008.
3 http://news.bbc.co.uk/1/hi/uk_politics/5382590.stm.
4 http://news.bbc.co.uk/1/hi/uk/7604808.stm.
5 *Terror in the Skies*.
6 Ibid.
7 Ibid.
8 http://news.bbc.co.uk/1/hi/uk/4778575.stm.
9 Ibid.
10 Ibid.
11 http://www.timesonline.co.uk/tol/news/uk/crime/article6824884.
   ece?token=null&offset=0&page=1.

Fourteen: Jihad.com

1 http://www.guardian.co.uk/uk/2008/aug/19/uksecurity.ukcrime.
2 Ibid.
3 http://www.timesonline.co.uk/tol/news/uk/crime/article4786555.ece.
4 Ibid.
5 http://www.justice.gov/opa/pr/2009/August/09-nsd-790.html.
6 http://sonyafatah.com/blog/2006/08/23/from-goth-chick-to-devout-wife/.
7 http://ca.news.yahoo.com/s/capress/100510/national/terror_trial.
8 http://www.jihadwatch.org/2010/05/hey-wanna-be-part-of-the-group-
   that-goes-up-to-parliament-man-cut-off-some-heads.html.

9 http://www.thestar.com/news/gta/crime/article/807202—toronto-18-ringleader-pleads-guilty-in-terror-trial.

10 http://edition.cnn.com/2009/CRIME/12/14/terror.sentence/index.html.

11 Ibid.

Fifteen: Talking to the Victims of Torture

1 'Reporting Northern Ireland', *Index on Censorship*, Vol. 7, No. 6, 1978.

2 Ibid.

3 McKittrick et al., *Lost Lives*, pp.1473–4.

4 Mayer, *The Dark Side*, p.147.

5 Ibid., p.183.

6 http://www.cageprisoners.com/page.php?id=10.

7 Ibid.

8 Combatant Status Review Board, 'Summary of Evidence for Combatant Status Review Tribunal'. Unclassified, 27 September 2004.

9 Ibid.

10 'Terror Watch: Al Qaeda in Yemen', NEFA Foundation, January 2009.

11 Ibid.

12 Evan F. Kohlmann, '"The Eleven": Saudi Guantánamo Veterans Returning to the Fight', NEFA Foundation, February 2009.

13 http://news.bbc.co.uk/1/hi/world/americas/7030383.stm.

14 Statement by Committee Chairman Senator Carl Levin, Senate Armed Services Committee's Inquiry into the Treatment of Detainees in US Custody, 11 December 2008.

15 US Department of Justice, Office of the Inspector General, 'A Review of the FBI's Involvement in and Observations of Detainee Interrogations in Guantánamo Bay, Afghanistan and Iraq', May 2008, pp.77ff.

16 http://www.timesonline.co.uk/tol/news/world/middle_east/article6813107.ece.

17 http://www.npr.org/templates/story/story.php?storyId=126889383.

18 Combatant Status Review Board, 19 October 2004.

19 *Guardian*, 26 October 2010.

Sixteen: Journey to the Dark Side

1 http://www.usatoday.com/news/sept11/2001/12/14/bush-binladen.htm.

2 US Department of Justice, Office of the Assistant Attorney General, Memorandum for John A. Rizzo, Acting General Counsel of the

Central Intelligence Agency, 'Interrogation of an Al Qaeda Operative'. Top Secret. 1 August 2002.

3 Ibid.

4 Ibid.

5 US Department of Justice, Office of Legal Counsel, Memorandum for John A. Rizzo, Senior Deputy General Counsel, Central Intelligence Agency. 'Re: Application of 18 U.S.C. 2340–2340A to the Combined Use of Certain Techniques in the Interrogation of High Value al Qaeda Detainees'. Top Secret. 10 May 2005.

6 Ibid.

7 Ibid.

8 Ibid.

9 Ibid.

10 US Department of Justice, 'Interrogation of an Al Qaeda Operative'.

11 US Department of Justice, 'Re: Application of 18 U.S.C. 2340–2340A to the Combined Use of Certain Techniques in the Interrogation of High Value al Qaeda Detainees'.

12 Ibid.

13 Ibid.

14 Central Intelligence Agency Inspector General, 'Special Review', 7 May 2004, paras 169, 173.

15 Ibid., para. 28.

16 Ali Soufan, 'My Tortured Decision', *New York Times*, 22 April 2009.

17 CIA Inspector General, 'Special Review. Counterterrorism Detention and Interrogation Activities (September 2001–October 2003)', para. 232.

18 Ibid., para. 231.

19 Ibid., paras 255, 266.

20 Bush, *Decision Points*, p.169.

21 http://www.dailymail.co.uk/news/article-1256796/Ex-MI5-boss-claims-U-S-waterboarded-9-11-chief-160-times.html.

22 Dame Eliza Manningham-Buller, 'Reflections on Intelligence', Mile End Group, MEG 64, 9 March 2010.

23 http://news.bbc.co.uk/1/hi/uk/8309919.stm.

24 Sir John Sawers, speech to the Society of Editors, 28 October 2010.

25 http://www.bbc.co.uk/news/10521326.

26 Combatant Status Review Board, 'Binyam Mohamed. To Personal Representative'. http://projects.nytimes.com/guantanamo/detainees/1458-binyam-mohamed#8.

27 Ibid.

28 Ibid.

29 US Department of Justice, Letter to US Court of Appeals re Mohamed et al. V. Jeppesen Dataplan. Inc. No. 08-15693 (9th Circuit). Argued 15 December 2009.

30 *Guardian*, 10 February 2010

31 http://www.statewatch.org/news/2009/feb/uk-binyam-mohamed-appeal-court-judgment-feb-2009.pdf.

32 US District Court for the District of Columbia, Farhi Saeed Bin Mohammed et al. v Barack H. Obama et al., 19 November 2009. [The following descriptions and quotes regarding the allegations are taken from the Judge's Opinion.]

33 Ibid.

34 http://www.reprieve.org.uk/static/downloads/2010_02_26_Judgment_Binyam_Mohamed_redacted_paragraph.pdf.

35 Bergen and Tiedemann, 'The Year of the Drone', New America Foundation, 24 February 2010.

36 Peter Bergen and Bruce Hoffman, 'Assessing the Terrorist Threat. A Report of the Bipartisan Policy Center's National Security Preparedness Group', 10 September 2010.

37 *Guardian*, 17 December 2010.

38 *Observer*, 31 October 2010.

39 Sir John Sawers, speech to the Society of Editors, 28 October 2010.

40 http://www.bbc.co.uk/news/uk-politics-11752897.

41 http://news.bbc.co.uk/2/hi/south_asia/8575623.stm.

42 http://www.bbc.co.uk/news/uk-10629358.

43 http://news.bbc.co.uk/2/hi/south_asia/7171205.stm.

44 http://www.guardian.co.uk/world/2008/may/30/alqaida.terrorism.

45 Ibid.

46 http://news.bbc.co.uk/2/hi/uk_news/politics/7299888.stm.

47 Ibid.

48 'The Betrayal of Palestine', Lawrence, *Messages to the World*.

49 http://www.guardian.co.uk/world/2010/jan/24/osama-bin-laden-abdulmutallab-detroit.

50 United States of America v Khalid Sheikh Mohammed [and others], 'The Islamic Response to the Government's Nine Accusations', 5 March 2009.

Epilogue

1 http://www.bbc.co.uk/news/mobile/world-south-asia-13279283.

2 http://www2.hn.psu.edu/faculty/jmanis/poldocs/ci-torture/
   olc_05302005_bradbury.pdf.

3 'Ex-CIA Counterterror Chief: "Enhanced Interrogation" Led US to bin
   Laden', *Time Swampland*, 4 May 2011.

4 Ibid.

5 http://english.aljazeera.net/news/middleeast/2011/05/
   201156203329911287.html.

6 Ibid.

7 http://www.bbc.co.uk/news/world-south-asia-13385597.

8 https://www.cia.gov/news-information/featured-story-archive/2011-
   featured-story-archive/the-operation-that-killed-bin-ladin.html.

9 http://www.economist.com/blogs/banyan/2011/06/death-ilyas-kashmiri.

10 http://www.bbc.co.uk/news/world-africa-13739567.

11 Ibid.

12 Presidential speech distributed by the Bureau of International
   Information Programs, US Department of State. Web site:
   http://iipdigital.usembassy.gov/iipdigital-en/index.html

13 Coroner's Inquests into the London Bombings of 7 July 2005, 6 May
   2011, para 15, p.4. https://wikispooks.com/w/images/1/19/7-7_.
   Inquest_Report.pdf

14 Ibid., para 12, p.3.

15 Ibid., para 81, p.18.

16 Ibid., para 41, p.10.

17 Ibid., para 71, p.16.

18 Ibid., para 1, p.17.

19 *The Secret War on Terror*, BBC2, 14 and 21 March 2011.

20 Ibid., 14 March 2011.

21 http://www.state.gov/secretary/rm/2011/02/156815.htm.

22 Ibid.

23 Ibid.

24 http://www.bbc.co.uk/news/world-south-asia-13821452.

25 http://www.bbc.co.uk/news/world-south-asia-13947169. The Taliban's
   assault also raised worrying questions over the ability of the Afghan
   National Army to take over once America and its allies had largely
   gone.

26 *The Secret War on Terror*, 21 March 2011.

BIBLIOGRAPHY

Books on the IRA and Al Qaeda are too many to enumerate. The following are some of those on which I have drawn and which I found valuable in the writing of this book.

Begg, Moazzam, *Enemy Combatant: The Terrifying True Story of a Briton in Guantánamo* (Pocket Books, 2007)

Bell, Stewart, *The Martyr's Oath: The Apprenticeship of a Homegrown Terrorist* [Mohammed Jabarah] (John Wiley and Sons Canada Ltd, 2005)

Bergen, Peter, *Holy War: Inside the Secret World of Osama Bin Laden* (Touchstone, 2002)

— *The Osama Bin Laden I Know: An Oral History of Al Qaeda's Leader* (Free Press, 2006)

Bew, Paul, and Gordon Gillespie, *Northern Ireland: A Chronology of the Troubles 1968–1999* (Gill and Macmillan, 1999)

Burke, Jason, *Al Qaeda: The True Story of Radical Islam* (Penguin Books, 2004)

Burleigh, Michael, *Blood and Rage: A Cultural History of Terrorism* (HarperPress, 2008)

Bush, George W., *Decision Points* (Virgin Books, 2010)

Coll, Steve, *Ghost Wars: The Secret History of the CIA, Afghanistan and Bin Laden from the Soviet Invasion to September 10, 2001* (Penguin Books, 2005)

Corbin, Jane, *The Base: Al-Qaeda and the Changing Face of Global Terror* (Pocket Books, 2003)

Evans, Martin, and John Phillips, *Algeria: Anger of the Dispossessed* (Yale University Press, 2007)

Gunaratna, Rohan, *Inside Al Qaeda: Global Network of Terror* (Columbia University Press, 2002)

Hamill, Desmond, *Pig in the Middle: The Army in Northern Ireland 1969–1984* (Methuen, 1985)

Kean, Thomas (Chair), Lee Hamilton (Vice Chair) and other members of the 9/11 Commission, *9/11 Commission Report: Final Report of the National Commission on Terrorist Attacks Upon the United States (with Index)* (Barnes and Noble Publishing, 2004)

Kepel, Gilles, *The War for Muslim Minds: Islam and the West* (The Belknap Press of Harvard University Press, 2008)

Kohlmann, Evan, *Al Qaeda's Jihad in Europe: The Afghan–Bosnian Network* (Berg, 2004)

Lacey, Robert, *Inside the Kingdom: Kings, Clerics, Modernists, Terrorists and the Struggle for Saudi Arabia* (Hutchinson, 2009)

Lawrence, Bruce, *Messages to the World: The Statements of Osama Bin Laden* (Verso, 2005)

McKittrick, David, Seamus Kelters, Brian Feeney and Chris Thornton, *Lost Lives: The Stories of the Men, Women and Children who Died as a Result of the Northern Ireland Troubles* (Mainstream Publishing, 1999)

Mayer, Jane, *The Dark Side: The Inside Story of How the War on Terror Turned into a War on American Ideals* (Anchor Books, 2009)

Miller, John, and Michael Stone with Chris Mitchell, *The Cell: Inside the 9/11 Plot, and Why the FBI and CIA Failed to Stop it* (Hyperion, New York, 2002)

Peirce, Gareth, *Dispatches from the Dark Side: On Torture and the Death of Justice* (Verso, 2010)

Powell, Jonathan, *Great Hatred, Little Room: Making Peace in Northern Ireland* (The Bodley Head, 2008)

Randal, Jonathan, *Osama: The Making of a Terrorist* (Vintage Books, 2009)

Rashid, Ahmed, *Taliban: The Story of the Afghan Warlords* (Pan Books, 2001)

Sands, Philippe, *Torture Team: Deception, Cruelty and the Compromise of Law* (Allen Lane, 2008)

Scheuer, Michael, *Imperial Hubris: Why the West is Losing the War on Terror* (Potomac Books, 2005)

— *Through Our Enemies' Eyes: Osama Bin Laden, Radical Islam, and the Future of America* (revised edition, Potomac Books, 2006)

— *Marching Toward Hell: America and Islam after Iraq* (Free Press, 2008)

Taylor, Peter, *Beating the Terrorists: Interrogation in Omagh, Gough and Castlereagh* (Penguin Special, 1980)

— *Stalker: The Search for the Truth* (Faber and Faber, 1987)

— *Families at War: Voices from the Troubles* (BBC Books, 1989)

— *States of Terror: Democracy and Political Violence* (BBC Books, 1993)

— *Provos: The IRA and Sinn Féin* (Bloomsbury Publishing, 1998)

— *Loyalists* (Bloomsbury Publishing, 1999)

— *Brits: The War Against the IRA* (Bloomsbury Publishing, 2001)

Walker, Clive, *The Anti-Terrorism Legislation* (Oxford University Press, 2002)

Worthington, Andy, *The Guantánamo Files: The Story of the 774 Detainees in America's Illegal Prison* (Pluto Press, 2007)

Wright, Lawrence, *The Looming Tower: Al-Qaeda and the Road to 9/11* (Knopf, Borzoi Books, 2006)

INDEX